Beginning Groovy and Grails

From Novice to Professional

Christopher M. Judd,
Joseph Faisal Nusairat, and
James Shingler

Apress®

Beginning Groovy and Grails: From Novice to Professional

Copyright © 2008 by Christopher M. Judd, Joseph Faisal Nusairat, James Shingler

ISBN-13 (pbk): 978-1-4302-1045-0

ISBN-13 (electronic): 978-1-4302-1046-7

Printed and bound in the United States of America 9 8 7 6 5 4 3 2 1

Trademarked names may appear in this book. Rather than use a trademark symbol with every occurrence of a trademarked name, we use the names only in an editorial fashion and to the benefit of the trademark owner, with no intention of infringement of the trademark.

Java™ and all Java-based marks are trademarks or registered trademarks of Sun Microsystems, Inc., in the US and other countries. Apress, Inc., is not affiliated with Sun Microsystems, Inc., and this book was written without endorsement from Sun Microsystems, Inc.

Lead Editors: Steve Anglin, Matthew Moodie
Technical Reviewer: Guilliaume Laforge
Editorial Board: Clay Andres, Steve Anglin, Ewan Buckingham, Tony Campbell, Gary Cornell, Jonathan Gennick, Matthew Moodie, Joseph Ottinger, Jeffrey Pepper, Frank Pohlmann, Ben Renow-Clarke, Dominic Shakeshaft, Matt Wade, Tom Welsh
Senior Project Manager: Kylie Johnston
Copy Editors: Nicole Abramowitz, Marilyn Smith
Associate Production Director: Kari Brooks-Copony
Senior Production Editor: Laura Cheu
Compositor: Kinetic Publishing Services, LLC
Proofreader: Liz Welch
Indexer: Julie Grady
Artist: Kinetic Publishing Services, LLC
Cover Designer: Kurt Krames
Manufacturing Director: Tom Debolski

Distributed to the book trade worldwide by Springer-Verlag New York, Inc., 233 Spring Street, 6th Floor, New York, NY 10013. Phone 1-800-SPRINGER, fax 201-348-4505, e-mail orders-ny@springer-sbm.com, or visit http://www.springeronline.com.

For information on translations, please contact Apress directly at 2855 Telegraph Avenue, Suite 600, Berkeley, CA 94705. Phone 510-549-5930, fax 510-549-5939, e-mail info@apress.com, or visit http://www.apress.com.

Apress and friends of ED books may be purchased in bulk for academic, corporate, or promotional use. eBook versions and licenses are also available for most titles. For more information, reference our Special Bulk Sales—eBook Licensing web page at http://www.apress.com/info/bulksales.

The information in this book is distributed on an "as is" basis, without warranty. Although every precaution has been taken in the preparation of this work, neither the author(s) nor Apress shall have any liability to any person or entity with respect to any loss or damage caused or alleged to be caused directly or indirectly by the information contained in this work.

The source code for this book is available to readers at http://www.apress.com.

To my supportive wife and best friend, Sue. To my son, Blake, who always makes me laugh. To all the individuals and organizations who have contributed to making Groovy and Grails amazing. And to my Heavenly Father, for all the blessings He has bestowed upon my family and me.
—Chris

To my family, for their love and support. And to my brother, Specialist Adam Nusairat, who is currently deployed to Afghanistan: stay safe; we miss you.
—Joseph

To my wonderful wife, Wendy, and my son, Tyler. None of this would have been possible without your love, support, and understanding. I love you!
—Jim

Contents at a Glance

Contents

Foreword

The year 2005 was a traumatic year for the Java web application development community. It was under fire for the unnecessary "fat" architecture of Java Platform, Enterprise Edition (Java EE) systems compared to the new kids on the block like Ruby on Rails and Django. The search began for Java's answer to these frameworks. I had an existing product that was heavily invested in Java frameworks such as Spring and Hibernate, but because I had been involved with the Groovy team for a while, I knew we could create the solution that people were looking for. Hence, Grails was born.

I knew Groovy itself was a phenomenal piece of technology that combined the best of the dynamic language worlds and Java. Innovation has been rife within the Groovy community since the early days with its builder concept. It had inspired other languages, and more recent languages such as ActionScript 3 and ECMAScript 4 had adopted its support for mixed typing. Groovy had proven to me that you can mix a dynamically typed language like Groovy with a statically typed language like Java in the same code base and get the best of both worlds without incurring the cost of context switching.

In addition, I knew that the Java community has invested years in building the largest amount of open source software in the world. Thousands of libraries exist for Java, built by years of best practice. Reinventing the wheel seemed like a crazy idea. Building Grails on top of existing technologies like Spring and Hibernate has proven to be one of the best decisions we have made. For me, Grails is the natural next step for Java EE developers. If Spring and Hibernate provided an abstraction over Java EE and simplified development, then Grails is an abstraction over Spring, Hibernate, and Java EE that can take you, the developer, to the next level.

Through the use of domain-specific languages and higher-level abstractions, Grails dramatically simplifies web development on the Java platform. By bundling a container and a database, we eliminated all barriers, and by supporting hot reloading during development, agile development became a reality. However, even with all this simplicity, as Grails has matured it has become much more than a web framework. It has become a web platform that participates in your entire project life cycle. Grasping all the concepts and conventions and applying them to your projects can be a challenge.

Fortunately, books like *Beginning Groovy and Grails* can help you get a grasp on the technology and guide you through the steps to make your application a reality. Chris, Joseph, and Jim do an excellent job of guiding you through the basics and then plunging headfirst into advanced topics like security, Asynchronous JavaScript and XML (Ajax), and deployment.

Books like this one take a while to write, and Grails itself was nearly three years in the making. However, what staggers me most is not the progress of Grails, but rather the progress of the community. The Groovy and Grails communities are some of the most vibrant around. The Grails mailing lists receive around 150 posts a day from enthusiastic users either asking questions or responding to questions from others.

During the development of Grails, we made a conscious decision to implement a plug-in system so that others could extend and embrace the Grails philosophy of convention over configuration. The idea was based on the success seen by other open source projects, like the Firefox browser, in allowing the user community to embrace and extend the core platform. This has resulted in more than 60 user-contributed plug-ins (`http://plugins.grails.org/`) that extend and enhance Grails' core functionality. They represent more than three million lines of user-contributed code.

It gives me great pleasure that *Beginning Groovy and Grails* takes a look at not only Grails, but also some of the excellent plug-ins made available by our users. So many problems out there already have excellent solutions; why reinvent the wheel?

Graeme Rocher
Grails Project Lead and CTO of G2One Inc. (`http://www.g2one.com`)

About the Authors

 **CHRISTOPHER M. JUDD** is the president and primary consultant for Judd Solutions, LLC (http://www.juddsolutions.com), an international speaker, an open source evangelist, the Central Ohio Java Users Group (http://www.cojug.org) leader, and the coauthor of *Enterprise Java Development on a Budget* (Apress, 2003) and *Pro Eclipse JST* (Apress, 2005). He has spent 12 years architecting and developing software for Fortune 500 companies in various industries, including insurance, retail, government, manufacturing, service, and transportation. His current focus is on consulting, mentoring, and training with Java, Java EE, Java Platform, Micro Edition (Java ME), mobile technologies, and related technologies.

 **JOSEPH FAISAL NUSAIRAT** is a software developer who has been working full time in the Columbus, Ohio, area since 1998, primarily focused on Java development. His career has taken him into a variety of Fortune 500 industries, including military applications, data centers, banking, internet security, pharmaceuticals, and insurance. Throughout this experience, he has worked on all varieties of application development, from design and architecture to development. Joseph, like most Java developers, is particularly fond of open source projects and tries to use as much open source software as possible when working with clients.

Joseph is a graduate of Ohio University with dual degrees in computer science and microbiology and a minor in chemistry. While at Ohio University, Joseph also dabbled in student politics and was a research assistant in the virology labs.

Currently, Joseph works as a senior partner at Integrallis Software (http://www.integrallis.com). In his off-hours, he enjoys watching bodybuilding competitions and Broadway musicals, specifically anything with Lauren Molina.

 **JAMES SHINGLER** is a senior consulting IT architect for a major midwestern insurance and financial services company. The focus of his career has been using cutting-edge technology to develop IT solutions for the insurance, financial services, and manufacturing industries. He has 11 years of large-scale Java experience and significant experience in distributed and relational technologies.

About the Technical Reviewer

GUILLAUME LAFORGE is the Groovy project manager and specification lead of Java Specification Request (JSR) 241, which standardizes the Groovy dynamic language in the Java Community Process (JCP). As the vice president of technology of G2One (http://www.g2one.com/), the company dedicated to the development of Groovy and Grails, he provides professional services for those technologies, including training, support, and consulting.

Guillaume coauthored the best-selling book, *Groovy in Action* (Manning Publications, 2007), and he reviewed and wrote forewords for most of the Groovy and Grails books on the market. You can meet him at conferences around the world, where he evangelizes the Groovy dynamic language and the agile Grails web framework.

Acknowledgments

This book is the culmination of the effort of a lot of people, without whom we would not have been able to accomplish its publication. We would like to begin by thanking Jason Gilmore for bringing this project to us and being our original managing editor. We really need to express our appreciation to our project manager, Kylie Johnston, for ultimately organizing the project to ensure we got the book done in a timely and organized manner. Thanks to our editorial director and associate publisher, Dominic Shakeshaft, for removing barriers. Thanks to our copy editors, Nicole Abramowitz and Marilyn Smith, for making our writing readable. Thanks to other Apress staff, including Steve Anglin, Laura Cheu, Stephanie Parker, and, of course, Gary Cornell.

It is important that a technical book be accurate, so we would like to thank our formal technical reviewers, Guillaume Laforge and Harshad Oak. We would also like to thank those who read the book and provided feedback during various stages of the book; thanks to Jeff Bailey, Matt Montgomery, and Stephen Thompson.

We would like to thank all those who have contributed to the Groovy and Grails projects, especially Graeme Rocher, Guillaume Laforge, and G2One. We would also like to thank other Groovy and Grails community contributors, including James Williams for SwingXBuilder, Andres Almiray for JideBuilder and Graphics Builder, and Marcos Fábio Pereira for the JasperGrails plug-in. They have created some great stuff and should be proud of themselves. Thanks to Sven Haiges and Glen Smith for their informative Grails podcast. Also, thanks to Dave Booth and JetBrains for providing us with licenses for IntelliJ IDEA, the best Groovy and Grails IDE.

I would like to personally thank my wife, Sue, and son, Blake, for being understanding and supportive through this long process. I would like to thank all those who have contributed to my personal and professional development over the years: David Bailey, Jim Shingler, Joseph Nusairat, Neal Ford, Brian Sam-Bodden, Steve Swing, Brian Campbell, Mike Rozlog, Geoff Goetz, Bob Myers, Ken Faw, Chris Nicholas, Rick Burchfield, Kevin Smith, Floyd Carver, Lee Hall, Seth Flory, David Lucas, BJ Allmon, Linc Kroeger, Doug Mair, Akin Oladoye, Tom Pugh, Drew Robbins, Angelo Serra, Hakeem Shittu, and Alex Terrazas. I'd also like to thank Jay Zimmerman, Andrew Glover, Dave Thomas, Venkat Subramaniam, Scott Davis, Ted Neward, and the other great speakers and influencers on the "No Fluff Just Stuff" tour.

Chris

Writing a book has been one of the most daunting tasks of my adult life. It is hard to write a book while still going to work and maintaining some semblance of a life. I thought writing with multiple authors would make it easier; however, it just gives more expectations to live up to. I'd like to first thank my coauthors for writing with me, and most importantly, for writing the chapters I didn't want to write. In fairness, I believe the way we divided up the chapters worked out well, because we were each able to focus on the areas we had the most passion about.

I'd also like to thank my business partner, Brian Sam-Bodden, for pushing me week after week and inspiring me to be a better developer.

I write these books in the hope that people will actually use the new technology we write about. For people to do that, companies need strong leaders who are willing to try something new. I'd like to thank those I have had the pleasure to work for who saw the power that new technologies bring—people like Chris Nicholas, Alberto Avila, Javier Sol, and Scott Carter, whose team I still keep running into at national conferences.

Finally, I'd like to thank my friends for their personal support and words of encouragement. Thank you Marie Wong, Joe O'Brien, Rob Stevenson, and all my tweets on twitter.

Joseph

I would personally like to thank my wife, Wendy, and son, Tyler, for their support and patience through the writing of the book and in our journey together through life. I would like to thank the many people who have contributed to my personal and professional growth: Wendy Shingler, James L. Shingler Sr., Linda Shingler, George Ramsayer, Tom Posival, Chris Judd, Rick Burchfield, David Lucas, Chris Nicholas, Tim Resch, Kevin Smith, Neal Ford, Seth Flory, Frank Neugebauer, David Duhl, Nate Beyene, Teresa Whitt, Jay Johnson, Gerry Wright, and the many other people who have touched my life.

Jim

Introduction

We live in interesting times. We are witnessing an amazing revolution. Over the last decade or so, two dominant platforms have emerged: Java and .NET. During their rise to power, promises of productivity were made and realized. Yet even with all the advancements in development tools, compilers, and virtual machine performance, and the multitude of frameworks available, developers began seeking the next level of productivity that the agile movement had introduced. Java and .NET developers began noticing that their counterparts who were using dynamic languages like Ruby, Python, and PHP were becoming increasingly productive, and these developers became jealous. The ever-moving technology pendulum began to swing back toward dynamic languages. And probably for the first time in history, the reigning platforms were ready to respond. Both Java and .NET have, for most of the decade, been able to run multiple languages, so they joined the race to see which platform would be able to add the right combination of dynamic languages and associated web frameworks. Meanwhile, a liberation of sorts took place as the mighty kingdoms embraced the open source community in order to gain more territory. On the .NET platform, Microsoft sought Ruby and Python and implemented its own versions of Ruby and Python with IronRuby and IronPython, respectively. The Java platform began by including in its distribution a scripting API and JavaScript using Mozilla's Rhino implementation. Then Sun embraced the Ruby community by hiring the developers who created the open source JRuby implementation.

As the revolution continues, a group in the Java community realized the same need for the productivity and flexibility offered by the dynamic languages yet understood the advantages of staying close to Java's roots. This group had witnessed the rise of Java a decade earlier, in part due to the ease of transition from the reigning C and C++ communities, and it realized the desire of large enterprises to take advantage of existing investments in infrastructure and education. The group knew that seamless interoperability and API consistency are important. Out of this group has come the dynamic language Groovy, specifically design for the Java Virtual Machine (JVM).

When Groovy was designed, it took many of the best features of the existing static and dynamic languages and fashioned them into a perfect complement to the Java language on the Java platform. Groovy is so good, in fact, that it has left the Java community in quite a quandary. Should the community continue to make investments into enhancing the Java language by adding some of the productivity features offered by dynamic languages, such as properties and closures? Or should it push the Java language down the stack to become the platform system language and embrace Groovy as the proper level of abstraction for developing applications, as has happened with so many technologies?

The Groovy revolution almost faltered in the early years with language instabilities, poor performance, and lack of focus. However, with the advent of the Grails framework, the web framework and development environment based on Groovy, the 1.0 release enabled developers to see that the early challenges were gone. This caused a renewed interest and even a passion for the technologies. Then with the 1.5 release, Groovy finally was able to perform all the metaprogramming that its rivals like Ruby were able to accomplish. Developers now see that developing scalable web applications can be productive and fun.

As more and more developers flock to Groovy and Grails, we realized that developers with no knowledge of Groovy and possibly little or no knowledge of the Java language and platform need a guide to lead them on their journey to quickly becoming productive with Groovy and Grails. This book combines our more than 30 years of Java and web development experience to assist developers in learning what they need to know to develop great, exciting, full-featured Web 2.0 applications using Groovy and Grails. It starts with the basic Groovy language features and ends with a complex web application that includes database persistence, Ajax, RSS feeds, searching, web services, reporting, batch processing, and even a desktop client to consume web services.

Who This Book Is For

This book is for Java developers and organizations looking to become more productive by taking advantage of dynamic languages and solid agile web frameworks while leveraging current investments in infrastructure, code, and education in the Java platform. It is for those who want to build internal applications and mission-critical, Internet-facing applications.

This book does not assume the reader has a strong Java or Groovy background, so those familiar with other dynamic languages like Perl, Ruby, Python, or PHP will find this a great source for investigating the Groovy and Grails alternative.

How This Book Is Structured

In this book, you'll explore how to build command-line, Swing, and web applications using the Groovy language and the Grails web framework. The step-by-step approach will take you from a simple to a complex and fully featured Web 2.0 application. Chapters 1–3 provide a basic Groovy language primer, while Chapters 4–12 explain how to build and deploy web applications using Grails. The final chapter explains how to use Groovy and Swing to build a desktop client that interacts with the Grails web application.

- *Chapter 1, "Introduction to Groovy"*: This chapter defines Groovy, explains how to install it, and then through example, demonstrates its power, flexibility, and readability compared to the Java language.

- *Chapter 2, "Groovy Basics"*: This chapter explains the basic Groovy syntax, structures, and tools.

- *Chapter 3, "More Advanced Groovy"*: This chapter goes beyond the Groovy basics to cover unit testing, XML processing, templating, and metaprogramming. It includes a discussion on domain-specific languages.

- *Chapter 4, "Introduction to Grails"*: This chapter defines the Grails architecture and its features. It then explains how to install Grails and get started developing applications with scaffolding.

- *Chapter 5, "Building the User Interface"*: This chapter explains how to combine Groovy Server Pages (GSP), controllers, Grails tags, templates, and Cascading Style Sheets (CSS) to build a basic user interface.

- *Chapter 6, "Building Domains and Services"*: This chapter explains how Grails uses a domain-driven approach to developing applications and how domain objects can be persisted using the powerful Grails Object Relational Mapping (GORM) framework. The chapter concludes by showing how you can organize application logic into reusable and injectable services.

- *Chapter 7, "Security in Grails"*: This chapter explains and demonstrates the alternative security options available in Grails.

- *Chapter 8, "Web 2.0—Ajax and Friends"*: This chapter explains how to add usability to your application through adding Ajax functionality, searching, and RSS.

- *Chapter 9, "Web Services"*: This chapter shows how to expose parts of your application to other clients using representational state transfer (REST) web services.

- *Chapter 10, "Reporting"*: This chapter explains how to use JasperReports and iReports to expose reports in multiple formats, including PDF, HTML, XML, and XLS.

- *Chapter 11, "Batch Processing"*: This chapter showcases how to schedule jobs to run automatically and how to generate e-mail messages.

- *Chapter 12, "Deploying and Upgrading"*: This chapter describes how to configure, package, and deploy Grails applications to alternative database and application servers.

- *Chapter 13, "Alternative Clients"*: This chapter builds a Swing client using Groovy that interacts with the Grails application through the RESTful web services built in Chapter 9.

Prerequisites

The code in this book requires Java Software Development Kit (SDK) 1.4 or greater.

Downloading the Code

The code for the examples in this book is available to readers in the Source Code/ Download section of the Apress web site at http://www.apress.com or on the book's web site at http://www.beginninggroovyandgrails.com.

Contacting the Authors

For more information about Groovy and Grails, visit the book's web site at http://www. beginninggroovyandgrails.com. We welcome any comments or feedback, so feel free to contact us directly. You can contact Chris directly via e-mail at cjudd@juddsolutions.com or visit his blog at http://juddsolutions.blogspot.com. You can contact Joseph directly via e-mail at jnusairat@integrallis.com or visit his blog at http://nusairat.blogspot.com or his company at http://www.integrallis.com. You can contract Jim directly via e-mail at shinglerjim@gmail.com or visit his blog at http://jshingler.blogspot.com.

CHAPTER 1

■ ■ ■

Introduction to Groovy

In 1995, Java changed the world. The Internet was in its infancy, and most web sites offered only static content. But Java changed that by enabling applications called *applets* to run inside the browser on many different platforms. Java became a popular general-purpose language, but its greatest growth and strength has been on the server side. It is now one of the dominant server-side platforms. But Java is starting to show its age. Many people are even beginning to call it the new COBOL.

With all these years of baggage, Java has become difficult. There are large barriers of entry, such as knowing which of the many competing frameworks and specifications to use. The language itself has remained pretty much unchanged since the early days to help support backward-compatibility. At this point, many organizations are faced with a dilemma. Should they switch to a platform like Ruby, LAMP (an open source platform based on Linux, Apache, MySQL, and PHP, Perl, or Python), or possibly even .NET to try to become more productive and agile at lower costs so they can better compete in the marketplace? Do they stick with Java and try to make the most of the large investments they have made in frameworks, code, education, and infrastructure? Or do they implement a hybrid and work through integration issues?

Fortunately, there is another option. Keep what is great about the Java platform, specifically the Java Virtual Machine (JVM) and the large library of Java Application Programming Interfaces (APIs), and augment the Java language with a more flexible and productive language. In recent years, many languages have competed to become the Java language replacement for the JVM. Implementations of languages like Ruby, Python, and JavaScript run on the JVM. But none of these languages show as much promise as Groovy, a dynamic language made specifically for the JVM.

In this chapter, we will introduce the Groovy language, describe how to install it, and give you an idea of the benefits of Groovy by working through an example.

Groovy Language Features

Groovy is a relatively new dynamic language that can either be interpreted or compiled and is designed specifically for the Java platform. It has been influenced by languages such as Ruby, Python, Perl, and Smalltalk, as well as Java.

Unlike other languages that are ported to the JVM, Groovy was designed with the JVM in mind, so there is little to no impedance mismatch, significantly reducing the learning curve. Java developers will feel right at home with Groovy. For example, Groovy relies on the Java API rather than supplying its own API, so developers do not need to decide between the IO package from Java and the IO methods from the other language libraries. In addition, because Groovy is built for the JVM, there is tight bytecode-level integration that makes it easy for Java to integrate with Groovy and Groovy to integrate with Java.

Groovy does not just have access to the existing Java API; its Groovy Development Kit (GDK) actually extends the Java API by adding new methods to the existing Java classes to make them more Groovy.

Groovy has support for many of the modern programming features that make other languages so productive, such as closures and properties. Groovy has also proven to be a great platform for concepts such as metaprogramming and domain-specific languages.

Groovy is a standard governed by the Java Community Process (JCP)[1] as Java Specification Request (JSR) 241.[2] It is hosted on Codehaus at `http://groovy.codehaus.org`.

Groovy Installation

Groovy comes bundled as a `.zip` file or platform-specific installer for Windows, and Ubuntu, Debian (as well as openSUSE until recent versions). This section will explain how to install the zipped version, since it covers the widest breadth of platforms.

■**Note** Because Groovy is Java, it requires Java Development Kit (JDK) 1.4 or above to be installed and the `JAVA_HOME` environment variable to be set.

To install Groovy, follow these steps:

1. Download the most recent stable Groovy binary release `.zip` file from `http://groovy.codehaus.org/Download`.

2. Uncompress `groovy-binary-X.X.X.zip` to your desired location.

---

1. `http://www.jcp.org`
2. `http://www.jcp.org/en/jsr/detail?id=241`

3. Set a `GROOVY_HOME` environment variable to the directory in which you uncompressed the `.zip` file.

4. Add the `%GROOVY_HOME%\bin` directory to your system path.

To validate your installation, open a console and type the following:

```
> groovy -version
```

You should see something like this:

```
Groovy Version: 1.5.6 JVM: 1.6.0_02-b06
```

Groovy by Example

The best way to grasp the power and elegance of Groovy is to compare it to Java using an example. In the remainder of this chapter, we will show you how to convert the simple Java class in Listing 1-1 into Groovy. Then we will demonstrate how to adapt the code to use common Groovy idioms.

Listing 1-1. *Simple Java Class*

```
01 package com.apress.bgg;
02
03 import java.util.List;
04 import java.util.ArrayList;
05 import java.util.Iterator;
06
07 public class Todo {
08   private String name;
09   private String note;
10
11   public Todo() {}
12
13   public Todo(String name, String note) {
14     this.name = name;
15     this.note = note;
16   }
17
18   public String getName() {
19     return name;
20   }
```

```
21
22    public void setName(String name) {
23      this.name = name;
24    }
25
26    public String getNote() {
27      return note;
28    }
29
30    public void setNote(String note) {
31      this.note = note;
32    }
33
34    public static void main(String[] args) {
35      List todos = new ArrayList();
36      todos.add(new Todo("1", "one"));
37      todos.add(new Todo("2", "two"));
38      todos.add(new Todo("3","three"));
39
40      for(Iterator iter = todos.iterator();iter.hasNext();) {
41        Todo todo = (Todo)iter.next();
42        System.out.println(todo.getName() + " " + todo.getNote());
43      }
44    }
45 }
```

If you have any Java experience, you will recognize Listing 1-1 as a basic Todo JavaBean. It has getters and setters for name and note attributes, as well as a convenience constructor that takes a name and note for initializing new instances. As you would expect, this class can be found in a file named Todo.java in the com.apress.bgg package.

The class includes a main() method, which is required for Java classes to be executable and is the entry point into the application. On line 35, the main() method begins by creating an instance of a java.util.ArrayList to hold a collection of Todos. On lines 36–38, three Todo instances are created and added to the todos list. Finally, on lines 40–43, a for statement is used to iterate over the collection and print the Todo's name and note to System.out. Notice that on line 41, the object returned from the iterator must be cast back to a Todo so the getName() and getNote() methods can be accessed. This is required because Java is type-safe and because prior to Java 1.5 and the introduction of generics, the Java collections API interface used java.lang.Object so it could handle any and all Java objects.

Converting Java to Groovy

To convert the Java Todo class in Listing 1-1 to Groovy, just rename the file to Todo.groovy. That's right, Groovy derives its syntax from Java. This is often referred to as *copy/paste compatibility*. So congratulations, you are a Groovy developer (even if you didn't know it)!

This level of compatibility, along with a familiar API, really helps to reduce the Groovy learning curve for Java developers. It also makes it easier to incorporate Java examples found on the Internet into a Groovy application and then refactor them to make them more Groovy-like, which is what we will do with Listing 1-1.

To run this Groovy application, from the command line, type the following:

```
> groovy com\apress\bgg\Todo.groovy
```

If you are coming from a Java background, you may be a little surprised that you did not need to first compile the code. Here's the Java equivalent:

```
> javac com\apress\bgg\Todo.java
> java com.apress.bgg.Todo
```

Running the Java application is a two-step process: compile the class using javac, and then use java to run the executable class in the JVM. But Groovy will compile to bytecode at runtime, saving a step in the development process and thereby increasing Groovy's productivity.

Groovy provides a lot of syntactic sugar and is able to imply more than Java. You'll see this in action as we make our Groovy application more Groovy by applying some of the Groovy idioms.

Converting a JavaBean to a GroovyBean

Let's begin by simplifying the JavaBean, which could also be referred to as a Plain Old Java Object (POJO). Groovy has the *GroovyBean*, which is a JavaBean with a simpler Groovy syntax, sometimes referred to as a Plain Old Groovy Object (POGO). GroovyBeans are publicly scoped by default. Listing 1-2 shows our example using a GroovyBean.

Listing 1-2. *Simple Example Using a GroovyBean*

```
01 package com.apress.bgg;
02
03 import java.util.List;
04 import java.util.ArrayList;
05 import java.util.Iterator;
06
07 public class Todo {
```

```
08
09   String name;
10   String note;
11
12   public static void main(String[] args) {
13     List todos = new ArrayList();
14     todos.add(new Todo(name:"1", note:"one"));
15     todos.add(new Todo(name:"2", note:"two"));
16     todos.add(new Todo(name:"3", note:"three"));
17
18     for(Iterator iter = todos.iterator();iter.hasNext();) {
19       Todo todo = (Todo)iter.next();
20       System.out.println(todo.name + " " + todo.note);
21     }
22   }
23 }
```

Listing 1-2 is significantly shorter than Listing 1-1, primarily because Groovy has a concept of native properties, which means getters and setters do not need to be declared. By default, all class attributes—such as the name and note attributes on lines 9 and 10—are public properties and automatically generate corresponding getters and setters in the bytecode. So if the class is used from Java code, or reflection is used to interrogate the class, you will see the getters and setters.

These properties also have a more intuitive usage model. They can be assigned or used directly, as on line 20, where the name and note properties, rather than the getters, are used to generate the output. Also, rather than needing to explicitly create a convenience constructor for initializing a GroovyBean, you can pass named parameters in the constructor to initialize any properties you want, as in lines 14–16.

Simplifying the Code

Some of the syntax sugar included in the Groovy language is making semicolons, parentheses, and data typing optional. Other interesting features to simplify code include implicit imports like the java.util.* package, common methods like println() applying to all objects including Java objects, and more flexible strings. Listing 1-3 applies these features to our example.

Listing 1-3. *Simple Example Applying Syntactic Sugar, Implicit Imports, Common Methods, and String Features*

```
01 package com.apress.bgg;
02
```

```
03 public class Todo {
04
05   String name
06   String note
07
08   public static void main(String[] args) {
09     def todos = new ArrayList()
10     todos.add(new Todo(name:"1", note:"one"))
11     todos.add(new Todo(name:"2", note:"two"))
12     todos.add(new Todo(name:"3", note:"three"))
13
14     for(Iterator iter = todos.iterator();iter.hasNext();) {
15       def todo = iter.next()
16       println "${todo.name} ${todo.note}"
17     }
18   }
19 }
```

In Listing 1-3, under the package declaration we no longer need to import `java.util.List`, `java.util.ArrayList`, and `java.util.Iterator`. These are implicitly imported since they are in the `java.util.*` package. Other implicitly included packages are `java.lang.*`, `java.net.*`, `java.io.*`, `groovy.lang.*`, and `groovy.util.*`.

Also notice that, other than in the `for` statement (which we will clean up in the next round of refactoring), all the semicolons have been removed.

On line 16, we have used optional parentheses with the implicit `println()` method. But that is not the only change to line 16. The `println()` method has been modified to use Groovy's GString format, which is similar to the Apache Ant[3] property format, rather than concatenating two strings. We'll cover Groovy strings in Chapter 2. At this point, just notice how much simpler this is to read.

Lines 9 and 15 have been changed to use optional typing. The variables `todos` and `todo` are no longer typed to `List` or `Todo`, respectively. Groovy uses "duck typing," which means if it sounds like a duck and walks like a duck, it must be a duck. Do you really care what the type of an object is, as long as you can pass it a message and it will handle the request if it can? If the object cannot handle the request, you will receive a `groovy.lang.MissingMethodException` or `groovy.lang.MissingPropertyException`. Of course, where you think typing is necessary, you always have the option of explicitly typing variables.

3. http://ant.apache.org

Using Groovy Collection Notation and Closure

The next step in refactoring the example is to take advantage of Groovy's collection and map notation, as well as replace the ugly for statement with a more elegant closure. Listing 1-4 shows this version.

Listing 1-4. *Example with the Groovy Collection Notation and Closure*

```
01 package com.apress.bgg;
02
03 public class Todo {
04
05    String name
06    String note
07
08    public static void main(String[] args) {
09       def todos = [
10          new Todo(name:"1", note:"one"),
11          new Todo(name:"2", note:"two"),
12          new Todo(name:"3", note:"three")
13       ]
14
15       todos.each {
16          println "${it.name} ${it.note}"
17       }
18    }
19 }
```

Notice how the ArrayList was replaced with [ ]. Again, this is just syntactic sugar; Groovy really is instantiating an ArrayList. Similarly, we can create maps with the [:] syntax.

Also to make the code more clean, we can initialize the list without needing to call the add( ) method for each entry. Then to simplify the iteration, we call the each( ) method, passing a closure that prints out the string. Notice that, by default, the iteration variable is it. Chapter 2 will provide more explanations and examples of Groovy lists, maps, and closures.

Getting Rid of Main()

One bit of Java ugliness left in our example is the main( ) method. After all these improvements, the main( ) method now just sticks out. Fortunately, Groovy has a concept of scripts as well as classes, and we can turn this into a script, removing the need for the main( ) method.

To begin, the file must be renamed to something like `Todos.groovy`. This is because a script will also be compiled to a class, and if we didn't change the name, there would be a name clash between the `Todo` class and the `Todo` script.

Then we simply move the code that currently exists in the `main()` method outside the `Todo` class. When the script is run, it will behave the same as before. Listing 1-5 shows the script version.

Listing 1-5. *Example As a Script*

```
package com.apress.bgg;

public class Todo {

  String name
  String note

}

def todos = [
  new Todo(name:"1", note:"one"),
  new Todo(name:"2", note:"two"),
  new Todo(name:"3", note:"three")
]

todos.each {
  println "${it.name} ${it.note}"
}
```

Finally, we have elegant, easy-to-read code at a fraction of what we started with in Java. It should be obvious that if we had started with the Groovy idioms to begin with, the Groovy approach would have been much more productive.

Summary

This chapter provided a brief introduction to Groovy. After describing how to install it, we demonstrated how you can dramatically reduce the code it takes to write the equivalent Java class in Groovy, while increasing the readability and expressiveness. In the next chapter, we will continue exploring Groovy by looking at its basic language features.

CHAPTER 2

■ ■ ■

Groovy Basics

Chapter 1 introduced you to Groovy, its relationship to Java, and where it differs. This chapter will delve into the Groovy language. The focus will be on language features commonly used to build Grails applications. First, you will learn about Groovy scripts, including compiling and running Groovy scripts using the command line, Groovy Shell, and Groovy Console. Then we will focus on specific aspects of the Groovy language: assertions, strings, methods, closures, collections, ranges, regular expressions, and operators.

Scripts

You will be using the Groovy language to build: domain objects, controllers, and services. But that isn't the only way to use Groovy. In addition to building classes, you can use Groovy as a scripting language.

You will see detailed examples of scripts in Chapter 12, which covers using scripts in an application context to access a web service. But here we'll start with a simple script. Listing 2-1 is an example of a very simple Groovy "Hello" script that takes an argument and uses it to print a message.

Listing 2-1. *A Simple Groovy Script, Hello.groovy*

```
println "Hello ${args[0]}, may Groovy be with you."
```

Execute the script by typing the following on the command line:

```
>groovy Hello "Luke Skywalker"
```

■Note If you are on Windows environment and installed Groovy with the installer, you can omit the `groovy` on the command line. By default, the installer is set up to map files with the `.groovy` file extension to the Groovy runtime.

The script will output the results:

```
Hello Luke Skywalker, may Groovy be with you.
```

On execution of the script, Groovy generates a class with the same name as the script source file, including a main method that contains the script source.

The equivalent Java application would look like Listing 2-2.

Listing 2-2. *The Java Version, HelloJava.java*

```
package com.apress.beginninggrails.cli.scripts;

public class HelloJava {
    public static void main(String[] args) {
        System.out.println( "Hello "+ args[0], may Java be with you.);
    }
}
```

Notice how much more verbose the Java version is compared to the Groovy version. With Java, you need to define a class and a main method. You also must fully qualify the println method, add parentheses, and terminate it with a semicolon. Then you need all of the closing curly braces. Even if you are a Java fan, you have to admit that the Groovy example is a good bit shorter and easier to read! Furthermore, you don't need to go through a separate step of compiling Groovy before it is executed.

Using Script Functions

Just like most scripting languages, Groovy scripts can be organized into blocks of reusable code. In scripts, these blocks are called *functions*. Listing 2-3 is an example of creating and using a function. It creates a simple function to print a name and calls the function with two different names.

Listing 2-3. *A Script Function, PrintFullName.groovy*

```
def printFullName(firstName, lastName) {
    println "${firstName} ${lastName}"
}

printFullName('Luke', 'SkyWalker')
printFullName('Darth', 'Vader')
```

This example defines the `printFullName` function, which takes two parameters. Next, the function is invoked twice: once to print `Luke Skywalker` and again to print `Darth Vader`.

Compiling Groovy

In the previous examples, we let Groovy compile the script on the fly. Like Java, Groovy can be compiled to Java bytecode. Listing 2-4 illustrates compiling the Groovy script in Listing 2-1.

Listing 2-4. *Compiling Groovy with groovyc*

```
groovyc Hello.groovy
```

As you might expect, compiling `Hello.groovy` results in `Hello.class`. Because `groovyc` compiles to Java bytecode, you can use the Java command line to execute it. Listing 2-5 illustrates running the program using Java.

Listing 2-5. *Running the Groovy Program Using Java*

```
java -cp %GROOVY_HOME%/embeddable/groovy-all-1.5.4.jar;. Hello "Luke Skywalker"
Hello Luke Skywalker
```

Being able to run the Groovy program using Java proves it—Groovy is Java. If you look at Listing 2-5, you'll see that the only thing special required to run the Groovy compiler is to include `groovy-all-<version>.jar` on the classpath.

The Groovy compiler is a joint compiler. It can compile Groovy and Java code at the same time. The joint compiler first became available in Groovy 1.5 through a generous donation by JetBrains, the makers of IntelliJ IDEA. The joint compiler allows you to compile Groovy and Java files with a single compile statement. Listings 2-6 and 2-7 are a Groovy file and a Java file, respectively, to demonstrate joint compilation.

Listing 2-6. *A Sample Groovy File, Name.groovy*

```
class Name
{
    String firstName
    String toString() { return "Hello ${firstName}, Java calling Groovy" }
}
```

Listing 2-7. *A Sample Java File, SayHello.java*

```java
public class SayHello
{
  public static void main( String args[] )
  {
    Name name = new Name();
    name.setFirstName( args[0] );

    System.out.println( name.toString() );
  }
}
```

The Java class, SayHello, instantiates the Groovy class Name and sets the firstName property to a value passed in on the command line. Listing 2-8 illustrates compiling and executing the programs.

Listing 2-8. *Joint Compile and Execute*

```
groovyc *.groovy *.java

java -cp %GROOVY_HOME%/embeddable/groovy-all-1.5.6.jar;. SayHello "Luke"
Hello Luke, Java calling Groovy
```

Compiling the Groovy and Java classes is accomplished by telling groovyc to compile files matching the file pattern ending in .groovy and .java. You run the program in the same way that you run any other Java program—just include groovy-all-<version>.jar in the classpath.

■**Caution** If you run groovyc without parameters, you will get the usage information. Looking at the usage information, you might come to the conclusion that you should use the -j switch. Groovy 1.5.0–1.5.5 had a bug[1] that would cause a compile error when using the -j switch. The bug was fixed in Groovy 1.5.6. If you are using an older version of Groovy and encounter an error, try not using the -j switch.

Running Groovy

You can run Groovy scripts and classes through the command line, Groovy Shell, or Groovy Console. Let's look at each technique.

---

1. https://jira.codehaus.org/browse/GROOVY-2747

Command Line

To run Groovy from the command line,[2] you have two or three options:

- Use Groovy directly by typing `groovy MyPgm` at the command line. (If you installed Groovy using the Windows installer, you can omit `groovy` and just type `MyPgm`.) If you are running a script, Groovy will generate a class with a `main` method containing the script commands, compile the script, and execute it. If you don't want to recompile the file each time it is run, you can use the third option.

- Compile the file using `groovyc` into a class and execute it using Java. You saw an example of this approach in the previous section.

- If you're in the Windows environment and Groovy was installed with the Windows Installer with the `PATHEXT` option, you can omit the leading `groovy` and just type `MyPgm.groovy`. The `PATHEXT` option associates files ending with `.groovy` to the Groovy runtime. On Unix platforms, you can use a shebang at the top of the file to get the same result:

```
#!/usr/bin/groovy
println "Hello ${args[0]}, may Groovy be with you."
```

Groovy Shell

The Groovy Shell[3] is an interactive command-line application (*shell*) that allows you to create, run, save, and load Groovy scripts and classes. To start the Groovy Shell, run groovysh. Figure 2-1 illustrates using the Groovy Shell to execute a simple script.

Figure 2-1. *Using the Groovy Shell*

---

2. `http://groovy.codehaus.org/Groovy+CLI`
3. `http://groovy.codehaus.org/Groovy+Shell`

As you can see, the script prints Hello Luke Skywalker. Then you see ===> null. As a matter of convention, Groovy always returns the results of methods. In this case, there is no result, so null is returned.

The Groovy Shell contains a built-in help facility that you can use to learn more about the shell. To access it, type help at the prompt. Figure 2-2 shows the help listing.

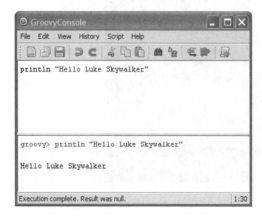

```
C:\Apps\groovy\Groovy-1.5.4\bin\groovysh.exe                    _ □ ×
groovy:000> help

For information about Groovy, visit:
    http://groovy.codehaus.org

Available commands:
  help       (\h) Display this help message
  ?          (\?) Alias to: help
  exit       (\x) Exit the shell
  quit       (\q) Alias to: exit
  import     (\i) Import a class into the namespace
  display    (\d) Display the current buffer
  clear      (\c) Clear the buffer
  show       (\S) Show variables, classes or imports
  inspect    (\n) Inspect a variable or the last result with the GUI object browse
r
  purge      (\p) Purge variables, classes, imports or preferences
  edit       (\e) Edit the current buffer
  load       (\l) Load a file or URL into the buffer
  .          (\.) Alias to: load
  save       (\s) Save the current buffer to a file
  record     (\r) Record the current session to a file
  history    (\H) Display, manage and recall edit-line history
  alias      (\a) Create an alias
  set        (\=) Set (or list) preferences

For help on a specific command type:
    help command

groovy:000>
```

Figure 2-2. *Groovy Shell help information*

Groovy Console

The Groovy Console,[4] shown in Figure 2-3, is a graphical version of the Groovy Shell. It is written using SwingBuilder, a Groovy module that makes building Swing user interfaces easier.

```
GroovyConsole                                      _ □ ×
File  Edit  View  History  Script  Help

println "Hello Luke Skywalker"




groovy> println "Hello Luke Skywalker"

Hello Luke Skywalker

Execution complete. Result was null.            1:30
```

Figure 2-3. *Groovy Console*

---

4. http://groovy.codehaus.org/Groovy+Console

You can start the Groovy Console in a number of ways, depending on your environment and how you installed Groovy. The easiest way is to execute groovyConsole, which is located in the Groovy bin directory.

The console provides the ability to create, save, load, and execute classes and scripts. Some of the nice features of the console are undo/redo and the ability to inspect variables.

If you have to choose between using the Groovy Shell and the Groovy Console, we recommend the Groovy Console. To a beginner, the Groovy Shell behavior can seem to be a bit unpredictable. For example, try the code from Listing 2-9 in the shell and then in the console.

Listing 2-9. *Shell/Console Experiment*

```
name = "Luke Skywalker"
def name = "Darth Vader"
println name
```

Running this code from the shell results in Luke Skywalker being printed. Running the code from the console results in Darth Vader being printed. The reason for the difference can be found in the Groovy Shell documentation.[5] The first instance of name causes a shell variable to be created and assigned the value Luke Skywalker. The second instance of name (def name) causes a local variable to be created and assigned the value Darth Vader. The shell executes expressions as soon as it sees a complete expression. In the case of the second instance of name, it was a complete expression that was executed and immediately went out of scope. When the final line of code (println) is executed, the only currently accessible name variable is assigned the value Luke Skywalker.

Assertions

As a developer, if you have used JUnit[6] (or any of the flavors of JUnit), you already have some idea what an assertion is. An *assertion* is used to validate that an expected condition is true. If the expected condition is not true, a java.lang.AssertionError[7] is thrown. You test that the expected condition is true by using Groovy expressions.

Taking advantage of Groovy's truth[8] required Groovy developers to create their own version of assert. They could not leverage the Java version of assert[9] because it is

---

5. http://groovy.codehaus.org/Groovy+Shell#GroovyShell-Variables

6. http://www.junit.org

7. http://java.sun.com/j2se/1.4.2/docs/api/java/lang/AssertionError.html

8. http://groovy.codehaus.org/Groovy+Truth

9. http://java.sun.com/j2se/1.4.2/docs/guide/lang/assert.html

restricted to Java's version of truth. You will also notice that the syntax is the same. Listing 2-10 illustrates the Java and Groovy versions of assert.

Listing 2-10. *Java and Groovy Assertions*

```
// Java assert
assert 1==2 : "One isn't Two";

// Groovy assert
assert 1==2 : "One isn't Two"
```

As you can see, the Groovy assert syntax is the same as Java's, except for the ending semicolon. The message is to the right of the expression and separated by a colon. As with Java, the message portion of the assert is optional.

Tip As a best practice, when you are using assertions, you should include a message. It will help the next person maintaining your code to understand its intent.

When an assertion fails, Groovy throws a java.lang.AssertionError. Listing 2-11 is an example of the Groovy assertion in Listing 2-10 failing.

Listing 2-11. *Sample Assertion Failure*

```
ERROR java.lang.AssertionError: One isn't Two Expression: (1 == 2)
```

As you can see, the error message from Listing 2-10 is embedded in Listing 2-11.

Assertions are very handy and one of the cornerstones of good testing. They also do a great job of clarifying intentions. You will see assertions in many of the examples throughout this book.

Strings

Like most modern languages, Groovy has the concept of a *string*. In Groovy, a string can be defined three different ways: using double quotes, single quotes, or slashes (called "slashy strings"). Listing 2-12 illustrates the three different ways to define a string.

Listing 2-12. *Groovy String Definition*

```
01 // Quote
02 def helloChris = "Hello, Chris"
03 println helloChris.class.name  // java.lang.String
04
05 // Single quote
06 def helloJoseph = 'Hello, Joseph'
07 println helloJoseph.class.name // java.lang.String
08
09 // Slashy string
10 def helloJim = /Hello, Jim/
11 println helloJim.class.name // java.lang.String
```

Just to prove that the variables are normal java.lang.String strings, run the code in Listing 2-12. The output should look like this:

```
java.lang.String
java.lang.String
java.lang.String
```

Groovy also supports a more advanced string called a GString. A GString is just like a normal string, except that it evaluates expressions that are embedded within the string, in the form ${...}. When Groovy sees a string defined with double quotes or slashes and an embedded expression, Groovy constructs an org.codehaus.groovy.runtime.GStringImpl instead of a java.lang.String. When the GString is accessed, the expression is evaluated. Listing 2-13 illustrates using a GString and embedded expressions.

Listing 2-13. *GString and Embedded Expressions*

```
01 def name = "Jim"
02 def helloName = "Hello, ${name}"
03 println helloName // Hello, Jim
04 println helloName.class.name // org.codehaus.groovy.runtime.GStringImpl
05
06 def helloNoName = 'Hello, ${name}'
07 println helloNoName // Hello, ${name}
08 println helloNoName.class.name  // java.lang.String
09
10 def helloSlashyName = /Hello, ${name}/
11 println helloSlashyName // Hello, Jim
12 println helloSlashyName.class.name  // org.codehaus.groovy.runtime.GStringImpl
```

Run the code in Listing 2-13 to see the expression evaluation and class names:

```
Hello, Jim
org.codehaus.groovy.runtime.GStringImpl
Hello, ${name}
java.lang.String
Hello Jim
org.codehaus.groovy.runtime.GStringImpl
```

Let's take a look at Listing 2-13 in a little more detail:

- Line 1 defines a variable, name, and assigns the value "Jim".

- Line 2 defines a GString, helloName, and assigns it to "Hello" plus the expression ${name}.

- Line 3 prints the GString. Accessing the GString causes the expression to be evaluated and results in Hello, Jim.

- Line 4 prints out helloName's class name to prove that it is a GString.

- Lines 6–8 take the same approach but define the string with single quotes. The result is a regular Java string, and the expression is *not* evaluated.

- Lines 10–12 take the same approach but define the string using slashes. The result is a GString, just as in the first example. When the string is printed, the expression is evaluated, and Hello, Jim is printed.

The evaluation of expressions within strings is called interpolation, as discussed next.

String Interpolation

String *interpolation* is the ability to substitute an expression or variable within a string. If you have experience with Unix shell scripts, Ruby, or Perl, this should look familiar. If you look closely at Listing 2-13, you can see string interpolation in action. Strings defined using double quotes and slashes will evaluate embedded expressions within the string (see lines 2 and 10 of Listing 2-13). Strings defined with single quotes don't evaluate the embedded expressions (see line 6 of Listing 2-13).

Java doesn't support string interpolation. You must manually concatenate the values together. Listing 2-14 is an example of the type of code you need to write in Java.

Listing 2-14. *Building Strings with Java*

```
String name = "Jim";
String helloName = "Hello " + name;
System.out.println(helloName);
```

While this is an extremely simple example, imagine what it might look like if you were building some XML or a SQL statement. It gets very difficult to read very quickly.

String interpolation is a nice feature and is used in the examples throughout this book to build up strings.

Multiline Strings

Groovy supports strings that span multiple lines. A multiline string is defined by using three double quotes or three single quotes.

Multiline string support is very useful for creating templates or embedded documents (such as XML templates, SQL statements, HTML, and so on). For example, you could use a multiline string and string interpolation to build the body of an e-mail message, as shown in Listing 2-15. String interpolation with multiline strings works in the same way as it does with regular strings: multiline strings created with double quotes evaluate expressions, and single-quoted strings don't.

Listing 2-15. *Using Multiline Strings*

```
def name = "Jim"
def multiLineQuote = """
Hello, ${name}

This is a multiline string with double quotes
"""
println multiLineQuote
println multiLineQuote.class.name

def multiLineSingleQuote = '''
Hello, ${name}

This is a multiline string with single quotes
'''
println multiLineSingleQuote
println multiLineSingleQuote.class.name
```

Running the code in Listing 2-15 results in the following output:

```
Hello, Jim

This is a multiline string with double quotes
org.codehaus.groovy.runtime.GStringImpl

Hello, ${name}

This is a multiline string with single quotes
java.lang.String
```

Slashy Strings

As mentioned earlier, slashes can be used to define strings. The slashy notation has a very nice benefit: additional backslashes are not needed to escape special characters. The only exception is escaping a backslash: \/. The slashy notation can be helpful when creating a regular expression requiring a backslash or a path. Listing 2-16 illustrates the difference between using regular quotes and slashes to define a regular expression to match a file system path.

Listing 2-16. *Using Slashy Strings*

```
def winpathQuoted='C:\\windows\\system32'
def winpathSlashy=/C:\windows\system32/
println winpathSlashy  // C:\windows\system32

assert winpathSlashy ==~ '\\w{1}:\\\\.+\\\\.+'
assert winpathSlashy ==~ /\w{1}:\\.+\\.+/
```

Listing 2-16 defines two variables and assigns them to a directory path. The first variable definition, winpathQuoted, uses the single-quote notation to define a string. Using the single-quote notation requires that the embedded backslash be escaped using an additional backslash. The first assert statement, which tests the regular expression defined using single quotes, also requires the addition of an extra backslash to escape a backslash. Notice how using the slashy notation doesn't require the additional backslashes.

Clearly, it is easier to write and read winpathSlashy, and the second regular expression is easier to write and read as well. Regular expressions and the ==~ operator will be covered in more detail in the "Regular Expressions" section later in this chapter.

Methods and Closures

You can define a block of reusable code in Groovy in two ways: as a method, as in Java, and as a closure.

Methods

Listing 2-17 illustrates defining a method in Groovy the Java way.

Listing 2-17. *Defining a Method the Java Way*

```
public String hello(String name) {
    return "Hello, " + name;
}
```

Listing 2-18 illustrates defining the method using the Groovy idiom.

Listing 2-18. *Defining a Method Using the Groovy Idiom*

```
def hello(name) {
    "Hello, ${name}"
}
```

The Groovy way of defining is method is a bit more compact. It takes advantage of a couple of Groovy's optional features:

- The return type and the `return` statement are not included in the body of the method. Groovy always returns the results of the last expression—in this case, the GString `"Hello, . . . "`.

- The access modifier `public` is not defined. By default, unless you specify otherwise, Groovy defaults all classes, properties, and methods to `public` access.

■Note Strictly speaking, the Groovy version of the `hello` method (Listing 2-18) is not exactly like the Java version (Listing 2-17). The corresponding Java signature of the method would be: `public Object hello(Object name)` But, functionally, they are very close to being the same.

Closures

A Groovy *closure* is a block of reusable code within curly braces {}, which can be assigned to a property or a variable, or passed as a parameter to a method.[10] The code within the curly braces is executed when the closure is invoked. In this form, the closure functions just like a Java method. The difference between methods and closures is that a closure is an object, and a method isn't. You will see why this is valuable in just a few moments. Listing 2-19 is an example of defining and invoking a closure.

Listing 2-19. *Using a Closure*

```
def name = "Chris"
def printClosure = { println "Hello, ${name}" }

printClosure()

name = "Joseph"
printClosure()
```

```
Hello, Chris
Hello, Joseph
```

This example demonstrates that just like methods, closures can access variables defined in the same scope as the closure.

And just as with methods, parameters can be passed to closures as well. Listing 2-20 shows an example of passing parameters to closures.

Listing 2-20. ■ *Passing Parameters to Closures*

```
def printClosure = {name -> println "Hello, ${name}" }

printClosure("Chris")
printClosure("Joseph")
printClosure "Jim"
```

---

10. http://groovy.codehaus.org/Closures+-+Formal+Definition and http://groovy.codehaus.org/Clo-sures+-+Informal+Guide

```
Hello, Chris
Hello, Joseph
Hello, Jim
```

In this example, `printClosure` takes a `name` parameter. Compare Listing 2-19 to Listing 2-20. Listing 2-19 is an example of closure accessing the `name` variable, and Listing 2-20 is an example of a closure taking a `name` parameter.

The third invocation of `printClosure` in Listing 2-20 does not include parentheses. This is not a typo. This is another one of the optional parts of Groovy. The fact that there is a parameter after the closure name helps Groovy infer that you want the closure invoked. This works only when a parameter is involved. In Listing 2-19, where there are no parameters, the parentheses are required.

Multiple parameters can be passed as well. Listing 2-21 illustrates calling a closure with multiple parameters.

Listing 2-21. *Passing Multiple Parameters to a Closure*

```
def printClosure = {name1, name2, name3 -> println "Hello, ${name1},
    ${name2}, ${name3}" }


printClosure "Chris", "Joseph", "and Jim"
```

```
Hello, Chris, Joseph, and Jim
```

In this example, the `"Hello, . . ."` and expressions were evaluated when the closure was invoked.

An advanced usage of closures is to bind the closure to values at the time it is defined. Listing 2-22 is an example of using this technique to create a timer.

Listing 2-22. *Binding Values to Closures*

```
01 def startTimer() {
02    def initialDate = new java.util.Date()
03    return { println "${initialDate} - ${new java.util.Date()} : Elapsed time
                  ${System.currentTimeMillis() - initialDate.time}" }
04 }
05
06 def timer = startTimer()
07 // Simulate some work
```

```
08 sleep 30000
09 timer()
10 // Simulate some more work
11 sleep 30000
12 timer()
13
14 // Reset the timer
15 println "Reset the Timer"
16 timer = startTimer()
17 timer()
18 sleep 30000
19 timer()
```

```
Sat Mar 01 09:29:27 EST 2008 - Sat Mar 01 09:29:57 EST 2008 : Elapsed time 29998
Sat Mar 01 09:29:27 EST 2008 - Sat Mar 01 09:30:27 EST 2008 : Elapsed time 59997
Reset the timer
Sat Mar 01 09:30:27 EST 2008 - Sat Mar 01 09:30:27 EST 2008 : Elapsed time 0
Sat Mar 01 09:30:27 EST 2008 - Sat Mar 01 09:30:57 EST 2008 : Elapsed time 29999
```

In Listing 2-22, lines 1–4 define a method, startTimer(), that returns a closure. The value of the variable initialDate, a java.util.Date object, is bound to the closure at the time it is defined, in line 6. In lines 7–12, when the closure is invoked, the expressions are evaluated. Line 16 invokes the startTimer() method, which causes the closure to be redefined and the results in the timer to be reset.

A closure is an object. You can pass closures around just like any other objects. A common example is iterating over a collection using a closure. Listing 2-23 illustrates passing a closure as a parameter.

Listing 2-23. *Passing a Closure As a Parameter*

```
def list = ["Chris", "Joseph", "Jim"]
def sayHello = { println it }
list.each(sayHello)
```

Notice that sayHello is a property whose value is a closure. It is passed to the each() method so that as each() iterates over the list, the sayHello closure is invoked.

Collections

Groovy supports a number of different collections, including lists, ranges, sets, arrays, and maps. Let's look at how to create and use each of the collection types.

Lists

A Groovy list[11] is an ordered collection of objects, just as in Java. It is an implementation of the `java.util.List`[12] interface. In the course of building Grails applications, it is common to see lists returned from the controllers and services. Listing 2-24 illustrates creating a list and common usages.

Listing 2-24. *Creating and Using Lists*

```
01 def emptyList = []
02 println emptyList.class.name //  java.util.ArrayList
03 println emptyList.size // 0
04
05 def list = ["Chris"]  // List with one item in it
06 // Add items to the list
07 list.add "Joseph"  // Notice the optional () missing
08 list << "Jim"  // Notice the overloaded left-shift operator
09 println list.size // 3
10
11 // Iterate over the list
12 list.each { println it } // Chris Joseph Jim
13
14 // Access items in the list
15 println list[1]  // Joseph  // Indexed access
16 list[0] = "Christopher"
17 println list.get(0)  // Christopher
18
19 list.set(0, "Chris") // Set the 0 item to Chris
20 println list.get(0)  // Chris
21
22 list.remove 2
23 list-= "Joseph"  // Overloaded - operator
24 list.each { println it } // Chris
```

---

11. http://groovy.codehaus.org/JN1015-Collections
12. http://java.sun.com/j2se/1.4.2/docs/api/java/util/List.html

```
25
26 list.add "Joseph"
27 list+="Jim" // Overloaded + operator
28 list.each { println it } // Chris Joseph Jim
29 println list[-1]  // Jim
```

On line 1 of Listing 2-24, an empty list is created by assigning a property the value of [ ]. Line 2 prints out the list's class name so that you can see that it is a java.util.ArrayList. Line 3 prints the list's size, which is 0.

Lines 5–9 create a list with an item already in it and show two ways to add items to the list. Line 12 iterates over the list, invoking the closure to print out the contents. The each() method provides the ability to iterate over all elements in the list, invoking the closure on each element. This is an example of using a closure as a parameter to a method.

Lines 15–17 illustrate using an index to access a list. Lists are zero-based. Line 15 shows accessing the second item in the list. Line 16 shows using an index to assign position 0 the value "Christopher". Line 17 accesses the list using the get() method. Lines 19–20 use the set() method to assign the first position in the list and then print it out.

Lines 22–24 remove items from the list using the remove() method and the minus operator. Lines 26–28 add items to the list using the add() method and the plus operator.

Line 29 is interesting—it uses the index value -1. Using a negative index value causes the list to be accessed in the opposite order, or from last to first.

Ranges

A range is a list of sequential values. Logically, you can think of it as 1 through 10 or *a* through *z*. As a matter of fact, the declaration of a range is exactly that: 1..10, or 'a'..'z'.

A range is a list of any objects that implements java.lang.Comparable.[13] The objects have next() and previous() methods to facilitate navigating through the range. This means that with a bit of work, it is possible to use your own Groovy objects within a range. Listing 2-25 illustrates some of things you can do with ranges.

Listing 2-25. *Creating and Using Ranges*

```
01 def numRange = 0..9
02 println numRange.size() // 10
03 numRange.each {print it}  // 0123456789
04 println ""
05 println numRange.contains(5)  // true
06
```

13. http://java.sun.com/j2se/1.4.2/docs/api/java/lang/Comparable.html

```
07 def alphaRange = 'a'..'z'
08 println alphaRange.size()    // 26
09 println alphaRange[1]     // b
10
11 def exclusiveRange = 1..<10
12 println exclusiveRange.size() // 9
13 exclusiveRange.each {print it}  // 123456789
14 println ""
15 println exclusiveRange.contains(10)  // false
16
17 def reverseRange = 9..0
18 reverseRange.each {print it} // 9876543210
```

Lines 1, 7, 11, and 17 illustrate defining ranges. Line 1 defines an inclusive range of numbers. Line 7 defines an inclusive range of lowercase letters. Line 11 defines an exclusive list of numbers. The range results in a range of numbers 1–9, excluding 10. Line 17 creates a range in reverse order, 9 through 0.

Frequently, ranges are used for iterating. In Listing 2-25, each() was used to iterate over the range. Listing 2-26 shows three ways you could use a range to iterate: one Java and two Groovy.

Listing 2-26. *Iterating with Ranges*

```
01 println "Java style for loop"
02 for(int i=0;i<=9;i++) {
03     println i
04 }
05
06 println "Groovy style for loop"
07 for (i in 0..9) {
08     println i
09 }
10
11 println "Groovy range loop"
12 (0..9).each { i->
13     println i
14 }
```

Listing 2-26 starts off by showing a classic Java style for loop. Lines 7–9 are an example of the same loop using the Groovy style for loop. Lines 12–14 illustrate yet another technique for looping, by using a range and the each() method.

Sets

A Groovy set[14] is an unordered collection of objects, with no duplicates, just as in Java. It is an implementation of java.util.Set.[15] By default, unless you specify otherwise, a Groovy set is a java.util.HashSet.[16] If you need a set other than a HashSet, you can create any type of set by instantiating it; for example, def aTreeSet = new TreeSet(). In general, we encourage you just to think of it as a regular set. Listing 2-27 illustrates creating sets and common usages.

Listing 2-27. *Creating and Using Sets*

```
01 def emptySet = [] as Set
02 println emptySet.class.name //  java.util.HashSet
03 println emptySet.size() // 0
04
05 def list = ["Chris", "Chris" ]
06 def set = ["Chris", "Chris" ] as Set
07 println "List Size: ${list.size()} Set Size: ${set.size()}" // List Size: 2 Set
Size: 1
08 set.add "Joseph"
09 set << "Jim"
10 println set.size() // 3
11 println set  // ["Chris", "Jim", "Joseph"]
12
13 // Iterate over the set
14 set.each { println it }
15 S
16 set.remove 2
17 set-= "Joseph"  // Overloaded - operator
18 set.each { println it } // Chris
19 set+= "Joseph"
20 set+= "Jim"
21 set.each { println it } // Chris Joseph Jim
22
23 // Convert a set to a list
24 List = set as List
```

---

14. http://groovy.codehaus.org/JN1015-Collections

15. http://java.sun.com/j2se/1.4.2/docs/api/java/util/Set.html

16. http://java.sun.com/j2se/1.4.2/docs/api/java/util/HashSet.html

```
25 println list.class.name // java.util.ArrayList
26 println set.asList().class.name // java.util.ArrayList
27 println set.toList().class.name // java.util.ArrayList
```

Creating an empty set is similar to creating an empty list. The difference is the addition of the as Set clause. Lines 5–7 illustrate that a list allows duplicates and a set doesn't. Lines 8–21 shouldn't be any surprise. One of the important differences between a list and a set is that a list provides indexed-based access and a set doesn't. Lines 24 and 26 show two different techniques to convert a Set into a List.

Arrays

A Groovy array[17] is a sequence of objects, just like a Java array.[18] Groovy makes working with arrays a little easier, but you have the same limitations as with Java arrays. Listing 2-28 illustrates creating and using arrays.

Listing 2-28. *Creating and Using Arrays*

```
01 def stringArray = new String[3]
02 println stringArray.size()
03 stringArray[0] = "Chris"
04 println stringArray  // {"Chris", null, null}
05 stringArray[1] = "Joseph"
06 stringArray[2] = "Jim"
07 println stringArray // {"Chris", "Joseph", "Jim"}
08 println stringArray[1] // Joseph
09 stringArray.each { println it} // Chris, Joseph, Jim
10 println stringArray[-1..-3] // ["Jim", "Joseph", "Chris"]
```

Line 1 creates a string array of size 3. Lines 3–8 use an index to access the array. Line 9 illustrates using the each() method to iterate through the array. That deserves a second look. Yes, the each() method is available on the array, which is very convenient. Line 10 also shows something interesting—it uses a range to access the array. In this case, the example goes one step further and shows accessing the array from left to right.

---

17. http://groovy.codehaus.org/JN1025-Arrays
18. http://codeguru.earthweb.com/java/tij/tij0053.shtml

Maps

A Groovy map[19] is an unordered collection of key/value pairs, where the key is unique, just as in Java. It is an implementation of java.util.Map.[20] By default, unless you specify otherwise, a Groovy map is a java.util.LinkedHashMap.[21] If you are familiar with LinkedHashMap maps, you know that they are ordered by insert.

If you need a map other than a LinkedHashMap, you can create any type of map by instantiating it; for example, def aTreeMap = new TreeMap(). In general, we encourage you just to think of it as a regular map.

Listing 2-29 illustrates creating maps and common usages.

Listing 2-29. *Creating and Using Maps*

```
01 def emptyMap = [:]
02 // map.class returns null, use getClass()
03 println emptyMap.getClass().name  //java.util.LinkedHashMap
04 println emptyMap.size() // 0
05
06 def todos = ['a':'Write the map section', 'b':'Write the set section']
07 println todos.size() // 2
08 println todos["a"] // Write the map section
09 println todos."a"  // Write the map section
10 println todos.a    // Write the map section
11 println todos.getAt("b") // Write the set section
12 println todos.get("b")   // Write the set section
13 println todos.get("c", "unknown") //  unknown, Notice "c" wasn't defined
14                                   // and now it is
15 println todos // ["a":"Write the map section", "b":"Write the set section",
16             // "c":"unknown"]
17
18 todos.d = "Write the ranges section"
19 println todos.d // Write the ranges section
20 todos.put('e', 'Write the strings section')
21 println todos.e // Write the strings section
22 todos.putAt 'f', 'Write the closure section' // Notice () are optional
23 println todos.f // Write the closure section
24 todos[null] = 'Nothing Set'  // Using null as a key
```

---

19. http://groovy.codehaus.org/JN1035-Maps

20. http://java.sun.com/j2se/1.4.2/docs/api/java/util/Map.html

21. http://java.sun.com/j2se/1.4.2/docs/api/java/util/LinkedHashMap.html

```
25 println todos[null] // Nothing set
26
27 // Print each key/value pair on a separate line
28 // Note: it is an implicit iterator
29 todos.each { println "Key: ${it.key}, Value: ${it.value}" }
30 // Print each key/value pair on a separate line with index
31 todos.eachWithIndex { it, i -> println "${i} Key: ${it.key},
32    Value: ${it.value}" }
33 // Print the value set
34 todos.values().each { println it }
```

In line 1, an empty map is created by assigning a property the value [:]. Compare the creation of an empty list to the creation of an empty map. An empty list is created using the value []; an empty map is created using the value [:]. You can see from line 2 that the map is implemented as a java.util.LinkedHashMap.

Line 6 illustrates defining a map with multiple entries. When using the square bracket notation, the colon separates the key from the value. Line 6 is [key1: value1, key2 : value2].

Lines 8–16 show several different techniques for accessing the map. The most interesting is line 10. It shows using the key as a property to the map. You can use this technique to read an item from the map and put an item into the map.

Lines 18–25 show several different techniques for putting items into the map. You can see that they mirror the techniques used on lines 8–16.

Lines 29, 31, 32, and 34 illustrate iterating. Line 29 iterates over the map to print the key and value. Lines 31 and 32 iterate with an index. Line 34 iterates over the map values.

Regular Expressions

Regular expressions, sometimes referred to as *regex*, are a technique for identifying and manipulating text using a pattern notation.[22] They have been popular in scripting languages such as Unix shell scripting and Perl for a long time, and were added to Java in version 1.4.[23]

■**Note** Regular expressions are extremely robust and powerful. This section discusses Groovy's support of regular expressions. For a full exploration of regular expressions, refer to a book devoted to that subject. You can also find many useful tutorials on the Internet.[24]

---

22. http://groovy.codehaus.org/Regular+Expressions

23. http://java.sun.com/j2se/1.4.2/docs/api/java/util/regex/Pattern.html

24. http://groovy.codehaus.org/Tutorial+4+-+Regular+expressions+basics and http://groovy.codehaus.org/Tutorial+5+-+Capturing+regex+groups, for example

A regular expression is a sequence of characters to create a pattern that is applied to a string. The pattern is defined by a pattern language. Table 2-1 shows some of the more common patterns in the Java regular expression language.[25]

Table 2-1. *Summary of Regular-Expression Constructs*

Construct	Matches
Characters	
x	The character *x*
\\	The backslash character
\t	The tab character (\u0009)
\n	The newline (line feed) character (\u000A)
\r	The carriage-return character (\u000D)
\f	The form-feed character (\u000C)
\e	The escape character (\u001B)
Character Classes	
[abc]	a, b, or c (simple class)
[^abc]	Any character except a, b, or c (negation)
[a-zA-Z]	a through z or A through Z, inclusive (range)
[a-d[m-p]]	a through d, or m through p: [a-dm-p] (union)
[a-z&&[def]]	d, e, or f (intersection)
[a-z&&[^bc]]	a through z, except for b and c: [ad-z] (subtraction)
[a-z&&[^m-p]]	a through z, and not m through p: [a-lq-z] (subtraction)
Predefined Character Classes	
.	Any character (may or may not match line terminators)
\d	A digit: [0–9]
\D	A nondigit: [^0–9]
\s	A whitespace character: [\t\n\x0B\f\r]
\S	A non-whitespace character: [^\s]
\w	A word character: [a-zA-Z_0-9]
\W	A nonword character: [^\w]

---

25. For a complete list of regular expressions, see http://java.sun.com/j2se/1.4.2/docs/api/java/util/regex/Pattern.html.

Construct	Matches
Boundary Matchers	
^	The beginning of a line
$	The end of a line
\b	A word boundary
\B	A nonword boundary
\A	The beginning of the input
\G	The end of the previous match
\Z	The end of the input but for the final terminator, if any
\z	The end of the input
Greedy Quantifiers	
$X?$	X, once or not at all
$X*$	X, zero or more times
$X+$	X, one or more times
$X\{n\}$	X, exactly n times
$X\{n,\}$	X, at least n times
$X\{n,m\}$	X, at least n but not more than m times
Reluctant Quantifiers	
$X??$	X, once or not at all
$X*?$	X, zero or more times
$X+?$	X, one or more times
$X\{n\}?$	X, exactly n times
$X\{n,\}?$	X, at least n times
$X\{n,m\}?$	X, at least n but not more than m times
Possessive Quantifiers	
$X?+$	X, once or not at all
$X*+$	X, zero or more times
$X++$	X, one or more times
$X\{n\}+$	X, exactly n times
$X\{n,\}+$	X, at least n times
$X\{n,m\}+$	X, at least n but not more than m times
Logical Operators	
XY	X followed by Y
$X\|Y$	Either X or Y
(X)	X, as a capturing group

Groovy Regular Expression Operators

Groovy leverages Java's regular expression support and makes it easier through Groovy's string support. Groovy also adds three convenience operators:

- The match operator (==~)

- The find operator (=~)

- The pattern operator (~*string*)

Match Operator

The match operator (==~) returns true if the regular expression *exactly* matches the subject. Listing 2-30 shows some examples of using the match operator.

Listing 2-30. *Using the Match Operator*

```
01 assert "abc" ==~ 'abc'
02 assert "abc" ==~ /abc/
03 assert "abcabc ==~ /abc/  // Fails - not an exact match
04 assert "abc" ==~ /^a.c/   // Starts with a, 1 char, ends with c
05 assert "abc" ==~ /^a../   // Starts with a, 2 chars
06 assert "abc" ==~ /.*c$/   // One or more chars end with c
07 assert "abc" ==~ ".*c\$"  // Slashy string is better
```

Line 3 shows that unless it is an exact match, the match will fail (return false). Lines 4–6 illustrate a couple of ways of defining a regular expression that matches the subject. Line 7 is another example of defining the regular expression on line 6, except it uses double quotes instead of slashes. The important thing to note is that using the double quotes requires the $ to be escaped using a (==~)backslash.

Find Operator

The find operator (=~) returns a java.util.regex.Matcher.[26] A *matcher* is a component that applies a regular expression to a string. The result is a two-dimensional array of matches. The first dimension contains the match, and the second dimension contains the groups within the match. A group is the defined within the regular expression using parentheses. In the example in Listing 2-31, the regular expression defines four groups. When the expression is applied to a string, the groups are individually accessible. This is useful for identifying and accessing portions of a string.

---

26. http://java.sun.com/j2se/1.4.2/docs/api/java/util/regex/Matcher.html

Listing 2-31. *Using the Find Operator*

```
01 def winpath=/C:\windows\system32\somedir/
02 def matcher = winpath =~ /(\w{1}):\\(\w+)\\(\w+)\\(\w+)/
03 println matcher
04 println matcher[0] // ["C:\windows\system32\somedir", "C", "windows",
05                     //  "system32", "somedir"]
06 println matcher[0][1] // C
07 def newPath = matcher.replaceFirst('/etc/bin/')
08 println newPath // /etc/bin
```

```
java.util.regex.Matcher[pattern=(\w{1}):\\(\w+)\\(\w+)\\(\w+) region=0,27
 lastmatch=]
["C:\windows\system32\somedir", "C", "windows", "system32", "somedir"]
C
/etc/bin/
```

Line 1 defines winpath as a directory path string. Line 2 applies a regular expression to the winpath variable using the find operator and returns a java.util.regex.Matcher. The regular expression is set up as a series of group-capturing expressions. Referring to Table 2-1, you can see that \w is a word character and the + means one or more. When the regular expression matches the variable, the individual group values are available from the matcher. When line 3 is invoked, you can see that matcher is in fact a java.util.regex.Matcher and the pattern is matching. Lines 4 and 5 illustrate printing the contents of the first match using an index notation. In this example, there will be only one match. If winpath had been a multiline string with multiple directory paths, then matcher would have had multiple matches. Line 6 shows accessing the first group within the match using a second index.

Now that you have a match, you can start applying java.util.regex.Matcher methods. Line 7 is an example of replacing the first match with a new value. When you replace a match, it returns a new string.

Pattern Operator

The pattern operator (~*string*) transforms a string into a pattern (java.util.regex.Pattern[27]), which is a compiled regular expression. When you are going to use a regular expression over and over, you should consider creating a pattern. Reusing a pattern will give the application a performance boost.[28] Listing 2-32 illustrates creating and using a pattern.

---

27. http://java.sun.com/j2se/1.4.2/docs/api/java/util/regex/Pattern.html
28. Section 3.5.4, *Groovy in Action* by Dierk Koenig et al. (Manning, 2007).

Listing 2-32. *Creating and Using a Pattern*

```
01 def saying = """Now is the time for all good men (and women) to come to the aid
02 of their country"""
03 def pattern = ~/(\w+en)/
04 def matcher = pattern.matcher(saying)
05 def count = matcher.getCount()
06 println "Matches = ${count}"
07 for(i in 0..<count) {
08   println matcher[i]
09 }
```

```
Matches = 2
["men", "men"]
["women", "women"]
```

Lines 1 and 2 assign a famous quote to the saying variable. Line 3 defines a regular expression pattern that should find the words that end in *en*, such as men and women.

■**Caution** Notice the space between the = and ~ for the pattern operator in Listing 2-32. Without the space, it would be the find operator.

Line 4 applies the pattern to the saying and returns a matcher that contains the results. Lines 5 and 6 print the number of matches. Lines 7–9 loop through and print the matches.

Common Uses of Regular Expressions

By now, you are starting to get an idea of how regular expressions work. Now let's see how they can be applied in real-world scenarios. It is common for web applications to allow the user to enter personal information such as a telephone number. Two common tasks are to check that the phone number is a valid format and to parse the phone number into the individual parts. Listing 2-33 is an example of using the match operator to validate a phone number.

Listing 2-33. *Validating a Phone Number*

```
def phoneValidation = /^[01]?\s*[\(\.-]?(\d{3})[\)\.-]?\s*(\d{3})[\.-](\d{4})$/
assert '(800)555-1212' ==~ phoneValidation
assert '1(800) 555-1212' ==~ phoneValidation
assert '1-800-555-1212' ==~ phoneValidation
assert '1.800.555.1212' ==~ phoneValidation
```

In this example, you see the same phone number in four different valid formats. The regular expression to validate the phone number format is assigned to the variable phoneValidation. The match operator is used to validate the phone numbers by applying the regular expression to the phone number. If the phone number is valid, the match operator returns true.

Another common task is parsing a phone number so that the values can be put into a domain class. Listing 2-34 illustrates parsing the phone number into the individual parts and loading it in the domain class.

Listing 2-34. *Parsing the Phone Number*

```
class Phone {
    String areaCode
    String exchange
    String local
}

def phoneStr = '(800)555-1212'
def phoneRegex = ~/^[01]?\s*[\(\.-]?(\d{3})[\)\.-]?\s*(\d{3})[\.-](\d{4})$/
def matcher = phonePattern.matcher(phoneStr)

def phone = new Phone(
    areaCode: matcher[0][1],
    exchange: matcher[0][2],
    local: matcher[0][3])

println "Original Phone Number: ${phoneStr}"
println """Parsed Phone Number\
        \n\tArea Code = ${phone.areaCode}\
        \n\tExchange  = ${phone.exchange}\
        \n\tLocal     = ${phone.local}"""
```

In this example, the Phone object, the phone number to parse (phone1), and the phone regular expression pattern (phoneRegex) are defined. Next, the phone pattern is applied to the phone number to be parsed. The pattern is defined with groups, which allows the regular expression to be used to parse the phone number into the individual parts. The construction of the Phone object illustrates accessing the individual parts using the second index. Lastly, we print out the phone number to prove that the parsing worked.

Operators

You use operators every day. They probably have become so familiar to you that you don't even think of them anymore. Common operators include = for assignment, + to add two numbers, * to multiply two numbers, and ++ to increment a number. Of course, there are many more, but you get the idea.

Operator Overloading

Operator overloading has been around for some time but absent from Java. Operator overloading was omitted from Java because of the bad experiences people had in C++. Groovy embraces operator overloading and makes it easy to define and use. An overloaded operator executes a method on object. Groovy has predefined the relationship between the overloaded operator and the object method. Table 2-2 lists the Groovy operators and their corresponding methods. When an overloaded operator is encountered, the corresponding method is invoked.

Table 2-2. *Operator Overloading*

Operator	Method
a + b	a.plus(b)
a - b	a.minus(b)
a * b	a.multiply(b)
a ** b	a.power(b)
a / b	a.div(b)
a % b	a.mod(b)
a | b	a.or(b)
a & b	a.and(b)
a ^ b	a.xor(b)
a++ or ++a	a.next()
a-- or --a	a.previous()
a[b]	a.getAt(b)
a[b] = c	a.putAt(b, c)
a << b	a.leftShift(b)
a >> b	a.rightShift(b)
switch(a) { case(b) : }	b.isCase(a)
~a	a.bitwiseNegate()
-a	a.negative()
+a	a.positive()

At first glance, you may not see the benefits of operator overloading. Groovy uses operator overloading to create shortcuts that make Java friendlier. For example, adding an object to a list in Java looks like this: `myList.add(someObject)`. The corresponding Groovy way of adding an object to a list is `myList << someObject`.

Operator overloading isn't limited to the predefined instances that Groovy supplies; you can add operator overloading to your Groovy classes by implementing the corresponding method.

Specialized Operators

Groovy includes many of the standard operators found in other programming languages, as well as operators that are specific to Groovy that enable it to be so powerful.

Spread Operator

The spread operator (`*.`) is a shorthand technique for invoking a method or closure on a collection of objects. Listing 2-35 illustrates two ways of iterating over a list: first using the `collect()` method and then using the spread operator.

Listing 2-35. *Using the Spread Operator*

```
class User {
    String firstName
    String lastName

    def printFullName = {
        println "${firstName} ${lastName}"
    }
}

// Instantiate a User using the named parameters constructor
User chris = new User(firstName:"Chris", lastName: "Judd")
User joseph = new User(firstName:"Joseph", lastName: "Nusairat")
User jim = new User(firstName:"Jim", lastName: "Shingler")

def list = [chris,joseph,jim]

println "Using collect closure"
list.collect { println it.printFullName() }

println "\n\nUsing Spread Operator:"
list*.printFullName()
```

This example shows creating a list of User objects and using two different techniques for printing the list. The first technique is using the collect() method to iterate over the list, applying the items' printFullName() closure. The second technique uses the spread operator to iterate over the list of users, invoking the users' printFullName() closure.

■Note Listing 2-35 includes a technique that we haven't discussed yet: *named parameters*. One of the neat things about Groovy is the ability to specify the property and value to be assigned as a parameter to a constructor. Using the code in Listing 2-35 as an example, we can instantiate a User object and set the firstName and lastName, just the lastName, or just the firstName without coding all of the different constructors that would be required.

Elvis Operator

The Elvis operator (?:) is a shorthand version of the Java ternary operator.[29] An example of using the Java-style ternary operator is a == 1 ? "One" : "Not One". If a is equal to 1, then "One" is returned; otherwise "Not One" is returned. It is literally a shorthand "if-then-else." As with most Java constructs, you can use the Java ternary operator in Groovy. In addition to the Java ternary operator, you can use an even shorter shorthand notation in Java: the Elvis operator. This can be very useful in defaulting values if they haven't been set already, meaning that they evaluate to null or false. Listing 2-36 illustrates using the Java ternary and Elvis operators in Groovy.

Listing 2-36. *Using the Elvis Operator*

```
def firstName = user.firstName == null ? "unknown" : user.firstName // Java ternary
def firstName2 = user.firstName ?: "unknown" // Groovy Elvis
```

In both cases, if the user.firstName is null, then the firstName is set to "unknown". The user.firstName portion of the Elvis operator example is known as the *expression*. If the expression evaluates to false or null, then the value after the : is returned. The two lines in the example are logically equivalent.

Safe Navigation/Dereference Operator

The safe navigation/dereference operator (?.) is used to avoid NullPointerExceptions, so it is incredibly handy. Consider the situation where you have a User object and you want to print the firstName. If the User object is null when you access the firstName property,

---

29. http://www.jguru.com/faq/view.jsp?EID=1300747

you will get a `NullPointerException`. Listing 2-37 illustrates the Java way of safe derefer-
encing and using the Groovy safe navigation/dereference operator.

Listing 2-37. *Using the Safe Navigation/Dereference Operator*

```
User user
println user.firstName    // Throws NullPointerException

// Adding a null check, the Java way
if (user != null) {
    println "Java FirstName = ${user.firstName}"
}

// Null check the Groovy way
println "Groovy FirstName = ${user?.firstName}"
```

This example shows using the standard Java technique of checking for `null` before
accessing an object and then using the Groovy safe navigation/dereference operator to
accomplish the same thing.

Field Operator

In Chapter 1, you learned about properties on a class and how Groovy automatically
supplies a getter. You also learned that in the event that special logic is required, you
can provide your own getter.

While not recommended because it is a major violation of encapsulation, Groovy
provides a way to bypass the getter and access the underlying field directly. Listing 2-38
shows an example of using the field operator (`.@`).

Listing 2-38. *Using the Field Operator*

```
class Todo {
    String name

    def getName() {
        println "Getting Name"
        name
    }
}

def todo = new Todo(name: "Jim")
println todo.name
println todo.@name
```

```
Getting Name
Jim
Jim
```

In this example, the first `println` uses the getter to access `name`, and the second `println` bypasses the getter to access `name` directly.

Method Closure Operator

Earlier in the chapter, you learned about closures and how some of the Groovy functions accept a closure as input. But what if you would like to pass a method around in the same way that you can pass a closure? Groovy provides the method closure operator (`.&`) for just this scenario. The method closure operator allows the method to be accessed and passed around like a closure. Listing 2-39 illustrates using a method as a closure.

Listing 2-39. *Using the Method Closure Operator*

```
def list = ["Chris","Joseph","Jim"]

// each takes a closure
list.each { println it }

String printName(String name) {
    println name
}

// & causes the method to be accessed as a closure
list.each(this.&printName)
```

```
Chris
Joseph
Jim
Chris
Joseph
Jim
```

This example creates a list of names and iterates through the list to print out the names. You have seen this before. A `printName()` method is created that prints the `name` parameter. Lastly and the main point of this example, the list is iterated over, executing the `printName()` method as a closure.

Now because this is a really simple example, you may be thinking, "Big deal." Well actually it is, especially if you are building a domain-specific language (DSL), which you will learn more about in Chapter 3.

The method really invokes `System.out.println`. How did the Groovy team get `println` to do that? The answer is that they used the method closure operator to assign `System.out.println` to a global property, as in `def println = System.out.&println()`. That is extremely powerful. Using the method closure operator, you are able to expose Java methods as closures.

Summary

The focus of this chapter was Groovy language basics. The goal was to teach you enough Groovy to get you started with Grails. In this chapter, you created a simple program (script) and compared it to what it would take to do the same thing in Java. Then you learned how to turn the script into a Groovy class, compile it, and run it using Java.

Once you learned about Groovy scripts and classes, we took a quick look at the Groovy Shell and Groovy Console. The shell and console are handy for writing and testing quick little programs. With some basic Groovy tooling under your belt, it was time to start taking a look at the Groovy language. Your journey into the Groovy language started with learning about Groovy's support of strings, closures and methods, and collections (lists, maps, sets, arrays, and ranges). Next, you had a high-level overview of Groovy's regular expression support. We covered the find (`=~`), match (`==~`), and pattern (`~string`) operators. Lastly, you learned about operator overloading and specialized operators. They are a major source of Groovy's power.

This chapter is by no means a comprehensive study of Groovy. Groovy is a very broad and deep topic. The goal was to give you enough Groovy knowledge to start building an application and know where to look for more information. The next chapter will introduce you to some of the Groovy frameworks and more advanced Groovy topics.

CHAPTER 3

More Advanced Groovy

Chapters 1 and 2 offered a glimpse into the power and capabilities of Groovy by providing a basic understanding of its language features and tools. But there is far more to know about Groovy. For example, Groovy provides an ideal framework for creating unit tests. It makes working with XML simple and straightforward, and it includes a great framework for templating text. Finally, Groovy has a meta programming model that you can use to do amazing things, such as enabling the creation of domain-specific languages and adding methods and functionality to the Java API classes, including classes that are marked as final, which prevents them from being extended in Java.

This chapter covers a variety of unrelated or loosely related advanced Groovy topics. It starts off by showing you how to use Groovy to write and execute unit tests, then it compares how to process XML documents with both Java and Groovy. The next section explains how you can use Groovy's templating to generate e-mails. The chapter concludes with three meta programming topics: implementing `Expando` classes, extending classes with Meta Object Protocol (MOP), and creating domain-specific languages (DSLs).

Groovy Unit Testing

One of Groovy's best value propositions is unit testing. Using Groovy to unit-test Groovy or Java code can make the code easier to read and maintain. Unit testing is a common way to introduce Groovy to an organization, because it doesn't affect the production runtime. Once developers and managers get comfortable with Groovy in a testing capacity, they eventually begin using it in production.

Unit testing is so fundamental to Groovy that it's built right in. You don't need to download a separate framework. Groovy already includes and extends JUnit,[1] which is a popular Java unit-testing framework. The primary extension is `groovy.util.GroovyTestCase`, which inherits from `junit.framework.TestCase` and adds the additional assert methods found in Table 3-1.

---

1. http://www.junit.org

Table 3-1. *GroovyTestCase Assert Methods*

Assert Method	Description
assertArrayEquals	Asserts two arrays are equal and contain the same values
assertContains	Asserts an array of characters contains the given characters or an array of ints contains a given int
assertEquals	Asserts two Objects or two Strings are equal
assertInspect	Asserts the value of the inspect() method
assertLength	Asserts the length of char, int, or Object arrays
assertScript	Asserts script runs without any exceptions being thrown
assertToString	Asserts the value of toString()

JUnit (and therefore Groovy unit testing) works by creating a class that inherits from TestCase or one of its descendants. GroovyTestCase is the appropriate class to extend for unit testing in Groovy. Notice that GroovyTestCase is found in the groovy.util package, so it is implicitly available and doesn't even require any imports. Tests can then be added by creating methods that have a name that begins with test and is followed by something descriptive about the test. For example, you could use testAlphaRanges for a test that validates the Groovy language feature of ranges. These test methods should take no parameters and return void. Unlike with JUnit tests written in Java, these methods don't have to declare exceptions that could be thrown, because Groovy naturally converts all checked exceptions into unchecked exceptions. This makes tests more readable than the equivalent Java implications.

Unit tests often require objects to be put into a known state. In addition, tests should be good test-harness citizens and clean up after themselves. Like JUnit tests, all Groovy tests can override the setUp and tearDown methods.

Unit tests are also a great way to learn new frameworks, libraries, and languages such as Groovy. You can use unit tests to validate your understanding of how they work. Listing 3-1 is a unit test used to validate some assumptions about Groovy ranges, including whether a range from 'a'..'z' contains uppercase letters and whether ranges can be concatenated together.

Listing 3-1. *Example Unit Test That Validates Assumptions About Groovy Ranges*

```
01 class RangeTest extends GroovyTestCase {
02
03    def lowerCaseRange = 'a'..'z'
04    def upperCaseRange = 'A'..'Z'
05
06    void testLowerCaseRange() {
```

```
07     assert 26 == lowerCaseRange.size()
08     assertTrue(lowerCaseRange.contains('b'))
09     assertFalse(lowerCaseRange.contains('B'))
10   }
11
12   void testUpperCaseRange() {
13     assert 26 == upperCaseRange.size()
14     assertTrue(upperCaseRange.contains('B'))
15     assertFalse(upperCaseRange.contains('b'))
16   }
17
18   void testAlphaRange() {
19     def alphaRange = lowerCaseRange + upperCaseRange
20     assert 52 == alphaRange.size()
21     assert alphaRange.contains('b')
22     assert alphaRange.contains('B')
23   }
24 }
```

Listing 3-1 shows a unit test that extends from GroovyTestCase and contains two variables that include a range of lowercase letters on line 3 and a range of uppercase letters on line 4. The test case also contains three tests. The first test, shown on lines 6–10, asserts that the range has a size of 26, representing each of the letters in lowercase. It also asserts that a lowercase 'b' is in the range but that an uppercase 'B' is not. The second test, shown on lines 12–16, is basically the same test but uses the uppercase range. The third test, on the other hand, validates that the two ranges can be concatenated together to produce a new range that includes both. Therefore, the new range is twice the size and includes both the lowercase 'b' and the uppercase 'B'.

Running a Groovy unit test is just like running a script. To run this test, execute the following:

```
> groovy RangeTest
```

Because a JUnit test runner is built into Groovy, the results of the tests are printed to standard out. The results identify how many tests ran, how many failed, and how many errors occurred. Failures indicate how many tests did not pass the assertions, and errors indicate unexpected occurrences such as exceptions. In addition, because GroovyTestCase extends JUnit, you can easily integrate the Groovy tests into automated test harnesses such as Apache Ant[2] and Apache Maven[3] builds so they can be run continually.

---

2. http://ant.apache.org
3. http://maven.apache.org

Working with XML

Extensible Markup Language (XML)[4] is a general-purpose markup language commonly used in enterprise applications to persist or share data. Historically, creating and consuming XML documents has been easier than working with other types of formats, because XML is text-based, follows a standard, is in an easily parsable format, and features many existing frameworks and libraries to support reading and writing documents for many different programming languages and platforms. Most of these frameworks, however, are based on the World Wide Web Consortium's (W3C's)[5] Document Object Model (DOM),[6] which can cause the code that manipulates XML documents to become difficult to write and read. Due to the popularity and complexity of working with XML, Groovy includes a framework that uses XML in a natural way. The next section demonstrates how complicated it is to write simple XML with standard Java code, then shows you how to process XML in the simple and elegant Groovy way.

Writing XML with Java

Generating a simple XML document like the one found in Listing 3-2 in Java is difficult, time consuming, and a challenge to read and maintain.

Listing 3-2. *Simple XML Output for To-Dos*

```
<todos>
  <todo id="1">
    <name>Buy Beginning Groovy and Grails</name>
    <note>Purchase book from Amazon.com for all co-workers.</note>
  </todo>
</todos>
```

Listing 3-3 shows the minimum Java code necessary to generate the XML shown in Listing 3-2.

Listing 3-3. *Java Code to Generate the Simple To-Do XML Found in Listing 3-2*

```
import org.w3c.dom.Document;
import org.w3c.dom.Element;
```

---

4. http://www.w3.org/XML/

5. http://www.w3c.org

6. http://www.w3.org/DOM/

```java
import javax.xml.parsers.DocumentBuilder;
import javax.xml.parsers.DocumentBuilderFactory;
import javax.xml.parsers.ParserConfigurationException;
import javax.xml.transform.stream.StreamResult;
import javax.xml.transform.Transformer;
import javax.xml.transform.TransformerFactory;
import javax.xml.transform.OutputKeys;
import javax.xml.transform.Source;
import javax.xml.transform.Result;
import javax.xml.transform.TransformerException;
import javax.xml.transform.dom.DOMSource;

/**
 * Example of generating simple XML in Java.
 */
public class GenerateXML {
  public static void main (String[] args)
      throws ParserConfigurationException, TransformerException {
    DocumentBuilder builder =
      DocumentBuilderFactory.newInstance().newDocumentBuilder();
    Document doc = builder.newDocument();

    Element todos = doc.createElement("todos");
    doc.appendChild(todos);

    Element task = doc.createElement("todo");
    task.setAttribute("id", "1");
    todos.appendChild(task);

    Element name = doc.createElement("name");
    name.setTextContent("Buy Beginning Groovy and Grails");
    task.appendChild(name);

    Element note = doc.createElement("note");
    note.setTextContent("Purchase book from Amazon.com for all co-workers.");
    task.appendChild(note);

    // generate pretty printed XML document
    TransformerFactory tranFactory = TransformerFactory.newInstance();
    Transformer transformer = tranFactory.newTransformer();
```

```
    transformer.setOutputProperty(OutputKeys.INDENT, "yes");
    transformer.setOutputProperty(
        "{http://xml.apache.org/xslt}indent-amount", "2");

    Source src = new DOMSource(doc);
    Result dest = new StreamResult(System.out);
    transformer.transform(src, dest);
  }
}
```

Notice how difficult it is to read Listing 3-3. It begins by using `DocumentBuilderFactory` to create a new `DocumentBuilder`. With `DocumentBuilder`, the `newDocument()` factory method is called to create a new `Document`. Elements are created using `Document`'s factory methods, configured by adding attributes or text content, and then finally appended to their parent element. Notice how difficult it is to follow the natural tree structure of the XML document by looking at the Java code. This is partly because most elements require three lines of code to create, configure, and append the element to its parent.

Finally, outputting the XML into a human-readable nested format isn't straightforward. Much like creating the document itself, it begins by getting a `TransformerFactory` instance and then using the `newTransformer()` factory method to create a `Transformer`. Then the transformer output properties are configured to indent, and the indent amount is configured. Notice that the indent amount isn't even standard. It uses an Apache Xalan[7]–specific configuration, which may not be completely portable. Ultimately, a source and result are passed to the transformer to transform the source DOM into XML output.

Groovy Builders

Groovy simplifies generating XML by using the concept of builders, based on the Builder design pattern from the Gang of Four.[8] Groovy builders implement a concept of Groovy-Markup, which is a combination of Groovy language features such as MOP (discussed later in the chapter), closures, and the simplified map syntax to create nested tree-like structures. Groovy includes five major builder implementations, as defined in Table 3-2. They all use the same format and idioms, so knowing one builder pretty much means you'll be able to use them all.

---

7. http://xalan.apache.org/

8. Erich Gamma, Richard Helm, Ralph Johnson, John Vlissides, *Design Patterns: Elements of Reusable Object-Oriented Software* (Boston, MA: Addison-Wesley Professional, 1994).

Table 3-2. *Groovy Builders*

Name	Description
AntBuilder	Enables the script and execution of Apache Ant tasks
DOMBuilder	Generates W3C DOMs
MarkupBuilder	Generates XML and HTML
NodeBuilder	Creates nested trees of objects for handling arbitrary data
SwingBuilder	Creates Java Swing UIs (discussed in detail in Chapter 13)

In general, you start using a builder by creating an instance of the builder. Then you call a named closure to create the root node, which could represent a root XML element, a Swing component, or a specific builder-appropriate node. You add nodes by nesting more named closures. This format makes it easy to read the hierarchical structures.

You add attributes by using Groovy's map syntax to pass name-value pairs into the named closures. Under the covers, MOP interprets the message passed to the object, usually to determine which method to invoke. When it realizes there is no method by that name, it creates the associated node or attribute.

Writing XML with Groovy MarkupBuilder

As noted in Table 3-2, you use MarkupBuilder to create XML and HTML. Listing 3-4 shows the Groovy code in action for creating the XML shown in Listing 3-2.

Listing 3-4. *Groovy Code to Generate the Simple To-Do XML Found in Listing 3-2*

```
01 def writer = new StringWriter()
02 def builder = new groovy.xml.MarkupBuilder(writer)
03 builder.setDoubleQuotes(true)
04 builder.todos {
05     todo (id:"1") {
06         name "Buy Beginning Groovy and Grails"
07         note "Purchase book from Amazon.com for all co-workers."
08     }
09 }
10
11 println writer.toString()
```

Looking at Listing 3-4, you can see how much easier it is to read than the Java equivalent shown in Listing 3-3. The example begins by creating StringWriter, so the final XML can be printed to system out on line 11. Then MarkupBuilder is created using StringWriter.

By default, MarkupBuilder uses single quotes for attribute values, so line 3 changes the quotes to double quotes to comply with the XML specification. Lines 4–9 actually build the XML document using named closures and map syntax. You can easily see that todos contains a todo with an id attribute of 1 and nested name and note elements.

Reading XML with XmlSlurper

Groovy makes reading XML documents equally as easy as writing XML documents. Groovy includes the XmlSlurper class, which you can use to parse an XML document or String and provide access to a GPathResult. With the GPathResult reference, you can use XPath[9]-like syntax to access different elements in the document.

Listing 3-5 shows how to use XmlSlurper and GPath to interrogate a todos XML document.

Listing 3-5. *Reading XML in Groovy*

```
01 def todos = new XmlSlurper().parse('todos.xml')
02 assert 3 == todos.todo.size()
03 assert "Buy Beginning Groovy and Grails" == todos.todo[0].name.text()
04 assert "1" == todos.todo[0].@id.text()
```

Listing 3-5 begins by using XmlSlurper to parse a todos.xml file containing three todo items. Line 2 asserts there are three todos in the document. Line 3 shows how to access the value of an element, while line 4 shows how to access the value of an attribute using @.

Generating Text with Templates

Many web applications generate text for e-mails, reports, XML, and even HTML. Embedding this text in code can make it difficult for a designer or business person to maintain or manage. A better method is to store the static portion externally as a template file and process the template when the dynamic portions of the template are known.

As shown in Table 3-3, Groovy includes three template engines to make generating text easier.

---

9. http://www.w3.org/TR/xpath

Table 3-3. *Groovy Template Engines*

Name	Description
SimpleTemplateEngine	Basic templating that uses Groovy expressions as well as JavaServer Pages (JSP) <% %> script and <%= %> expression syntax
GStringTemplateEngine	Basically the same as SimpleTemplateEngine, except the template is stored internally as a writable closure
XmlTemplateEngine	Optimized for generating XML by using an internal DOM

The SimpleTemplateEngine usually is appropriate for most templating situations. Listing 3-6 shows an HTML e-mail template that we'll use in Chapter 11 for sending e-mail during a nightly batch process.

Listing 3-6. *HTML E-mail Template Found in nightlyReportsEmail.gtpl*

```
<!DOCTYPE HTML PUBLIC "-//W3C//DTD HTML 4.01 Transitional//EN">

<html>
<head>
  <title>
    Collab-Todo Nightly Report for
    ${String.format('%tA %<tB %<te %<tY', date)}
  </title>
</head>

<body bgcolor="#FFFFFF" style="margin:0;padding:0;">
  <div style="padding: 22px 20px 40px 20px;background-color:#FFFFFF;">
    <table width="568" border="0" cellspacing="0" cellpadding="1"
        bgcolor="#FFFFFF" align="center">
      <tr>
        <td>
          Dear ${user?.firstName} ${user?.lastName},
          <p />
          Please find your attached nightly report for
          ${String.format('%tA %<tB %<te %<tY', date)}.
        </td>
      </tr>
    </table>
    <!-- static HTML left out for brevity -->
  </div>
</body>
</html>
```

The template in Listing 3-6 is mostly HTML with a couple of Groovy expressions thrown in for the dynamic portions of the e-mail, such as formatting the date and user's name. The e-mail produces the image shown in Figure 3-1.

Dear Christopher Judd,

Please find your attached nightly report for Thursday May 15 2008.

© 2008 Beginning Groovy and Grails by Christopher Judd, Joseph Faisal Nusairat, and James Shingler

Figure 3-1. *HTML e-mail*

To process the template, you create an instance of a template engine and use the overloaded createTemplate() method, passing it a File, Reader, URL, or String containing the template text to create a template. Now with the template loaded and parsed, you call the make() method, passing it a map that binds with the variables in the template that are based on the names in the map. Listing 3-7 shows what the code that generates the e-mail in Figure 3-1 looks like.

Listing 3-7. *E-mail Template-Processing Code*

```
01 import groovy.text.SimpleTemplateEngine
02
03 /**
04 * Simple User Groovy Bean.
05 */
06 class User {
07   String firstName;
08   String lastName;
09 }
10
11 def emailTemplate = this.class.getResource("nightlyReportsEmail.gtpl")
12 def binding = [
13    "user": new User(firstName: "Christopher", lastName: "Judd"),
14    "date": new Date()
15 ]
16 def engine = new SimpleTemplateEngine()
17 def email = engine.createTemplate(emailTemplate).make(binding)
18 def body = email.toString()
19
20 println body
```

Listing 3–7 begins by importing the `SimpleTemplateEngine` on line 1 so you have access to it on line 16. Lines 6–9 declare a simple `User` GroovyBean. The template is loaded from the `nightlyReportsEmail.gtpl` file found on the classpath on line 11. It contains the template text found in Listing 3-6. Lines 12–15 create the map containing the passed user and date data, which will be bound to the template when the template is processed. `SimpleTemplateEngine`, created on line 16, is used on line 17 to create and process the template.

Expandos

There are times in an application when you need an object to hold data or behaviors, but it is not used enough to warrant creating an entire class definition for it. For example, the `User` GroovyBean from Listing 3-7 is used simply to pass data to the template engine; it provides no other value, so it's a great candidate for an `Expando` object.

The `Expando` class is found in the `groovy.util` package and is a dynamically expandable bean, meaning you can add properties or closures to it at runtime. Combine this with Groovy's duck typing, and `Expandos` are also a great way to implement mock objects during unit testing.

■**Note** Duck typing refers to the concept that if it walks like a duck and talks like a duck, it must be a duck. In Groovy speak, if an object has properties and methods similar to another object, the two objects must be of the same type.

The best way to understand `Expandos` is to see them in action. Listing 3-8 shows code that creates the `User` GroovyBean from Listing 3-7 using `Expandos` rather than a concrete class.

Listing 3-8. *Alternative to the User GroovyBean*

```
01 def user = new Expando()
02
03 user.firstName = 'Christopher'
04 user.lastName = 'Judd'
05
06 user.greeting = { greeting ->
07   "${greeting} ${firstName} ${lastName}"
08 }
09
10 assert user.greeting("Hello") == 'Hello Christopher Judd'
```

Listing 3-8 uses an Expando as a replacement for a concrete GroovyBean class. On line 1, a new instance of the Expando is created. On lines 3 and 4, the firstName and lastName properties are added to the object dynamically and assigned values. Properties are not the only things that you can add. You can also add behaviors using closures. Lines 6–8 create and assign a closure to greeting that concatenates the greeting parameter with the properties for the first and last names. Finally, line 10 executes greeting.

You can also initialize Expandos with properties using the overloaded constructor that takes a map. Listing 3-9 uses this technique to reimplement the template example found in Listing 3-7.

Listing 3-9. *Template Example Using Expandos Instead of User GroovyBean*

```
import groovy.text.SimpleTemplateEngine

def emailTemplate = this.class.getResource("nightlyReportsEmail.gtpl")
def binding = [
        "user": new Expando([ firstName: 'Christopher', lastName:'Judd']),
        "date": new Date()
]
def engine = new SimpleTemplateEngine()
def template = engine.createTemplate(emailTemplate).make(binding)
def body = template.toString()

println body
```

Notice that Listing 3-9 reduces the amount of code and increases the readability of the earlier template example by replacing the User class definition with Expando, which contains the firstName and lastName properties.

Meta Object Protocol

Another important concept to Groovy and Grails is Meta Object Protocol (MOP). This protocol enables you to add properties and behaviors to existing classes, much like the Expando class discussed in the previous section. The capability of MOP to extend classes doesn't just exist for classes you write or Groovy classes. MOP enables you to add functionality to the Java API, including classes such as java.lang.String, which is marked as final to prevent standard Java classes from extending it and adding functionality. This is how the Groovy JDK[10] provides more Groovy idiomatic behavior to the standard Java classes. You will learn in Chapter 6 how Grails uses this technique to add amazing persistence features to your domain classes.

---

10. http://groovy.codehaus.org/groovy-jdk/

■**Note** An in-depth explanation of the entire MOP and dispatch mechanism is beyond the scope of a book aimed toward beginners. However, this section provides a brief introduction to the topic, so you can understand how parts of the Grails framework might be implemented.

In Groovy, all classes—including all Java classes—have a property of metaClass of type groovy.lang.MetaClass, similar to how all Java classes have a property of class of type java.lang.Class. The groovy.lang.MetaClass interface is similar to the Expando object in that you can add behavior at runtime. During the dispatching of a message to an object, the MetaClass helps to determine which behavior should be invoked. In addition, you can use the MetaClass to provide behavior if the class doesn't implement the specific behavior requested. This is how the builders discussed earlier in the chapter work. When you add closures to the builder, MetaClass interprets this as a call to a missing method and provides the specific builder functionality. For example, it might add an XML element to the enclosing parent element.

In the previous template examples, a template URL was found for the template file on the classpath using the following line, which by now may seem a little more like Java than Groovy:

```
def emailTemplate = this.class.getResource("nightlyReportsEmail.gtpl")
```

Listing 3-10 shows how MOP could make this a little more Groovy by adding the getResourceAsText() method to java.lang.Class, which actually loads the file and gets the contents of the file as text rather than just the URL to the file.

Listing 3-10. *Adding the getResourceAsText() Method to java.lang.Class*

```
01 import groovy.text.SimpleTemplateEngine
02
03 Class.metaClass.getResourceAsText = { resource ->
04   this.class.getResourceAsStream(resource).getText()
05 }
06
07 def emailTemplate = this.class.getResourceAsText('nightlyReportsEmail.gtpl')
08 def binding = [
09        "user": new Expando([ firstName: 'Christopher', lastName:'Judd']),
10        "date": new Date()]
11 def engine = new SimpleTemplateEngine()
12 def template = engine.createTemplate(emailTemplate).make(binding)
13 def body = template.toString()
14
15 println body
```

Notice how line 7 expresses much more explicitly that it is loading the template as text and not as a URL. This is accomplished by extending the final java.lang.Class on lines 3–5 by accessing the metaClass property and adding the getResourceAsText() method that takes a parameter of resource, which is the name of a file on the classpath. The implementation of this method found on line 4 uses the getResourceAsStream() technique to load a file as a stream. This is generally safer than using a URL, because not everything is easily addressable with a URL. The closure then finishes by using the getText() method, which Groovy includes in the Groovy JDK on all java.io.InputStreams by means of MOP. Finally, line 7 shows what a call to the getResourceAsText() method would look like on java.lang.Class.

There are additional ways in which you might want to do the same thing and make it a little more expressive. Listing 3-11 shows another implementation of doing the same thing by adding behavior to java.lang.String, which is also a class marked as final.

Listing 3-11. *Adding the fileAsString() Method to java.lang.String*

```
01 String.metaClass.fileAsString = {
02    this.class.getResourceAsStream(delegate).getText()
03 }
04
05 println 'nightlyReportsEmail.gtpl'.fileAsString()
```

Listing 3-11 begins by adding the fileAsString() method to the metaClass property of the java.lang.String class, similar to the previous example. However, it uses a delegate variable instead of a passed-in parameter. The delegate is a reference to the object instance of which the method was called, which in this case would be the String containing the file name to be loaded. Notice how nicely line 5 reads. It is almost like reading an English sentence. The next section continues with a technique for making code easier to read.

Domain-Specific Languages

With the realization that code is read more frequently than it is written and the popularity of more expressive and flexible languages such as Groovy, domain-specific languages (DSLs)—languages written to solve a problem using the particular problem's vernacular—are becoming increasingly popular.

For example, using Groovy's optional parameters and MOP, you can turn this code that only a programmer can love:

```
println this.class.getResourceAsStream('readme.txt').getText()
```

into:

```
write 'readme.txt'.contents()
```

Notice that with the second option, even a nonprogrammer has a chance of under-stating the intent of the code.

Listing 3-12 shows how to implement this simple DSL for writing files.

Listing 3-12. *Implementation of a Simple DSL*

```
01 String.metaClass.contents = {
02   this.class.getResourceAsStream(delegate).getText()
03 }
04
05 def write = { file ->
06   println file
07 }
08
09 write 'readme.txt'.contents()
```

Lines 1–3 use the same metaprogramming implementation from the previous section to add a `contents` closure to the `String` class. The `contents` closure loads a file from the classpath as text based on the value of the `String`. Lines 5–7 implement a closure named `write` that simply does a `println` on whatever is passed as a parameter. This ultimately enables line 9 to read like a sentence when the optional parentheses for the `write` call are not included.

Summary

Combined with the Groovy topics from the previous chapters, the Advanced Groovy topics in this chapter—such as unit testing, XML processing, templates, `Expandos`, and meta-programming—have prepared you for developing web-based applications using the Groovy-based Grails framework that is the focus of the remainder of the book.

■**Note** You can explore many other advanced topics in Groovy. To learn more, check out the Groovy docu-mentation[11] or *Groovy in Action*[12] by Dierk Koenig.

---

11. http://groovy.codehaus.org/Documentation

12. Dierk Koenig with Andrew Glover, Paul King, Guillaume Laforge, and Jon Skeet, *Groovy in Action* (Greenwich, CT: Manning Publications, 2007), http://www.manning.com/koenig/.

CHAPTER 4

■■■

Introduction to Grails

Let's face it: developing web applications is hard. This problem has been exacerbated in today's environment, where applications deemed to fall into the Web 2.0 category involve lots of technologies, such as HyperText Markup Language (HTML), Cascading Style Sheets (CSS), Asynchronous JavaScript and XML (Ajax), XML, web services, Java, and databases. Then on top of the technologies sit lots of open source framework choices like model-view-controller (MVC) frameworks and Ajax frameworks. To make matters worse, while the complexity of building applications continues to grow, expected turnaround times continue to shrink.

In recent years, the Java community has tried solving these issues by building applications using Java Platform, Enterprise Edition (Java EE) and its predecessor, Java 2 Platform, Enterprise Edition (J2EE). While these platforms have proven to be scalable and robust, they don't allow for rapid agile development. Java EE has proven over and over again that it was not written with an application level of abstraction but rather with a much lower technical level. This is the reason that all the recent application frameworks have been created and most notably the popularity in such frameworks as Struts, Spring, and Hibernate. Furthermore, the development cycle of coding, compiling, packaging, deploying, testing, and debugging takes entirely too long for any real productivity and requires developers to switch context too frequently.

Enter Grails. Grails is an open source web development framework that packages best practices such as convention over configuration and unit testing with the best-of-the-best open source application frameworks such as Spring, Hibernate, and SiteMesh. Together with the productivity of the Groovy scripting language, everything runs on top of the robust Java and Java EE platforms.

In this chapter, you will learn about the features and open source frameworks included with Grails. Then you'll learn how to take advantage of Grails' powerful scaffolding feature to build your first Grails application.

What Is Grails?

Grails is not only an open source web framework for the Java platform, but a complete development platform as well. Like most web frameworks, Grails is an MVC framework, but it's not your average Java MVC framework. Like other Java MVC frameworks, it does have models referred to in Grails as *domain classes* that carry application data for display by the view. However, unlike other MVC models, Grails domain classes are automatically persistable and can even generate the underlying database schema. Like other MVC frameworks, Grails controllers handle the requests and orchestrate services or other behavior. Unlike most MVC frameworks, though, services and other classes can be automatically injected using dependency injection based on naming conventions. In addition, Grails controllers are request-scoped, which means a new instance is created for each request. Finally, the default view for Grails is Groovy Server Pages (GSP) and typically renders HTML. The view layer also includes a flexible layout, a templating feature, and simple tag libraries.

Other Grails advantages include minimal configuration and a more agile development cycle. Grails eliminates most of the standard MVC configuration and deployment descriptors by using initiative conventions. Also, because Grails takes advantage of Groovy's dynamic language features, it is usually able to shorten the development cycle to just coding, refreshing, testing, and debugging. This saves valuable development time and makes development much more agile than with other Java MVC frameworks or Java EE.

Grails is also a complete development platform, including a web container, database, build system, and test harness out of the box. This combination can reduce project startup time and developer setup time to minutes rather than hours or days. With Grails, you typically don't have to go find and download a bunch of server software or frameworks to get started. You also don't have to spend time creating or maintaining complicated build scripts. Everything you need to get started comes bundled in one simple-to-install package.

■**Note** Grails is licensed under the flexible Apache 2.0 license and is hosted by the Codehaus open source community.[1]

Grails has an impressive list of features and is able to provide so much by integration of proven open source projects.

Grails Features

Grails really has too many features to mention them all. In this section, we'll highlight some of the more important ones.

---

1. http://grails.codehaus.org, http://www.grails.org

Convention Over Configuration

Rather than using lots of XML configuration files, Grails relies on conventions to make application development easier and more productive. This also helps encourage the Don't Repeat Yourself (DRY) principle. Many of the conventions relate to its directory structure, which we'll discuss later in this chapter in the "Creating the Application" section. However, Grails also includes a command-line interface that you use to generate Grails artifacts and enforce the conventions.

Unit Testing

Unit testing is now recognized as a critical best practice to improving the quality of software deliverables and enabling long-term maintainability of an application. Furthermore, unit testing is even more important for applications written using dynamically typed languages such as Groovy, because identifying the effects of changes without the help of the compiler and unit tests can be difficult. This is why unit testing is a major Grails convention. As you will learn later in this chapter in the "Implementing Integration Tests" section, a unit test is created automatically when you use Grails to generate domain or controller classes.

Grails separates its unit tests into two categories: unit and integration. Grails unit tests are freestanding unit tests with no dependencies other than possibly mock objects. Integration tests, on the other hand, have access to the entire Grails environment, including the database.

Grails also includes functional testing for automating the web interface. In Chapter 5, you'll learn how to write functional tests.

Scaffolding

As you'll experience in the second half of this chapter, Grails has a scaffolding framework that generates applications with create, read, update, and delete (CRUD) functionality with very little code, allowing you to focus on defining the Groovy domain by creating classes with properties, behaviors, and constraints. At either runtime or development time, Grails can generate the controller behavior and GSP views associated with the domain classes for CRUD functionality. At the same time, it can even generate a database schema, including tables for each of the domain classes.

Object Relational Mapping

Grails includes a powerful object relational mapping framework called Grails Object Relational Mapping (GORM). Like most object-relational mapping (ORM) frameworks, GORM can map objects to relational databases and represent relationships between those objects, such as one-to-one or one-to-many. But what sets GORM apart from other

ORMs is the fact it is built for a dynamic language like Groovy. It injects the CRUD methods right into the class without having to implement them or inherit from a persistent super classes. Once more, it is able to provide an ORM DSL for dynamic finder methods and search criteria. You will learn more about GORM in Chapter 6.

Plug-Ins

Grails does not propose to have all the answers to every web development problem. Instead, it provides a plug-in architecture and a community where you can find plug-ins for things like security, Ajax, testing, searching, reporting, and web services. This plug-in architecture makes it easy to add complicated functionality to your application. For example, Chapter 7 will show how to use a CAPTCHA plug-in to ensure real people are registering with your application.

Integrated Open Source

Grails does not suffer from the Not Invented Here (NIH) syndrome. Rather than reinvent the wheel, it integrates the best of the best industry-standard and proven open source frameworks, as you'll see in the "Grails Architecture" section.

Groovy

Groovy is one of the pillars of Grails. As you learned in Chapters 1–3, Groovy is a powerful and flexible open source language that stands on its own. However, its integration with Java, dynamic scripting features, and simple syntax makes it a perfect complement to Grails and provides the agile nature of the entire solution.

Spring Framework

Spring Framework[2] (Spring) is best described by its creator Rod Johnson as providing an application level of abstraction on top of the Java EE API. For example, rather than having to deal with the details of handling transactions, Spring provides a means for declaring transactions around regular Plain Old Java Objects (POJOs), so you can focus on implementing business logic. In addition, because Spring brings Java EE features to POJOs, you're able to develop and test your application code outside a Java EE container, thereby increasing productivity. Along with Hibernate, Spring was a major influence on the new Enterprise JavaBeans (EJB) 3.0 spec, which attempts to simplify Java EE development.

Grails implicitly handles much of the Spring integration. However, in the "Injecting into the Service" section of Chapter 6, you will learn how to explicitly configure and integrate with Spring if you find it necessary.

---

2. `http://www.springframework.org`

Hibernate

Hibernate[3] is an object-relational persistence framework that provides the foundation for GORM. It's able to map complex domain classes written as POJOs or POGOs to relational database tables, as well as map relationships between the tables. As mentioned in the previous section, Hibernate had a big influence on the EJB 3.0 specification, specifically the Java Persistence API (JPA). Hibernate is one of the many JBoss projects.

SiteMesh

SiteMesh[4] is a web page layout framework that implements the decorator design pattern for rendering HTML with constant components such as the header, footers, and navigation. It is one of the components found in the OpenSymphony suite and is hosted on the OpenSymphony site.[5] Grails hides most of the SiteMesh details from you as a developer, but in Chapter 5, you'll see how to create page layouts and other web components such as GSP.

Ajax Frameworks

Web 2.0 functionality has become so popular that Grails includes three popular Ajax frameworks by default in every web application: script.aculo.us,[6] Rico,[7] and Prototype.[8] Some of the Grails tag libraries even integrate with them to make standard Ajax behavior simple even for the Ajax beginner. Chapter 8 will explain how to add Ajax functionality to your application to increase usability.

Jetty

To ensure Grails has a complete development environment, it includes the popular and fast Jetty web container/server.[9] Grails makes application and container life-cycle management easy by using its command-line interface to start and stop the server while taking care of packaging and deploying the application behind the scenes. But by no means are Grails applications limited to running in a Jetty container. Chapter 12 will explain how to deploy Grails applications to other containers.

---

3. `http://www.hibernate.org`
4. `http://www.opensymphony.com/sitemesh/`
5. `http://www.opensymphony.com`
6. `http://script.aculo.us`
7. `http://openrico.org`
8. `http://www.prototypejs.org`
9. `http://www.mortbay.org`

HSQLDB

Having a complete development environment out of the box requires a relational database. Grails includes the 100% Java database called HSQLDB.[10] You can use this database either as a standalone database server or as an embedded database. You can also configure it to run in memory or persisted to disk. By default, Grails uses the embedded in-memory configuration, so that each time the application is run, the database is rebuilt from scratch and all data is lost. Chapter 12 will explain how to configure Grails to use other databases such as MySQL.[11]

JUnit

For unit testing, Grails uses the popular JUnit framework.[12] In the "Implementing Integration Tests" section, you will learn to write and run unit tests.

Grails Architecture

Now that you know some of the features and open source frameworks included in Grails, you are more prepared to understand the Grails architecture. Figure 4-1 depicts the architecture graphically.

Figure 4-1. *Grails architecture*

In Figure 4-1, notice that the foundation of Grails is the Java Virtual Machine (JVM). Also, notice the separation in the architecture from the Java language and the JVM. In the past couple of years, the Java community has seen a rash of new and ported languages being run on the JVM. This is particularly important in Grails, because in the next level up from the JVM, you see that both the Java and Groovy languages are being used.

---

10. http://hsqldb.org

11. http://www.mysql.com/

12. http://www.junit.org

Above the languages you find the Grails framework itself, which, as you know from the previous section, is made up of several industry-standard open source projects such as Spring, SiteMesh, and GORM/Hibernate, to name just a few. However, as an application developer, you're not limited to the libraries and frameworks Grails has to offer. Your application can use just about any Java library, whether open source or proprietary. The final layer of the architecture is the applications you will build with Grails. Typically, this layer follows the MVC pattern. Grails also makes it easy to organize your application to make coarse-grained services.

To simplify development, Grails includes a command-line tool for creating many Grails artifacts and managing Grails projects. The Grails command line is built on top of Gant,[13] a build system that uses the Groovy language to script Apache Ant[14] tasks rather than Ant's XML format. You will learn more about Gant and adding your own scripts to the Grails command line in Chapter 12.

From a runtime perspective, you can think of Grails out of the box as looking like Figure 4-2.

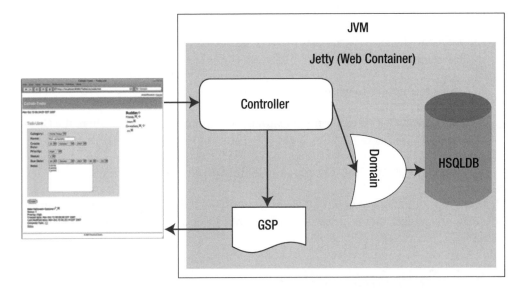

Figure 4-2. *Grails default runtime*

In Figure 4-2, you see a web browser making a request to a Jetty web container. The container forwards the request on to a controller in a similar fashion to the standard MVC model. The controller may set or use data from a domain class (model). As mentioned earlier, all Grails domain classes are persistable through the GORM framework.

---

13. http://gant.codehaus.org

14. http://ant.apache.org

You don't need to use a Data Access Object (DAO) pattern or write SQL to persist objects. In Chapter 6, you will learn how to take full advantage of the persistable domain classes.

Out-of-the-box Grails uses an embedded HSQLDB database, which means the database runs in the same JVM as your application and the Jetty web container. When the controller is done, it forwards the request to a GSP, which is the view technology to render the HTML that is returned to the requesting browser.

Installing Grails

Considering the alternative to using Grails—downloading and installing a web container or application server, database, and MVC framework—installing Grails seems almost too easy. All you need to do is uncompress a file and set up some environment variables, and you're done. Most everything is self-contained. Grails does require two prerequisites, though: you must have a JDK 1.4 or greater, and you must have the JAVA_HOME environment variable configured for that JDK.

Follow these steps to install Grails:

1. Download the latest Grails .zip or .tar/.gz file release from http://grails. codehaus.org/Download.

2. Extract the archive to your preferred location.

3. Create a GRAILS_HOME environment variable that points to the path where the Grails archive was extracted.

4. Append the GRAILS_HOME\bin directory to the PATH environment variable.

Once you complete these steps, the Grails command line will be available. You can use it to create the project, create artifacts, run the application, and package the application.

Collab-Todo Application

Throughout this book, we'll use a single web application example to demonstrate how to write a web application using the Grails framework. The application name is Collab-Todo, and it is a collaborative Web 2.0 to-do application. The application allows users to create and manage to-dos in categories. It also allows users to create buddy lists of other Collab-Todo users to make it easy to assign tasks to other users. In addition, it includes reports and batch e-mails, along with a thick client and web service access. Figure 4-3 shows what Collab-Todo will look like by the end of the book.

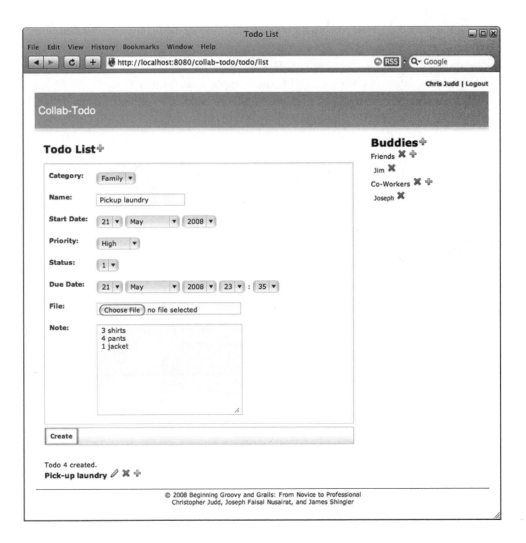

Figure 4-3. *Final version of the Collab-Todo application*

Getting Started with Scaffolding

We feel it is important for you to experience for yourself the power and productivity of Grails early on. So for the remainder of this chapter, you will be learning to take advantage of Grails conventions and scaffolding to create a simple but functional version of the Collab-Todo application. This initial version of the application will not be a production-suitable application from a usability and design perspective. However, the Grails scaffolding is able to render a simple but functional CRUD web application with almost no code besides your domain class code. In addition, Grails will generate a database schema and populate a database with the schema when the application is run. This scaffolding-based version of the application is suitable for testing domain objects as well as quick application prototyping.

Figure 4-4 shows an example of what the CRUD to-do pages will look like by the end of the chapter.

Figure 4-4. *Todo List page*

As you can see in Figure 4-4, the Todo List page provides the ability to view all the to-dos in the database as well as create new to-dos or delete existing to-dos. It also provides a link to the edit page, where you can create a new to-do or updating an existing to-do.

Figure 4-5 shows the Edit Todo page, which is basically the same page used for updating and creating to-dos.

Figure 4-5. *Edit Todo page*

As you can tell from Figures 4-4 and 4-5, this is not the most attractive application, and you probably won't want to release this to your users. In Chapter 5, you'll learn how to make the application more usable and pleasing to your users' eyes, and in Chapter 8, you'll learn how to make it even better by adding Web 2.0 features.

Figure 4-6 is a Unified Modeling Language (UML) diagram of a subset of the Collab-Todo domain classes you'll be creating in this chapter.

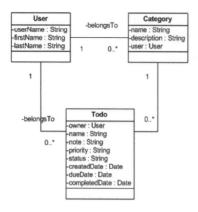

Figure 4-6. *Subset of the Collab-Todo domain classes*

Notice the domain class in Figure 4-6 is very simple and includes only three domain classes. In Chapter 6, you will extend this domain model and learn about the Grails persistence framework, GORM. Initially, the domain consists of a User class, which has a Todo (task) class, and user-defined Category classes used for organizing to-dos into logical groups.

Understanding the Scaffolding Process

Creating a Grails application using its scaffolding is really quite simple. The following seven basic steps summarize the process:

1. Create an application.

2. Run the application.

3. Create the domain class.

4. Implement the integration test.

5. Run the test harness and update the domain classes until the tests pass.

6. Create the controller.

7. Repeat steps 3 through 6 until the domain class and the controllers are complete.

Notice that none of these steps say anything about creating a view, HTML, or anything related to the user interface (UI). You don't even have to run anything to generate the presentation. The scaffolding uses introspection to determine the appropriate interface to render at runtime.

Because Grails is an agile framework that tries to provide feedback quickly, you want to run the application immediately after creating it so you can observe how changes to the domain class or controllers affect the application.

Creating the Application

To create the application, you follow a pattern that is repeated for creating just about everything in Grails: you execute a Grails target on the command line. You use the `create-app` target to create a new application. This generates the basic application structure and populates the structure with some basic files.

To create the Collab-Todo application, you need to execute the `create-app` target using an optional project name, as shown here:

```
>grails create-app collab-todo
```

If you don't supply the project name, you will be prompted for one.

The output of executing the `create-app` target is shown here:

```
Welcome to Grails 1.0 - http://grails.org/
Licensed under Apache Standard License 2.0
Grails home is set to: C:\devl\java\grails-1.0

Base Directory: C:\devl\workspace
Environment set to development
Note: No plugin scripts found
Running script C:\devl\java\grails-1.0\scripts\CreateApp.groovy
    [mkdir] Created dir: C:\devl\workspace\collab-todo\src
    [mkdir] Created dir: C:\devl\workspace\collab-todo\src\java
    [mkdir] Created dir: C:\devl\workspace\collab-todo\src\groovy
    [mkdir] Created dir: C:\devl\workspace\collab-todo\grails-app
    [mkdir] Created dir: C:\devl\workspace\collab-todo\grails-app\controllers
    [mkdir] Created dir: C:\devl\workspace\collab-todo\grails-app\services
    [mkdir] Created dir: C:\devl\workspace\collab-todo\grails-app\domain
    [mkdir] Created dir: C:\devl\workspace\collab-todo\grails-app\taglib
    [mkdir] Created dir: C:\devl\workspace\collab-todo\grails-app\utils
    [mkdir] Created dir: C:\devl\workspace\collab-todo\grails-app\views
    [mkdir] Created dir: C:\devl\workspace\collab-todo\grails-app\views\layouts
    [mkdir] Created dir: C:\devl\workspace\collab-todo\grails-app\i18n
    [mkdir] Created dir: C:\devl\workspace\collab-todo\grails-app\conf
    [mkdir] Created dir: C:\devl\workspace\collab-todo\test
    [mkdir] Created dir: C:\devl\workspace\collab-todo\test\unit
    [mkdir] Created dir: C:\devl\workspace\collab-todo\test\integration
    [mkdir] Created dir: C:\devl\workspace\collab-todo\scripts
    [mkdir] Created dir: C:\devl\workspace\collab-todo\web-app
    [mkdir] Created dir: C:\devl\workspace\collab-todo\web-app\js
    [mkdir] Created dir: C:\devl\workspace\collab-todo\web-app\css
```

```
   [mkdir] Created dir: C:\devl\workspace\collab-todo\web-app\images
   [mkdir] Created dir: C:\devl\workspace\collab-todo\web-app\WEB-INF\classes
   [mkdir] Created dir: C:\devl\workspace\collab-todo\web-app\META-INF
   [mkdir] Created dir: C:\devl\workspace\collab-todo\lib
   [mkdir] Created dir: C:\devl\workspace\collab-todo\grails-app\conf\spring
   [mkdir] Created dir: C:\devl\workspace\collab-todo\grails-app\conf\hibernate
[propertyfile] Creating new property file:
         C:\devl\workspace\collab-todo\application.properties
    [copy] Copying 2 files to C:\devl\workspace\collab-todo
    [copy] Copying 2 files to C:\devl\workspace\collab-todo\web-app\WEB-INF
    [copy] Copying 5 files to C:\devl\workspace\collab-todo\web-app\WEB-INF\tld
    [copy] Copying 87 files to C:\devl\workspace\collab-todo\web-app
    [copy] Copying 16 files to C:\devl\workspace\collab-todo\grails-app
    [copy] Copying 1 file to C:\devl\workspace\collab-todo\grails-app\conf\spring
    [copy] Copying 1 file to C:\devl\workspace\collab-todo
    [copy] Copying 1 file to C:\devl\workspace\collab-todo
    [copy] Copying 1 file to C:\devl\workspace\collab-todo
[propertyfile] Updating property file:
         C:\devl\workspace\collab-todo\application.properties
Created Grails Application at C:\devl\workspace/collab-todo
```

After the create-app target has run, you will have a new directory matching the name of your project. This will be the root of your new project, and you must make all subsequent Grails command-line calls from within this directory. It's a good idea to use the cd command to get into the directory now so you don't forget. Within the new project directory, you will find a structure matching the directory structure found in Figure 4-7.

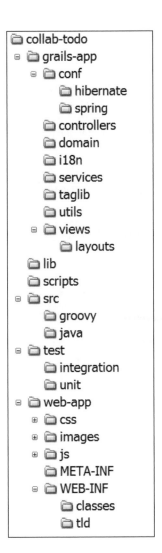

Figure 4-7. *Directory structure created by running the create-app target*

As mentioned earlier, the directory structure generated from the create-app target is a part of the Grails practice of convention over configuration. The target provides locations for placing common artifacts. Throughout the book, you will learn details about each directory. For now, Table 4-1 provides a summary of the more important directories.

Table 4-1. *Important Directories in the Grails Convention*

Directory	Description
grails-app/conf	Common configuration files such as bootstrapping, logging, data source, and URL mapping (see the "Configurations" sidebar)
grails-app/conf/hibernate	Custom Hibernate mappings, which are rarely needed (covered in Chapter 6)
grails-app/conf/spring	Custom Spring mapping files
grails-app/controllers	Application controllers that handle requests (covered in Chapter 5)
grails-app/domain	Domain model classes (covered in Chapter 6)
grails-app/i18n	Internationalized message bundles (covered in Chapter 5)
grails-app/services	Services (covered in Chapter 6)
grails-app/taglib	Custom dynamic tag libraries
grails-app/views	GSP (covered in Chapter 5)
grails-app/views/layout	Commonly shared page layouts (covered in Chapter 5)
lib	Third-party JAR files, such as database drivers
scripts	Gant script for automating tasks (covered in Chapter 12)
src/java	Additional Java source files
src/groovy	Additional Groovy files
test/integration	Integration tests (covered in Chapter 5)
test/unit	Unit tests (introduced later in this chapter)
web-app	Web artifacts that will ultimately comprise a web application archive (WAR) (many of the artifacts are covered in Chapter 5)
web-app/css	Cascading Style Sheets (covered in Chapter 5)
web-app/images	Web graphics (covered in Chapter 5)
web-app/js	JavaScript (covered in Chapter 8)
web-app/WEB-INF	Common Servlet specification WEB-INF directory containing private artifacts such as configuration files like web.xml, the Spring application context, and the SiteMesh config

At this point, you're able to open the project in your development tool of choice. Not only does the create-app target generate the directory structure, but it also generates project files for Eclipse[15] and TextMate.[16] Another option is to use IntelliJ IDEA,[17] because it understands how to consume Eclipse project files.

---

15. http://www.eclipse.org

16. http://macromates.com

17. http://www.jetbrains.com/idea/

CONFIGURATIONS

Grails includes four configuration files in the `grails-app/config` directory. Two of these files are environmentally aware, meaning you can have different configurations for different environments like the built-in `development`, `test`, and `production` environments. In Chapter 12, you will learn how to add custom development environments. The following table describes the standard configuration files.

Grails Configuration Files

Name	Environmentally Aware	Description
`BootStrap.groovy`	No	Life-cycle–aware configuration containing callbacks for initializing and destroying the application
`Config.groovy`	Yes	Catchall configuration files containing logging, Multipurpose Internet Mail Extensions (MIME) typing, and other configurations
`DataSource.groovy`	Yes	Java Database Connectivity (JDBC) or Java Naming and Directory Interface (JNDI) configurations
`UrlMappings.groovy`	No	Customizable URL mapping file

Running the Application

At this point, you have a functional application that you can run and access via a web browser. It really does not do much yet, but running it now will enable you to get instant feedback as you add domain and controller classes.

To run a Grails application, execute the `run-app` target from your project root directory as shown here:

```
> grails run-app
```

The output of executing the `run-app` target is shown here:

```
...
Running script C:\devl\java\grails-1.0\scripts\RunApp.groovy
    [mkdir] Created dir: C:\devl\workspace\collab-todo\web-app\WEB-INF\lib
    [mkdir] Created dir:
    C:\Documents and Settings\Administrator\.grails\1.0\projects\collab-todo\classes
Compiling 4 source files to
```

```
C:\Documents and Settings\Administrator\.grails\1.0\projects\collab-todo\classes
  [mkdir] Created dir:
  C:\devl\workspace\collab-todo\web-app\WEB-INF\grails-app\i18n
   [copy] Copying 8 files to
  C:\devl\workspace\collab-todo\web-app\WEB-INF\grails-app\i18n
   [copy] Copying 1 file to C:\devl\workspace\collab-todo\web-app\WEB-INF\spring
   [copy] Copying 1 file to
  C:\Documents and Settings\Administrator\.grails\1.0\projects\collab-todo\classes
   [copy] Copying 1 file to
  C:\Documents and Settings\Administrator\.grails\1.0\projects\collab-todo\classes
Running Grails application..
2007-10-12 23:16:09.891::INFO:  jetty-6.1.4
...


2007-10-12 23:16:09.891::INFO:  Started SelectChannelConnector@0.0.0.0:8080
Server running. Browse to http://localhost:8080/collab-todo
```

Running the run-app target does some initial project setup by copying files into your web application's WEB-INF directories. Then it starts a Jetty web container that listens on localhost port 8080. Jetty then loads the application, causing the Grails internal classes to get initialized for filtering URL mappings and requests along with GrailsDispatchServlet. Ultimately, you will know that the application server is available and you can start testing your application when you see this:

```
Server running. Browse to http://localhost:8080/collab-todo.
```

To test your app, point your web browser of choice to that URL, as shown in Figure 4-8.

Figure 4-8 shows the standard default Grails page. As you can see, it is not very interesting; it looks like a static page. However, as you'll see soon, there is some dynamism to this page. If you wish to modify this page, it is the GSP web-app\index.gsp.

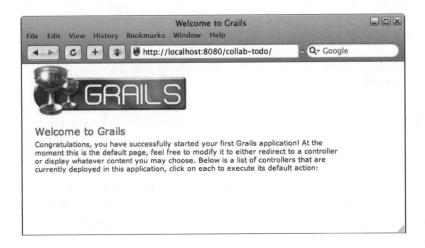

Figure 4-8. *Default Grails page*

Creating a Domain Class

At this point, the application doesn't really do anything, so you will have to add some additional classes for the application to take shape. Typically, you begin by creating a domain class and then follow it up with an associated controller class. To create a domain class, use the Grails `create-domain-class` target. This creates a new Grails domain class in the `grails-app/domain` directory, as well as an integration test for the domain class in `test/integration`.

Note The `create-domain-class` target creates an integration test rather than a unit test, because as you will learn in Chapter 6, domain classes have dependencies on the database. Making the domain test an integration test by putting it in the `test/integration` directory enables the test to have access to the entire Grails environment, including the database. Without this, the domain class would not have access to the dynamic methods available to domain classes for persistence.

To create the `Todo` domain class, you need to execute the `create-domain-class` target using an optional class name, as shown here:

```
> grails create-domain-class todo
```

If you don't supply the class name, you will be prompted for one.

The output of executing the `create-domain-class` target is shown here:

```
Running script C:\devl\java\grails-1.0\scripts\CreateDomainClass.groovy
    [copy] Copying 1 file to C:\devl\workspace\collab-todo\grails-app\domain
Created  for Todo
    [copy] Copying 1 file to C:\devl\workspace\collab-todo\test\integration
Created Tests for Todo
```

Notice that when running the `create-domain-class` target with the optional class name, you can leave the class name in lowercase, and Grails will automatically uppercase it for you so that it follows the standard Groovy class-naming convention. Listing 4-1 shows the generated Todo domain class.

Listing 4-1. *Grails-Generated Todo Domain Class*

```
class Todo {
}
```

The Todo domain class in Listing 4-1 appears to be the most basic of Groovy classes. As you will learn in the next couple of sections and in the next two chapters, there is more to Grails domain classes than meets the eye.

Implementing Integration Tests

As you saw in the previous section, Grails is true to its testing convention by generating a corresponding integration test every time you create a domain class. Listing 4-2 shows the generated integration test for the Todo domain class.

Listing 4-2. *Grails-Generated Integration Test for the Todo Domain Class*

```
class TodoTests extends GroovyTestCase {

  void testSomething() {
  }
}
```

Notice that the integration test in Listing 4-2 extends the standard Groovy test case, which extends the JUnit test case and adds some convenience assert methods. The generated integration test also includes a test method template.

■**Note** As is true with all JUnit test cases, any method prefixed with `test` will be treated as a test and is executed when the test harness is run.

Listing 4-3 shows the `Todo` integration tests updated with two tests: one for testing the `toString()` method and one for persisting `Todo` objects.

Listing 4-3. *Todo Integration Tests*

```
1  class TodoTests extends GroovyTestCase {
2
3    void setUp() {
4      Todo.list()*.delete()
5    }
6
7    void testPersist() {
8      new Todo(name: "1", createdDate:new Date(), priority: "", status:"").save()
9      new Todo(name: "2", createdDate:new Date(), priority: "", status:"").save()
10     new Todo(name: "3", createdDate:new Date(), priority: "", status:"").save()
11     new Todo(name: "4", createdDate:new Date(), priority: "", status:"").save()
12     new Todo(name: "5", createdDate:new Date(), priority: "", status:"").save()
13
14     assert 5 == Todo.count()
15   }
16
17   void testToString() {
18     def todo = new Todo(name: "Pickup laundry")
19     assertToString(todo, "Pickup laundry")
20   }
21 }
```

The integration test in Listing 4-3 contains three methods. The `setUp()` method on lines 3–5 is a standard JUnit life-cycle method. It is called prior to executing any method prefixed with `test` and should be used to put your tests into a known state. In this case, the known state is making sure there are no `Todos` in the database. It does this by using the dynamic `list()` method on the `Todo` class. You were warned that Grails domain classes are more complicated than they appear.

On a Grails domain class, GORM provides the `list()` method, which returns a list containing all the records of that type in the database. In the `setup()` method, you want to delete all the `Todos` returned in the list. Rather than iterate through each object in the list, you can use the Groovy spread operator (`*.`) to call the following method on each of the objects in the list. In this case, the delete() method removes that object instance from the database.

■**Caution** Take care when using the list() method, because it returns *all* records of the specified type and can cause large memory consumption, depending on the number of records in the database.

The testPersist() method on lines 7–15 creates five new instances of the Todo domain class and then saves them to the database using another dynamic Grails domain class method, save(). Finally, this test method validates that there are five Todos in the database by using another dynamic Grails domain class method of count() to get the number of records in the database. It also uses the Groovy assert keyword to validate the proper number of records.

■**Note** Whenever unit tests are run or the default configured application is started, an in-memory HSQLDB database is loaded. This in-memory database does not save anything to disk, so each time the application or tests are run, you will have a new, clean database. In addition, Hibernate will use the domain classes to create or update a schema in that database.

The testToString() test on lines 17–20 is a pretty basic and self-explanatory unit test that tests the toString() method of the Todo domain class. The only item of interest is the assertToString() method. You may not recognize this as the standard JUnit assert method. That's because it is implemented by the GroovyTestCase class.

Running the Test Harness

At this point, you want to run the test harness. Tests are expected to fail, because the Todo class still has no implementation. After seeing the failures, you add functionality to the Todo class and iterate over implementing and testing until all the tests pass.

To run the test harness, simply execute the Grails test-app target. This executes all the unit and integration tests and displays the results of each test. In addition, it creates several reports for diagnosing any test errors or failures:

```
>grails test-app
```

The output of executing the `test-app` target is shown here:

```
...
Running script C:\devl\java\grails-1.0\scripts\TestApp.groovy
...
No tests found in test/unit to execute ...
--------------------------------------------------------
Running 2 Integration Tests...
Running test TodoTests...
                        testPersist...SUCCESS
                        testToString... FAILURE
Integration Tests Completed in 711ms
--------------------------------------------------------
[junitreport]
  Processing C:\devl\workspace\collab-todo\test\reports\TESTS-TestSuites.xml
[junitreport]
  Loading stylesheet jar:file:/C:/devl/java/grails-1.0/lib/ant-junit.jar
  !/org/apache/tools/ant/taskdefs/optional/junit/xsl/junit-frames.xsl
[junitreport] Transform time: 751ms
Tests failed: 0 errors, 1 failures, 0 compilation errors. View reports in
  C:\devl\workspace\collab-todo/test/reports
```

The results of running the test harness show no unit tests were run, because no unit tests have been added to the `test/unit` directory yet. They also show that two integration tests were run—one that was successful, and one that failed. Because the Todo class does not have any implementation yet, you expected both tests to fail. So, you should evaluate the `testPersist` test to understand why it passed and to improve the test to make sure it fails before writing the Todo implementation.

Listing 4-4 shows the original implementation of the `testPersist` test.

Listing 4-4. *Original testPersist*

```
void testPersist() {
  new Todo(name: "1", createdDate:new Date(), priority: "", status:"").save()
  new Todo(name: "2", createdDate:new Date(), priority: "", status:"").save()
  new Todo(name: "3", createdDate:new Date(), priority: "", status:"").save()
  new Todo(name: "4", createdDate:new Date(), priority: "", status:"").save()
  new Todo(name: "5", createdDate:new Date(), priority: "", status:"").save()

  assert 5 == Todo.count()
}
```

In Listing 4-4, five Todos are saved to the database and the count of the inserted Todos are validated. This currently works because even at this point with no Todo implementation, Todo objects can be saved to the database. However, looking at the database, you should see a record with no name, createdDate, priority, or status, because those properties don't exist yet. The parameterized constructor happily accepts parameters that do not map to properties, so this test passes with no problems. To make the test more valuable, try retrieving at least one of the Todos based on the value of one of its properties, as shown in Listing 4-5.

Listing 4-5. *Improved testPersist*

```
void testPersist() {
  new Todo(name: "1", createdDate:new Date(), priority: "", status:"").save()
  new Todo(name: "2", createdDate:new Date(), priority: "", status:"").save()
  new Todo(name: "3", createdDate:new Date(), priority: "", status:"").save()
  new Todo(name: "4", createdDate:new Date(), priority: "", status:"").save()
  new Todo(name: "5", createdDate:new Date(), priority: "", status:"").save()

  assert 5 == Todo.count()
  def actualTodo = Todo.findByName('1')
  assert actualTodo
  assert '1' == actualTodo.name
}
```

Listing 4-5 is the same as Listing 4-4 with three additional lines at the end. After the saves and validating the count, the test now looks up a Todo by name, using the dynamic findByName() method that we'll discuss in Chapter 6. Then the test asserts the object returned is not null, and then it validates a value.

Running the test harness again shows that both integration tests fail. In addition, it produces a JUnit HTML report, shown in Figure 4-9 and found in the test/reports/html directory. This can help you determine why the tests failed.

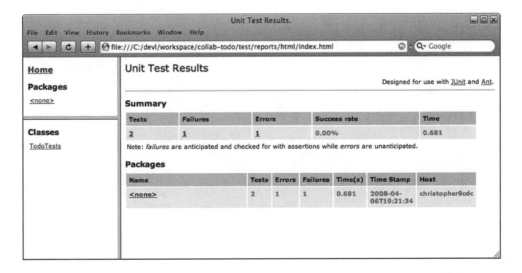

Figure 4-9. *Example unit test report*

Drilling into `TodoTests`, you can see that `testPersist` errored because there is no property of `name` found on `Todo`, so the `findByName()` method could not be invoked properly. You also learn `testToString()` fails because the return value does not equal the expected value. Until you override `toString()` in the `Todo` class, the class returns the Grails domain class default `toString()`.

In addition to the HTML report shown in Figure 4-9, a text version and an XML version of the unit test results are also generated in the `test/reports/plain` and `test/reports` directories, respectively.

Implementing a Domain Class

Now that the tests are implemented and failing as expected, it is time to update the domain class until all tests pass. Listing 4-6 shows the `Todo` domain class after adding the fields shown in the UML diagram in Figure 4-6.

Listing 4-6. *Todo Domain Class After Adding Attributes, Constraints, and the toString() Method*

```
1  class Todo {
2
3      String name
4      String note
5      Date createdDate
6      Date dueDate
```

```
7     Date completedDate
8     String priority
9     String status
10
11    static constraints = {
12       name(blank:false)
13       createdDate()
14       priority()
15       status()
16       note(maxSize:1000, nullable:true)
17       completedDate(nullable:true)
18       dueDate(nullable:true)
19    }
20
21    String toString() {
22       name
23    }
24  }
```

In Listing 4-6, you see that lines 3–9 are several fields of both String and Date types that you would expect to find in a Todo domain class. However, there are some additional properties you don't see that are implicit to a Grails domain class by convention. They include the id and version properties.

The id property, as you might expect, represents a unique autoincrementing identifier and is null until the object is initially saved. The version property is a Hibernate mechanism for managing optimistic locking. Each time an object is saved, its version number gets incremented, and like the id, it is initially null. Before Hibernate saves any object, it first checks the version number in the database, and if the versions don't match the object about to be saved—meaning it was already modified since the last read—Hibernate will throw an org.hibernate.StaleObjectStateException.

Lines 11–19 demonstrate the Grails construct of constraints. These are basically rules governing the values of the properties. For example, line 12 states the name property is required and may not be empty using a blank:false constraint, while the note, completedDate, and dueDate properties on lines 16–18 are allowed to be null. Also, note that the note property on line 16 has a maximum length of 1,000 characters. In addition to constraining the properties, the constraints dictate the order of fields on the edit pages as well as the types of HTML form fields rendered by the Grails scaffolding. The order of the constraints represents the order of the fields on the page. While a String is usually represented by an HTML input field of type text, a String property with a maxSize is usually rendered as an HTML input field of textarea to support the larger amounts of input data.

Domain classes can also have behavior implemented as methods. Lines 21–23 show the `toString()` method being overridden. The default `toString()` behavior of a Grails domain class is to print the class name followed by a colon and the object ID. To make the `toString()` a little more helpful, line 21 prepends the `name` property of the `Todo` instance.

This section has not even scratched the surface of domain classes. You will learn lots more about them in Chapter 6.

Now that the `Todo` class is complete, rerunning the test harness will result in both tests passing.

VERSION-CONTROLLING GRAILS FILES

A Grails application includes lots of files, most of which should be version-controlled. However, both the running of unit tests and the application generate and copy files that should not be version-controlled in a source code repository like Subversion or Concurrent Versions System (CVS). The following table includes a list of directories that should be ignored by version control.

Grails Directories Not to Version-Control

Directory	Description
`web-app/WEB-INF/classes`	Contains class files that get recompiled at runtime
`web-app/WEB-INF/lib`	Contains JAR files copied from the `lib` directory and Grails at runtime
`web-app/WEB-INF/grails-app`	`grails-app` contents get copied here at runtime
`web-app/WEB-INF/spring`	`grails-app/config/spring` contents get copied here at runtime
`test/classes`	Contains class files that are recompiled during testing
`test/reports`	Contains text and HTML reports that get generated during testing
`staging`	Temporary directory for staging the building of WAR files

---

Creating the Controller

The last step before iterating over these steps over and over again is to create the controller. As mentioned earlier, the controller is responsible for the interaction between the view and the domain classes. Fortunately, the Grails scaffolding makes this simple. The controller consists of only a single line of code that instructs the scaffolding to do its magic and generate the basic CRUD UI.

To create a controller class, use the Grails `create-controller` target. This creates a new Grails controller class in the `grails-app/controllers` directory, as well as an integration test for the controller class in `test/integration`. It also creates a `grails-app/views/<controller name>` directory if it doesn't exist already.

To create the `TodoController` class, you need to execute the `create-controller` target using an optional class name, as shown here:

```
>grails create-controller todo
```

If you don't supply the class name, you will be prompted for one.

The output of executing the `create-controller` target is shown here:

```
...
Running script C:\devl\java\grails-1.0\scripts\CreateController.groovy
    [copy] Copying 1 file to C:\devl\workspace\collab-todo\grails-app\controllers
Created Controller for Todo
    [mkdir] Created dir: C:\devl\workspace\collab-todo\grails-app\views\todo
    [copy] Copying 1 file to C:\devl\workspace\collab-todo\test\integration
Created ControllerTests for Todo
```

Notice that when running the `create-controller` with the optional class name, you can leave the class name in lowercase, and Grails will automatically uppercase it for you so that it follows the standard Groovy class-naming convention. Listing 4-7 shows the generated `TodoController` class.

Listing 4-7. *Grails-Generated TodoController Class*

```
class TodoController {
  def index = { }
}
```

The `TodoController` class in Listing 4-7 contains an empty `index` action. Chapter 5 will explain actions on the controller.

For now, to use the Grails scaffolding, change the `index` action to a `scaffold` property and assign it the domain class, as shown in Listing 4-8. That's all there is to it. This causes List Page, Create Page, Edit Page, and Show Page views, as well as delete functionality, to be generated for the specified domain class.

Listing 4-8. *Scaffolding-Enabled TodoController*

```
class TodoController {

  def scaffold = Todo
}
```

After changing `TodoController` to look like it does in Listing 4-8, refresh your browser to reveal a new `TodoController` link on the initial page, as shown in Figure 4-10.

■Tip You can make most changes, including changes to the domain and controller classes, without having to restart the web server. Sometimes, however, changes require a restart. Creating a new controller sometimes requires a restart, so if the controller doesn't appear in the controllers list, stop the server using Ctrl+C and the Grails `run-app` target to restart.

Figure 4-10. *Initial Grails page with the TodoController link added*

Selecting the `TodoController` link in Figure 4-10 brings you to the Todo List page shown in Figure 4-11. The Todo List page is a paginated list of domain objects.

Figure 4-11. *Todo List page*

From the list page shown in Figure 4-11, you have the ability to create new domain objects (as shown in Figure 4-12) by clicking the New button on the navigation bar. You can also show domain objects (as shown in Figure 4-14) by clicking on the ID.

The save page displays the list of properties in the order in which the constraints are ordered as shown in the Create Todo page in Figure 4-12. Note that the Grails scaffolding displays the edit fields in the appropriate date type format. A String is displayed as an HTML text input field, while createdDate is displayed as a series of drop-downs for the day of month, month, year, hour, and seconds. In addition, the note property is displayed as an HTML text-area input due to the maxSize constraint. That's not all: the Grails scaffolding is also smart enough to use the constraints for doing form validation, as shown in Figure 4-13.

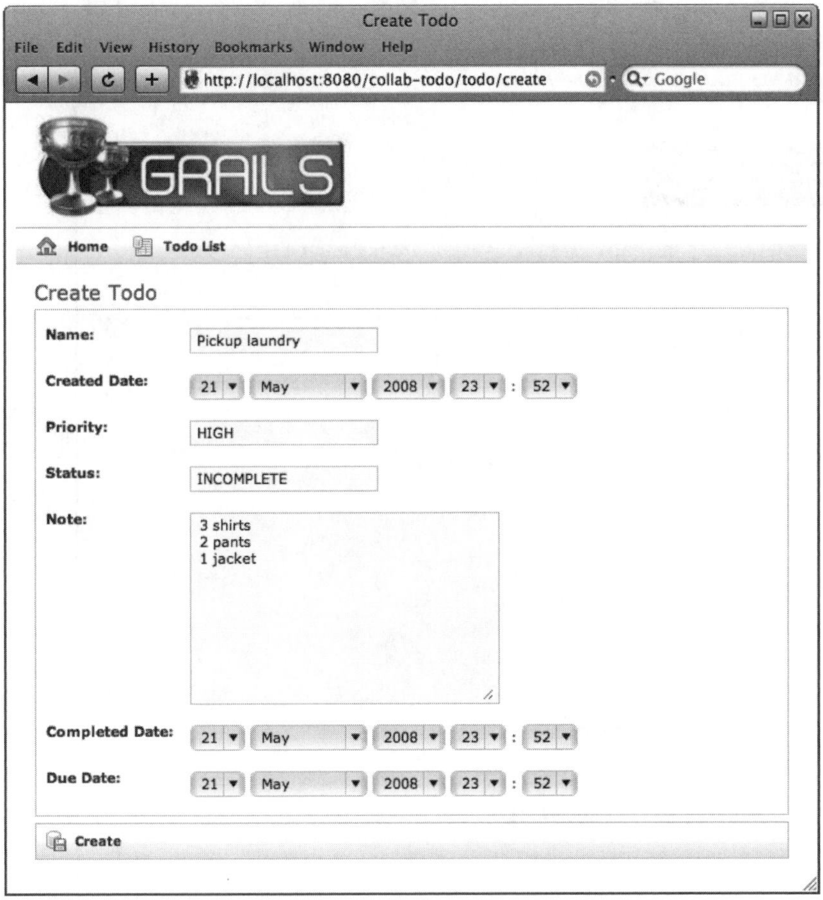

Figure 4-12. *Create Todo page*

Figure 4-13. *Validation errors*

Notice in Figure 4-13 that a validation message is displayed at the top of the page if the form is submitted with an empty name. The blank:false constraint makes the name property required.

Figure 4-14 shows a read-only view that gets displayed when the ID is selected from the Todo List page.

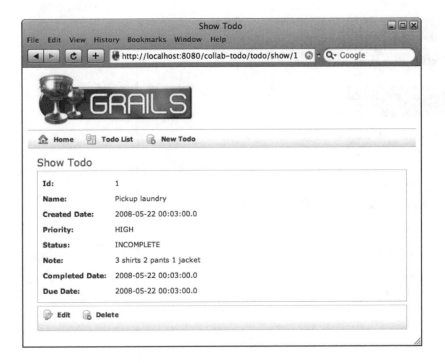

Figure 4-14. *Show Todo page*

The Show Todo page displays all the properties and values. It also provides access to the Edit Todo page, as shown in Figure 4-15, where you can delete the domain object.

Figure 4-15. *Edit Todo page*

The Edit Todo page, shown in Figure 4-15, is really the same as the Create Todo page, except the data is repopulated with the domain object values, and it has Update and Delete buttons at the bottom of the page.

Finishing the Remaining Domain and Controllers

Now that you've created the Todo domain and controller classes, the steps for creating the domain classes and controller classes can be repeated for the remaining domain and controllers: Category and User. Then you can add the relationships between the domain classes.

As illustrated in the UML diagram in Figure 4-6, the Category class is very simple. Listing 4-9 shows the code after generating the class using the Grails create-domain-class target and adding the properties from the UML diagram.

Listing 4-9. *Category Domain Class*

```
class Category {
  String name
  String description

  static constraints = {
    name(blank:false)
  }

  String toString() {
    name
  }
}
```

In Listing 4-9, you see the Category class just has name and description properties and an overloaded toString() method that returns the name property. This overloaded toString() method will become important later, because it is used to populate an HTML select field. Without it, the select field would only display the category's id, making it difficult to differentiate categories in the list. The Category class also includes a constraint, which requires the name property.

The User domain class follows the same pattern as both the Todo and Category classes. Listing 4-10 shows the code after generating the class with the Grails create-domain-class target and adding the properties from the UML diagram.

Listing 4-10. *User Domain Class*

```
class User {
  String userName
  String firstName
  String lastName

  static constraints = {
    userName(blank:false,unique:true)
    firstName(blank:false)
    lastName(blank:false)
  }

  String  toString () {
    "$lastName, $firstName"
  }

}
```

In Listing 4-10, you see the User class contains userName, firstName, and lastName properties. It also contains constraints that make all properties required and forces the userName property to be unique in the database. Finally, the overridden toString() method returns the user's name in a last-name-first format.

Note If you're making changes to domain or controller classes while the application is running with the default development data-source configurations, it is common for all the data to disappear. This happens because the changes to the domain class cause Hibernate to regenerate the schema. In Chapter 12, you'll learn how to change the default development data-source configurations once the domain classes have been completed.

The controller classes are carbon copies of TodoController. Listing 4-11 shows CategoryController after it has been created with the Grails create-controller target and the scaffolding variable set.

Listing 4-11. *CategoryController*

```
class CategoryController {

  def scaffold = Category
}
```

Listing 4-12 shows UserController.

Listing 4-12. *UserController*

```
class UserController {

  def scaffold = User
}
```

After completing the Category and User domain and controller classes, the application start page displays all three controllers. In addition, CRUD pages for both Category and User are available when clicking on the respective controller links.

Creating Domain Relationships

At this point, you have three standalone domain classes—Todo, Category, and User—with no relationships between them. But remember that the UML diagram in Figure 4-6 showed that users had user-defined categories as well as to-dos that were organized by categories.

Now it's time to represent those one-to-many relationships between the domain classes using the belongsTo and hasMany properties.

Listing 4-13 shows the new Todo class, which shows the relationships with User and Category.

Listing 4-13. *Todo Domain Class with Relationships to the User and Category Domain Classes*

```
class Todo {
  String name
  String note
  Date createdDate
  Date dueDate
  Date completedDate
  String priority
  String status
  User owner
  Category category

  static belongsTo = [User, Category]

  static constraints = {
    name(blank:false)
    createdDate()
    priority()
    status()
    note(maxSize:1000, nullable:true)
    completedDate(nullable:true)
    dueDate(nullable:true)
  }

  String toString() {
    name
  }

}
```

Notice in Listing 4-13 that the relationship is defined with the belongsTo property to the User and Category classes. We've also added new owner and category properties. belongsTo tells GORM to delete the to-do if either the associated user or the category is deleted. Scaffolding renders these relationships as the select fields on the Create Todo and Edit Todo screens, as shown in Figure 4-16.

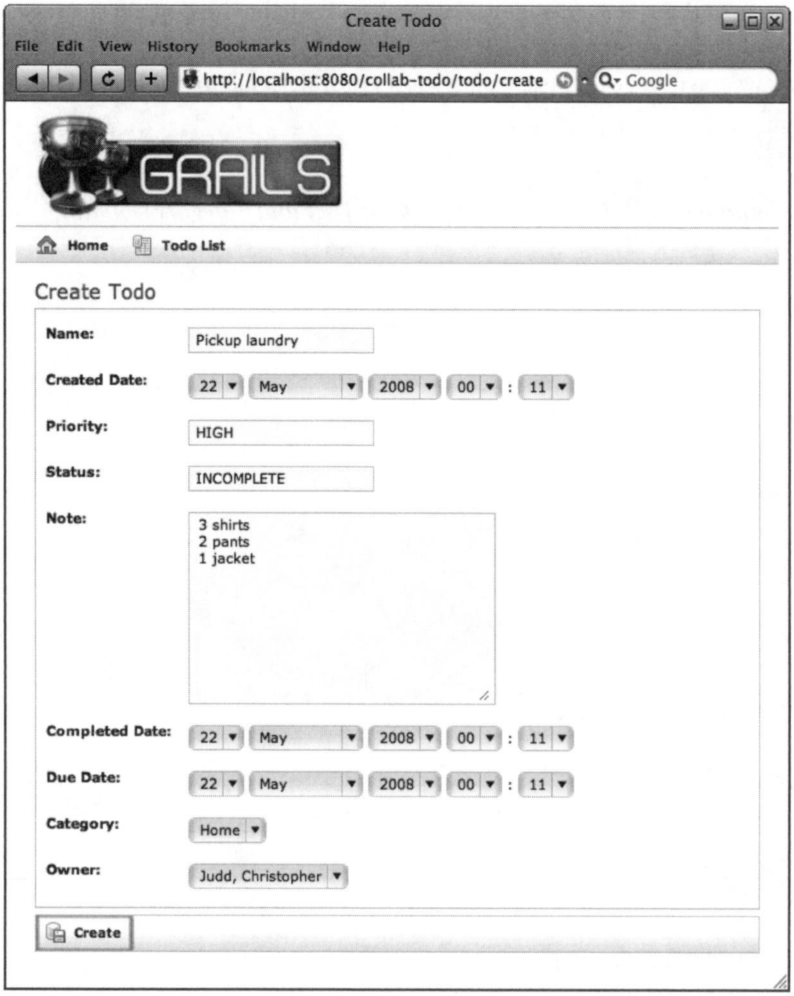

Figure 4-16. *Create Todo edit page with Category and Owner select fields*

Notice in Figure 4-16 that Category and Owner are select fields that display the domain class toString() method results.

Like the Todo class, the Category class has a belongsTo relationship with User, but it also has a collection of Todos, as shown in Listing 4-14.

Listing 4-14. *Category Domain Class with Relationships to the User and Todo Domain Classes*

```
class Category {
  String name
  String description
  User user
```

```
static belongsTo = User
static hasMany = [todos: Todo]

static constraints = {
  name(blank:false)
}

String toString() {
  name
}

}
```

Notice that in addition to belongsTo associated with User, Category contains a hasMany property, which is a map designating a one-to-many relationship with the Todo class. Also, the collection is available via the todos property.

Finally, the User class in Listing 4-15 has now defined its relationships with Todo and Category.

Listing 4-15. *User Domain Class with Relationships to the Todo and Category Domain Classes*

```
class User {
  String userName
  String firstName
  String lastName

  static hasMany = [todos: Todo, categories: Category]

  static constraints = {
    userName(blank:false,unique:true)
    firstName(blank:false)
    lastName(blank:false)
  }

  String  toString () {
    "$lastName, $firstName"
  }

}
```

As shown in Listing 4-15, the changes required to include the relationships with the Todo and Category classes only take a single line. The hasMany property identifies collections named todos and categories.

■**Note** We'll discuss relationships in more detail in Chapter 6.

As stated earlier, when you run the application, Hibernate creates a database schema based on domain classes. Figure 4-17 shows an entity relational diagram of the domain classes so far.

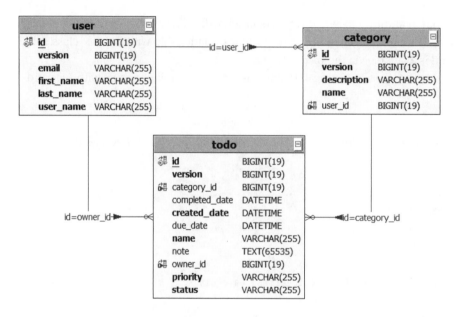

Figure 4-17. *Entity relational diagram*

Notice that the entity relational diagram looks almost identical to the UML diagram shown in Figure 4-6. Hibernate creates three tables with table names based on the class names. It also creates fields for each of the properties using underscores instead of CamelCase. Also, notice the id and version columns are the Hibernate columns for object identity and optimistic locking. Hibernate also creates foreign keys to represent the relationships between the domain classes.

During development, out-of-the-box Grail uses a Jetty web container and an embedded HSQLDB database. However, many operational environments use other web containers or applications servers and use server-based databases. In Chapter 12, we will look at how to package and deploy an application to an alternative operating environment.

Summary

In this chapter, you were introduced to the fact that Grails is a new web development framework that combines the best of Java open source, conventions, the Groovy dynamic language, and the power of the Java platform.

You also saw how easy it is to develop a fully functional application using Grails scaffolding to do most of the work. In Chapter 5, you will learn how to make the application pretty and customize it to your own look and feel, as well as make the controllers more functional. Then in Chapter 6, you will learn how to enhance the domain classes, including accessing more of the persistence features of GORM.

■ ■ ■

CHAPTER 5

Building the User Interface

Chapter 4 introduced the layering and components of Grails, and it showed you how to create a simple application using Grails scaffolding. In this chapter, you'll use the domain objects from Chapter 4 to start the process of creating an attractive, full-featured application.

You will learn how to use GSP, Grails tags, Grails templates, and CSS to create a look and feel that will be common across the application. You will create the login view and controller actions to support it. Once you have some code, you will start building a testing harness that will include integration tests and functional tests. Next, you will start to focus on user experience. You will look at validation, errors, and messages, and you'll learn how to customize them. You'll further enhance the view and controllers by removing unnecessary information, and you'll use actions to set properties on the domain object. To support the application, you will create a simple audit logging facility that leverages the Grails log controller property.

Starting with the End in Mind

The goal for this chapter is to create the look and feel for the Collab-Todo application's layout. Figure 5-1 shows a wireframe to give you an idea of how the application is laid out.

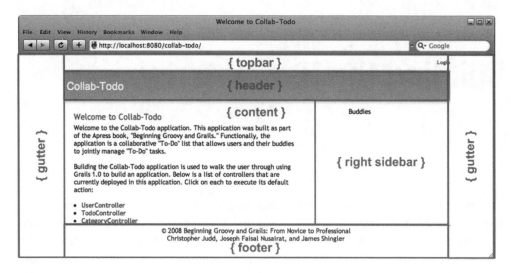

Figure 5-1. *The Collab-Todo wireframe*

The wireframe follows a common format: two columns centered on the page, gutters on both sides for spacing, and a header and a footer. Table 5-1 describes each component.

Table 5-1. *Wireframe Components*

Component	Description
gutter	Provides whitespace on the edges of the browser so that the main content area is centered in the browser.
topbar	Provides the ability to log in and log out, and displays the user's first and last name when he or she is logged in.
header	Displays the application's title, "Collab-Todo."
content	This is the main content area of the application. The majority of the application data is displayed here.
right sidebar	Chapter 8 will use the right sidebar to display buddy list information.
footer	Displays copyright information.

Like most modern view technologies, Grails uses a layout and template-based approach to assemble the view/UI. A template is a view fragment that resides in the `grails-app/views` directory and starts with an underscore. The underscore is Grails' convention for signifying that GSP is a template. Best practices dictate that you should put templates that are associated with a specific domain, such as `User`, in the domain's view directory, such as `grails-app/views/user/_someTemplate.gsp`. You should put templates that are more generic or shared across views in a common place, such as `grails-app/views/common`.

A layout assembles the templates and positions them on the page. You create the layout using `main.gsp` (grails-app/views/layouts/main.gsp) and CSS (web-app/css/main.css). Create a couple of templates (_topbar.gsp and _footer.gsp) that will be common across all views, then apply some CSS styling and leverage it in `main.gsp`.

Let's start with a simple footer to illustrate the point.

Creating the Footer

The goal is for a simple copyright notice to be displayed at the bottom of every page in the web site. As you might have guessed, you need to create a GSP fragment named _footer.gsp in the `grails-app/views/common` directory, then add the _footer.gsp template to the layout using the `<g:render template="/common/footer" />` tag. You then need to style the footer by adding a `<div>` section to the main layout using a style class that you define in the `main.css`. Listing 5-1 shows what you need to do.

Listing 5-1. *The Footer Template (_footer.gsp)*

```
<span class="copyright">&copy;  2008 Beginning Groovy and Grails: From Novice
to Professional<br />
Christopher Judd, Joseph Faisal Nusairat, and James Shingler
</span>
```

You need to add the copyright to the main layout (`main.gsp`) so that it's included on every page. This is where the `<g:render>` tag[1] comes to your aid. You use the `<g:render>` tag, which has a template attribute, to insert templates into GSPs. All you have to do is add `<g:render template="/common/footer" />` to the bottom of `main.gsp`. Listing 5-2 shows the content of `main.gsp`.

■**Note** By convention, the underscore and .gsp are omitted from the `template` attribute.

Listing 5-2. *The Main Layout (main.gsp)*

```
<html>
    <head>
        <title><g:layoutTitle default="Grails" /></title>
        <link rel="stylesheet"
            href="${createLinkTo(dir:'css',file:'main.css')}" />
```

---

1. http://www.grails.org/Tag+-+render

```
        <link rel="shortcut icon" href="${createLinkTo(dir:'images',
            file:'favicon.ico')}" type="image/x-icon" />
        <g:layoutHead />
        <g:javascript library="application" />
    </head>
    <body>
        <div id="spinner" class="spinner" style="display:none;">
            <img src="${createLinkTo(dir:'images',file:'spinner.gif')}"
                alt="Spinner" />
        </div>

        <div class="logo"><img src="${createLinkTo(dir:'images',
            file:'grails_logo.jpg')}" alt="Grails" /></div>
        <g:layoutBody />
        <g:render template="/common/footer" />

    </body>
</html>
```

Figure 5-2 shows what happens when you reload the home page.

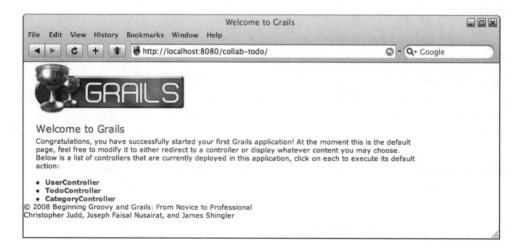

Figure 5-2. *Adding a copyright notice*

The copyright footer is on the page, but it isn't really what you want. It would be nice if it were centered and had a separator. You could just put the style information directly in the footer template, but a better solution, and a best practice, is to use CSS.[2] You need

---

2. http://www.w3schools.com/css, http://www.glish.com/css

to add a `<div>` tag with the `id` attribute set to `"footer"` in the main layout, and you need to define the `"footer"` style in `main.css`. Listing 5-3 shows the changes you need to make to `main.gsp`.

Listing 5-3. *The Enhanced Main Layout (main.gsp)*

```
<html>
    <head>
        <title><g:layoutTitle default="Grails" /></title>
        <link rel="stylesheet"
            href="${createLinkTo(dir:'css',file:'main.css')}" />
        <link rel="shortcut icon" href="${createLinkTo(dir:'images',
            file:'favicon.ico')}" type="image/x-icon" />
        <g:layoutHead />
        <g:javascript library="application" />
    </head>
    <body>
        <div id="spinner" class="spinner" style="display:none;">
            <img src="${createLinkTo(dir:'images',file:'spinner.gif')}"
                alt="Spinner" />
        </div>

        <div class="logo"><img src="${createLinkTo(dir:'images',
            file:'grails_logo.jpg')}" alt="Grails" /></div>
        <g:layoutBody />

        <div id="footer">
            <g:render template="/common/footer" />
        </div>
    </body>
</html>
```

Listing 5-4 shows how to define the `footer` style.

Listing 5-4. *The Footer Style*

```
#footer {
    clear:both;
    text-align: center;
    padding: 3px;
    border-top: 1px solid #333;
}
```

Figure 5-3 shows the results.

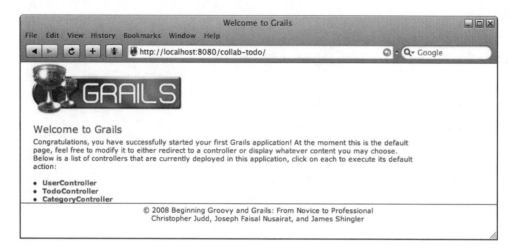

Figure 5-3. *Styling the footer*

Let's review how to add the footer. First, you create the `_footer.gsp` template and locate it in the `grails-app/views/common` directory. Second, you add the `_footer.gsp` template to the layout using the `<g:render template="/common/footer" />` tag. Third, you style the footer by adding a `<div>` section to the main layout using a style class that you defined in the `main.css`.

Now, you are going to take what you learned by creating the footer and start building the login/logout functionality.

Creating the Topbar

You create the topbar by adding a topbar (`_topbar.gsp`) template to the main layout. The topbar template is common and should be located in the `grails-app/view/common` directory. Listing 5-5 shows the content of the topbar template.

Listing 5-5. *The Topbar Template (_topbar.gsp)*

```
01    <div id="menu">
02        <nobr>
03          <g:if test="${session.user}">
04            <b>${session.user?.firstName} ${session.user?.lastName}</b> |
05             <g:link controller="user" action="logout">Logout</g:link>
06          </g:if>
```

```
07        <g:else>
08          <g:link controller="user" action="login">Login</g:link>
09        </g:else>
10      </nobr>
11    </div>
```

Listing 5-5 uses three Grails tags that you haven't seen yet: <g:if>,[3] <g:else>,[4] and <g:link>.[5] The <g:if> and <g:else> tags work together to create "if-then-else" logic. The <g:link> tag creates a hypertext link (i.e., http://localhost:8080/collab-todo/user/logout). In lines 3–6, you check if the session has a User object. If the session has a User object, the user's name followed by a | and a Logout link is printed. Lines 7–9 shows the else condition of the if statement, which displays the Login link. Listing 5-6 shows how to add the topbar to the main layout.

Listing 5-6. *Enhancing the Main Layout for the Topbar (main.gsp)*

```
<html>
  . . .
  <body>
    <div id="spinner" class="spinner" style="display: none;">
      <img src="${createLinkTo(dir:'images',file:'spinner.gif')}"
        alt="Spinner" />
    </div>

    <div id="topbar">
      <g:render template="/common/topbar" />
    </div>

    <div class="logo">
      <img src="${createLinkTo(dir:'images',file:'grails_logo.jpg')}"
        alt="Grails" />
    </div>
      . . .
```

Now add the CSS fragments found in Listing 5-7 to main.css.

---

3. http://www.grails.org/GSP+Tag+-+if
4. http://www.grails.org/GSP+Tag+-+else
5. http://www.grails.org/Tag+-+link

Listing 5-7. *The Topbar Styles*

```
#topbar {
    text-align:left;
    width: 778px;
    margin: 0px auto;
    padding: 5px 0;
}

#topbar #menu {
    float: right;
    width: 240px;
    text-align: right;
    font-size: 10px;
}
```

Figure 5-4 shows the results.

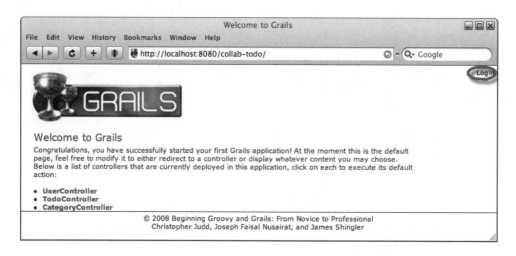

Figure 5-4. *Adding the topbar template*

Notice that the Login/Logout link is located in the upper-right corner of the browser.

Adding More Look and Feel

Now you need to finish the transformation so that Collab-Todo has its own look and feel instead of appearing that it came right out of the box. Do this by adding the right sidebar, replacing the Grails header, and setting the default title. As noted earlier, Chapter 8 will use the right sidebar to display the user's buddies. Start off with some CSS styling by adding the CSS snippet in Listing 5-8 to the main style sheet (main.css).

Listing 5-8. *CSS Styling*

```css
#header {
    width: 778px;
    background: #FFFFFF url(../images/header_background.gif)  repeat-x;
    height: 70px;
    margin: 0px auto;
}

#header h1 {
    font-family:Arial,sans-serif;
    color: white;
    padding: 20px 0 0 6px;
    font-size:1.6em;
}

body {
    margin: 0px;
    padding: 0px;
    text-align:center;
    font-family: "Trebuchet MS",Arial,Helvetica,sans-serif;
    font-style: normal;
    font-variant: normal;
    font-weight: normal;
    font-size: 13px;
    line-height: normal;
    font-size-adjust: none;
    font-stretch: normal;
    color: #333333;
}

#page {
    width: 778px;
    margin: 0px auto;
    padding: 4px 0;
    text-align:left;
}
```

```
#content {
    float: left;
    width: 560px;
    color: #000;
}

#sidebar {
    float: right;
    width: 200px;
    color: #000;
    padding: 3px;
}
```

■**Note** You can find `header_background.gif` in the project source.

Now, you need to take advantage of the CSS styling in the main layout (main.gsp), as shown in Listing 5-9.

Listing 5-9. *Finishing the Layout (main.gsp)*

```
01    <html>
02        <head>
03            <title><g:layoutTitle default="Collab Todo" />
04            </title>
05            <link rel="stylesheet"
06                href="${createLinkTo(dir:'css',file:'main.css')}" />
07            <link rel="shortcut icon"
08                href="${createLinkTo(dir:'images',file:'favicon.ico')}"
09                type="image/x-icon" />
10            <g:layoutHead />
11            <g:javascript library="application" />
12        </head>
13        <body>
14            <div id="page">
15                <div id="spinner" class="spinner" style="display: none;">
16                    <img src="${createLinkTo(dir:'images',   file:'spinner.gif')}"
17                        alt="Spinner" />
18                </div>
19
```

```
20              <g:render template="/common/topbar" />
21
22          <div id="header">
23              <h1>Collab-Todo</h1>
24          </div>
25
26          <div id="content">
27              <g:layoutBody />
28          </div>
29
30          <div id="sidebar">
31              <g:render template="/common/buddies" />
32          </div>
33
34          <div id="footer">
35              <g:render template="/common/footer" />
36          </div>
37      </div>
38   </body>
39 </html>
```

BUDDIES TEMPLATE

We'll cover the _buddies.gsp template in detail in Chapter 8. Until then, add the following snippet to the /common/_buddies.gsp template:

```
<div id="buddies">
    <div class="title">Buddies</div>
</div>
```

Let's talk about the changes you made to the layout. Line 3 uses the <g:layoutTitle> tag. If the view being decorated doesn't have a title, then the default "Collab Todo" will be applied to the page. Line 14 adds a <div> that uses the page style. Together with the body style, the page style creates a container that's 778 pixels wide and centered on the page. Lines 22–24 replace the Grails header with the Collab-Todo header. If you look carefully at the CSS header style, you'll see that it defines a header image (header_background.gif). Lines 26 and 28 wrap the view's body with the content style. This means that pages decorated by main.gsp are inserted here. The content style creates a container 560 pixels wide and left-aligns it within the page container. Lines 30–32 wrap the buddies template with the `sidebar` style, which creates a container 200 pixels wide and right-aligns it within the page container.

You can see the results of your work in Figure 5-5.

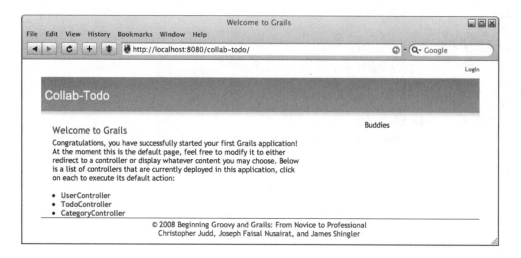

Figure 5-5. *The completed layout*

It's starting to look good; you have just one more thing to do. You won't use the default index page for long, but let's change "Welcome to Grails" and the body. You can find the HTML for this in `web-app/index.gsp`. Replace the contents of `index.gsp` with the contents found in Listing 5-10.

Listing 5-10. *A New Index Page (index.gsp)*

```
01  <html>
02      <head>
03          <title>Welcome to Collab-Todo</title>
04        <meta name="layout" content="main" />
05      </head>
06      <body>
07          <h1 style="margin-left:20px;">Welcome to Collab-Todo</h1>
08          <p style="margin-left:20px;width:80%">
09            Welcome to the Collab-Todo application.  This application was built
10            as part of the Apress Book, "Beginning Groovy and Grails."
11            Functionally, the application is a collaborative "To-Do"
12            list that allows users and their buddies to jointly
13            manage "To-Do" tasks.</p><br />
14          <p style="margin-left:20px;width:80%">Building the Collab-Todo
```

```
15          application is used to walk the user through using Grails 1.0 to
16          build an application.  Below is a list of controllers that are
17          currently deployed in this application. Click on each to execute
18          its default action:</p>
19          <br />
20        <div class="dialog" style="margin-left:20px;width:60%;">
21            <ul>
22              <g:each var="c" in="${grailsApplication.controllerClasses}">
23                    <li class="controller"><a href="${c.logicalPropertyName}">
24                      ${c.fullName}</a></li>
25            </g:each>
26          </ul>
27        </div>
28      </body>
29  </html>
```

A couple of items in the file deserve explanation. Lines 22–25 illustrate the usage of
<g:each>, an iteration tag. In this case, it is iterating over a collection of all controller
classes that are a part of the application to display the name of the controller class in a list.

Line 4 is an example of using layouts by convention. In this case, the layout metatag
causes the "main" layout (main.gsp) to be applied to the page. You might recall that all layouts reside within the grails-app/views/layouts directory.

You have created the layout, and it's looking good. You can see the results of your
work in Figure 5-6.

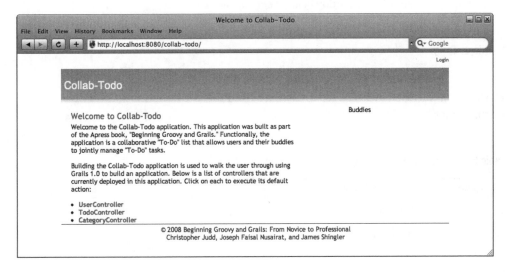

Figure 5-6. *Layout results*

Setting up the wireframe exposes you to layouts, templates, CSS, and a couple of Grails tags. Grails, like all modern web frameworks, supports tag libraries. The Grails tag library is similar to the JavaServer Pages Standard Tag Library (JSTL) and Struts tags. It contains tags for everything from conditional logic to rendering and layouts. The following section provides a quick overview of the Grails tags.[6]

Grails Tags

Part of Grails' strength in the view layer is its tag library. Grails has tags to address everything from conditional logic and iterating collections to displaying errors. This section provides an overview of the Grails tags.

Logical Tags

Logical tags allow you to build conditional "if-elseif-else" logic. Listing 5-5 demonstrated the use of the `<g:if>` and `<else>` tags in `topbar.gsp`. Table 5-2 contains an overview of the logical tags.

Table 5-2. *Grails Logical Tags*

Tag Name	Tag Description
`<g:if>`	Logical switch based upon a test expression
`<g:else>`	The `else` portion of an `if` statement
`<g:elseif>`	The `else if` portion of an `if` statement

Iteration Tags

Iteration tags are used to iterate over collections or loop until a condition is false. The `<g:each>` tag was used in `index.gsp` in Listing 5-10. Table 5-3 contains an overview of the iteration tags.

Table 5-3. *Grails Iteration Tags*

Tag Name	Tag Description
`<g:while>`	Executes a loop while a test condition is true
`<g:each>`	Iterates over a collection

---

6. http://www.grails.org/GSP+Tag+Reference

Tag Name	Tag Description
`<g:collect>`	Iterates over a collection and transforms the results as defined in the `expr` parameter
`<g:findAll>`	Iterates over a collection where the elements match the GPath defined in the `expr` parameter
`<g:grep>`	Iterates over a collection where the elements match the filter defined in the `expr` parameter

Assignment Tags

You use assignment tags to create and assign a value to a variable. Table 5-4 contains an overview of assignment tags.

Table 5-4. *Grails Assignment Tags*

Tag Name	Tag Description
`<def>` (deprecated)	Defines a variable to be used within the GSP page; use `<set>` instead
`<set>`	Sets the value of a variable used within the GSP page

Linking Tags

Linking tags are used to create URLs. The `<g:link>` tag was used in `topbar.gsp` (shown in Listing 5-5), and `<g:createLinkTo>` was used as an expression in `main.gsp` (shown in Listing 5-9). Table 5-5 contains an overview of the linking tags.

Table 5-5. *Grails Linking Tags*

Tag Name	Tag Description
`<g:link>`	Creates an HTML link using supplied parameters
`<g:createLink>`	Creates a link that you can use within other tags
`<g:createLinkTo>`	Creates a link to a directory or file

Ajax Tags

You use Ajax tags to build an Ajax-aware application. Chapter 8 uses some of these tags to enhance the user interface. Table 5-6 contains an overview of the Ajax tags.

Table 5-6. *Grails Ajax Tags*

Tag Name	Tag Description
`<g:remoteField>`	Creates a text field that invokes a link when changed
`<g:remoteFunction>`	Creates a remote function that is called on a DOM event
`<g:remoteLink>`	Creates a link that calls a remote function
`<g:formRemote>`	Creates a form tag that executes an Ajax call to serialize the form elements
`<g:javascript>`	Includes JavaScript libraries and scripts
`<g:submitToRemote>`	Creates a button that executes an Ajax call to serialize the form elements

Form Tags

Form tags are used to create HTML forms. Table 5-7 contains an overview of form tags.

Table 5-7. *Grails Form Tags*

Tag Name	Tag Description
`<g:actionSubmit>`	Creates a submit button
`<g:actionSubmitImage>`	Creates a submit button using an image
`<g:checkBox>`	Creates a check box
`<g:currencySelect>`	Creates a select field containing currencies
`<g:datePicker>`	Creates a configurable date picker for the day, month, year, hour, minute, and second
`<g:form>`	Creates a form
`<g:hiddenField>`	Creates a hidden field
`<g:localeSelect>`	Creates a select field containing locales
`<g:radio>`	Creates a radio button
`<g:radioGroup>`	Creates a radio button group
`<g:select>`	Creates a select/combo box field
`<g:textField>`	Creates a text field
`<g:textArea>`	Creates a text area field
`<g:timeZoneSelect>`	Creates a select field containing time zones

UI Tags

You use UI tags to enhance the user interface. The only official UI Grails tag is the rich text editor, but several UI tags built by the Grails community are available as plug-ins. Table 5-8 contains an overview of the UI tag.

Table 5-8. *Grails UI Tag*

Tag Name	Tag Description
`<g:richTextEditor>`	Creates a rich text editor, which defaults to fckeditor

Render and Layout Tags

Render and layout tags are used to create the layouts and render templates. As you might expect, several render and layout tags were used in `main.gsp`. Table 5-9 contains an overview of the render and layout tags.

Table 5-9. *Grails Render and Layout Tags*

Tag Name	Tag Description
`<g:applyLayout>`	Applies a layout to a body or template
`<g:encodeAs>`	Applies dynamic encoding to a block of HTML to bulk-encode the content
`<g:formatDate>`	Applies a `SimpleDateFormat` to a date
`<g:formatNumber>`	Applies a `DecimalFormat` to number
`<g:layoutHead>`	Displays a decorated page's header, which is used in layouts
`<g:layoutBody>`	Displays a decorated page's body, which is used in layouts
`<g:layoutTitle>`	Displays a decorated page's title, which is used in layouts
`<g:meta>`	Displays application metadata properties
`<g:render>`	Displays a model using a template
`<g:renderErrors>`	Displays errors
`<g:pageProperty>`	Displays a property from a decorated page
`<g:paginate>`	Displays Next/Previous buttons and breadcrumbs for large results
`<g:sortableColumn>`	Displays a sortable table column

Validation Tags

Validation tags are used to display errors and messages. Table 5-10 contains an overview of the validation tags.

Table 5-10. *Grails Validation Tags*

Tag Name	Tag Description
<g:eachError>	Iterates through errors
<g:hasErrors>	Checks if errors exist within the bean, model, or request
<g:message>	Displays a message
<g:fieldValue>	Displays the value of a field for a bean that has data binding

Making the Topbar Functional

Now that you have the layout, let's make the topbar functional. You want the topbar to provide the user the ability to log in. Once the user has logged in, the topbar should display the username and provide the ability for the user to log out. When the user selects the Login link, he or she should be presented with a Login form.

■Note The login functionality you are building initially is simply to identify who is using the system. It's not meant to provide a full, robust security system. Because the login you are constructing is temporary, adding authentication logic to all controller actions is out of scope at this time. In Chapter 7, you will add a fully functional security system.

The Login View

Creating the login view requires you to create a GSP in the appropriate directory. The GSP contains a form that has a single selection field of usernames and a submit button. When the user submits the selection, the form invokes the handleLogin action on the UserController. Figure 5-7 illustrates the login view.

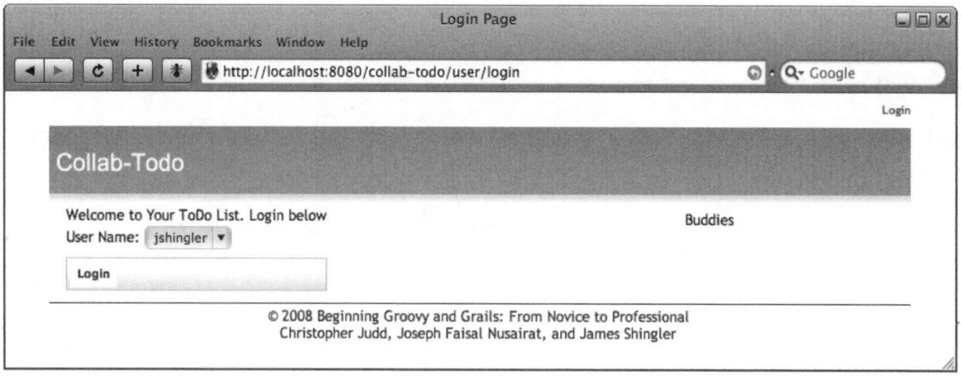

Figure 5-7. *The login view*

Let's take a look at the Login link, `<g:link controller="user" action="login">`
`Login</g:link>`. When the user selects the Login link, the `login` action on the
`UserController` is invoked. We'll explain the `login` action in the next section.

Based upon convention, `login.gsp` should go in the `grails-app/views/user` directory.
Listing 5-11 shows the contents of `login.gsp`.

Listing 5-11. *The Login View (login.gsp)*

```
01  <html>
02      <head>
03          <title>Login Page</title>
04          <meta name="layout" content="main" />
05      </head>
06      <body>
07          <div class="body">
08              <g:if test="${flash.message}">
09                  <div class="message">
10                      ${flash.message}
11                  </div>
12              </g:if>
13              <p>
14                  Welcome to Your ToDo List. Login below
15              </p>
16              <form action="handleLogin">
17
18                  <span class='nameClear'><label for="login">
19                      Sign In:
20                  </label>
21                  </span>
22                  <g:select name='userName' from="${User.list()}"
23                      optionKey="userName" optionValue="userName"></g:select>
24                  <br />
25                  <div class="buttons">
26                      <span class="button"><g:actionSubmit value="Login" />
27                      </span>
28                  </div>
29              </form>
30          </div>
31      </body>
32  </html>
```

Let's review the form. Lines 1–5 define the title and determine that the page is decorated by the main layout. This means that main.gsp acts as a container for login.gsp. Take a look at line 26 in Listing 5-9. In this case, the body of login.gsp is inserted at the <g:layoutBody> tag. Remember that the main layout contains a default title, <g:layoutTitle default="Collab Todo" />. When login.gsp is decorated with the main layout, the title in login.gsp is used instead of the default that was defined in the layout.

Lines 6–31 define the body of the page. Lines 9–12 display flash messages, which we'll cover shortly in the "Flash and Flash Messages" section. Lines 16–29 create the form with a selection field. Line 16 specifies that when the form is submitted, the handleLogin action of the UserController is invoked. In lines 22–23, the Grails select tag creates an HTML selection element. The name attribute sets the selection name to userName (which in turn is passed to the login action). When evaluated, the form attribute results in a collection that Grails uses to create the options. optionKey and optionValue are special attributes used to create the HTML <option> element ID and the text display in the selection field. Lines 25–28 use the Grails <g:actionSubmit> tag to create a form submission button.

If you run the application and access the view right now, you'll get a 404 error. This is because the topbar links to the login view via the UserController login action, which hasn't been created yet.

The login Action

Currently, the UserController is set up with dynamic scaffolding. You will continue to use the dynamic scaffolding and add the login action to it. Listing 5-12 shows the updated version of the UserController class.

Listing 5-12. *The login Action*

```
class UserController {

    def scaffold = User


    def login = {}
}
```

A common best practice on the Web is to use actions as a redirection mechanism. By convention, Grails uses the name of the action to look up a GSP of the same name.

If you click on the Login link now, the login view will be displayed, and the User Name selection field will be blank. Recall from Listing 5-11 that you call User.list() to populate the selection with a collection of users. You haven't added any users yet, so the list is empty. Test the functionality of the form by creating two users. From the home page, select UserController ➤ New User. Now when you select Login, the User Name selection field is populated (see Figure 5-8).

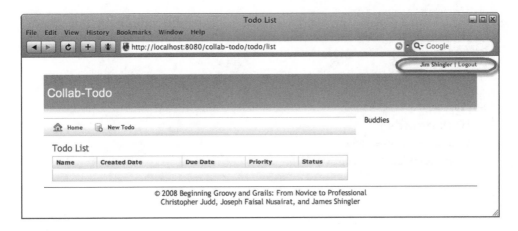

Figure 5-8. *A logged-in user*

Next, you need to implement the login logic through the UserController handleLogin action.

Handling the Login and Logout Actions

You call the handleLogin action to log in a user. When you call the action, the Login form is passed the userName of the user to be signed in. Logging in is accomplished by adding the user object associated with the userName to the session. If the user cannot be found, an error message is created, and the user is redirected to the login view. In this particular example, there shouldn't be any way for the login to fail, but it is still good practice. You use the logout action to remove the user from the session, so he or she can log out. Listing 5-13 shows how you enhance the UserController.

Listing 5-13. *Enhanced UserController*

```
class UserController {

    def scaffold = User

    def login = {}

    def handleLogin = {
        def user = User.findByUserName(params.userName)
        if (!user) {
          flash.message = "User not found for userName: ${params.userName}"
          redirect(action:'login')
```

```
        }
        session.user = user
        redirect(controller:'todo')
    }

    def logout = {
        if(session.user) {
            session.user = null
            redirect(action:'login')
        }
    }
}
```

Now, when the user logs in, he or she will be taken to the Todo List view when you log in, and the topbar will contain the user's first name, last name, and a Logout link. Line 8 in Listing 5-5 shows how selecting the Logout link invokes the UserController logout action.

Now that you have written code, you must make sure that you don't break it as you make other enhancements. That's next to impossible, but the next best thing is to steal an idea from Six Sigma,[7] Poka Yoke.[8] Poka Yoke is a Japanese word that means *mistake proofing*. The idea is to make mistakes so obvious that in effect, you prevent them. You accomplish this by creating tests. The next section will help you write tests for the code you just wrote.

Testing

Grails uses two popular testing frameworks—JUnit[9] and Canoo[10]—to implement unit tests, integration tests, and functional tests. The purpose of testing is to verify that the application works as expected and to confirm that you haven't broken the application as you iterated over it. It is extremely valuable to have a good test framework.

In this section, you'll use JUnit to perform integration testing on the UserController, and you'll use Canoo to perform functional testing on the presentation. First, you will create a JUnit integration test for the UserController handleLogin and logout actions. Then you will create a test using the Canoo WebTest plug-in to functionally test the topbar.

■**Note** Purists may suggest that you should have written the tests before you wrote the code. This has merit, but for the purposes of this book, it was more straightforward to show the code first. The important thing is that you have good tests that give you faith that the application works as intended.

---

7. http://en.wikipedia.org/wiki/Six_Sigma

8. http://en.wikipedia.org/wiki/Poka-yoke

9. http://www.junit.org

10. http://webtest.canoo.com

Integration Testing Using JUnit

In Chapter 4, when you ran the `grails create-controller` command to create the `UserController`, the command not only created the controller, but it also created an empty test in the `test/integration` test directory. Take a peek in the `test/integration` directory, and you'll see `UserControllerTests.groovy`. Listing 5-14 shows you the contents of the test when first generated.

Listing 5-14. *UserControllerTests.groovy*

```
class User ControllerTests extends GroovyTestCase
{
    void testSomething() {
    }
}
```

■**Note** If `UserControllerTests.groovy` doesn't exist for some reason, you can create it by executing `grails create-integration-test` and specifying `UserController` when prompted.

As you can see, a Grails test extends/inherits from `GroovyTestCase`,[11] which in turn extends from `junit.framework.TestCase`.[12] This means that Grails tests have all the features of JUnit and `GroovyTestCase`, including all the standard JUnit `assert*`, `setUp`, and `tearDown` methods and Groovy `assert` methods.

It is important to understand the distinction between integration and unit tests. A unit test is created with the `grails create-unit-test` command and results in a skeleton unit test in the `tests/unit` directory. One of the interesting things about Grails unit tests is that Grails dynamic methods, such as `save`, `delete`, and `findBy*`, are not available. Grails does this to help you understand the difference between unit tests and integration tests. The purpose of a unit test is to test the logic in a piece of code, not how the code and everything else around it (e.g., the database) interact—that is the purpose of integration tests. Right about now, you might be saying, "It's going to be awfully hard for me to test the logic in the code if I can't use dynamic methods." This is where Groovy's `MockFor*` and `StubFor*` methods come to your aid.

You're going to test the `UserController` `handleLogin` and `logout` actions using an integration test. Take a look at Listing 5-13, which contains the logic you want to test. The `handleLogin` action tries to find the user using the `userName`. If it finds the user, it adds the

---

11. http://groovy.codehaus.org/api/groovy/util/GroovyTestCase.html
12. http://junit.sourceforge.net/javadoc/junit/framework/TestCase.html

user object to the session, and the user is redirected to the Todo List view. If it doesn't find the user, it redirects the user to the login view. The logout action removes the user object from the session, and the user is redirected to the login view. You need two tests—one positive (a login with a valid user) and one negative (a login with an invalid user)—for handleLogin and one test for logout. Listing 5-15 contains the tests.

Listing 5-15. *UserController Integration Test*

```
01    class UserControllerTests extends GroovyTestCase {
02
03    User user
04    UserController uc
05
06    void setUp() {
07      // Save a User
08      user = new User(userName:"User1", firstName:"User1FN", lastName:"User1LN")
09      user.save()
10
11    // Set up UserController
12      uc = new UserController()
13  }
14
15  void tearDown() {
16    user.delete()
17  }
18
19    /**
20    * Test the UserController.handleLogin action.
21    *
22    * If the login succeeds, it will put the user object into the session.
23    */
24    void testHandleLogin() {
25
26      // Setup controller parameters
27      uc.params.userName = user.userName
28
29      // Call the action
30      uc.handleLogin()
31
32      // If action functioned correctly, it put a user object
33      // into the session
34      def sessUser = uc.session.user
```

```
35      assert sessUser
36      assertEquals("Expected ids to match", user.id, sessUser.id)
37      // And the user was redirected to the Todo Page
38      assertEquals "/todo", uc.response.redirectedUrl
39    }
40
41    /**
42     * Test the UserController.handleLogin action.
43     *
44     * If the login fails, it will redirect to login and set a flash message.
45     */
46      void testHandleLoginInvalidUser() {
47      // Setup controller parameters
48      uc.params.userName = "INVALID_USER_NAME"
49
50      // Call the action
51      uc.handleLogin()
52      assertEquals "/user/login", uc.response.redirectedUrl
53      def message = uc.flash.message
54      assert message
55      assert message.startsWith("User not found")
56    }
57
58    /**
59     * Test the UserController.login action
60     *
61     * If the logout action succeeds, it will remove the user object from
62     * the session.
63     */
64    void testLogout() {
65      // make it look like user is logged in
66      uc.session.user = user
67
68      uc.logout()
69      def sessUser = uc.session.user
70      assertNull("Expected session user to be null", sessUser)
71      assertEquals "/user/login", uc.response.redirectedUrl
72    }
73 }
```

If you have used JUnit before, this will look familiar. Lines 3–17 contain the test setup
and teardown functionality. The setup runs before each test, and the teardown runs after

each test. The only interesting thing to point out here is that lines 9 and 16 use dynamic methods.

Lines 24–39 contain the handleLogin action positive test. The action takes userName as a parameter. Line 27 adds user.userName to the parameters to be passed to the action. Line 30 calls the handleLogin action using the parameters you just defined. Lines 34–36 validate that the action set the user into the session. If you look closely, you'll see that the test uses the Groovy assert and the JUnit assertEquals. In Groovy, assert considers null to be false. If the user wasn't put in the session, assert would fail. Line 38 looks in the UserController response to validate that the user was redirected to the Todo List view.

Lines 46–56 contain the handleLogin action negative test and use an invalid userName. As you might expect, lines 48–51 create an invalid username and call the action. Line 52 validates that the user is redirected to the proper view. Lines 53–55 validate that a flash message was generated to tell the user that he or she was not logged in. We'll cover flash messages in more detail shortly in the "Flash and Flash Messages" section.

Lines 64–71 contain the logout action test. Lines 66–68 manually add the user to the session and call the action. Lines 69 and 70 validate that the session doesn't contain a user object. Line 71 validates that the user is redirected to the login view.

Now for some fun. You run all the tests with the grails test-app command, and you run individual tests by appending the test name, as shown here:

```
grails test-app UserController
```

The command executes the UserControllerTest and produces the following output:

```
--------------------------------------------------------
Running 3 Integration Tests...
Running test UserControllerTests...
                    testHandleLogin...SUCCESS
                    testHandleLoginInvalidUser...SUCCESS
                    testLogout...SUCCESS
Integration Tests Completed in 2110ms
--------------------------------------------------------
[junitreport] Transform time: 719ms
Tests passed. View reports in <<PROJECT>>/test/reports
```

As you can see, everything passed. The test also generated a JUnit report under the test/reports directory. Figure 5-9 shows the JUnit HTML report.

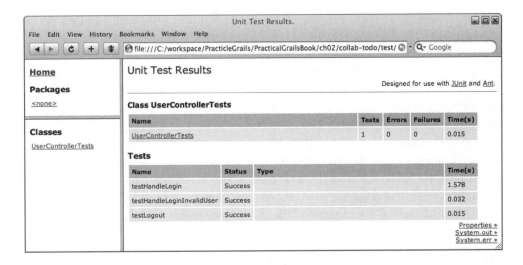

Figure 5-9. *JUnit report*

Now you have some confidence that when you change code, you can make sure the `handleLogin` and `logout` actions function correctly. Now that you know that your actions are working individually, you need to create a test to verify that the topbar renders correctly when the user logs in.

■**Note** As a side project, you could take a look at continuous integration (CI) tools[13] and have the system execute your tests automatically. For more information, check out Martin Fowler's article.[14]

Functional Testing Using Canoo WebTest

If you recall, when the user first comes to the page, the topbar displays a link for the user to log in. Once the user has logged in, the topbar displays a link to log out. When you were testing manually, you had to add the user to the system, log in, and then check to make sure the topbar displayed the user's name. While this isn't a lot of work, do you really want to do this manually every single time you enhance the application? We hope the answer is no. Instead, you can create a suite of functional tests and let the computer do the regression testing of the presentation. All you have to do is kick it off or add it to your CI environment.

Grails has a Canoo WebTest plug-in, thanks to Dierk Koenig, founder and project manager of the Canoo WebTest plug-in. Canoo WebTest is a free open source tool that

---

13. http://en.wikipedia.org/wiki/Continuous_integration

14. Martin Fowler, "Continuous Integration," http://martinfowler.com/articles/continuousIntegration.html, 2006.

allows you to create functional tests. You start by installing the Canoo WebTest plug-in, then you generate and code a functional test for the user CRUD operations. Next, you create a functional test by hand to test the topbar functionality.

Install the WebTest plug-in by executing `grails install-plugin webtest`. Grails downloads the plug-in and installs it under the application's `plugins` directory. Next, generate a functional test by executing `grails create-webtest`. Grails first creates a `webtest` directory in the current project, then it creates a configuration file (`webtest/conf/webtest.properties`) and a test suite (`webtest/tests/testsuite.groovy`).

When prompted for a WebTest domain name, specify `user`. Grails uses WebTest templates to generate CRUD operation tests for the `user` object. Under normal circumstances, you shouldn't have to change the WebTest configuration, but in case you do, check out Table 5-11, which defines the contents of the configuration file.

Table 5-11. *webtest.properties*

Name	Initial Value	Description
webtest_host	localhost	The name of the host server
webtest_port	8080	The port number to start the test server on
webtest_protocol	http	The protocol used to communicate with the server
webtest_summary	true	Determines whether a summary report should be printed
webtest_response	true	Determines whether a response should be saved to view from the report
webtest_resultpath	webtest/reports	Determines where to put the reports
webtest_resultfile	WebTestResult.xml	Specifies the name of the report results file
webtest_haltonerror	false	Determines whether execution should be stopped if an error occurs
webtest_errorproperty	webTestError	Specifies the name of the Ant property to set when an error occurs
webtest_haltonfailure	false	Determines whether execution should be stopped if a failure occurs
webtest_failureproperty	webTestFailure	Specifies the name of the Ant property to set when a failure occurs
webtest_showhtmlparseroutput	true	Determines whether to show parsing warnings and errors in the terminal window

The other generated file, `testsuite.groovy`, uses Ant `fileScanner` to load all classes in the `webtest/tests` directory that end with `Test`. It then executes them by calling their `suite` method. When you first start an application, the default behavior is probably good enough. As the application becomes more sophisticated, though, it may become necessary to have more control over the order in which the functional tests are executed. You can accomplish this by loading and executing the tests manually. Listing 5-16 shows an example.

Listing 5-16. *Loading and Executing a Functional Test Manually*

```
new MyTest(ant:ant, configMap:configMap).suite()
new MyOtherTest(ant:ant, configMap:configMap).suite()
```

Now that WebTest is installed, you can start creating the functional test. When Grails generates the WebTest, it does the best it can using a template. To make the test able to run, you need to add test values to the test.

■**Note** Grails 0.6 featured a UI face-lift, which caused some challenges in the WebTest template. This may or may not have been fixed by the time you read this. In either case, tweaking the test is pretty straightforward.

Listing 5-17 contains a simple functional test that validates the usage of the user domain object through the presentation.

Listing 5-17. *User WebTest*

```
01   class UserTest extends grails.util.WebTest {
02
03     // Unlike unit tests, functional tests are often sequence dependent.
04     // Specify that sequence here.
05     void suite() {
06         testUserListNewDelete()
07         // add tests for more operations here
08     }
09
10   def testUserListNewDelete() {
11       webtest('User basic operations: view list, create new entry, view,
12                edit, delete, view'){
13           invoke(url:'user')
14           verifyText(text:'Home')
```

```
15
16                  verifyListPage(0)
17
18              clickLink(label:'New User')
19              verifyText(text:'Create User')
20              clickButton(label:'Create')
21              verifyText(text:'Show User', description:'Detail page')
22              clickLink(label:'List', description:'Back to list view')
23
24              verifyListPage(1)
25
26           group(description:'edit the one element') {
27               clickLink(label:'Show', description:'go to detail view')
28               clickButton(label:'Edit')
29               verifyText(text:'Edit User')
30               clickButton(label:'Update')
31               verifyText(text:'Show User')
32               clickLink(label:'List', description:'Back to list view')
33           }
34
35              verifyListPage(1)
36
37           group(description:'delete the only element') {
38               clickLink(label:'Show', description:'go to detail view')
39               clickButton(label:'Delete')
40               verifyXPath(xpath:"//div[@class='message']",
41                   text:/User.*deleted./, regex:true)
42           }
43
44              verifyListPage(0)
45
46      }   }
47
48      String ROW_COUNT_XPATH = "count(//td[@class='actionButtons']/..)"
49
50      def verifyListPage(int count) {
51          ant.group(description:"verify User list view with $count row(s)"){
52              verifyText(text:'User List')
53              verifyXPath(xpath:ROW_COUNT_XPATH, text:count,
54                  description:"$count row(s) of data expected")
55      }   }
56 }
```

Use the `grails run-webtest` command to run the test and see what happens. When the test completes, it shows you the results in your default browser. Figure 5-10 is an example of what you'll see.

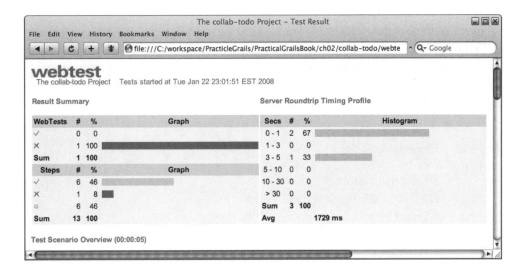

Figure 5-10. *WebTest results*

Looking at the results, you can see that the test failed. In the WebTests section of the report, you can see that zero tests passed (shown by the green check mark) and one test failed (shown by the red X). In the Steps section of the report, you can see that six steps passed (green check mark), one step failed (red X), and six steps were not executed (shown by the yellow o). Some steps failing can be expected, because Grails generates a skeleton implementation that you need to fill in. If you scroll down in the browser, you'll see more information about where it failed. The test failed in step 7, where the test verifies the text "Show User." Take a look at line 21 of Listing 5-17. The step failure means that it wasn't able to find the text "Show User" on the page. Most likely, something right before this didn't work as anticipated. Let's review the test.

■**Tip** Because the meanings of WebTest commands are pretty clear, you can follow along and execute the same commands in a browser. It's almost like a checklist.

The core of the test starts on line 13. Lines 13–14 invoke the user URL, `http://localhost:8080/collab-todo/user`, and verify that the page contains the word "Home." Line 16 calls a method to verify that the page contains no items in the list.

■**Note** If you take a look at the `verifyListPage` method, you'll see that it's using XPath expressions to count the number of entries in the list. Learn more about XPath on the W3Schools site.[15]

Lines 18–19 select the New User link and verify that the page contains the text "Create User." Line 20 selects the Create link. If you don't input anything in the User Name, First Name, or Last Name fields and you select the Create link, a flash message will appear telling you that the information is required. That's why line 21 failed. To fix the test, insert the code shown in Listing 5-18 right after line 20.

Listing 5-18. *Setting Input Fields*

```
// Set Inputs Start
setInputField(name:'userName', 'User1')
setInputField(name:'firstName', 'User1FN')
setInputField(name:'lastName', 'User1LN')
// Set Inputs End
```

This is how you insert values into the User Name, First Name, or Last Name fields using WebTest. Rerun the WebTest and take a look at the results.

■**Caution** At the time of this writing, the template used to generate the WebTest wasn't integrated with the new look and feel of Grails. As a result, you may experience some additional errors. The errors are easier to resolve if you follow along with the test in your browser and then go to View ➤ View Source in the browser to see the resulting HTML. Doing so will give you an idea of how you can modify the test.

Now you can build upon what you have learned to create a WebTest for the topbar functionality.

The `grails create-webtest` command assumes that you are creating a WebTest for a domain object. The topbar isn't a domain object, so you need to create the topbar test by hand. You can use the User WebTest (`webtest/tests/UserTest.groovy`) as a guide.

Create `TopBarTest.groovy` in the `webtest/test` directory. Make sure `webtest/tests/TopBarTest` extends `grails.util.WebTest`, and be sure to include the `suite` method. You need to follow these steps to test the topbar:

---

15. W3Schools, "XPath Tutorial," http://www.w3schools.com/xpath/.

1. Create a user.

2. Log in.

3. Verify the topbar.

4. Log out.

5. Delete the user.

You could do all of the steps in one test method, but it makes more sense to divide them up into separate tests and use the `suite` method to control the sequence in which the tests are executed. A logical breakup would be `testCreateNewUser`, `testLoginTopBarLogout`, and `testDeleteUser`. Listing 5-19 contains an implementation of the WebTest to test the topbar.

Listing 5-19. *WebTest to Test the Topbar*

```
class TopBarTest extends grails.util.WebTest {

  // Unlike unit tests, functional tests are often sequence dependent.
  // Specify that sequence here.
  void suite() {
    testCreateNewUser()
    testLoginTopBarLogout()
    testDeleteUser()
  }

  /**
   * Create the user that will be used in the login
   */
  def testCreateNewUser() {
      webtest('Test TopBar: create new user'){
        invoke(url:'user')
          verifyText(text:'Home')

          clickLink(label:'New User')
          verifyText(text:'Create User')
          // Set Inputs Start
          setInputField(name:'userName', 'User1')
          setInputField(name:'firstName', 'User1FN')
```

```
            setInputField(name:'lastName', 'User1LN')
            // Set Inputs End
            clickButton(label:'Create')
        }
    }


    /**
     *  Login, look for name on TopBar, and log out
     */
    def testLoginTopBarLogout() {
        webtest('Test TopBar: login, verify topbar, logout'){
          invoke(url:'user/login')
            verifyText(text:'Login below')
            setSelectField(name:'userName', value:'User1')
            clickButton(label:'Login')
            // after login should be on the todo view
            verifyText(text:'Todo List')
            // look for topbar information
            verifyText(text:'User1FN')
            verifyText(text:'User1LN')
            verifyText(text:'Logout')
            // logout
            clickLink(label:'Logout')
            // should be on the login view
            verifyText(text:'Login below')
        }
    }


    /**
     * Clean up after ourselves, delete the user we added.
     */
    def testDeleteUser() {
        webtest('Test TopBar: delete user'){
          invoke(url:'user')
            verifyText(text:'Home')

            // delete the first user.
            clickElement(xpath:'//td/a',description:'go to detail view')
            clickButton(label:'Delete')
            // Handle the javascript popup
            expectDialog(dialogType:'confirm', response:'true', description:
                'Are you sure')
```

```
            verifyText(text:'Home')
            verifyText(text:'User List')
        }
    }
}
```

Listing 5-19 almost reads like a checklist of instructions that you would have to give someone to test it manually. Verify that the test works as expected by running the WebTest.

You now have a testing framework. You created integration tests on the `handleLogin` and `logout` actions of the `UserController`. You also created a functional test for the `user` domain object using the generated templates and a custom functional test for the topbar. The best source for help with WebTest is the Canoo WebTest manual,[16] which contains some good examples. Translating the information in the manual to a Groovy implementation is straightforward.

■**Note** Throughout the rest of the book, we will assume that you're maintaining tests and creating new tests for every enhancement you make. Periodically, we will revisit testing to focus on a particular aspect, tip, or gotcha that is related to the topic being covered.

Externalizing Strings

Like all modern Java web frameworks, Grails supports the concept of message bundles. It uses the `<g:message>` tag to look up a properties file for the text to be displayed. For example, say you're having a difficult time deciding if the topbar should say "Login" or "Sign In." You could externalize the string and just change the `messages.properties` file whenever you change your mind. Grails uses the message bundles to display errors. So, if you don't like the error message you're getting back, you can make it friendlier by modifying the message in the message bundle. The `messages.properties` file is located in the `grails-app/i18n` directory. Listing 5-20 shows the default contents of the `messages.properties` file.

Listing 5-20. *messages.properties*

```
default.doesnt.match.message=Property [{0}] of class [{1}] with value [{2}] does \
not match the required pattern [{3}]
default.invalid.url.message=Property [{0}] of class [{1}] with value [{2}] is not \
a valid URL
```

---

16. http://webtest.canoo.com/webtest/manual/manualOverview.html

```
default.invalid.creditCard.message=Property [{0}] of class [{1}] with value [{2}] \
is not a valid credit card number
default.invalid.email.message=Property [{0}] of class [{1}] with value [{2}] is \
not a valid e-mail address
default.invalid.range.message=Property [{0}] of class [{1}] with value [{2}] \
does not fall within the valid range from [{3}] to [{4}]
default.invalid.size.message=Property [{0}] of class [{1}] with value [{2}] does \
not fall within the valid size range from [{3}] to [{4}]
default.invalid.max.message=Property [{0}] of class [{1}] with value [{2}] \
exceeds maximum value [{3}]
default.invalid.min.message=Property [{0}] of class [{1}] with value [{2}] is \
less than minimum value [{3}]
default.invalid.max.size.message=Property [{0}] of class [{1}] with value \
[{2}] exceeds the maximum size of [{3}]
default.invalid.min.size.message=Property [{0}] of class [{1}] with value \
[{2}] is less than the minimum size of [{3}]
default.invalid.validator.message=Property [{0}] of class [{1}] with value
[{2}] does not pass custom validation
default.not.inlist.message=Property [{0}] of class [{1}] with value [{2}] is \
not contained within the list [{3}]
default.blank.message=Property [{0}] of class [{1}] cannot be blank
default.not.equal.message=Property [{0}] of class [{1}] with value [{2}] \
cannot equal [{3}]
default.null.message=Property [{0}] of class [{1}] cannot be null
default.not.unique.message=Property [{0}] of class [{1}] with value [{2}] \
must be unique

default.paginate.prev=Previous
default.paginate.next=Next
```

Let's go back to the topbar WebTest example to demonstrate how to externalize strings. Take a look at Listing 5-5 to see the current topbar template. Change lines 5 and 8 to use the `<g:message>` tags. When completed, the topbar template should look something like what's shown in Listing 5-21.

Listing 5-21. *Topbar Template with Messages*

```
<div id="menu">
  <nobr>
    <g:if test="${session.user}">
      <b>${session.user?.firstName} ${session.user?.lastName}</b> |
```

```
        <g:link controller="logout"><g:message code="topbar.logout" /></g:link>
    </g:if>
    <g:else>
      <g:link controller="login" action="auth">
          <g:message code="topbar.login" /></g:link>
    </g:else>
  </nobr>
</div>
```

Now just add `topbar.logout` and `topbar.login` to the messages bundle:

```
topbar.login=Login
topbar.logout=Logout
```

You can easily change the text to display whatever you want without modifying the GSP. You still have to be careful, though. Depending upon how you modify the text associated with the message code, you may have to adjust the WebTest if it is looking for specific text. In a sophisticated application, you will have to make some decisions about functional testing. You need to ask yourself, "Should the functional test be run against a single locale or multiple locales?" If you decide on multiple locales, you will have to write a more robust functional test and pay particular attention to the usage of `verifyText`.

If you're an experienced web developer, you won't be surprised to find out that using the `<g:message>` tag also starts you on the path of internationalizing the application. The `<g:message>` tag is locale-aware; the `i18n` in the directory name to the `messages.property` file is a giveaway. By default, the tag uses the browser's locale to determine which message bundle to use.

Now that you understand message bundles, you can change the default messages displayed to something user friendly when errors occur.

Errors and Validation

In this section, you'll learn the difference between errors and flash messages, and you'll discover how to customize the messages.

If you try to submit a user form without entering a username, you will see error messages in action. When you violate a domain object's constraints, the red text that you see is an example of an error message. Figure 5-11 shows an example.

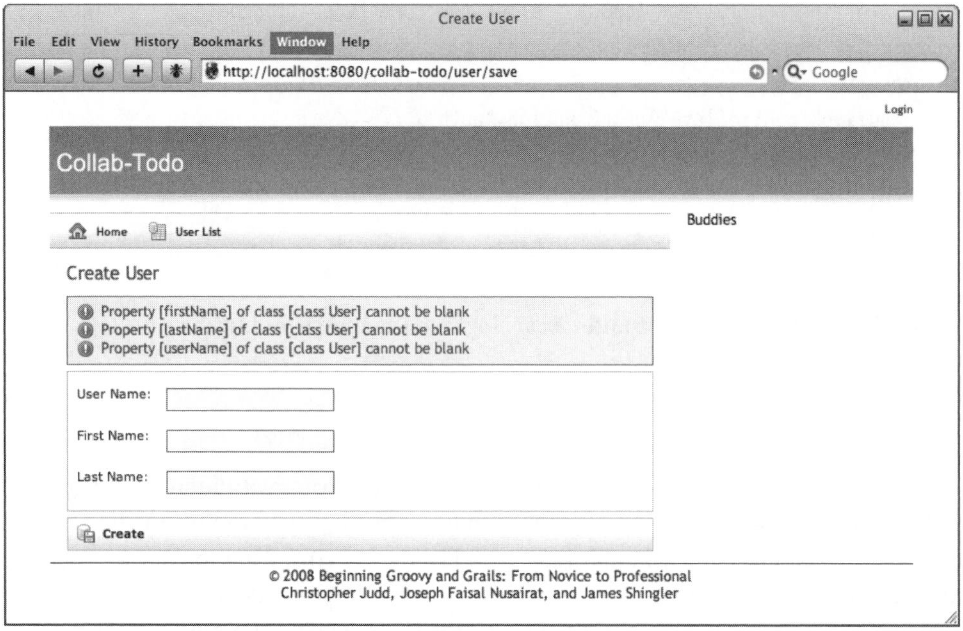

Figure 5-11. *Error message*

This screen shows the default error messages. As you saw previously in Listing 5-20, you can customize the message using the `messages.properties` file located in the `grails-app/i18n` directory. To get a better understanding of how this works, you need to switch the views and the controller from dynamic scaffolding to static scaffolding. Grails generates dynamic scaffolding on the fly when the application starts. If Grails can generate the code at runtime, it makes sense that it can generate the code at development time so you can see it. The generated code is called *static scaffolding*. Take a precaution against losing the existing implementation of the `UserController` by making a backup copy.

You can create the views for the `User` domain object by executing the command `grails generate-views User`. The command uses Grails templates to generate four new GSP pages in the `grails-app/views/user` directory: `create.gsp`, `edit.gsp`, `list.gsp`, and `show.gsp`. Now you need to create static scaffolding for the controller. You can create the controller for the `User` domain object by executing the command `grails generate-controller User`. Grails will detect that you already have an implementation of the controller and ask for permission to overwrite it. Give it permission; this is why you made a backup copy. After the `UserController` is generated, you need to copy the `login`, `handleLogin`, and `logout` actions from the backup to the newly generated controller. Listing 5-22 contains the contents of the `save` action.

Listing 5-22. *The UserController.save Action*

```
01      def save = {
02          def user = new User()
03          user.properties = params
04          if(user.save()) {
05              flash.message = "User ${user.id} created."
06              redirect(action:show,id:user.id)
07          }
08          else {
09              render(view:'create',model:[user:user])
10          }
11      }
```

The save action is called when the user clicks the Create button from the New User view. When line 4 is executed, Grails validates the user constraints before attempting to persist the user in the database. If validation succeeds, the user is redirected to the Show User view with the message "User ${user.id} created." If the save fails, the Create User view is rendered so that you can correct the validation errors without losing the previous input. When validation fails, Grails inserts an error message in the user object's meta-data, and the user object is passed as a model object to the view. When the Create User view is rendered, it checks to see if there are any errors and displays them if appropriate. Listing 5-23 contains a short snippet that shows how to display the errors.

Listing 5-23. *Display Errors*

```
<g:hasErrors bean="${user}">
<div class="errors">
    <g:renderErrors bean="${user}" as="list" />
</div>
</g:hasErrors>
```

As you can see, the generated GSP uses the <g:hasErrors> and <g:renderErrors> tags to detect and display the errors. The <g:hasErrors> tag uses the bean attribute to detect errors in the user object. If errors are detected, the body of the tag is evaluated, which results in the error being displayed by the <g:renderErrors> tag. The <g:renderErrors> tag iterates through the errors in the user object and displays them as a list. The display process knows that it is receiving an error code and error attributes. The tag looks up the error code in the message bundle, and the attributes are substituted in the message before it is displayed.

This technique works because the page is rendered from the controller. Take another look at line 6 in Listing 5-22. In the case of a redirect, the controller instructs the browser to go to the Show User view. The browser does this by calling the `show` action on the `UserController`. The controller then executes the `show` action and renders `show.gsp`. With all of this back and forth between the controller and the browser, can you imagine what it would take to make sure that all of the message information stays intact so it can be displayed by `show.gsp`? Well, this is where flash messages come to your rescue.

Flash and Flash Messages

What is flash scope and why do you need it? The short answer is that it is a technique implemented by Grails to make passing objects across redirects much easier. In other words, it addresses the problem described at the end of the previous section.

Figure 5-12 illustrates the problems associated with normal techniques of passing information from the controller to the view when a redirect is involved.

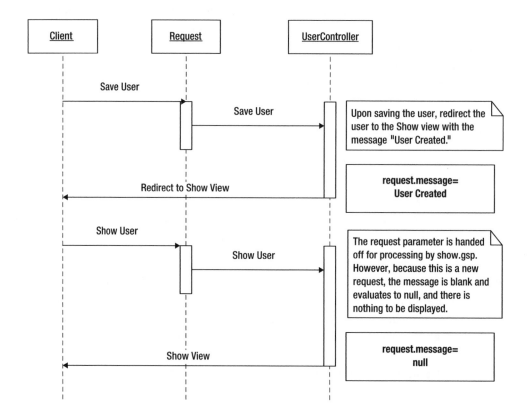

Figure 5-12. *Redirect problem*

On a redirect, if you try to use the request to carry the message to the Show view, the message gets lost when the browser receives the redirect. Another option would be to stick the message in the session and have the Show view pick it up from the session. However, in the Show view, you have to remember to delete the message from the session once it has been displayed; otherwise, the same message might be displayed on multiple views. The problem with this approach is that it depends upon you doing the right thing, and it's tedious.

This is where Grails comes to the rescue: it takes the last option and implements it for you and makes it part of the Grails framework. This is the flash scope. The flash scope works just like the other scopes[17] (application, session, request, and page) by operating off a map of key/value pairs. It stores the information in the session and then removes it on the next request. Now you don't have to remember to delete the object in the flash scope. Figure 5-13 illustrates the concept of the flash scope.

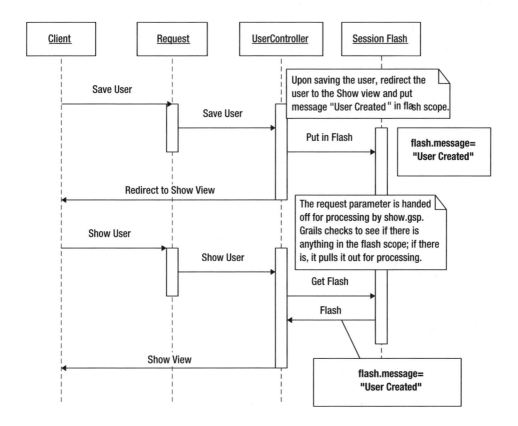

Figure 5-13. *Flash scope*

---

17. http://java.sun.com/blueprints/guidelines/designing_enterprise_applications_2e/
    web-tier/web-tier5.html#1079198

The Show view can access the flash scope objects—a message, in this case—and display them using the tags and techniques illustrated in Listing 5-24.

Listing 5-24. *Access and Display a Flash Message*

```
<g:if test="${flash.message}">
   <div class="message">${flash.message}</div>
</g:if>
```

Grails isn't the only modern web framework that implements this technique. Ruby on Rails (RoR) developers should find this familiar.

Accessing a message from a flash scope looks pretty easy, but how do you put a message in flash? Listing 5-25 illustrates how the save action on the UserController puts a message into the flash scope.

Listing 5-25. *Putting a Message in the Flash Scope*

```
. . .
if(user.save()) {
    flash.message = "User ${user.id} created."
    redirect(action:show,id:user.id)
}
...
```

Grails implements a flash scope using a map. In this case, message is the key, and "User ${user.id} created." is the value.

What if you need to internationalize the code or want to change the message without editing the GSP? (Currently, the message is essentially hard-coded.) You can set it up to use message bundles just like errors do. Earlier in the chapter, you used the <g:message> tag to pull error messages from message bundles. You can do the same thing for flash messages using a couple of attributes. Listing 5-26 illustrates how to use the <g:message> tag to display flash messages.

Listing 5-26. *Using the <g:message> Tag to Display a Flash Message*

```
<g:message code="${flash.message}" args="${flash.args}"
    default="${flash.defaultMsg}"/>
```

Listing 5-27 illustrates the enhancements to the save action to set the values that the message tag will use.

Listing 5-27. *Setting Values in a Flash Scope for Use by the <g:message> Tag*

```
...
if(user.save()) {
    flash.message = "user.saved.message"
    flash.args = [user.firstName, user.lastName]
    flash.defaultMsg = "User Saved"
    redirect(action:show,id:user.id)
}
...
```

The `flash.message` property is the message code to be looked up in the message bundle, `flash.args` are the arguments to be substituted into the message, and `flash.defaultMsg` is a default message to display in the event of a problem.

Only one thing left to do: create an entry in the message bundle with the `user.saved.message` code and whatever you would like the text to be. See Listing 5-28 for an example.

Listing 5-28. *Flash Message Code Example*

```
user.saved.message=User: {0} {1} was saved
```

The results should look something like what's shown in Figure 5-14.

Figure 5-14. *Customized flash message*

Note Any action can call or redirect to the Show view. At this point, you may be wondering what happens if `flash.args` and `flash.defaultMsg` aren't set. The `<g:message>` tag is pretty smart; it does the logical thing. It displays the contents of `flash.message`. To see it in action, update an existing user and take a look at the message displayed.

Now that you know about the flash scope and messages, you can create customized and internationalized application messages with a minimal investment.

You have learned quite a bit about Grails user interfaces and have established the basic look and feel. Now it's time to start implementing some logic and control.

Controlling the Application

The application has the ability to create users, log in as a user, log out, and even create categories and to-do items. However, if you spend some time playing around with multiple users, you'll discover that users can modify and delete each other's information. That's not good.

Controlling Users

In this section, you will modify the controllers to prevent user 1 from accidentally changing user 2's information, and you'll add a simple audit log using an interceptor. Let's start with the user information. It is not a problem for users to see each other's user details, but they shouldn't be able to change them or delete another user.

Let's analyze the problem for a second. You might take a UI-centric approach, and in the GSP, just don't show the link to edit the user unless the ID of the current user is the same as the ID being displayed. If everyone in the world were trustworthy, that might work, but it has some serious flaws.[18] For example, a large system might have multiple places that implement the logic you're trying to guard against. A controller/action-centric approach is a better answer and probably sufficient for a simple application. Centralizing the authorization check in the controller/action has the benefit of guarding the update logic no matter how it is called.

Note The UI approach might still be worthwhile from a user experience perspective, but you should *never* use it as a replacement for the more centralized controller/action approach. The two approaches are not mutually exclusive; you can use them together.

---

18. You will learn more about security in Chapter 7.

Listing 5-29 contains the default implementation of the edit action.

Listing 5-29. *The edit Action*

```
def edit = {

    def user = User.get( params.id )

    if(!user) {
            flash.message = "User not found with id ${params.id}"
            redirect(action:list)
    }
    else {
        return [ user : user ]
    }
}
```

As you can see, the edit action retrieves the user to be edited based upon params.id. In this case, params.id is the ID of the user to be edited. If the user ID to be edited isn't the same as the currently logged-in user, then the user should be returned to the User List view and view a message that states, "You can only edit yourself." You can accomplish this by changing the implementation of the edit action to match Listing 5-30. Don't forget that when a user logs into the application, that user is put into the session.

Listing 5-30. *The edit Action with User Check*

```
def edit = {
    if (session.user.id != params.id) {
        flash.message = "You can only edit yourself"
        redirect(action:list)
        return
    }

    def user = User.get( params.id )

    if(!user) {
            flash.message = "User not found with id ${params.id}"
            redirect(action:list)
    }
    else {
        return [ user : user ]
    }
}
```

Make sure to include the `return` statement. Failure to do so will result in the action continuing to process after the browser has been instructed to go to a different action. As you can see, you use `flash.message` to make the error message available to the List view. You should apply the same logic to the `update` and `delete` actions to prevent users from updating or deleting a record other than their own. Let's explore this action a little deeper.

`params` is a mutable map of request parameters. The fact that it is mutable allows you to add or modify request parameters. You can even pass them to other actions. You use the dot dereference operator to access the value for the key `id`. This works well and is the preferred method for accessing a map when the key is not an invalid identifier—in other words, when it doesn't have invalid characters such as dot or /. For special cases, you can use the subscript operator to access `params`. Listing 5-31 illustrates using the subscript operator. This technique is also useful when the key is not known until runtime (i.e., passed in as a variable).

Listing 5-31. *Accessing Request Parameters Using the Subscript Operator*

```
def user = User.get(params['id'])
```

This brings up an additional point of interest. Because `params` is a request parameter map, you have been accessing request parameters in the controller actions. You might be wondering, "How did the parameters get passed into the action?" Go to the User List view and select a user to show. Now take a close look at your browser URL, which should look something like the screen shown in Figure 5-15. The callouts aren't part of the URL; they are used to identify the different parts of the URL.

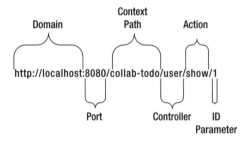

Figure 5-15. *The URL*

Remember that not everyone in the world is trustworthy. This is why it isn't good enough to just not show the link on the view. A mischievous person could type the URL directly into the browser and bypass the view. Figure 5-16 illustrates passing additional request parameters on the URL.

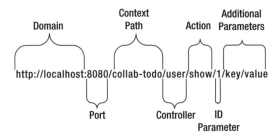

Figure 5-16. *Additional request parameters*

Another interesting point in Listing 5-30 is the last `return` statement. In Grails, actions can do many things, one of which is returning a model that is used by the view to display information. A model is a map of key/value pairs. The `return [user : user]` statement returns a Groovy map.[19] This can be a little confusing. Grails leverages Groovy's ability to create a map using the `[:]` notation. The entry before the : is the key, and the entry after the : is the value (i.e., `[key:value]`).

■**Note** Groovy provides an implicit return. The value returned is the value of the last statement in the action/closure. For example, take a look at the `show` action on the `UserController`.

Listing 5-32 illustrates how `show.gsp` uses the information in the `User` object to display the user's name.

Listing 5-32. *Using the User Object in a View*

```
<tr class="prop">
    <td valign="top" class="name">User Name:</td>
    <td valign="top" class="value">${user.userName}</td>
</tr>
```

`${user.userName}` is accessing the model map by the `user` key and then accessing the `userName` property from the value object. In this case, the value object is the `User` domain object. You can think of this as `${modelMapKey.modelMapValue}`.

Before you move on with the application, let's take a look at some other actions in the `UserController`. Listing 5-33 shows the implementation of the `save` action.

---

19. http://groovy.codehaus.org/Collections#Collections-Maps

Listing 5-33. *The UserController save Action*

```
01     def save = {
02         def user = new User()
03         user.properties = params
04         if(user.save()) {
05             flash.message = "user.saved.message"
06             flash.args = [ user.firstName, user.lastName]
07             flash.defaultMsg = "User Saved"
08             redirect(action:show,id:user.id)
09         }
10         else {
11             render(view:'create',model:[user:user])
12         }
13     }
```

Line 3 demonstrates a powerful feature of Grails called *data binding*. The save action is typically called from the Create view. Taking a quick look at the user Create view will help you understand how the save action works. The view is used to create users. In the process of creating users, the view supports creating userName, firstName, and lastName using a form component. When the form is submitted, userName, firstName, and lastName are put in the parameters map. Line 3 sets the domain properties from the request parameters. In Chapter 6, you will learn more about domain objects and properties; this is just a preview.

Data binding is handy and saves lots of code. If you're an experienced web developer, go take a look at one of your existing applications to see how much effort it took to assign form data to domain objects. As an aside, you can also use an overridden constructor to assign the values (e.g., def user = new User(params)).

After assigning the domain object properties, the action attempts to save the object. In the process of saving the object, it is validated. If the object passes validation and the save succeeds, the user is redirected to the Show view, and the user.saved.message message is displayed. If the save fails, the Create view is redisplayed, and the validation errors are displayed.

Line 11 demonstrates using the render method to display the Create view and pass the failed user object to the model. You may be asking, "Why would it pass the user back?" The view uses the user object to repopulate the form so that the user can correct mistakes. That's great, and it saves a good deal of development effort too. But how does the view know what failed in validation? We'll cover this more in Chapter 6, but the short answer is that Grails adds an error collection to the domain object. The view retrieves the error messages from the domain object.

Let's review some of what you have learned while restricting modification of user information. You learned how to introduce logic into the edit, update, and delete actions to prevent users from modifying information unless the users themselves are making the change. You explored request parameters and the Grails URL when examining why the check must be in the controller action. While you were looking at the UserController, you also took a quick look at how information is passed back to the view in the form of a model and how parameters are set into domain objects using data binding. You also had a preview into Chapter 6's discussion of domain object validation, and you learned that when validation fails, the view can ask the domain object for the error messages. With this information, you're now ready to further enhance the application by controlling what category and to-do information is displayed.

Controlling Categories

When the user navigates to the Category List view, all of the categories are displayed, including other users' categories. When a user is maintaining categories, having other users' categories in the list is just a distraction and provides no value. The goal is to take what you just learned about controller actions and apply it to the Category controller. The first step is to generate the category views and controller by executing the commands grails generate-views Category and grails generate-controller Category. The second task is to restrict the categories displayed in the List view by restricting the categories returned from the list action. Listing 5-34 contains the contents of the list action before you enhance it.

Listing 5-34. *The list Action*

```
01    def list = {
02        if(!params.max)params.max = 10
03        [ categoryList: Category.list( params ) ]
04    }
```

Line 2 checks to see if the params map contains a key named max. If it doesn't, the code creates a new key/value pair in params, called max, with a value of 10. The dynamic method, list, uses the max parameter to limit the number of categories returned. Line 3 calls the dynamic method list on the category domain object and returns the results to the List view. You will learn more about dynamic methods[20] in Chapter 6. You need to make the changes illustrated in Listing 5-35 to restrict categories to the currently logged-in user.

---

20. http://www.grails.org/DomainClass+Dynamic+Methods#DomainClassDynamicMethods-list

Listing 5-35. *Restricting the list Action*

```
01    def list = {
02        if(!params.max)params.max = 10
03        def user = User.get(session.user.id)
04        [ categoryList: Category.findAllByUser(user, params) ]
05    }
```

Line 3 retrieves the current user based upon the user information in the session. Line 4 finds all the categories for the user retrieved on line 3. Line 4 is an example of using a dynamic finder method. You will learn about dynamic finder methods in Chapter 6. When that application is run, you will see that the display now restricts the List view to the currently logged-in user. Figure 5-17 illustrates the Create view.

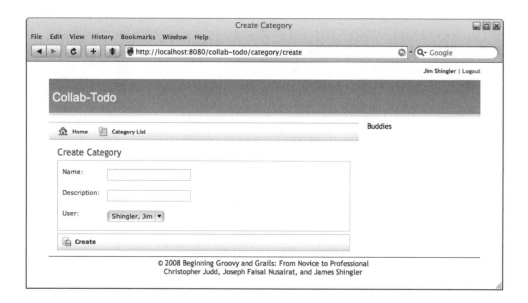

Figure 5-17. *Create view*

Now that the category views are restricted to the currently logged-in user, having the user displayed in any of the views is redundant. Removing the user selection component is a two-step process. First, you need to remove it from the views (`grails-app/views/category/*.gsp`), and default the user to the currently signed-on user when the `save` and `update` actions are called. This process is straightforward, and I'll leave it up to you. Let's focus on the second step, in which you default the user in the `save` and `update` actions. Listing 5-36 highlights the enhancements to the `save` and `update` actions to enable defaulting the users.

Listing 5-36. *Defaulting the User*

```
def update = {
    def category = Category.get( params.id )

    if(session.user.id != category.user.id) {
        flash.message = "You can only delete your own categories"
        redirect(action:list)
        return
    }

    def user = User.get(session.user.id);
    if(category) {
        category.properties = params
        category.user = user
        if(category.save()) {
            flash.message = "Category ${params.id} updated."
            redirect(action:show,id:category.id)
        }
    }

. . .

def save = {
    def category = new Category()
    category.properties = params
    def user = User.get(session.user.id);
    category.user = user
    if(category.save()) {
        flash.message = "Category ${category.id} created."
        redirect(action:show,id:category.id)
    }
    else {
        render(view:'create',model:[category:category])
    }
}
}
```

Take a look at `flash.message`. This is a Groovy String, or GString.[21] The `${}` allows you to insert an expression into a string. In this case, the value of `category.id` is inserted into the string. Figure 5-18 shows the cleaned-up Create view.

---

21. http://groovy.codehaus.org/Strings#Strings-GStrings

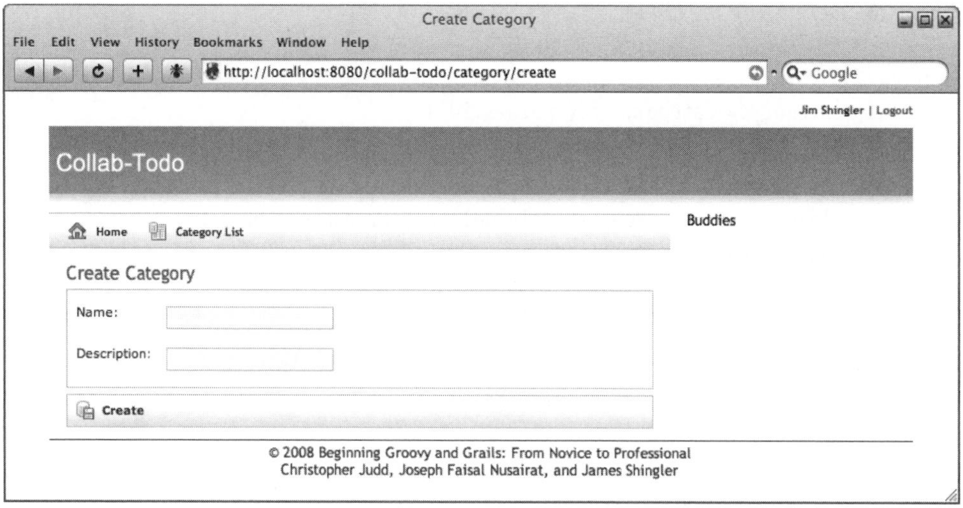

Figure 5-18. *Cleaned-up Create view*

The Category ID doesn't provide any value. Remove it from the List and Show views. The user experience is improved dramatically without the Category ID and User Name fields on the views.

Tip In the List view, the ID field has a link to show a specific category. Make sure that you move the link to the category name; otherwise, you won't be able to navigate to the Show view.

You should also apply the user check that you added to the UserController's edit, update, and delete actions to the CategoryController's edit, update, and delete actions. Additionally, you should apply the enhancement you made to the category controller and view to the to-do controller and views. From this point forward, we'll assume that you have completed both exercises.

Tip On the Todo domain object, the user owns to-do items. The property that represents the user is owner.

Now that you have experience enhancing controllers, it's time to learn about another controller technique: action interceptors. You will use interceptors to construct a simple audit log.

Creating an Audit Log Using Action Interceptors

Occasionally, you'll have problems with the application. When this happens, it is useful to know the input and results of the actions being executed. This entails displaying the inputs to the action before the action is executed and the results before control is passed to the next step in the process. You could modify every action to print the inputs before executing the body of the action and then again at the end of the action. However, that's way too much work and difficult to maintain.

Grails provides a mechanism called *action interceptors* that you can use to provide the desired functionality. Experienced developers will see that this is similar to aspect-oriented programming (AOP). If you aren't familiar with AOP, you might be familiar with servlet filter interceptors for servlets, which are similar. The good news is that Grails makes it easier than either one of these.

■**Note** Ruby on Rails developers will recognize this as a Rails filter.

Grails provides *before* and *after* interceptors. You will use both to provide the audit log functionality. You will use a before interceptor to log the userName, controller, action, and input parameters. To accomplish this, you will add the beforeInterceptor closure to the TodoController. Listing 5-37 is an example of the beforeInterceptor for you to add to the controller.

Listing 5-37. *beforeInterceptor*

```
def beforeInterceptor = {
    log.trace("${session?.user?.userName} Start action ${controllerName}
        Controller.${actionName}() : parameters $params")
}
```

If defined and unless otherwise instructed, the beforeInterceptor is called just before the action is invoked. Since it is a closure, it has full access to all of the controller properties as well as the request parameters. It uses logging (see the "Logging" sidebar) to output the audit information. Notice that it's using the ?. safe dereference operator. The safe dereference operator checks to see if the current expression so far is null before evaluating the next portion of the expression. So, if session or user is null, userName will never be accessed. This helps you avoid the infamous NullPointerException. beforeInterceptor allows you to perform logic before an action is invoked, while afterInterceptor allows you to perform logic after the action has executed. Listing 5-38 is an example of afterInterceptor for you to add to the controller.

Listing 5-38. *afterInterceptor*

```
def afterInterceptor = { model ->
   log.trace("${session?.user?.userName} End action
   ${controllerName}Controller.${actionName}() : returns $model")
 }
```

As you would expect, the afterInterceptor looks similar to the beforeInterceptor. The one additional piece is the passing of the model object to the interceptor; this allows you to output it to the audit log.

■**Caution** This implementation of audit logging is a potential security hole for sensitive data. If the parameters or model contain sensitive data, you will want to take extra care to filter it out before logging any audit information.

---

beforeInterceptor and afterInterceptor are invoked for every action in the controller. Suppose you didn't want to invoke the audit log for every action. What if you didn't want to collect audit log information for the list action? You could write an if statement around the log statement. That would work, and it would work well. Grails provides an additional mechanism, called *interceptor conditions*, which allow interceptors to be applied conditionally. Listing 5-39 is an example of the before and after interceptors using conditions to exclude the list action from the audit log.

Listing 5-39. *Before and After Interceptors with Conditions*

```
def beforeInterceptor = [action:this.&beforeAudit,except:['list']]
def afterInterceptor = [action:{model ->this.&afterAudit(model)},
    except:['list']]

def beforeAudit = {
    log.trace("${session?.user?.userName} Start action
        ${controllerName}Controller.${actionName}() : parameters $params")
}

def afterAudit = { model ->
    log.trace("${session?.user?.userName} End action
        ${controllerName}Controller.${actionName}() : returns $model")
}
```

■Note *The Definitive Guide to Grails* shows you how to use action interceptors to build a simple security framework.[22]

Using Filters

Filters[23] are similar to action interceptors in that they give you the ability to execute logic before and after an action. They differ from action interceptors in that they are more flexible and can be used in situations other than actions. For example, you can define a filter that applies across multiple controllers.

Let's see how you can use filters to simplify the UserController. The UserController's edit, delete, and update actions all contain guard logic that allows users to edit only their own user data. The actions contain logic similar to Listing 5-40.

Listing 5-40. *User Modification Guard*

```
. . .
    if (session.user.id != params.id) {
       flash.message = "You can only edit yourself"
       redirect(action:list)
       return
    }
. . .
```

While the logic in Listing 5-40 isn't complex, it would be repeated for each action that requires a guard. You can use filters to extract and centralize the logic to a single location. This may sound familiar to those of you who have worked with AOP. The basic idea is to extract the logic to a central location and then configure when that logic should be applied.

In Grails, you extract the logic into a class ending with the name Filters.groovy and place it in the grails-app/conf directory. Each filter is contained within a method that takes parameters to define the scope of the filter, when it is applied. Listing 5-41 shows how you would centralize the user modification logic.

Listing 5-41. *Filter Scope*

```
class UserFilters {
    def filters = {
        userModificationCheck(controller: 'user', action: '*') {
```

22. Graeme Rocher, *The Definitive Guide to Grails* (Berkeley, CA: Apress, 2006).

23. http://grails.org/Filters

```
                . . .
            }
        someOtherFilter(uri: '/user/*') { }
    }
}
```

The userModificationCheck filter is scoped and applied to the UserController on all actions. Another way of scoping the filter is to use a URL. You can see an example of this option on the someOtherFilter filter.

Next, you need to determine if the filter should be applied before the action, after the action, and/or afterView rendering. In this case, the goal is to determine if the person using the system should be allowed to modify the user. This means the guard logic should be applied before the edit, update, and delete actions. Listing 5-42 illustrates how to specify the before condition.

Listing 5-42. *before Filter*

```
class UserFilters {
    def filters = {
        userModificationCheck(controller: 'user', action: '*') {
            before = {

                . . .

            }
        }
    }
}
```

Finally, you need to limit the guard logic to the edit, update, and delete actions. Listing 5-43 shows the complete userModificationFilter.

Listing 5-43. *User Modification Filter*

```
01 class UserFilters {
02     def filters = {
03         userModificationCheck(controller: 'user', action: '*') {
04             before = {
05                 def currActionName = actionName
06                 if (currActionName == 'edit' ||
07                         currActionName == 'update' ||
08                         currActionName == 'delete') {
09                     String userId = session?.user?.id
10                     String paramsUserId = params?.id
```

```
11                    if (userId != paramsUserId) {
12                        flash.message = "You can only modify yourself"
13                        redirect(action: 'list')
14                        return false
15                    }
16                }
17            }
18        }
19    }
20 }
```

Let's review the new lines. Line 5 gets the current action. Remember, you should apply the filter to the edit, update, and delete actions, as shown in lines 6–8.

Line 11 determines if the person attempting the modification—the logged-in user—is modifying his or her own user record. If not, an appropriate flash message is created, and the user is redirected to the UserController list action. Line 14 returns false to tell Grails that it shouldn't execute any other filters.

Now that you have the userModificationCheck filter, you can remove the redundant guard code from the edit, update, and delete actions.

LOGGING

While everyone uses println from time to time, a more mature approach is to use logging. Grails controllers are preconfigured with a log property. Each controller receives its own instance of org.apache. commons.logging.log. Apache Commons Logging component[24] is an abstraction that allows you to plug in different logging packages. Grails comes prepackaged with log4j.[25]

The Apache Commons Logging abstraction provides the interface seen in the following code.

The org.apache.commons.logging.log Interface

```
public interface log {
    void debug(java.lang.Object message)
    void debug(java.lang.Object message, java.lang.Throwable t)
    void error(java.lang.Object message)
    void error(java.lang.Object message, java.lang.Throwable t)
    void fatal(java.lang.Object message
    void fatal(java.lang.Object message, java.lang.Throwable t)
    void info(java.lang.Object message)
```

---

24. http://commons.apache.org/logging
25. http://logging.apache.org/log4j

```
        void info(java.lang.Object message, java.lang.Throwable t)
        void trace(java.lang.Object message)
        void trace(java.lang.Object message, java.lang.Throwable t)
        void warn(java.lang.Object message)
        void warn(java.lang.Object message, java.lang.Throwable t)
        boolean isDebugEnabled()
        boolean isErrorEnabled()
        boolean isFatalEnabled()
        boolean isInfoEnabled()
        boolean isTraceEnabled()
        boolean isWarnEnabled()
    }
```

Messages have a severity level. The possible severity levels (from least severe to most severe) are

- Trace

- Debug

- Info

- Warning

- Error

- Fatal

Since Grails version 0.6, logging is configured through the `Config.groovy` file found in the `grails-app/conf` directory. By default, Grails is configured for info-level logging. To enable trace-level debugging in the development environment, add the definitions found in the following code to the `Config.groovy` file.

Configure Development Environment Logging

```
environments {
    development {
        log4j {
            logger {
                grails.'app.controller'="trace,stdout"
                grails.app="error,stdout"
```

```
            }
        }
    }
}
```

For more information on logging configuration, see the online log configuration documentation at http://www.grails.org/Logging.

Summary

Views and controllers are broad and deep topics. We have used the construction of the Collab-Todo wireframe and customization of the views and controllers to help you learn about some of the more important aspects to these topics.

In the process of building the Collab-Todo application, you have learned how to use layouts, templates, and CSS to build the wireframe. The wireframe was composed of top-bar, header, content, sidebar, and footer components. Building the wireframe also exposed you to some of the Grails tag libraries.

Once you built the wireframe, you learned how to build a temporary login facility that allowed you to exercise the topbar login/logout functionality. Building the login facility involved creating a customized view and customized actions on the UserController.

You used JUnit to write integration tests for the actions, and you used Canoo WebTest to write functional tests for the application. Building the integration and functional tests relieved you from manual testing every time you enhanced the application, and it allowed you to focus on the next set of enhancements: externalizing strings to property files and messages.

You also learned about errors, validation, and flash messages. This gave you insights into how Grails renders errors and messages and how you can control them. You also learned about the redirect message problem and how using flash-scoped messages solves the problem.

Once you had the basic mechanics of the application down, your attention turned to the user experience by restricting the information users were shown to the information that was relevant to them. You accomplished this by enhancing the controller actions so that they restricted the model information returned to the views to only the information users were permitted to see. You learned about the URL and request parameters. Then you enhanced the view by removing the ID and user fields from the category and to-do views, and you enhanced the save and update actions to set the user information to the currently logged-in user.

You learned how to use interceptors for things like auditing. Finally, you created a simple audit log using action interceptors and logging.

It's important to remember that even though we covered a lot, there are even more advanced things you can do with views and controllers. We'll cover more of the advanced topics in the coming chapters. The next step on your journey is to learn more about domain models and services.

■ ■ ■

CHAPTER 6

Building Domains and Services

KING ARTHUR. *The Lady of the Lake, her arm clad in the purest shimmering samite held aloft Excalibur from the bosom of the water, signifying by divine providence that I, Arthur, was to carry Excalibur. THAT is why I am your king.*

DENNIS, *interrupting. Listen, strange women lyin' in ponds distributin' swords is no basis for a system of government. Supreme executive power derives from a mandate from the masses, not from some farcical aquatic ceremony.*

Just as King Arthur and his knights embarked on a quest to find the Holy Grail in *Monty Python and the Holy Grail*, the next step in our discovery of Grails is to search for its very heart and soul . . . or in Java terms, its *domain*. Those of you familiar with Ruby on Rails and other web frameworks know the domain as a model. These synonymous terms are most often used in conjunction with the objects that are persisted against the database. Although the terms are interchangeable, for the purpose of this book, we will follow Grails' (and Java's) lead and refer to the *domain*.

You received your first taste of the domain in Chapter 4 when you learned how to scaffold the application. In Chapter 5, we broke out a few of those controllers to show actual calls against the domain. However, we didn't dive too much into the functionality of the domain. Well, here is where we take it up a notch. We'll show you the full power of Grails database persistence and explain all the options available to you. In addition, we'll discuss the idea of services—something that should be familiar to any enterprise developer. Unlike controllers, services don't contain any specific web knowledge like sessions and request parameters do.

GORM

We've shown you how to interact with the database, but we've left the process a bit nebulous until now. In this chapter, we'll go over the specifics behind how GORM works. Most frameworks, especially those straight out of the box, have their own mechanism for persisting to the database. Ruby on Rails uses ActiveRecord as the persistence mechanism.

Java EE frameworks use the JPA (which, if you're on JBoss Application Server, is simply Hibernate underneath the covers). WebSphere uses iBATIS.

Grails uses GORM. However, GORM is not its own creation; under the covers, it uses Hibernate for its persistence implementation. GORM simply wraps Hibernate in Groovy layers. This is a blessing, because Hibernate gives GORM all of the necessary plumbing code, allowing GORM to focus on the usability instead. In fact, if you're familiar with ActiveRecord and Hibernate, then you should be about 95% good to go when it comes to writing domain objects in Grails. GORM truly is an amalgamation of the ActiveRecord and Hibernate, giving you the best of both worlds. As we move along with examples on how to use GORM, the similarities and differences will become more apparent.

Collab-Todo's Domain

Before going into depth about how to create domains in Groovy, let's start by explaining what you'll be creating. In Chapter 4, we gave you the base of the domain structure with the Todo, Category, and User classes. However, this application wouldn't be that interesting if we kept just those three domain objects. We decided to wait to show you the entire domain for two major reasons:

- We didn't want to overwhelm you with the domain when you were just starting to learn the system.

- Without more background, you might not be entirely familiar with the way the domain is created.

However, now we're at that stage where we can introduce you to the entire domain. We'll start off by going over what the Java class domain looks like. Then we'll explain the options you have for creating and configuring the domain components. Finally, we'll show you the database you'll create with the domain configurations.

Figure 6-1 shows a class-level diagram filled with connectors and columns. This should give you an overview of the application you'll be building and explain what the individual parts mean. We suggest you also look at the source code to get an idea of how you'll transition from the diagram in Figure 6-1 to the actual code you'll be using throughout the book. (You can find the code samples for this chapter in the Source Code/Download area of the Apress web site [www.apress.com].) Please note that this diagram contains two domains that we'll use in the next chapter as part of the security apparatus.

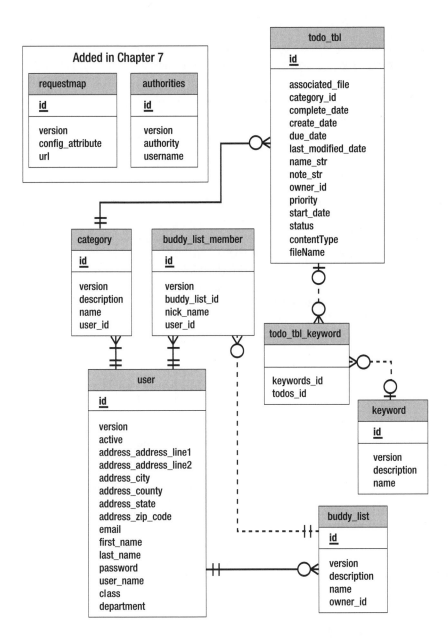

Figure 6-1. *Class-level diagram of the domain*

■**Note** We're using the domain model to map the database; we're not using the database to map the domain model. This is becoming a fairly standard practice, although you're more than welcome to do the reverse.

A few of these tables should seem familiar to you. Table 6-1 provides a list of each domain object and a brief description of its purpose.

Table 6-1. *Domain Classes Used for the Collab-Todo Application*

Domain Name	Description
Address	An inner domain object that we have stored inside the User.groovy file, because you'll use it as an embedded class anyway.
Admin	Extends the User class. You'll use it for administrators, where you'll track what department they are with. You will *not* use this class in permissioning, though.
Authorities	Used as part of the Acegi security plug-in that we'll get into in Chapter 7.
BuddyList	Defines the buddy lists for each of the users.
BuddyListMember	Each person the users want in their buddy lists must be referenced in this class. The other purpose of this class is to assign nicknames.
Category	Creates specific names to categorize to-dos by.
Keyword	Creates keywords to differentiate the individual to-dos.
Requestmap	Used as part of the Acegi plug-in discussed in Chapter 7.
Todo	The holder for all the to-dos. This is the main object of the application.
User	Stores information about the person creating the to-do.

As we move through this chapter, we will add various relations and constraints to the domain model. Let's start with how you actually create the domain object.

Creating Domain Objects

Because we're discussing how to create the domain objects that create the database, it's best to start off small by examining just one table at first. In the previous two chapters, we showed you how to start the domain collection and add to it. Now we'll dive into all the options and the specifics of how domain creation works. Luckily, even if you've never worked with Hibernate or Java Data Objects (JDO), learning how to use GORM will be easy. For one, it's intuitive. For example, with normal JDOs, you have to memorize what *many-to-one, one-to-one*, and so on mean. With GORM, relationships are easier to define.

The relationships are defined in a DSL syntax so that domain A *belongs to* domain B or domain A *has many* domain Bs associated with it. GORM was built with a DSL, so the terms you use to create the area sound like how you speak.

We're going to take a few steps back before we take a few steps forward. We'll start with basic domain creation, and we'll dive into the details of what's going on under the covers. Then we'll go into some more advanced settings for the domain, including how to create complex object types and how to overwrite the storage of the domain. By the end of this section, you should be ready to create and customize almost any domain object you need.

Basic Domain Creation

Figure 6-1 showed the domain model you'll be using, and in the previous chapters, you saw the implementation of a few domain objects. However, we have not detailed how you create a domain object of your own, your options in creating it, or even how it affects the underlying database. We have now come to that time. We'll detail two sets of concepts:

- Creating a fully functional domain model with constraints and relationships

- Understanding how these domain objects create and interact with the database

First, let's re-create the Todo domain object. We're doing this not because we want to waste more of your time, or because we get paid by the page (we don't). We're doing this because you should see what's occurring to the database under the covers when you create the tables we have defined for Collab-Todo application. While it's nice that the ORM tools isolate you from having to create the database tables directly with SQL commands, you still need to have a grasp on what happens behind the scenes.

If you have ever created a domain object in EJB3 or Hibernate, this will seem familiar. Let's refresh our memory of the Todo domain and see how it interacts with the database. Listing 6-1 contains a partial listing of the domain; we're only showing the domain properties.

Listing 6-1. *Revisiting the Todo Domain*

```
class Todo {

    static belongsTo = [User, Category]

    User owner
    Category category
    String name
    String note
```

```
    Date createdDate
    Date dueDate
    Date completedDate
    String priority
    String status


    ...

}
```

You might be wondering, "What is GORM doing when it stores the domain in the database?" Well, that's actually pretty simple. Figure 6-2 shows a snapshot of the table from a MySQL database. Note how it is the implementation of the todo table seen in Figure 4-17 from Chapter 4.

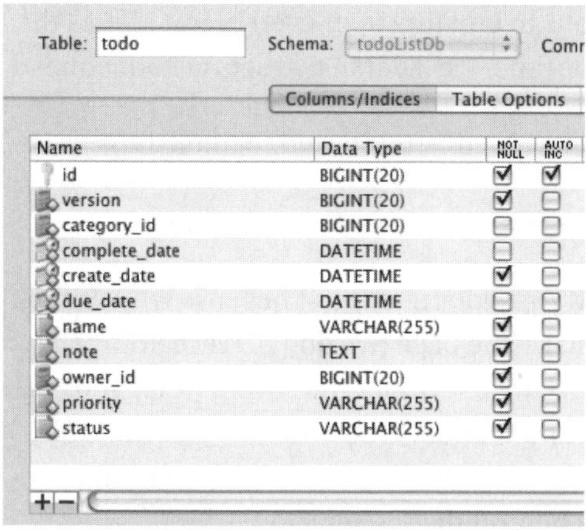

Figure 6-2. *The todo table*

If you compare this table to the domain, you'll notice a few differences. Let's break them down into a few areas.

New Columns

Probably the first things you'll notice are the auto-generated primary key ID and the version. The ID is always used as the reference for the primary key; you can access it off the domain object at any time. The ID ties the particular detached domain object to the persisted one. Hibernate also uses a version field for transactional integrity and to support optimistic locking. This works much like ActiveRecord in Rails, which allows you to have the primary key and version created for you; unfortunately, the downside is that you cannot overwrite the primary key by hand.

■**Note** It may seem like a downside that the primary key is set for you by default, but in practice, using a single unique ID primary key with Hibernate allows for the best performance when interacting with the database. We'll show you how to use mappings to change the primary key in the "Changing the Primary Key" section of the chapter.

Naming

Next, notice that the table name and column names are assigned. The names that were in CamelCase before are now switched to snake_case (lowercased and separated by an underscore).

Foreign Keys

In most databases, foreign keys or foreign key indices are created between the User and Category tables. GORM sets up the foreign key by taking the class that has the belongsTo reserved word—in this case, the Category class has belongsTo = User—and saving the user_id column in the category table to the database. The user_id column is the concatenation of the belongsTo table name with _id.

Data Type

The last thing you'll notice is the data types. For the most part, they're derived from the types you set in the domain itself. So Strings become VARCHARs, Dates become DATETIMEs, and so on. Of course, the exact type is dependent on the actual database you're using and the constraints applied to the property.

Setting Default Values

Many applications have a default value to store in the database if you don't select one for them. Setting a default value is easy in GORM; simply set the value as you would to a normal domain object. In general, a status usually has a starting value. In the Collab-Todo application, your value will not be "Completed" from the get-go, so start the status at "Started". If the user wants to change this upon creation, he or she will be able to. Listing 6-2 showcases the updated change.

Listing 6-2. *The Todo with a Default Value for Status*

```
class Todo {

    static belongsTo = [User, Category]

    User owner
    Category category
    String name
    String note
    Date createdDate
    Date dueDate
    Date completedDate
    String priority
    String status = "Started"


    ...
}
```

Large Object Types

Before we move on to relationships, let's discuss the treatment of large object types. Large objects are generally binary large objects (BLOBs) and character large objects (CLOBs) that get persisted to the database. Although we're storing objects to the database as an example and will be using it to highlight features in Chapter 8 on downloading and uploading files, we don't necessarily suggest using a database to store files. Files can be *very* large, and unless you need to version those files, it is unwise to waste the database as a storage place. Instead, use the file system to keep files. Remember that the point of a file system is to store files.

Of course, there are legitimate reasons to store files in the database, so if you want to store BLOBs, simply set the datatype to byte[]. Note that we've added an item to Todo called associatedFile. When you update the database in MySQL, you will notice that the object type created is TINYBLOB. In addition, setting the maxSize on the constraints produces a longtext column in the database when using MySQL.

Creating Relationships

Unless you're building a domain structure with only a few classes, you're bound to have relations to other classes. For example, the Todo object belongs to one Category and one User. Conversely, a User can have many Todos. We'll discuss the following four relationship types:

- One-to-one

- One-to-many

- Many-to-one

- Many-to-many

Writing relationships in Grails is relatively easy. In fact, the syntax and usage are virtually identical to Ruby on Rails' ActiveRecord. Knowing that GORM is based on Hibernate, you might expect the syntax and usage to be more like Hibernate or JPA, but this isn't the case. With standard JPA, you can create relations using annotations solely on one side of the bean. However, these annotations can get entirely too complex. For example, take the many-to-many relationship in JPA shown in Listing 6-3.

Listing 6-3. *Example of a Many-to-Many Relationship in JPA*

```
@ManyToMany
@JoinTable(name="COURSE_TO_STUDENT_TBL",
    joinColumns=@JoinColumn(name="courseId"),
    inverseJoinColumns=@JoinColumn(name="studentId"))
private Collection<Student> students;
```

Note that there are different annotations for each type of relationship. In reality, JPA configures more from the database level, whereas GORM is programmed more from the verbal level. First, we'll review the players involved, then we'll show you how to create the relationships.

Players Involved

As you saw in Chapter 4, creating relationships is quite easy. However, we'll provide an example for those who need a refresher. You'll need to modify only two pieces of code in your classes. You'll use the following two keywords:

- hasMany

- belongsTo

The next section shows examples of these in action.

One-to-One

A one-to-one relationship exists when one record in table A references exactly one record in table B, and vice versa. For example, the User table contains a reference to the Address table. There is exactly one user at one particular address. Listing 6-4 shows an example of each table.

Listing 6-4. *Example of a One-to-One Relationship*

```
class User {
    ...
    Address address
}
class Address {
    User user
}
```

■**Note** The code for the book doesn't contain a reference to User in Address, because we're going to treat Address as an embedded class. This is merely one way of doing it. We actually have no pure one-to-one relationships in our code base.

One-to-Many

A one-to-many relationship exists when a record in table A can reference many records in table B, but when those records in table B can *only* reference one record in table A. Our application contains many examples of one-to-many relationships, one of which is the relationship between the user and the buddy lists. A user can have multiple buddy lists, but the buddy list can only be referenced to one user. Listing 6-5 shows an example of this in the code.

Listing 6-5. *Example of a One-to-Many Relationship*

```
class User {
    ...
    static hasMany = [buddyLists: BuddyList]
}
class BuddyList {
    static belongsTo = User
}
```

hasMany, which is put on the consuming domain, tells you that this domain "has many" of this domain. The belongsTo keyword is on the other side of the object—in this case, the BuddyList. The belongsTo keyword refers to what properties are referencing.

Let's look at another example in the BuddyList domain that has many BuddyListMembers, as shown in Listing 6-6.

Listing 6-6. *Defining hasMany on BuddyListMember*

```
class BuddyList {
    static hasMany = [members: BuddyListMember]
    ...
}
```

Here, members references the variable name you'll use to retrieve the BuddyListMembers from the BuddyList object. This is just one side of the relationship. The other side is actually the more important side and is what ties the constraints together in the database.

Listing 6-7 shows how to define belongsTo on the BuddyList object.

Listing 6-7. *Defining belongsTo on BuddyListMember*

```
class BuddyListMember {
    static belongsTo = BuddyList
}
```

Putting this static reference on belongsTo tells the BuddyListMember class to put a reference to BuddyList in BuddyListMember's table upon database creation.

Managing Relationships

Adding to the relationships is quite easy and makes use of Groovy dynamic syntax. Listing 6-8 shows how to add and remove members from BuddyList.

Listing 6-8. *Adding BuddyList to and Removing BuddyList from BuddyListMember*

```
BuddyList myList
myList.addToMembers(someMember)
myList.removeFromMembers(someMember)
```

Many-to-One

As you've probably guessed, a many-to-one relationship is a complete inverse of the one-to-many relationship. Listing 6-5 shows a many-to-one relationship from the point of view of the buddy list. This is an example of what we meant when we said that GORM is more intuitive than JPA. JPA would have included an @ManyToOne annotation.

Many-to-Many

The many-to-many relationship further demonstrates the distinction between the way GORM and JPA implement relationships. A many-to-many relationship looks much different and is more readable than the many-to-many relationships in JPA. Readability is part of the goal of using dynamic languages such as Groovy and Ruby.

In a many-to-many relationship, a record in table A can reference multiple records in table B. Conversely, a record in table B can reference multiple records in table A. To set this up, you use the same keywords you used previously, so you have nothing new to learn. Both records contain hasMany, because they both reference many records in the other table. In addition, at least *one* class needs belongsTo to create the relation (it doesn't matter which one). Listing 6-9 shows an example of implementing a many-to-many relationship between the Todo and Keyword domains.

Listing 6-9. *Example of a Many-to-Many Relationship*

```
class Todo {
    static hasMany = [keywords: Keyword]
}
class Keyword {
    static belongsTo = Todo
    static hasMany = [todos: Todo]
}
```

Here, you can add and remove the keywords the same way you did in Listing 6-8.

DOMAIN-TO-DATABASE TRANSLATION

One of the biggest challenges when using JDO is successfully translating your domain objects to the database. With Hibernate and EJB3, you can easily add options to change anything, including intermediate tables.

However, this is not always the case with Grails. While it is possible in Grails to be fully customized (because you can create your own mapping files), it is not advisable. In some of Grails' earlier releases, you could only change the name of the tables without having to create your own Hibernate configuration files. With the advent of mappings in more recent releases, you can change more and more areas. You're still somewhat limited (mostly in regards to intermediary tables), but for the most part, you can still make your DBAs happy with standard naming conventions.

Overwriting Default Settings

Now that we've established the basic rules of domain creation, you should be able to do everything you need to create your domain objects. There are a few items we have not covered yet, such as constraints, but we'll wait until the "Validation" section. In this section, we'll go over a few "advanced" settings for domain items. First, we'll show you how to fine-tune your tables, columns, and indexes for specific names and values. You could configure these items in a Hibernate configuration file, but we'll show you how to configure them in DSLs. In addition, we'll show you how to add properties to domains that are not persisted, and we'll explain how to fire events when inserting, updating, and deleting a table.

Adjusting the Mappings

One of the downsides to Ruby on Rails' ActiveRecord is the lack of ease in being able to adjust the names of the tables and columns on the database itself. This might seem like a trivial problem to have, but the truth is that if you've ever worked in any large corporate environment, you've probably encountered database administrators who want the database tables and columns to be named a certain way. Sometimes it's for good readability, and other times it's just they way they've been doing things for 30 years. The fact remains, you'll have to conform to their standards to push your application to production.

Luckily, GORM allows you to adjust these settings in a DSL way without the need for extra configuration files, as Hibernate requires. To demonstrate, we'll customize the Todo domain. By the end, you'll be able to see those changes reflected.

To make these adjustments, you need to add a static mapping closure to the domain object. The additional code simply adds to those static mappings. Check out the adjustment to Todo in Listing 6-10.

Listing 6-10. *Todo with the Mapping Closure Defined*

```
class Todo {
    ...
    static mapping = {
        // insert mappings here
    }
}
```

Now you can start adding to the static mappings, slowly growing the mapping for added functionality.

Table and Column Naming

First, change the table name and a column name; these are common changes to those in an enterprise environment. To change the table name persisted from `todo` to `todo_tbl`, add the following line to the mapping:

```
table 'todo_tbl'
```

This simply tells GORM that the `table` is named `todo_tbl`.

That was easy enough. Now, let's update the column names. Because a table can have multiple columns, column names are grouped together under one subblock in the mapping. Change the name of the `name` and `note` to `name_str` and `note_str`. This naming convention is somewhat common for DBAs, who like to see the column type simply by glancing at the column name. To do this, add the following code to the mapping:

```
columns {
        name column:'name_str'
        note column:'note_str'
    }
```

GORM reads this as, "For `columns`, the `name` property references `column name_str`."

Changing the Primary Key

Earlier versions of Grails provided no easy way of changing the primary key that the column goes off of. Even worse, you couldn't change the generation method. While this probably didn't affect smaller shops, it likely affected large companies, many of which demanded that DBAs use stored procedures or other techniques to generate a primary key. First, we'll go over how to change the generator, then we'll discuss how to change the primary key itself.

By default, the generator uses the native implementation of the database. This could be an identity or a sequence, depending on the database. However, let's say you want to change it to use a high-low method of determining the number. You would add this entry to your mapping:

```
id generator:'hilo', params:[table:'hi_value',column:'next_value',max_lo:100]
```

This entry starts off with identifying itself by referencing to the `id` property, which is the default property on the domain. Next, `generator` defines the generator to be used, and `params` defines the parameters to pass into the generator. For a high-low calculation, the generator needs a table name, a column in the table, and a maximum low. Remember, this is all based off of what Hibernate expects as parameters for each of the generations. We're not going to go over them here, but you can view the Hibernate generator documentation.[1]

---

1. http://www.hibernate.org/hib_docs/v3/reference/en/html_single/
    #mapping-declaration-id-generator

The other common approach to creating primary keys is to use a composite key, which has multiple attributes. In the example, this could be a combination of the name and the due date, the name and the user ID, and so on. Before we explain how to change the primary key to a composite key, we recommend that you don't do this unless you have to. Many would think of it as just poor design; however, the more important reason not to change it from a single ID is the fact that Hibernate performs *best* when using a primary key generated by one column.

This being said, let's take a look how to do it. Suppose you want the primary key to be the name plus the due date, because you cannot have the same named item due on the same date. Defining it is as simple as adding a composite ID entry in the mapping:

```
id composite:['name', 'dueDate]'
```

Note You cannot define a composite ID with a generated ID. In addition, because you can't have two different primary key techniques on one table, we've only made use of the generated ID for this chapter's source code.

Disabling Versioning

By default, GORM uses versioning to help maintain a version number in the database. Having versions is Hibernate's way of checking to make sure that as you're updating a record, someone doesn't update it underneath you. Whenever you update a record in the table, the version number gets incremented. Before the actual save occurs, Hibernate checks the version for the record you're trying to save against the record in the database. If they're different, Hibernate doesn't allow the save to occur.

While this sounds great, there may be legitimate reasons you don't want to use versioning. In some applications, it may not matter if the record has been updated by two people at the same time. To turn off versioning, simply type this command in the mapping:

```
version false
```

This eliminates the column version from your table, and Hibernate will no longer perform any version checking.

Changing Eager Fetching and Locking

When you retrieve embedded domains from the database, GORM tells Hibernate to fetch them lazily. However, if you want to fetch them eagerly, you must disable lazy fetching for the column.

The Todo object offers no good example of this, so we'll use the User object, which has an embedded address property. In Listing 6-11, you can see an example of Todo with the embedded address domain being fetched eagerly.

Listing 6-11. *Todo with the Embedded address Fetched Eagerly*

```
class User {
    static mapping = {
        columns {
            address lazy:false
        }
    }
}
```

Creating Database Indices

You can also tune the database indices from the GORM domain level. DBAs can then these by hand in the database, but many people (especially those without full-time database architects) find it easier to tune them via the application framework. This ensures that if you're using the automatic update feature of the database, the indexes will also get updated.

In the example, you'll define the name and createDate indexes. You'll name the first index Name_Idx, and you'll name the createDate index Name_Create_Date_Idx. Listing 6-12 shows you how to define the index in the columns section.

Listing 6-12. *Defining Indexes for the Todo Domain*

```
class Todo {
    static mapping = {
        columns {
            name index:'Name_Idx, Name_Create_Date_Idx'
            createDate index:'Name_Create_Date_Idx'
        }
    }
}
```

Class Inheritance

It's typical of a domain diagram to have class inheritance, but this concept isn't always typical in database design. Luckily, with GORM, it's literally as easy as extending a class. For the data model, the Admin class extends the User class. Listing 6-13 shows the Admin class.

Listing 6-13. *The Admin Class That Extends the User Class*

```
class Admin extends User {
    String department
}
```

The real question is, "What goes on in the underlying database below?" By default, it keeps only one table for your entire hierarchy. So instead of having a User and an Admin table, it has only a User table with all the data in it for all the classes. Besides the combined columns and the other normal columns, you will also notice a class column in the database, which serves as the differentiator when creating an object so you can know exactly which object you're creating it from.

This situation works well for the example, but there are some drawbacks. To begin with, if you have complex inheritance with lots of properties in the child domains, you would be creating artificially big tables that aren't always getting the maximum use. Furthermore, you wouldn't be able to set non-null columns on the child objects. If that's the position you're in, you can set the following line in the static mapping:

```
tablePerHierarchy true
```

When set to true, this tells GORM to create a different table for each object in the class, so you'll have separate Admin and User tables. Of course, the drawback in this scenario is that they will both contain duplicate data from the base class. Furthermore, if you want to query all users, you'll have to join User and Admin.

■**Note** Hibernate and JPA offer a few additional configurations that aren't implemented directly in GORM. So if having one table per hierarchy or having all the properties in one table don't fit what you're looking for, you can look at using Hibernate configuration files for these domains instead.

Turning on the Cache

One of the big pluses with Hibernate is its ability to use second-level caching, which stores data associated with the domain class to the Hibernate cache. The advantage to this is that if you retrieve the data, it will pull it from the cache instead of making a call to the database. This is a great mechanism for retrieving data that is accessed often and is rarely changed. To configure the second-level cache, you have to follow a few steps. First, update the DataSource.groovy file, then update the domain object in question.

Configuring the cache in the data source is easy. Add the code from Listing 6-14 into your DataSource.groovy file.

Listing 6-14. *The Entry to Initialize the Hibernate Second-Level Cache*

```
hibernate {
    cache.use_second_level_cache=true
    cache.use_query_cache=true
    cache.provider_class='org.hibernate.cache.EhCacheProvider'
}
```

This tells Hibernate that you want to use second-level caching and that the provider you're going to use is `EhCacheProvider`. You can swap this line out with another provider if you like; this just happens to be the de facto Hibernate cache.

Next, initialize the cache for the individual domain objects you want to associate it with. You initialize it for `Todo` by inserting the cache entry into the mapping constraints. Add the following line to your mapping:

```
cache true
```

When using `true`, it signals that the object should be stored in the cache. By default, this initializes the cache to `read-only` and `non-lazy`. However, you can further adjust the cache settings to be `read-write`, `transactional`, or even `lazy`. To do this, you use a similar entry to the previous one but with more specifics. You would create the following entry to make it `read-write` and `lazy`:

```
cache usage:'read-write', include:'lazy'
```

Besides configuring the cache at the class level, you can also configure it for embedded classes at the domain level. The configuration is virtually identical to what you did previously, except you specify the column that will be cached, as shown in Listing 6-15.

Listing 6-15. *Configuring the Cache for the Address on the User*

```
class User {
    static mapping = {
        address cache:true
    }
}
```

In addition, the same optional configurations (`lazy`, `read-write`) you applied previously can be applied to this configuration as well.

Transient Properties

In JPA and GORM, all the properties on your domain (or entity) objects are persisted to the database by default. This can be disadvantageous when you want to have properties on your domains that either are amalgamations of other properties or simply don't need to be persisted. Luckily, in GORM, you can easily mark properties to not be persisted.

In GORM and JPA, properties that you don't want to persist are called *transient properties*. In JPA, you mark each property with the `@Transient` annotation. In GORM, you create a transient mapping of all these properties.

For the example, you'll use the `User` table. Inside `User`, you want to have a `comfirmPassword` property, so you can make sure the user typed in the correct password. Obviously, you don't need the password persisted twice, so you mark it as transient. In Listing 6-16, you can see that you add `confirmPassword` to the `transients` mapping.

Listing 6-16. *User Object with the Transient confirmPassword*

```
class User {
    static transients = [ "confirmPassword" ]

    String firstName
    String lastName
    String userName
    String password
    String email
    String confirmPassword
}
```

As you can see, you still add the `confirmPassword` to the normal domain, but you also add it to a list of strings called `transients`, marking it as transient.

GORM Events

Often in normal domain and DAO architectures, you could have base save/update/delete methods. However, if you ever want to add a universal concept for a particular domain, such as updating timestamps or writing to a log, you could overwrite the method, add your own custom needs, and then call the parent method. However, GORM and some of these other more modern frameworks eliminate the need for the DAO classes and allow you to access the domain class directly. However, this can pose a problem, because now the individual developers are responsible for updating fields (such as a last-modified date) that always need to be run when updating, and writing to the log file. Yuck; this could lead to disaster.

Luckily, GORM has an answer to this problem. It gives you the ability to define these types of transitions at the domain level. `Todo` has `lastModifiedDate` and `createDate`. In GORM, you can add two methods to the domain that are called automatically before inserting and before updating the database. Obviously, the `beforeInsert` method is called before insertion, and beforeUpdate is called before updating. Listing 6-17 shows the code you need to add to Todo in order to have your dates modified at insertion and creation.

Listing 6-17. *Code for Adding the Automatic Events for Todo*

```
def beforeInsert = {
    createDate = new Date()
    lastModifiedDate = new Date()
    }
def beforeUpdate = {
    lastModifiedDate = new Date()
}
```

Now whenever a save or update is called, these two methods will be called regardless from where the save or update is called from. In addition, a beforeDelete event will be called before a deletion.

Do you detect a pattern here? Having create and modify dates is a fairly standard pattern. In order to have this same functionality on more than one class, you would have to add those seven lines of code plus the two lines to define the domains in each of your domain classes.

Luckily, as you may have guessed, GORM has a way around this. If you have lastUpdated and dateCreated named properties, you can configure GORM to automatically update them by adding the following line in the mapping:

```
autoTimestamp false
```

Note that the properties *have* to be named lastUpdated and dateCreated. In addition, lastUpdated only gets updated when the domain is actually updated and *not* on a creation like before.

Finally, there is one other way to adjust items, and that is on the actual loading of the item, or rather after the item has been loaded and all the properties have been set. Listing 6-18 contains a method that displays a message upon loading the domain object.

Listing 6-18. *Method Called upon Loading the Domain*

```
def onLoad = {
    print 'We have loaded the item'
}
```

Database Model

Before moving onto validation, let's see how all the updates to the domain model affect a MySQL database.

In Figure 6-3, you can see the output of the database structure after being created by GORM.

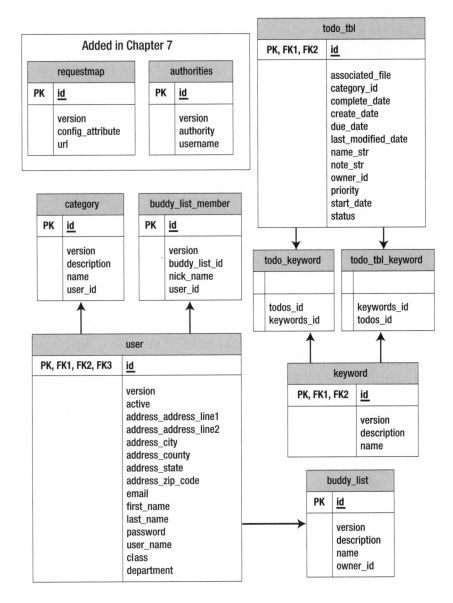

Figure 6-3. *The database model after being created by GORM*

■**Note** We kept the modifications to the generator, and we included the lack of versioning and the name change, so Figure 6-3 includes some extra tables you might not have expected.

Validation

In the previous chapters, you saw that when you executed save() on the Todo instance, GORM would only persist the data if the validations (set in the constraints) passed for the domain. The save() would return a true or false depending on if persisting was successful or not. Now the real question is, "How do you know what to validate?"

Constraints are somewhat of a dual-use item. Their main functionality is to validate items before they're persisted to the database, but they also can adjust some of the settings on the database itself for the column. For example, if you mark a column in your constraints as nullable or set a maximum length, then these changes will be reflected at the database level as well. Out of the box, GORM comes with quite a few validations, and it even provides the framework for creating a few custom validations of your own.

For the purpose of the sample application, you only need a small subset of those validations, so while we will list all of them here, you'll only use a few. In addition, just like any application, it would be impossible for all the built-in validations to cover every situation, so we'll also introduce the idea of custom validations. We will then close with a discussion about how to change the messages to something a bit more meaningful.

Constraints

You've already seen constraints in Chapter 4. These were used to determine whether some properties had to be filled in on the domain object, and also to set the order of display when scaffolding the domain. Let's expand a bit and look at what other features you can use constraints for.

You have seen the nullable constraint, which not only verifies that the object is not null, but also sets the database property to "not null" (in Figure 6-2, you can see many properties are set to "not null"). Of course, this assumes you're using GORM to create or update your database.

Let's start with the familiar Todo object, since this is the object you're going to want to apply the most validations to. Start with the basic skeleton shown in Listing 6-19.

Listing 6-19. *The Todo Object with the Validation Constraints*

```
01 class Todo {
02     ...
03     static constraints = {
04         owner(nullable:false)
05         name(blank:false)
06     }
07 }
```

In line 3, `static constraints = {` starts the constraint area. This line makes sense when you think about it. Constraints are static because they span multiple instances. The next two lines define two of constraints for you. Line 4 tells you that the owner cannot be `nullable`; however, it could be a blank string. Line 5 not only doesn't allow for `nulls`, but it also doesn't allow the name to be blank.

Using Built-In Constraints

You can add quite a few different constraints to your domain object, including everything from `null` checking to credit-card validation. In our application, we will use quite a bit of these validations, although there's no way for us to use them all. Table 6-2, however, shows all the possible constraints provided by GORM.

Table 6-2. *Constraints Built into GORM*

Name	Description
blank	Validates that the string either is or is not blank
creditCard	Validates that the string either is or is not a valid credit-card number
email	Validates that the string either is or is not a valid e-mail address
inList	Validates that the constraint is contained within the supplied list
matches	Validates that the object matches the supplied regular expression
max	Validates that the number is not larger than the supplied maximum value
min	Validates that the number is not smaller than the supplied minimum value
minSize	Validates that the object's string's length or collection's size is larger than the supplied amount
maxSize	Validates that the object's string's length or collection's size is smaller than the supplied amount
notEqual	Validates that the object is not equal to the supplied object
nullable	Validates that the object is not `null`
range	Validates that the object falls within the given range
scale	Constrains the supplied number to a particular decimal place
size	Validates that the object's string's length or collection's size is equal to the supplied amount
url	Validates that the supplied string is formatted as a valid URL

Of course, it is impossible for the Grails team to predict all the possible constraints needed by an application. Using precreated constraints is the easy part. In the next section, we'll show you how to create your own customized constraints using closures.

Creating Custom Constraints

Let's take another look at that Todo object and what other constraints you need to define for it. Let's start off by examining the startDate property and see what you need to constrain on it. For starters, you don't want to allow users to use start dates in the past. The purpose of this application is to create tasks that start now or in the future; in theory, this is something that is probably created at the beginning and never changed. Nothing in the built-in constraints shown in Table 6-2 do what you need, so you need to create your first custom constraint. You need to allow the constraint to be null, and if the constraint is filled in, you need to make sure the date doesn't occur in the past.

To define custom constraints in GORM, you will mark the custom constraint with validator. Take a look at this in action in Listing 6-20.

Listing 6-20. *Applying a Simple Custom Validator to Todo*

```
static constraints = {
    ...
    startDate(nullable:true,
        validator: {
            if (it?.compareTo(new Date()) < 0 ) {
                return false
            }
            return true
    })
}
```

As you can see, this starts off like normal validations with nullable:true, but then it adds custom validation. All custom validators start off with the word validator, followed by a closure. Inside the closure, you need to return true if the validation passes, and false if the validation doesn't pass. Of course, you cannot create a decent validation with a random closure that has no information. However, that is why you have access to the property, demarked with it, inside the validator closure. The it represents the item that is being validated. For our validation, we are going to check that the start date doesn't occur before the current date. As you can see, it's pretty easy to create a custom validation, but you can make it even more advanced.

For this next example of functionality, let's take a look at the completedDate field. It makes sense that completeDate has to occur after startDate. To create a custom validator to show this, you need to have access to the startDate object. No problem. Check out its implementation in Listing 6-21.

Listing 6-21. *Applying a More Complex Validator to Todo*

```
static constraints = {
    ...
    completeDate(nullable:true,
        validator: {
            val, obj ->
                if (val != null) {
                    return val.after(obj.createDate)
                }
                return true
        })
}
```

As you can see, this looks similar to the validator you defined in Listing 6-20, with one small change: you also pass in the variables val, obj ->. val is the variable that is passed in; the previous example used it to represent the value of startDate. In addition, you're now also passing in obj, which is the domain object you're using—in this case, the Todo object. This allows you to compare completeDate directly with that domain's createDate.

This gives you a fairly dynamic way of creating validations. In fact, you can even create queries inside the validator, allowing for some pretty slick validations. Let's take a look at the Keyword domain, which is one of the constraints. To reduce redundancy, you want to put a constraint on the name, because you don't want to have any names that are also used as names for the description. You can easily make the name a unique field, but you also want to make sure that no description is the same as the name. If there is, you're probably creating a name twice or not defining the other one properly. Listing 6-22 shows how to find all the instances of description to make sure it doesn't have the same text as the name property.

Listing 6-22. *A Custom Constraint That Performs a Query*

```
class Keyword {
    ...
    String name
    String description
    static constraints = {
        name(validator: {
            if (Keyword.findAllByDescription(it).size() > 0) {
                return false
            }
            return true
        })
    }
}
```

Calling the Validator

Validation is called behind the scenes when you do a save or when there is an update to the domain object. Of course, this prevents you from persisting objects that don't pass your own validations. However, there may be times when you'll want to call the validator manually, so you can do some additional checking on it or test that specific messages get returned. Listing 6-23 shows a simple check for a validation that is called twice. The first time it fails, and the second time it passes.

Listing 6-23. *Example of a Validation Called Twice*

```
void testValidationsOnTodo() {
    def todo = new Todo(
        owner: user1, name: "Validation Test", note:"Detailed web app description",
        createDate: new Date(), dueDate: new Date(), lastModifiedDate:
        new Date(), priority: '1', status: '1' )
    assert true == todo.validate()

    // shouldn't validate
    todo.completeDate = new Date() - 1
    todo.name = null
    assert false == todo.validate()

    // readjust the date to be in the future
    todo.completeDate = new Date() + 3
    assert true == todo.validate()
}
```

In this example, you can see that you set completedDate to the past, which is not allowed with the constraints. When the first validation fails, you update the completed date to the future; now, as you can see, the validation passes. This example shows you how you can use validation in your test cases to make sure you have an item works. This isn't as necessary for out-of-the-box validators, but for your custom validators, you're going to want to use this to make sure you wrote the validation correctly.

Validation Messages

In Chapters 4 and 5, we showed the error messages that Grails provides when a validation fails on a page. In Chapter 5, we went over more extensively how to write the error outputs to the page without using scaffolding. However, we haven't yet explained how those messages names are derived. Now that we've gone over constraints, we'll explain the validation messages.

As you may have guessed from looking at the messages in `messages.properties` and looking at the constraints, there is a roughly one-to-one ratio between constraints and messages, with an added error message for the custom constraints.

Let's take a look at the `Todo` example. We'll be focusing on three constraints: `name`, `priority`, and `completeDate`. Listing 6-24 shows what those three validations look like.

Listing 6-24. *The name, priority, and completeDate validations in Todo*

```
name(blank:false)
priority(blank:false)
completeDate(nullable:true,
    validator: {
        val, obj ->
            if (val != null) {
                return val.after(obj.createDate)
            }
            return true
    }
)
```

If you run this on one of the `Todo` pages and don't fill in the name or a date that comes after the create date, Grails will display the page shown in Figure 6-4.

As you can see, it's a normal validation; however, the messages are ugly and not something you'd want to show to your end users. As we said in Chapter 5, you could easily change these error messages to something a bit less ugly, but they would still lack specificity. In other words, right now, the messages in the message bundles are geared toward the type of validation, as opposed to being tied to the screen they originated from.

Grails does something pretty interesting. It has a hierarchy lookup of messages, and that hierarchy is based on many things, including the name of the domain object, the column, the type of validation, and the type of object involved. Table 6-3 lists the order of the validation lookup for the `Todo` domain and `name` property having a `blank` validation.

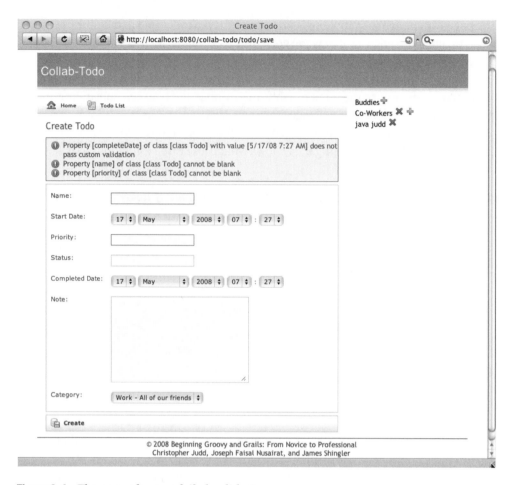

Figure 6-4. *The page after two failed validations*

Table 6-3. *Hierarchy Error-Messaging Lookup*

Order	Name
1	todo.name.blank.error.Todo.name
2	todo.name.blank.error.name
3	todo.name.blank.error.java.lang.String
4	todo.name.blank.error
5	todo.name.blank.Todo.name
6	todo.name.blank.name
7	todo.name.blank.java.lang.String
8	todo.name.blank

Order	Name
9	blank.Todo.name
10	blank.name
11	blank.java.lang.String
12	blank

As you may be able to tell by looking at the list, validation message lookup goes from most specific to least specific. At the end, if it doesn't find any matching messages, it will look up the default one originally in the `messages.properties` resource you saw previously.

Let's take a look at how to adjust these settings. As you saw in Listing 6-24, two were of the same type: `blank`. Let's start by changing that. Add the following line to `messages.properties`:

```
blank.java.lang.String=Blank strings are not good.
```

The result of changing this produces the errors shown in Figure 6-5.

ℹ Property [completeDate] of class [class Todo] with value [4/5/08 1:35 PM] does not pass custom validation
ℹ Blank strings are not good.
ℹ Blank strings are not good.

Figure 6-5. *The error message displayed after changing the first error*

As you can see, that worked. Now let's be a bit more specific. Adjust the error message *only* for the name itself. Using the uppermost name will cut down on the time of the lookup, but some of the later ones look cleaner. Let's add line 9 from Table 6-3, which creates the following text to add to `messages.properties`:

```
blank.Todo.name=The name for your To Do must be filled in.
```

Figure 6-6 shows the results this change produced.

ℹ Property [completeDate] of class [class Todo] with value [4/5/08 1:35 PM] does not pass custom validation
ℹ The name for your To Do must be filled in.
ℹ Blank strings are not good.

Figure 6-6. *The final change with the two custom validators*

Because the message is higher up in the hierarchy, both messages are now displayed: one for the priority being blank, and the other for the name being blank.

■**Note** For the custom validator, the differentiator will be the term "validator." In the example, the top line
would have `todo.completeDate.validator.error.Todo.completeDate`.

Querying the Database

Starting in Chapter 4, we gave you a fully functioning web site with database persistence. In
this chapter, we have expanded that relatively crude database, and now you essentially have
a fully functioning schema complete with constraints and relations. Now that you have this
wonderful database to use, it's time to start using it. We're going to assume that if you're reading this book, you have at least cursory knowledge of creating SQL queries. However, if that's
not the case, don't worry. Grails has made creating SQL queries extremely easy—in fact, it's
almost too easy, if you ask us.

To begin, we'll go over four different ways to query the database. This might seem
like an overly excessive way of querying the database, but in the end, you will find that
you have the flexibility to create a query with as little or as much information as you
need to provide.

We'll show you how to do simple CRUD operations. We demonstrated this in the
previous two chapters, but we'll briefly rehash it so you can see how to build up your
querying ability. We'll then explain how GORM really shows off its DSL capabilities by
being able to create dynamic queries in the form of method names. You saw a bit of this
in the earlier chapters when we did `findBy`, but now we'll show you all the options and
parameters available to you. We'll cover this for both straight single retrievals and for
retrieving multiple objects.

Finally, we'll show you how to use Hibernate Query Language (HQL) queries instead
of the more dynamic DSL queries. Sometimes using HQL is the only way to get the query
you want.

GORM's CRUD Support

When interacting with a database, you need to know how to do basic CRUD operations.
Most Java developers reading this are probably used to the standard DAO domain model,
where after you create the domain, you create a DAO with various operations. These DAO
models usually have the standard `void delete(Domain d)` and `get(String primaryKey)` methods. Before Hibernate, these methods would usually interact with the database directly
with straight SQL calls. This kind of methodology made a bit of sense when you had to write
the SQL code directly, but with today's tools and a dynamic language like Groovy, these
constraints are no longer necessary.

Hibernate helped eliminate the problem of having to hard-code SQL by allowing you
to use more abstract terminology to persist to the database. But that solved only half the

problem. Why do you even need DAO at that point? It's still a waste of programmers' time to create these DAO objects, and time is money.

Because we're using Groovy as the underlying language for Grails, we now have many more options available to us. We'll start off by looking at a test case that steps through the individual CRUD operations. Afterwards, we'll discuss the ease of operations. Listing 6-25 shows a test case for updating the User object.

Listing 6-25. *Performing CRUD Operations on the User*

```
void testCRUDOperations() {

    // Let's create the user
    def userTemp = new User(userName: 'testUser', firstName:'John',
                            lastName:'Smith', password:'pass',
                            email:"smith@gmail.com")

    // Create - let's save it
    userTemp.save()
    // grab the user id
    def userId = userTemp.id

    // Update - since we are still within the session we caught it
    // we shouldn't need to do anything explicit
    userTemp.password = 'A new password'
    // let's see if it got updated
    userTemp = User.get(userId)
    assert "A new password" == userTemp.password
    assert "John" == userTemp.firstName

    // let's show the delete
    userTemp.delete()
    // let's make sure it got deleted
    assert null == User.get(userId)
}
```

As you can see, creating, updating, and deleting are as easy as pie. None of the domain objects have a get, delete, or save method, and there are no base classes. So how does this work? It's a simple method interception, as we discussed in Chapter 3. Grails has the ability to intercept methods and provide functionality for them. The same functionality of retrieving, deleting, and saving could be done in straight Java with aspects or dynamic proxies, but you wouldn't be able to get that far, because the previous tests wouldn't compile in straight Java. Using a dynamic language like Groovy really gives you the best of both worlds. It keeps the object a lightweight object for passing between layers and storing into `HttpSession`, and it gives you the functionality of a bloated object with the get, save, and delete methods on it.

CRUD operations don't give you everything you'll need to do in an application, so you still need to create some dynamic queries. You need the options to select one or more than one record. You also may want to select records based on parameters or by interacting with multiple tables. In the next section, we'll go over creating these dynamic queries.

Creating Queries

To create the code for the Collab-Todo project, you're going to have to create many dynamic queries throughout the book. You'll use these queries later on for a variety of things, from creating user-registration pages to creating the fancier Ajax items in Chapter 8. All of these actions require various types of dynamic support, and although the query portion will not be the focus of those chapters, you'll need to understand how those queries are created and how to create some of your own queries.

Queries in GORM are different than queries in ActiveRecord or in EJB3. Because we're using Hibernate as the back end, they're obviously more like Hibernate queries. Actually, GORM has *more* options than Hibernate, because it makes use of Groovy's dynamic ability to make some DSL-type queries. The amount of options you have are the same here. Each type serves its own purpose. If you want to become a Grails guru, it's important to understand the different types. In the next few sections, we'll show you how to create the following queries:

- GORM's dynamic queries

- HQL queries

- Hibernate's criteria queries

GORM's Dynamic Queries

As you just saw, creating dynamic CRUD queries is fairly easy. However, you're only able to do a simple retrieval based on the primary key (the ID). While this is necessary to most applications, you obviously need to do more than that. In the example application, you'll need to retrieve not only lists, but also lists of people and ever more specific queries.

In the upcoming sections, we'll go over multiple types of queries, ranging from fairly simple single finds to lists, criteria queries, and HQL queries. The criteria queries will make use of Groovy the most by allowing you to create a DSL of the query you want to create. This makes for some wonderfully easy queries to create. The downside is, unlike with the HQL queries, the criteria queries are limited to querying off only one class.

We'll start by showing you how to grow some single result-set queries, then we'll go over how they work. We'll list out the options you have to create the queries, and finally, we'll show you how to create the query lists.

Note In these sections, we're going to go over many types of queries. Where we can, we'll reference code that we're actually using in our application. However, we can't show *all* the possible ways to create the queries. So to that extent, you'll also be able to find these queries in the code base integration tests in the Source Code/Download area of the Apress web site (`http://wwww.apress.com`).

Counts

Probably the easiest query to create a query is to do a simple count. The code in Listing 6-26 counts the amount of Todos.

Listing 6-26. *Counting the Amount of Todos*

```
Todo.count()
```

Besides the standard count, you can also count the amount of Todos where the columns equal a particular value. Listing 6-27 counts the amount of Todos that have a priority of "1".

Listing 6-27. *Example of a countBy Query*

```
Todo.countByPriority('1')
```

Single Result-Set Queries

Now we'll take a look at queries that return a single result set back to you. You use these when you want to find one item. We'll go over these two types in this section:

- findBy

- findWhere

Although there are two different ways of performing a query, the end result and the usefulness are mostly equal. The main difference is how the query looks and how you pass the values into the query.

Let's take a look first at the findBy example, as shown in Listing 6-28. In this query, you find where Todo has a priority of "2" and a status of "3".

Listing 6-28. *Example of a findBy Query*

```
Todo.findByPriorityAndStatus("2", "3")
```

As you can imagine, there actually is no method called `findByPriorityAndStatus` on Todo. This is one of our first examples of a dynamic query. In Figure 6-7, we have broken up this query into its individual parts.

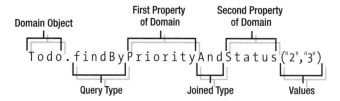

Figure 6-7. *The dynamic query broken up into its parts*

As you can see, the DSL method starts with a static `findBy` call. It then has a property name separated with an `And` and another property name. In fact, we could have added a few more `And`s if we wanted to; you're only limited by the amount of properties on the domain object. Additionally, you can separate the properties with either an `And` or an `Or`.

This approach is very useful, especially if you want to mix `And`s and `Or`s. However, if you want to build something simpler that contains only `And`s, you can use the query shown in Listing 6-29.

Listing 6-29. *Example of a findWhere Query*

```
Todo.findWhere([ "priority": "1", status: "2"])
```

Although this is a bit simpler than the previous example, in this one you're passing the properties and values into the class as a map. You pass the name of the domain's property as the key, and you pass the item you want it to equal as the value. This query is also more useful if you received a map of name values from another call.

Multiple Results Queries

The previous queries were only able to return single results; they would have thrown errors much like Hibernate does if you returned multiple results. In this section, we'll show you how to return multiple results. The way these are written looks much like the previous examples, except they return much more. In this section, we'll also add a few more select types:

- findAllBy

- findAllWhere

- getAll

- listOrderBy

- list

findAllBy The findAllBy call is similar in functionality and use to the findBy method we used earlier. Listing 6-30 shows an example of two findAllBys.

Listing 6-30. *Two Examples of a findAllBy Query*

```
Todo.findAllByName("Our First Web App")
Todo.findAllByPriorityOrStatus("2", "4")
```

In the first one, you're finding all records where the name equals one item; in the second, you're separating the retrieval with an Or, so that if a record has a status with a "2" or a "4". As with findBy, this query is able to use And or Or operations to separate the domain properties.

findAllWhere Again, findAllWhere is similar to findWhere defined previously. Listing 6-31 shows an example of using findAllWhere to retrieve all Todos that have a priority of "1" and a status of "2".

Listing 6-31. *Example of a findAllWhere Query*

```
Todo.findAllWhere([ "priority": "1", status: "2"])
```

getAll getAll is much like the get method we covered in the "GORM's CRUD Support" section. However, get retrieves one item for an ID, while this method allows multiple items to be passed through. This is a basic convenience method when you already have the IDs. Listing 6-32 shows an example of retrieving three Todos with the IDs of 1, 3, and 5.

Listing 6-32. *Retrieving Three Todos*

```
Todo.getAll(1,3,5)
Todo.getAll([1,3,5])
```

This code contains two examples, because you can pass in the objects either as a comma-separated list or as a map.

list The next method we are going to go over is probably the most basic type of retrieval: retrieving all records. This returns all the items of the domain. Listing 6-33 retrieves all the items in Todo.

Listing 6-33. *Example of a list Query*

```
Todo.list()
```

listOrderBy listOrderBy also retrieves the complete list of records from a domain, but it lets you arrange them by column. Listing 6-34 retrieves the entire list ordering by the name column.

Listing 6-34. *Example of a listOrderBy Query*

```
Todo.listOrderByName()
```

Filtering Queries

We haven't actually gone over *all* the options for queries, because there are some overlapping configurations. In this section, we'll look at those overlapping configurations, which provide the ability to set the maximum results, the fetch modes, what to sort on, and the ordering. We'll only show the code for one type, but you can use the query types equally with any of these options:

- list

- listOrderBy

- findAllBy

- findBy

Some of this code can be useful when you're attempting to get a partial set of records back—for example, when doing pagination. Listing 6-35 gets results that should be 20 through 30 back, sorting on priority and the order to be descending.

Listing 6-35. *Example of Filtering the Results*

```
Todo.list(max: 10, offset: 20, sort: "priority", order "desc")
```

HQL Queries

The previous methods for query creation allowed you to use powerful DSLs to create simple user queries. However, using these queries is like eating sushi—an hour later, you're hungry for more. These GORM dynamic queries could not perform anything too complex, such as ranges, and more importantly, they were only querying off themselves.

In many applications, you not only need to query other tables to get the data, but you also often want bits and pieces of the data back—for example, a few columns from table A mixed with a few columns from table B. With HQL queries, you can perform this task easily.

Once again, if you're familiar with Hibernate, this is going to be second nature to you. However, if you're new to Hibernate, understanding HQL is simply realizing that you're creating a query based off of what the domain says as opposed to what is actually in the database (like in a SQL query).

In the "GORM's Dynamic Queries" section, we went over two sets of queries: returning one result set and returning multiple result sets. With HQL queries, you have the same scenario plus a more general query mechanism with executeQuery:

- find

- findAll

- executeQuery

find

The first query type we'll look at is find. Listing 6-36 shows a few examples of setting up a find query.

Listing 6-36. *An HQL Query with find*

```
01 Todo.find("From Todo as t order by t.priority asc")
02 Todo.find("From Todo as t
                  where t.name = ?
                  and t.priority = ?
                  order by t.priority asc", ["Test", "2"])
03 Todo.find("From Todo as t
                  where t.name = :name
                  and t.priority = :priority
                  order by t.priority asc", [priority :"2", name : "Test"])
04 def todo = new Todo()
   todo.name = "Test"
   todo = Todo.find(todo)
```

As you can see, the one thing they all have in common is an HQL query. In the first example, the `find` retrieves all the items in the database. However, being that this is only a `find`, you better hope you have only one item in the database. The next three queries are much more specific. In the second and third ones, you're searching for a query with the name "Test" and the priority of "2". The difference between the two is how you label the variables. In second one, you do it by the order of variables. This works well in the example, because we know the order. However, if you had more of a dynamic query coming in from another source, the key/value map of the third one might be a better fit. The fourth example is what is called a *query by example*. Basically, you pass in a partially completed `Todo`, and GORM finds a match based off the items passed in.

findAll

`findAll` looks the same as the examples in Listing 6-36, except this time, you're able to return multiple entries. As you were able to filter your list and other queries previously, now you will be able to do the same here with `max`, `offset`, and so on. For example, if you took the example in Listing 6-35 and converted it to a `findAll` HQL query, you would get the following code:

```
Todo.findAll("From Todo t", max: 10, offset: 20, sort: "priority", order "desc")
```

If you'd like, you could even add a selection based on priority with this query:

```
Todo.findAll("From Todo t where t.priority = ?",
                    ["1"], max: 10, offset: 20, sort: "priority", order "desc")
```

executeQuery

`executeQuery` is a bit different than the other queries, because you don't necessarily need to retrieve an actual domain object. You can simply return columns off the domain. For example, if you want to get the names of every `Todo` with a priority of "1", you would use the query shown in Listing 6-37.

Listing 6-37. *Query to Find the Names of All the Todos with a Priority of "1"*

```
Todo.executeQuery("select t.name from Todo t where t.priority = ?, "1")
```

In addition, all the normal rules of passing parameters work for executing the query.

Hibernate's Criteria Queries

If you've ever worked with Hibernate, you're probably familiar with Hibernate's Criteria API. Perhaps you tried to do some of the concepts of projections and so on, then got confused. Sometimes the simplest criteria query seems overly complex. For those of you not familiar with the Criteria API, it's a Hibernate API designed to provide elegance to creating dynamic queries. You might be wondering why this is necessary. Well, let's think back to the HQL queries we created previously.

What if you want to create a dynamic query? Doing so would require multiple dynamic where clauses, which would require you to do multiple string concatenations and a bunch of if-then-else statements. Yuck! That just gets messy fast, and lends itself to easy runtime SQL errors—and that's never a good thing. Using the Criteria object allows you to abstract away creating the query and make it in a readable DSL way.

As we said, creating the Criteria queries in pure Hibernate is a bit of a pain; however, with the Groovy language, GORM has created some fairly smooth ways for creating these queries. In this section, we'll go over how to create advanced Criteria queries. First, we'll show a small example that demonstrates the difference between creating a query with Criteria and creating a query with HQL.

Comparing HQL and Criteria

Our first example is a relatively simple problem that you could have with any web application—even ours. Take Todo—what if you want to search based on the note, the description, or whatever field you want? This requires you to create a dynamic query. You need to store the possible values in the map where the key is the name of the field and where the value is the value.

We'll build this in a few steps to make this as easy as possible. First, we'll create the base test methods for TodoTest. Next, we'll show you the implementation of this logic if we did it in HQL. Finally, we'll show you how to do this the proper way in Criteria.

You'll be creating a query that can take in this map and do multiple ands of it on the key/value pair. Listing 6-38 shows the parameters you're going to pass through to the query runners.

Listing 6-38. *The Entry Test Case*

```
void testFindingTodosWithHQL() {
    def params = [ name: '%Second%', status: '4' ]
    def todos = executeHQLQuery( params )
    assert todos[0].name == "Our Second Web App"
}

void testFindingTodosWithCriteria() {
    def params = [ name: '%Second%', status: '4' ]
    def todos = executeCriteriaQuery( params )
    assert todos[0].name == "Our Second Web App"
}
```

These tests are relatively simple; they look on the Todo list for a name with the word
Second in it and a status of '4'. With our sample data, this should only return one record
with the name "Our Second Web App". This is the easy part. Now let's take a look at how to
implement this for an HQL query. Listing 6-39 defines executeHQLQuery.

Listing 6-39. *The Dynamic* HQL Query

```
List executeHQLQuery(def params) {

    def hqlQuery = "Select t From Todo t "

    if (params.size() > 0) {
        def first = true
        params.each { key, value ->
        if (first) {
            hqlQuery += ' where '
        } else {
            hqlQuery += ' and '
        }
        first = false
        hqlQuery += " t.${key} like :${key} "
        }
        }
        return Todo.executeQuery(hqlQuery, params)
    }
```

We won't try to claim that this is the *only* way of creating the necessary query, but it is
one of the ways. The solution contains multiple steps:

1. Create the select—in this case, Select t From Todo t.

2. Check whether there are any parameters. This is necessary because you don't want
a where clause if there are no parameters.

3. Add where or and depending on whether it's the first or subsequent property you're
electing.

4. Add the comparison. The key is the name of the property, and the value is the value
to be compared to. You see the word key twice, because the second instance will be
replaced by a prepared statement when executeQuery is called.

5. Execute the query, pass in the supplied parameters, and voilà.

If you look at that code and explanation, you'll see that it's not a pretty way of performing that query. Luckily, Hibernate has an easier solution: the Criteria query. With this, you can write dynamic queries without ever having to write any SQL or HQL code. And with Groovy, this gets even easier, because you get to use builders to create your Criteria query instead. Listing 6-40 defines the method you'll use for creating the Criteria query.

Listing 6-40. *The Criteria Query*

```
List executeCriteriaQuery(def params) {
        def todos = Todo.createCriteria().list {
            and {
                params.each {key, value ->
                    like(key, value)
                }
            }
        }
    }
```

Not only does this look better, but it's much easier to read as well. Here's the breakdown for this one:

1. Create a dynamic query on the `Todo` domain.

2. Use `and` to define a closure that then allows you to iterate through a list of expressions.

3. Set `like` with a name/value pair without any formatting.

As you can see, this is much easier than creating a dynamic HQL query. Once you're familiar with creating Criteria queries in your average Java code, you'll see that the ability to use the Groovy builder with closures is cleaner and more robust. This will become even more apparent when we increase the complexity of our Criteria examples throughout the book.

CREATING NATIVE QUERIES

GORM, like Hibernate, lets you create native queries, which go directly against the database names, columns, and semantics. We suggest that you use these *only* as a last resort, because using native queries adds an extra layer to worry about when changing the database.

Creating native queries is fairly simple. As shown here, inject Hibernate's `org.hibernate.SessionFactory`, get a current session, and create the query:

```
def sessionFactory
```

```
...
def session = sessionFactory.getCurrentSession()
def result = session.createSQLQuery("SELECT * FROM TODO_TBL").list()
```

You inject `sessionFactory` at the class level; we'll discuss injection at the end of this chapter. Please note, though, that this query has the overhead of using `ResultSetMetaData`. To avoid this, you need to add a method call to `addScalar` or `addEntity`, as shown here:

```
def result = session.createSQLQuery("SELECT * FROM TODO_TBL")
                     .addScalar("ID", Hibernate.LONG).list()
def result = session.createSQLQuery("SELECT * FROM TODO_TBL")
                     .addEntity(Todo.class).list()
```

Database Migration

Those of you familiar with Ruby on Rails are probably used to the migrations built into the Rails system. In Grails, the built-in system only allows for database creation or updates; there is no way to segregate out migrations when you remove columns, rename them, and so on. The step-like migration system of Rails is not built into Hibernate.

But don't fret; the Grails plug-in community has stepped up and offered two plug-ins that tackle database migrations. Our application doesn't really have much need for migrations, because we are creating and using the database in one shot. However, let's take a look at the power these two plug-ins can provide. Before we go on, it's important to note that although these have similar end results to Rails migrations, they're really nothing alike in execution. It's also wise to remember that if you're performing a step such as a column change, the scripts won't be able to detect this, and you should create a migration for this on your own.

The dbmigrate Plug-In

The dbmigrate plug-in is by far the simpler of the two; however, it still provides enough support so that most users could easily stick to this one without any problems. dbmigrate has two basic commands for completing the migration. The first one is:

```
grails create-migration
```

This inspects the current state of the database and the content of your domain objects. The plug-in then generates a SQL file that allows you to adjust the database to reflect what's in your domain. Then to actually update the database, dbmigrate calls the `grails migrate` command.

The LiquiBase Plug-In

LiquiBase is a bit more advanced in that it gives you many more options and allows for greater feedback if you need it. In addition, unlike the previous example that creates a SQL script for the migration, LiquiBase creates a more generic XML file that it has to reinterrupt to update the database.

You can install LiquiBase as a plug-in with the following command line:

```
grails install-plugin liquibase
```

Once installed, you have to create a change log file in `grails-app/migrations/changelog.xml`. Listing 6-41 shows an example.

Listing 6-41. *Example of a changelog.xml File*

```
<databaseChangeLog
        xmlns="http://www.liquibase.org/xml/ns/dbchangelog/1.4"
        xmlns:xsi="http://www.w3.org/2001/XMLSchema-instance"
        xsi:schemaLocation="http://www.liquibase.org/xml/ns/dbchangelog/1.4
        http://www.liquibase.org/xml/ns/dbchangelog/dbchangelog-1.4.xsd">
</databaseChangeLog>
```

Once the file is set up, you can then execute commands on it. You can find the commands at `http://www.liquibase.org/manual/grails`.

While this explanation has been brief, you can find much more detailed information about LiquiBase on its web site at `http://www.liquibase.org/`.

GORM OUTSIDE OF GRAILS

On the list of future enhancements for Grails is making GORM an independent part of Grails. This will make it much easier to use GORM outside of your Grails application. Right now, it's an integrated part of the application, but you can still use GORM outside of Grails; it just requires a few more steps.

The following is a summary of the instructions contained at `http://grails.codehaus.org/GORM+-+StandAlone+Gorm`. You must start by downloading a separate GORM JAR file from that site. Remember that the current download is basically Grails with all the extras stripped out, such as the tag libraries and GSP. The following instructions will look similar to how the Grails environment is set up:

1. Modify the `hibernate.properties` file to point to the environment you want it deployed to.

2. Put the JDBC driver for the appropriate environment into the `lib` directory.

3. Put all your domain classes in the `grails-app/domain` directory (which is the same as a normal Grails install).

4. Move the Groovy scripts that perform actions against the domain classes to the `grails-app/scripts` directory.

5. To compile and run the scripts and domain classes, you need to choose from one of three options on the Ant script: `run`, `build`, or `clean`. Run the following command to execute your specific script:

```
ant run -Drun=YourScript
```

Services

If you're a Java developer who has spent the last few years doing "enterprise development" work, you'll have to get used to the idea of controllers. It can be hard sometimes to get used to putting so much business logic inside the controller. On top of that, sometimes it's not even the correct answer. Many times, it is necessary to send the code off to a service class where you can also control the transactioning of it, the scope, and so on.

Enter Grails services. These classes are stored in the `grails-app/services` directory. Like other Groovy objects in Grails, these classes are simple POJOs.

Of course, the next logical question is, "If they're Groovy POJO scripts, why use them instead of controllers? Is it segregation for segregation's sake?" As you can guess, the answer is no. Controllers differ by the fact that they are the only items accessible directly via the GSP UI. As such, they're where the bulk of your initial interactions should go. However, imagine something like e-mail, which needs to be reused over and over again. Why would you want it in a controller? The answer is, you wouldn't. (By the way, we mention an e-mail service as an example here, because that's exactly what we're going to build in Chapter 8.)

Besides the ability to segregate reusable data, services serve two other purposes as well: one is controlling transactioning, and the other is controlling the context for the service.

Creating a Service

Creating a service is a relatively simple task, and like other Grails items, there is a command-line call. If you want to make a `todo` service, you would type the following command:

```
grails create-service todo
```

This creates two classes, as always: the service class and a test case. Listing 6-42 lists both classes.

Listing 6-42. *The TodoService and TodoServiceTests Classes*

```
class TodoServiceService {

    boolean transactional = true

    def serviceMethod() {

    }
}

class TodoServiceTests extends GroovyTestCase {

    void testSomething() {

    }
}
```

This looks like a fairly normal class that defaults with transactioning turned on; we'll discuss that in a bit. In the service, you can do whatever you'd want to do in a controller; you can call other classes, access the domain, pass in parameters, and so on.

Calling the Service

As we said earlier, you still have to go through the controller first when calling from a web page. To access the service, you use simple injection. In Listing 6-43, the controller accesses the service you just created.

Listing 6-43. *TodoController Accesses TodoService*

```
class TodoController {

    def todoService

    def process = {
        todoService.serviceMethod()
    }
}
```

If you've used Spring, Seam, HiveMind, or any other injection framework out there, this concept should be familiar to you.

Injecting into the Service

In addition to being able to inject the service into the controller, you can inject other services into the service as well. If want to use Spring, or if you have some legacy Spring code, you can also inject Spring beans into the service.

If you had the following bean defined in spring\resources.xml:

```
<bean id="customBean" class="com.CustomBeanImpl"/>
```

you could inject this bean into your bean using the ID as the name. Simply define it as def customBean inside your service. This works by using Spring's functionality to auto-wire by name.

Initializing the Service

If you recall, Spring and EJB don't always rely on constructors for initialization. The main reason for this is because often a constructor might rely on items that need to be injected (like Spring services), but these items may not be available during instantiation. If you have any items that need to be looked up at creation, use Spring's InitializingBean, which calls the afterPropertiesSet() method. Listing 6-44 shows TodoService with a post-initialization method.

Listing 6-44. *TodoService with a Post-Initialization Method*

```
import org.springframework.beans.factory.InitializingBean

class TodoService implements InitializingBean
{

    boolean transactional = true

    void afterPropertiesSet()
    {
        println "Post Initialization"
    }

    def serviceMethod() {
        println "TodoService - serviceMethod"
    }
}
```

The bold areas are the new sections. As you can see, calling an initialize method is quite simple to do, and you have access to any other services that have been injected into that service.

Setting a Bean to Be Transactional

As you might have noticed, `transactional` = `true` exists everywhere. You can control the transaction boundaries of items inside the services. When set to `true`, Grails defaults the service to `PROPAGATION_REQUIRED`. Within the services, you can even inject the data sources and get even finer-grain control.

Service Context Available in the Service

The last subject we'll cover is service contexts. Contexts have been around for a while; for a long time, we've had application, request, session, and page contexts. However, in recent years with frameworks such as Seam and, more recently, Spring, contexts have expanded to include the conversation context and others.

You can think of the conversation context as more than a request and less than a session. The data has a start, a middle, and an end. For example, take a credit-card application, which can take multiple pages to complete. It contains data that you'll want to have until the end.

We won't cover conversation contexts (also known as *flows*) in this book. However, here we'll show you how you can set the service for these contexts. By default, every context is a singleton, meaning that the whole application shares this one instance. This means that you don't want to have any data as a global property with its state specific to the user. To adjust the context of a service, add the following line to your service:

```
static scope = "singleton"
```

The `"singleton"` is the default, and if you don't define the scope, the service will be automatically assumed to be a singleton. Table 6-4 provides a list of the available contexts.

Table 6-4. *Available Contexts for Services*

Name	Description
prototype	Every time the service is injected in a new class, a new service is instantiated.
request	Each time a request to the server is made, a service is instantiated.
flash	The service is instantiated for the current and next requests only.
flow	The service lives for the lifetime of a controller's web flow.
conversation	The service lives for the lifetime of a controller's web flow and subflows.
session	The service is instantiated and kept for the life of the user's HttpSession.
singleton	This default service is treated like a singleton and shared across the application scope.

Summary

In this chapter, we covered quite a bit of information in a relative short amount of space. Database interaction is an important piece of the framework puzzle, and many books and sites are devoted to it alone.

We showed you how to create domain objects, and we explained the options used to create them. This is important to understand, so you know how our domains operate. Hopefully, you'll be able to create some of your own.

From there, we showed you how to query the domains; as you saw, there are quite a few options. Throughout the rest of this book, we will use bits and pieces of each, basically picking the best one that suits our needs at the time. Hopefully, you've gotten an idea of when to use each, but be forewarned that for many, there is no one right answer.

We briefly covered the ability to use database migrations, which is useful on systems that can change from time to time in production and when you want accurate scripts to go from each level.

Lastly, we dove into services. We will use them in various forms as the book progresses. In future chapters, you'll see how services can be useful and also how the different scopes can boost your applications performance, especially when coupled with web flows.

REFERENCES

Before we move on to the next chapter, we want to say one last thing about GORM. While covering every aspect of it is out of the scope for this book, you shouldn't feel intimidated by it. As we mentioned earlier, GORM is built on top of Hibernate, and numerous free sites and books are written on using Hibernate. If you get stuck on the HQL syntax, take a look at a few of these.

In addition, the http://grails.org web site keeps up to date on changes to GORM. Finally, if that's not enough, we want to mention one final place you can look, and that's the code itself. Often, developers write fairly ugly, hard-to-read code, especially in some frameworks. Without giving too much praise, GORM is not like that. The GORM classes are easy to read, and more importantly, they're *very* well documented in the Javadoc, and the classes are segregated logically. For example, if you want to know all the `findBy` or `list` options, look in the `org.codehaus.groovy.grails.orm.hibernate.metaclass` package (on either the source or the API). We actually came up with much of the material for this chapter by simply looking at what the code does and trying it out. We welcome you to do the same if you get the chance.

Now that the domain is all ready to go, we'll start to dive into some more interesting code in the next few chapters. First, though, you need to secure the application so you don't have other people changing your ToDos. That's what we'll tackle next in Chapter 7.

CHAPTER 7

■ ■ ■

Security in Grails

Now that you have a good foundation in Grails, it's time to move on in our programming adventure. We have already gone over how to create a basic application and completed the domain model. So what's next? We now need to address security.

Security concerns can range from actually securing a server to securing the application itself. Since this is a book about the Grails application framework, we are going to discuss only the latter. So when you read about "securing the application" or "security," we will be referring to *application-level security*.

So far, we have not addressed security at all. In Chapter 5, we used an extremely unsafe generic login, which allows you to choose the user you want to log in as. This was certainly easy to implement, but now we can move on to a more mature approach to web security.

So, what are the goals of security? One goal of security is to allow the ability to sign on as a specific user. We will want to know how to secure certain pages for those who have logged in. In addition, many web sites require different levels of access for different users. Designing your security model can get fairly convoluted, depending on your application's needs, and we have seen it reach the point where the application's design is wrapped around the security. The security needs of this book's sample application, Collab-Todo, are middle ground—requiring access control but nothing so complex that we need to build an entire system from scratch.

The security apparatus we are going to use is not just to meet the needs of the application we have created so far, but also the needs of the application going forward. Let's quickly examine what those needs are:

- *Domain/model-level security for a user*: We need to make sure that when users retrieve their to-dos, they are retrieving theirs and no one else's. We don't want people to view other's to-dos. If they could, it would quickly make our application unpopular.

- *Administrator vs. regular user access*: In Chapter 10, we are going to create a few reports that are for only administrators. This means we need to be able to secure certain pages of the site for administrators.

- *Basic access authentication*: For the web services we'll add in Chapter 9, we need to secure the site so it can be accessed through basic URL authentication.

If we dove straight into a solution for just our sample application's security needs, not only would that be a bit dull, but it also wouldn't help you out if your application happens to have different requirements.

In some Java frameworks, like JBoss Seam, there is a built-in security framework. That is not the case for Grails. However, quite a few security plug-ins are available for Grails. In this chapter, we will go over three of the plug-ins, along with our very own custom security implementation for the application. But before we start looking at the different security solutions, let's take a step back and review what we actually mean by *security*.

What Is Security?

Before we dive into our security examples with Grails, we should reach a common understanding of what security means for a web application and the issues involved with adding security to a web application. Depending on your experience in web development, this may or may not be familiar.

Although there are many aspects to security, two techniques are very common: authentication and access control. These two basic areas will serve as the core aspects for each of the security plug-ins and the custom solution covered in this chapter.

Authentication

Even part-time web surfers are familiar with *authentication*, which is the process of logging in to and logging out of a site. A client (typically the user on a web browser) sends over a username and a password. The client is then either authenticated and forwarded to a welcome screen or rejected and kept on the login page. Figure 7-1 illustrates basic authentication.

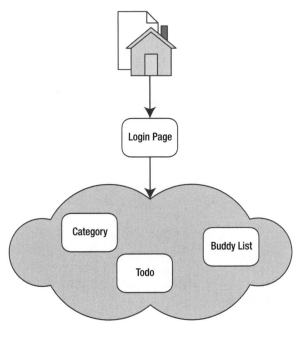

Figure 7-1. *Basic authentication*

The login username and password sent to the server typically correspond with entries in a database. Since this information is in a database, it is not really that secure, so most web sites will not store the password in clear text. Generally, the password will be hashed, and the hash of it will be saved. The value of using a hash is that it is only a one-way manipulation of the data, as opposed to encryption, where data can be scrambled and then unscrambled given the right key. When a password is hashed, if someone gains access to the database and retrieves the password in an illegal way (like hacking the box), he will need to spend some trying to determine what the original string was.

HASHING TECHNIQUES

Throughout this chapter, we will be hashing passwords prior to storing them in the database. *Hashing* is a cryptographic technique to take a string and output a fixed-length string that is unintelligible. Here are two examples of hashing a word with Message Digest algorithm 5 (MD5), a commonly used hash function:

```
password                - 5f4dcc3b5aa765d61d8327deb882cf99
josephsPassword         - 32c6f5140cbd510d57e87bc5aeea1f60
```

As you can see, although the lengths of the strings to be hashed differ, the hash length is the same—a 32-character hex string.

A variety of techniques to produce hashes are available. The more secure the hash, the longer it will take to create and the more space it will consume in the database.

For hashing in Java, and specifically Grails, a common technique is to use `DigestUtils` in the package `org.apache.commons.codec.digest.DigestUtils`. This class contains a variety of methods to produce different types of hashes. Let's take a quick look at the three methods we will be using in this chapter:

- `DigestUtils.md5(java.lang.String data)`: This method will produce a 16-element `byte[]` using MD5 as its digest mechanism.

- `DigestUtils..md5Hex(java.lang.String data)`: This method also uses MD5, but will create a 32-character hex string.

- `DigestUtils.shaHex(java.lang.String data)`: This method will create a 32-character hex string as well, but uses SHA-1 as the digest mechanism.

See the `DigestUtils` API for other hashing options.[1]

When creating authentication for a corporate web site, you don't want to overburden the user with the need to remember a lot of login credentials, nor do you want to overburden yourself with the task of managing them. If you are creating an internal site for a big business, or even an external site where multiple business entities can interact, you probably do not want a person to need to create a new username and password for each site. For one thing, it's annoying. For another, if you need to remove that person's login credentials (for example, because she has left her job and should no longer be able to log in to an internal site), it would be difficult to contact every single business unit that the user may have an account with and get them to delete the user. That is why many companies use a centralized authentication server, something like a Lightweight Directory Access Protocol (LDAP) server.

As we go through each of the solutions in this chapter, you will notice that there are slightly different ways to authenticate a user.

Access Control

So now that we have discussed the ability to log in, what's next? We also need some sort of permissions mechanism. The following are common forms of access control:

---

1. `http://commons.apache.org/codec/apidocs/org/apache/commons/codec/digest/DigestUtils.html`

Session validation: This is probably the simplest form of authentication. It just involves checking if there is a valid session. Generally, this is used in conjunction with user authentication. For the Collab-Todo site, we will take this approach to make sure that users have been authenticated and their session is active.

User: One way to secure pages and data is on the user level itself. Many web sites that require authentication use data at the user level to retrieve items that are specific to a particular user. With this level, you store user data to the session, and then whenever you need to do a query against a back-end system, you retrieve only the data for that user. This is how our application will work.

Roles: You can assign users to roles to provide coarse-grained permissions to pages or even just areas of a page. An internal site may have roles like manager, developer, trainee, and so on. For example, a site that handles work orders could allow a worker to work on a variety of tickets, but the page that assigns or approves the tickets is accessible only to the manager. In addition, the ticket itself may have a Delete button available only to the manager. A more common approach, and the one we will take for our application, is to have two roles: an admin and a regular user. The admin role can access more functionality than is available to the regular user role. The nice thing about roles is that you can assign multiple people to a single role, and even provide multiple roles to a single user. Unfortunately, roles do not, in general, provide for fine-grained control.

Permissions: For fine-grained control, we turn to permissions. With permissions, you can give only certain users access to certain portions of a site. Returning to the example of work order tickets, what if you wanted to allow some users to create and delete tickets; others to just view them; and others to create, edit, and delete them? This could be accomplished with roles, but you would need a lot of them, so it would get messy fast. Both assigning and managing all those roles would be a burden. Using permissions is easier.

Rules: Some sites use a rule-based access control. Systems like JBoss Seam use a rules engine (like JBoss Drools) to determine authentication privileges while also using permissions and roles. This provides for an extremely flexible authentication mechanism. However, it also requires more configuration and general knowledge of how to use the rules engine.

These are basic security concepts. As you may have noticed, each successive one provides more flexibility, but with the added flexibility comes more overhead. So the trick for you as the developer will be to pick the items you need that give you a balance between flexibility and ease of implementation. Keep this in mind as we discuss each security solution in this chapter.

BOOTSTRAPPING

One of the directories that Grails creates for you when you create a Grails application is `grails-app/conf`. This directory contains configuration files, including a bootstrap file, `Bootstrap.groovy`. We have not made use of this file yet; however, that will change in this chapter. If you are familiar with the Java Persistence API (JPA), the `Bootstrap.groovy` is much like the `import.sql` file, only smarter and more powerful.

The traditional Java EE bootstrapping mechanism is to preload the database. This could be to populate a preferences type table or to load some sample data. However, Grails not only allows for the population of the database, but also to the servlet context if desired. You can use actual Groovy code for the bootstrap file, as opposed to just SQL code, as in JPA.

When we add security in this chapter, we will want to do some prepopulation of the database. One reason is that we are going to store permissions in the database. Additionally, we want to have a few users prepopulated for the examples.

Bootstrapping itself is relatively easy. Here is an example of the bare minimum code in the `Bootstrap.groovy` file:

```
class BootStrap {
    def init = { servletContext ->
    }
}
```

The `init` method is the method the application will call, passing in the `servletContext`. This will allow us to have access to the servlet context in case we need to add data to it. Within this context, we can do normal database insertions to add sample data. For example, to insert a user, you would add the following line:

```
new User(userName: 'joseph', firstName: 'Joseph', lastName: 'Nusairat',
        email: 'jnusairat@integrallis.com', password: pass).save()
```

You just instantiate a `new User` and then save it. This method of adding data will be the same throughout this chapter and the rest of the book.

While using the bootstrap file can be a useful tool to warm the database, if you are using this in a full development, test, or production environment, you should consider one additional item. If you are using it to prepare static tables like roles or permission names, these are, across the board, global constraints. However, if you are going to prepare sample data, like users and to-dos, you do not want this data in your production database. Luckily, within Grails, there is an easy way to configure your bootstrap file to only write to different environments. You can detect the environment you packaged the application to be deployed to and specify that variable in the bootstrap file. For example, using the following code, you can create common methods or custom methods for the development and production environments:

```
import grails.util.GrailsUtil
. . .
```

```
switch(GrailsUtil.environment) {
    case "development":
        configureForDevelopment()
        break
    case "production":
        configureForProduction()
        break
}
```

In this chapter, we will not present all of the `Bootstrap.groovy` file, but will show bits and pieces of what we are adding to it. The complete file is available with this book's downloadable source code.

An Overview of Grails Security Solutions

Two of our favorite shows on TV right now are *Project Runway* and *Hell's Kitchen*. These shows have experts in their fields (either designers or chefs) who are given the task of creating something unique and awesome, and then their efforts are judged. It's decided which is best, or at least which one each judge likes the best. Security, and especially security in Grails, is something like that. You have many experts in the field creating different security frameworks, each with pluses and minuses, and you must judge which one is better.

Grails is truly a unique Java framework. While some frameworks suffer from the underlying code being unstable, Grails really does not have this problem since it uses two well-established frameworks at its core (JBoss Hibernate and Spring). However, it suffers from being new, which brings about a lack of 100% mature plug-ins for it. Although the developers of these plug-ins are working hard to keep up-to-date with changes in Grails, all of the plug-ins are relatively new, as indicated by their .1 or .2 statuses. Therefore, when you deal with these plug-ins, you may encounter some not-so-polished features.

Much like our favorite TV shows, when it comes to security plug-ins, there is rarely a clear winner, and odds are there never will be. Each plug-in serves a particular niche market. Which one you choose will greatly depend on your specific requirements.

The Grails security plug-ins we will examine in this chapter are JSecurity, CAS, and Acegi. Additionally, we will demonstrate how to implement your own custom security, which can work well for either simple sites or very complex sites where control is strict.

We will start with the custom security implementation, and then move on to the different plug-ins (note that the order we are discussing the solutions in is purely arbitrary and does not represent any superiority of each). In the end, we will use the Acegi plug-in as our solution, because it meets the needs outlined at the beginning of this chapter.

> ■**Note** When examining the plug-ins in this chapter, keep in mind that none of these is in itself a specific security solution for Grails. What has been developed thus far are wrappers for existing security mechanisms.

Because our approach in this chapter is to show you multiple paths but only go with one, we decided to do something a bit different with the code examples in this chapter. Normally, each chapter's code builds on the previous chapter's code—that is the nature of building an application. In the previous chapter, we added quite a bit to our domain model. Most of this is unnecessary from a pure security point of view. We feel it's not necessary to add that complexity here. So for all the examples (except the Acegi one), we will be using the code from Chapter 5. For the Acegi plug-in example, we will use the code from Chapter 6.

One of the first items you will notice when we talk about the plug-ins is that many have their own User classes. This can pose a problem, because you are going to want to tie your User object on your domain to the plug-in's user class. You will want to tackle this problem during authentication, and there are essentially two ways to solve this problem:

- If the domain model is created after plug-in creation, the set of user domain objects the plug-in creates can either be moved into the grails-app/domain directory or referenced directly in your application. The only reason to move them is if you want to make changes to the domain.

- You can have the plug-in's domain object and your domain object linked by username after authentication. Since this is a unique field, after authentication has been verified, you can look up your user in the database and save your user to the session. This provides a nice balance of keeping your application uncoupled while at the same time totally relying on the plug-in for security. This is the approach we'll take in this chapter.

Custom Security Implementation

We are starting with the most basic approach to securing a web site, which is our custom security implementation. But using a simple security apparatus does not means your web site is simple. The two are not really related. It is just about picking the right security for your application.

> ■**Note** The term *custom implementation* may be a bit confusing. This approach is not truly "custom." Many applications use this same approach. In fact, it's a very common implementation. We call it custom because it doesn't use a security plug-in (other than the CAPTCHA one).

One of the main needs of any user-based application is to authenticate the users. With our application, the majority of the pages are driven by which user is accessing the page. The to-dos that appear are only for the logged-in user, users add buddy lists for themselves, and so on. We also need to make sure the user is authenticated before accessing any page except the login page. This is a fairly simple authentication pattern, and we will be using a User object in the session to check the access to the pages. (We will use the User object in the session in the other plug-ins, but the difference is we are not using it for page-level authentication purposes.)

In this section, we are going to adjust the user-creation procedure. Note that for our custom security implementation, we do not need any new domain classes. We will use the domain classes we created in Chapter 5. Our main focus will be on manipulating the User class. Now we will be adding a password confirmation and a CAPTCHA challenge.

CAPTCHA

While you may not be familiar with the term *CAPTCHA*, you probably have encountered such a challenge. For example, you may have gone to a web site and seen an image like this:

This image is part of a CAPTCHA (for Completely Automated Public Turing Test to Tell Computers and Humans Apart). You're asked to type in the text you see in the image. The purpose is to help prevent automated computer programs from gaining access to your site, and for the most part, CAPTCHAs work. They are not unbreakable, but depending on the complexity of the CAPTCHA, decoding the image requires a fairly complex neural network. CAPTCHAs are used on a variety of sites. For example, ticketmaster.com has a fairly complex set (and we admit to missing a few on that site).

Even simple sites are subject to spammers. When we launched our company's web site at http://www.integrallis.com, within a few days, we were getting hit by spam via our Contact Us link. Now that we have added the CAPTCHA, the only e-mail we get is from real people.

In order to create the custom security solution, we will cover three aspects of its design and implementation:

- Registering a user

- Logging users in and out

- Securing the controllers

Registering a User

In order to register a user, we will need to add two items: a registration page (`register.gsp`) and an action to register the user in the `UserController`. As noted, we will use a CAPTCHA challenge on the registration page, so we need to install the plug-in for that.

Installing the Captcha Plug-in

The CAPTCHA is being added only to the registration page because it is the only page on the site that could be easily affected by spammers. The other parts of the application require authentication before users even get to the page.

For the registration page with the CAPTCHA, we will be using the Simple Captcha plug-in[2] for the creation of the CAPTCHA. Let's install the plug-in:

```
> grails install-plugin /home/user/captcha.zip
```

■**Note** You will need to download this plug-in directly, as there is no registered shortcut for it at the time of writing.

JCAPTCHA

There actually is another, more advanced CAPTCHA plug-in out there called JCaptcha.[3] It allows for more customization on the output of the look of the CAPTCHA. It also lets you use a `.wav` file CAPTCHA (which would be used by web users with vision difficulties).

JCaptcha does require a bit more configuration, and we did not include it here for that reason. But we highly recommend it for a production site (there actually have been lawsuits against sites that are not usable by the blind).

Now that we have the Grails Captcha plug-in installed, and we have the domain objects from Chapter 5 installed, it's time to go ahead and get this working. Let's start with the registration page section.

---

2. http://grails.org/Simple+Captcha+Plugin
3. http://grails.org/JCaptcha+Plugin

Implementing the Registration Page

Our registration page is going to look like the page to add a user, except we will have a field to confirm the password and the CAPTCHA image. So, we will start by copying the file views/user/add.gsp to register.gsp. This allows us to preserve the add.gsp page.

Listing 7-1 shows the code for register.gsp, with the new sections for the password confirmation and the CAPTCHA link in bold.

Listing 7-1. *The Form Section of register.gsp*

```
<g:form action="handleRegistration" method="post" >
  <div class="dialog">
    <table>
      <tbody>
        <tr class='prop'>
          <td valign='top' class='nameClear'>
            <label for="login">Login:</label>
          </td>
          <td valign='top'
              class='valueClear ${hasErrors(bean:user,field:'userName','errors')}'>
            <input type="text" name="userName" />
          </td>
        </tr>
        <tr class='prop'>
          <td valign='top' class='nameClear'>
            <label for="password">Password:</label>
          </td>
          <td valign='top'
              class='valueClear ${hasErrors(bean:user,field:'password','errors')}'>
            <input type="password" name="password" />
          </td>
        </tr>
        <tr class='prop'>
          <td valign='top' class='nameClear'>
            <label for="confirm">Confirm Password:</label>
          </td>
          <td valign='top'
              class='valueClear
                    ${hasErrors(bean:user,field:'password','errors')}'>
            <input type="password" name="confirm" />
          </td>
        </tr>
```

```
        <tr class='prop'>
          <td valign='top' class='nameClear'>
            <label for="firstName">First Name:</label>
          </td>
          <td valign='top'
             class='valueClear
                      ${hasErrors(bean:user,field:'firstName','errors')}'>
            <input type="text" name="firstName" />
          </td>
        </tr>
        <tr class='prop'>
          <td valign='top' class='nameClear'>
            <label for="lastName">Last Name:</label>
          </td>
          <td valign='top'
             class='valueClear ${hasErrors(bean:user,field:'lastName','errors')}'>
            <input type="text" name="lastName" />
          </td>
        </tr>
        <tr class='prop'>
          <td valign='top' class='nameClear'>
            <label for="email">Email:</label>
          </td>
          <td valign='top'
             class='valueClear ${hasErrors(bean:user,field:'email','errors')}'>
            <input type="text" name="email" />
          </td>
        </tr>
        <tr class='prop'>
          <td valign='top' class='nameClear'>
            <label for="code">Enter Code:</label>
          </td>
          <td valign='top' class='valueClear'>
            <input type="text" name="captcha"><br/>
            <img src="${createLink(controller:'captcha', action:'index')}" />
          </td>
        </tr>
      </tbody>
    </table>
  </div>
```

```
<div class="buttons">
  <span class="button">
    <input class="save" type="submit" value="Register"></input>
  </span>
</div>
</g:form>
```

The line with the `captcha` reference is the plug-in's CAPTCHA controller. The controller will create a word, save the word in clear text to a session variable, and then output the image in a distorted manner. Figure 7-2 shows the registration page.

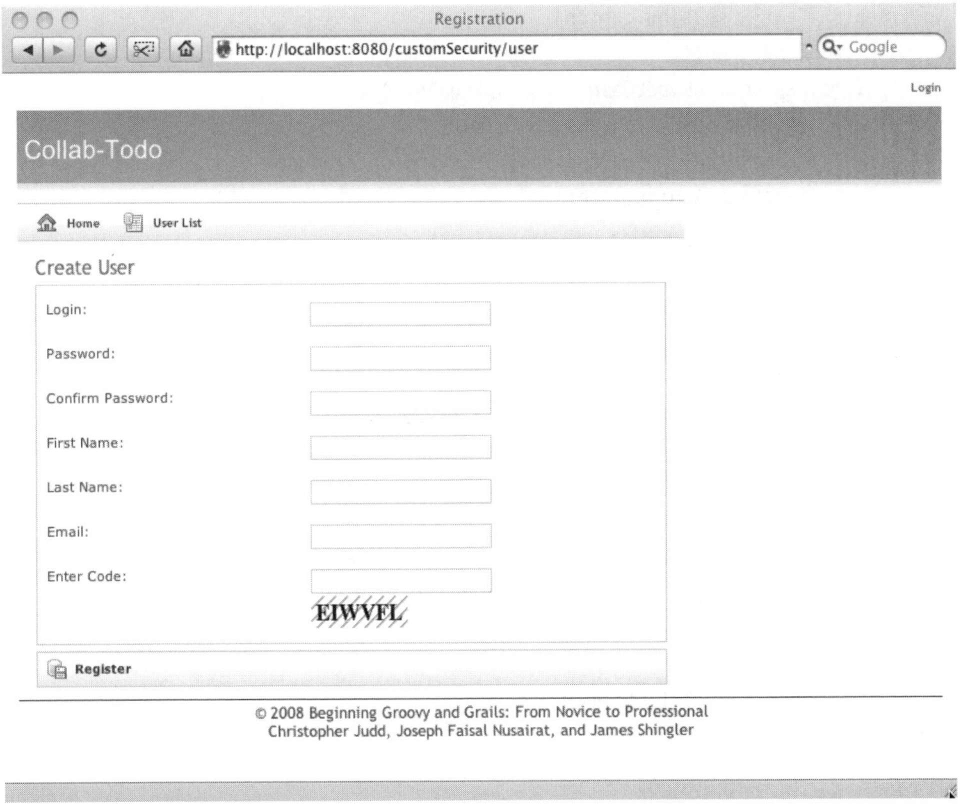

Figure 7-2. *The register.gsp page with the password confirmation and CAPTCHA image*

Adding the Registration Action to the Controller

Putting the CAPTCHA on the GSP is only half the battle in creating our CAPTCHA challenge. The other half is handling it on the server side. Unfortunately, there is nothing that automatically intercepts the CAPTCHA when used to verify the image. We need to code this by hand.

In our UserController registration action, we will add a check to make sure the CAPTCHA the user entered matches the CAPTCHA given. You can see our registration action in Listing 7-2. This will check that the CAPTCHA matches, and then if it passes validation, allow for the user to register.

Listing 7-2. *The Action That Will Register a User in the UserController*

```
def handleRegistration = {
    def user = new User()
    log.info("HANDLE REGISTRATION")
    // Process the captcha request
    def captchaText = session.captcha
    session.captcha = null
    if (params.captcha.toUpperCase() == captchaText) {
        if(params.password != params.confirm) {
            flash.message = "The two passwords you entered don't match!"
            redirect(action:register)
        }
        else {
            log.info "before save"
            // Let's hash the password
            user.properties = params
            println(user.dump())
            if(user.save()) {
                log.info "saved redirecting to user controller"
                // Let's log them in
                session.user = user
                redirect(controller:'todo')
            }
            else {
                log.info "didn't save"
                flash.user = user
                redirect(action:register)
            }
        }
    }
    else {
        log.info "Captcha Not Filled In"
        flash.message = "Access code did not match."
        redirect(controller:'user')
    }
}
```

You may notice that the CAPTCHA created is in the session scope. Unfortunately, at the time of writing, this was necessary to allow the image to spawn multiple requests (with some of the new service-level scopes written after the plug-in's creation, this requirement may change in the future). We have overcome this issue slightly by saving the data from the session to a local variable, then removing the CAPTCHA information from that session.

In addition, you will notice that, as a convenience factor, we have set the `session.user` to the user that was just created. We did this because once users are logged in, we will want other pages to know that. This information can be used to display the username or simply to get the ID for querying.

Also notice that we've hashed the password. As mentioned earlier in the chapter, hashing is a critical step, because we do not want to keep a password in the database in clear text form.

■**Note** Remember that many people use the same password for multiple sites. If you stored a clear text password and your site was compromised, you could potentially expose users' passwords to all sorts of sites and therefore valuable data. The one downside (and it's arguable if it's a downside) is that if you have a password-reminder routine, it cannot remind people of their password; instead, it will simply need to reset the password to a random string.

Logging In and Out

Now that the user is registered, the next step is to log the user in and out. This could be difficult depending on your back-end system. Logging in could involve going through an LDAP server or whatever other systems you are using. However, for our example, logging in is relatively simple, as we are just authenticating against a local database.

We will preserve the general feel of the login page we had before, except now instead of choosing from a drop-down list, the user must actually enter a proper username and password. The modified login page is shown in Figure 7-3.

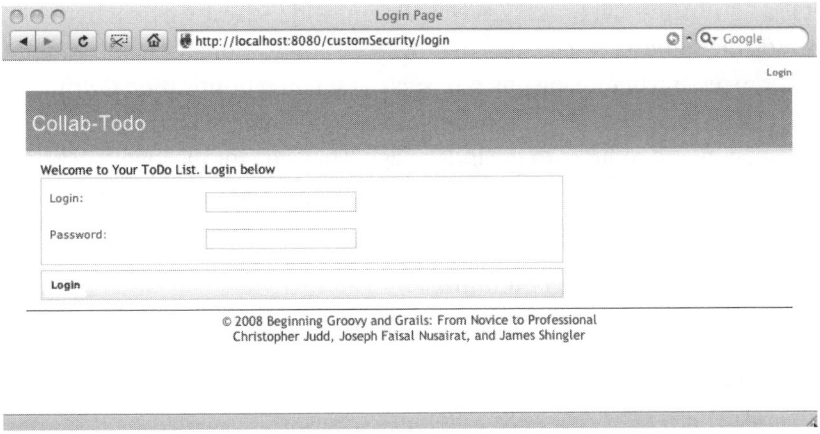

Figure 7-3. *The login page with username and password validation*

As you see in Listing 7-3, we check the user and the password in the database for a match, hashing the password passed in by the front end with an MD5 hash. If a user is not found, we will send a message to the page and redirect back to the login page. If a match is found, we will set the user in the session and redirect to the to-do page.

Listing 7-3. *The handleLogin Action of the LoginController*

```
def handleLogin = {
        def hashPassd = DU.md5Hex(params.password)
        // Find the username
        def user = User.findByUserNameAndPassword(params.userName, hashPassd)

        if (!user) {
           flash.message = "User not found for userName: ${params.userName}"
            redirect(action:'index')
           return
      } else {
            session.user = user
            redirect(controller:'todo')
      }
}
```

■**Note** You will notice that we send one generic message back. Some sites will search for the user first, and then do a check against the password. This is done so that a more specific message is sent back to the user. While this can be helpful for the user, it is also another point of exposure—it can tell a would-be hacker which part of his attempt was successful.

Logging out is a fairly universal process in web design, and the way we do it here will more than likely look the same as you've seen in other web applications. The only differences can lie in preprocessing before logging out, such as sending notifications, writing to an events table, and so on. However, we do not need any of that for our system. We will just invalidate the session and redirect to the index page. The code for the logout action is shown in Listing 7-4.

Listing 7-4. *The Logout Action of the LogoutController*

```
def logout = {
        log.info 'logout'
        if(session.user) {
```

```
        session.user = null
        session.invalidate()
        redirect(controller:'login')
    }
}
```

Securing the Controllers

So far, we have covered the ability to log in and out of the site and to register a user. These are the first two steps in securing the site. Now what's left? We need to secure the actual controller pages so that a nonauthenticated user cannot access the TodoController and other controllers. The registration and logging in and out were relatively simple to code. Controller security is a slightly more difficult piece of our authentication model.

We will control access to the pages using tried-and-true servlet technology: filters. Filters are great for simple, all-encompassing procedural capture. And since all but three pages (the index, login, and registration pages are the exceptions) require a session, filters are the cheapest and most effective way to implement access control.

Filters are relatively easy to create in Grails. Unlike servlet filters, they do not require any web.xml configuration. Here, we will walk through the steps to create the filter.

■**Note** We will be using filters in the other security solutions covered in this chapter. The configuration here applies to those other solutions as well.

Let's start with the filter's name and location. Filters must be placed in the grails-app/ conf directory, and the name of the Groovy class must end with the word Filters. Since our filters are for security, we will name the file SecurityFilters:

```
class SecurityFilters {
}
```

The next part is defining the filters. We will be defining an action called filters. This is the method that the Grails framework will use to look for any and all filters we have created:

```
class SecurityFilters {
    def filters = {
    }
}
```

With the framework set up to have the filters, now we define the filters. We can have one or more filters defined inside the same class. If you have programmed regular servlet filters before, you will realize that this is a huge advantage; with regular servlet filters, you must define a different class for each filter.

You can create two types of filters:

- The more traditional type, where you define the URI to be intercepted, like this: uriCheck(uri: /user/*). The method defining this check will be intercepted anytime anyone calls anything with the /user URI.

- Capture based on the controller and action. This way, you can capture all controllers and actions or just selective ones. This is the approach we will take here.

For our application, we can either capture all controllers or be selective and individually capture certain controllers. We opted for the capture-all approach and will ignore the login and registration page in the code. Otherwise, if we added more controllers later, we would need to keep adding the login check code to each filter, which could get messy fast, depending on how much functionality we add to the site. Listing 7-5 shows the final definition of the filter.

Listing 7-5. *The Filter for Securing the Application*

```
def filters = {
    collabTodoFilter(controller:'*', action:'*') {
        before = {
            if(!session.user
                && !controllerName.equals('login')
                && !controllerName.equals('captcha')
                && ( !controllerName.equals('user')
                && !actionName.equals("register"))
                ) {
                // There is no log access in the filter
                //log.info('Redirect to login page')
                redirect(controller:'login')
                return false
            }
        }
    }
}
```

Here, we are checking the session as well as the controller and action names. The controllerName will tell us the controller that was just accessed. The actionName tells us the action that was accessed. Grails injects several properties and makes them accessible in the filters, including the following:

- request

- response

- session

- servletContext

- applicationContext

- params

Our custom security solution is a fairly lightweight security wrapper. For many applications, all you need to worry about is whether or not users are logged in, and this solution handles that. However, some applications have more complex requirements. For example, a banking application might have an administration portion of the site. The admin could log in to the same application as the regular user, so that he could mimic being a particular user if necessary (such as to assist a customer if she were having a problem with the online application). At the same time, you *wouldn't* want the admin to be able to do some things, such as actually submitting a payment. Creating such a solution requires more than just a simple authenticated validation. It requires assigning roles and permissions, and then giving each task access based on the roles and permissions. The plug-ins covered in the remainder of this chapter provide mechanisms for this type of security.

JSecurity

Of the roles-and-permissions–based plug-ins we cover in this chapter, JSecurity[4] is the simplest. In fact, this plug-in looks much like a role/permission system that you would create for yourself. So why use it? The answer is because it offers simplicity and time-savings. This plug-in allows you to use a system with code that has already been tested and created, and which is not overly intrusive to your system. Additionally, it is fairly simple to use.

Like other plug-ins, JSecurity is not just a Grails-specific framework. It is a regular Java framework with an architecture that supports multiple clients accessing a common authentication.[5] The framework even allows authentication to be specified from different providers, although we are going to go with a simple database as the provider.

In this section, we will go over the installation and basic usage of the JSecurity plug-in.

---

4. http://grails.codehaus.org/JSecurity+Plugin
5. http://www.jsecurity.org

JSecurity Installation

The installation process is as straightforward as the usual plug-in installations. Simply execute the following:

```
> grails install-plugin jsecurity
```

Alternatively, you can download the plug-in from `http://grails.codehaus.org/JSecurity+Plugin` and install it by hand.

After installing the plug-in, you need to create the realm and domain objects, as follows:

```
> grails create-db-realm
```

JSecurity Domain Classes

With the plug-in is installed, we are ready to go. However, before we delve into the details of how to use the plug-in, let's take a look at what it brings us. With the plug-in, we get a few extra domains, controllers, and GSP pages. Table 7-1 lists the domain objects provided by JSecurity.

Table 7-1. *JSecurity Domain Objects*

Name	Description
JsecUser	User object to be used for authentication
JsecRole	Role object to be used for all the roles
JsecPermission	Permission object
JsecRolePermissionRel	Object to tie the role and the permission together
JsecUserRoleRel	Object to tie the user and the role together
JsecUserPermissionRel	Object to tie the user and the permission together

One of the interesting features about the plug-in is the location of these domain objects. The `create-db-realm` call places these domain objects into your `grails-app`. (Later, you will notice the Acegi plug-in will do the same thing.) Copying the domain objects to `grails-app/domain` gives you a much easier way to customize some of those classes. However, if you do that, and the plug-in authors update the plug-in later, it could pose problems if the update wants you to re-create those classes to add new functionality. Therefore, we advise leaving the classes where and how they are created.

Now let's take a closer look at the domain objects listed in Table 7-1.

JsecUser

The JsecUser object will be used as the focal point for logging in to an application. Table 7-2 lists the attributes of the JsecUser object.

Table 7-2. *JsecUser Attributes*

Attribute	Description
username	Unique name used to log in to the web site
password	Hashed password that is used for authentication

Recall that our custom security implementation employed MD5 hashing. In the case of JSecurity, a shaHex algorithm is used instead.

JsecRole

The JsecRole object is made up of just one attribute, name, which will be the unique name of the role. Remember the role names you create, since you will reuse the names when you assign them to a user.

JsecPermission

The JsecPermission object contains the two attributes listed in Table 7-3.

Table 7-3. *JsecPermission Attributes*

Attribute	Description
type	Unique name for the permission type
possibleActions	Comma-separated list of possible actions

While a string is easier to use in a test case like this, a collection is handy if you want to create permissions in a dynamic way. The possible actions will be the actions you want to control. In our case, we will create a permission for the create, update, and delete actions, since these actually change data.

JsecRolePermissionRel

The JsecRolePermissionRel relationship is used to tie roles with permissions. Table 7-4 shows its attributes.

Table 7-4. *JsecRolePermissionRel Attributes*

Attribute	Description
role	JsecRole associated with this permission relationship
permission	JsecPermission on which this relationship is based
target	Controller associated with the relationship
actions	Actions that will be targeted by this permission relationship

JsecUserRoleRel

As you will see, roles do not have fine-grained control. A user either has a role or does not have a role; there is no halfway point. As a result, JsecUserRoleRel is a simple relationship between the user and the role. Table 7-5 lists its attributes.

Table 7-5. *JsecUserRoleRel Attributes*

Attribute	Description
user	JsecUser associated with this relationship
role	JsecRole associated with the role part of the relationship

JsecUserPermissionRel

Now that we have established a user and permission, we need to have a domain to correlate the user with a permission. Table 7-6 shows the attributes of this domain.

Table 7-6. *JsecRolePermissionRel Attributes*

Attribute	Description
user	JsecUser associated with this permission relationship
permission	JsecPermission on which this relationship is based
target	Controller associated with the relationship
actions	Actions that will be targeted by this permission relationship

As you can see from the properties on the domain, when using a permission, you can narrow the user's access with the permission based on the controller and specific actions. This allows for fine-grained control associated with permissions.

JSecurity Domain Data

Now that we have the domains established, it is time to load some extra data so that we can test the application. We will use the `Bootstrap.groovy` file to preload some temporary data. The domain objects added by this role-and-permission–based application should give you an idea of the kind of temporary data we are going to create.

We will create three different sets of data:

- *Roles*: We will create two basic roles to assign to the users.

- *Permissions*: We will create one basic permission.

- *Users*: We will create two users: an admin and a basic user.

Finally, we will assign the users to the roles and permissions.

The code described in the following sections should be placed in the `init()` method of the `Bootstrap.groovy` file.

Role Definition

The following code defines two roles: one for admin privileges and another for general privileges.

```
def adminRole = new JsecRole(name: 'Administrator').save()
def generalRole = new JsecRole(name: 'General').save()
```

Note the names. We will reuse the names when we assign them to a user.

Permission Definition

We next create a basic permission, named `BasicPermission`. Possible actions will be the actions you want to control: `create`, `update`, and `delete`.

```
def perm = new JsecPermission(type: 'BasicPermission',
                            possibleActions: 'create,delete,update')
```

User Definition

We define `user` and `admin` users. These usernames correspond with the usernames that we are creating on the `User` class in the `Bootstrap.groovy` file as well.

```
def user =
  new JsecUser(username: 'user', passwordHash: DigestUtils.shaHex('password'))
def admin =
  new JsecUser(username: 'admin', passwordHash: DigestUtils.shaHex('password'))
```

The password is a shaHex hash, and we process it through the DigestUtils utility. (We are encoding it as shaHex because JSecurity's built-in login controllers will use shaHex when we pass a password through to them.)

Role and Permission Assignment

Now that we have all the pieces of our puzzle, it is time to put them in place. We have created our roles, permissions, and users. Now we need to correlate them for the various relationships.

Let's start with the roles and the users. We created two roles and two users. We assign one role to each user. As you may have guessed, the admin role is going with the admin user and the general role is going with the general user. We save to the JsecUserRoleRel class. This class takes two attributes: a user object and a role object.

```
new JsecUserRoleRel(user: admin, role: adminRole).save()
new JsecUserRoleRel(user: user, role: generalRole).save()
```

Assigning the permissions is not as straightforward as assigning the roles, due to the generally complex nature of permissions. With each of the permissions, you have four items to worry about:

- User

- Permission previously created

- Target controller

- Target actions

The user is easy—it is the previously defined user we created earlier. The permission refers to that all-encompassing basic JsecPermission we created earlier. The next two will be items that we are creating on the fly now. These give the permission the specificity it needs. The target controller is the name of the controller you are referring to—in our case, the Todo class. The target actions are the actions this particular permission relationship relates to. This could be all of the actions or a subset. For this example, we will create only permissions to do updates and creations, not deletions.

```
new JsecUserPermissionRel(user: user, permission: perm, target: 'todo',
                          actions: 'create,update').save()
```

Now that we have all the pieces in place, let's see how we can use them together.

JSecurity Usage

With the plug-in installed and the database populated, you could, in theory, run the application, go to the to-do page, and so on. Of course, it would not really work, since we have not told JSecurity when to log in or what to control yet. Remember this is not securing the whole web site haphazardly. We need to take care of tying everything together.

Saving the User in Session

The first problem we have is that the only thing the plug-in is saving is its own user information. This will not help us, since all of our controllers require us to have a user in the session. We could solve this problem in a few different ways:

- Go into the JSecurity's AuthController class itself and add a user lookup and save to the session. But this means updating a JSecurity plug-in class directly, and that could cause problems if you ever want to upgrade to a new version of the plug-in.

- Have a base class that will look up the user each time from the username that is stored by JSecurity. This approach is effective but would become repetitive.

- Take the filter route again. You know which controller method is doing the authentication, so it's a simple matter of intercepting it and saving the user to the session on a successful authentication. This is the technique we'll use.

Listing 7-6 shows the code for a security filter that will check after authentication if the user was authenticated. If so, our User object is then set in the session.

Listing 7-6. *The Security Filter Set to Intercept and Check Authentication*

```
class SecurityFilters {

    def filters = {
        signInFilter(controller:'auth', action:'signIn') {
            after = {
                def securityContext = new ThreadLocalSecurityContext()
                if (securityContext.authenticated) {
                    def user = User.findByUserName(params.username)
                    session.user = user;
                }
            }
        }
    }
```

```
        signOutFilter(controller:'auth', action:'signOut') {
            after = {
                // Put redirect here
                redirect('/auth')
            }
        }
    }
}
```

Notice we reference `ThreadLocalSecurityContext`, which is a JSecurity-specific file that keeps track of the user, roles, and so on. We are using it here to check to make sure the user has been authenticated. Also notice that we have added a `signOutFilter`, which will be used to redirect the user to our own custom page on logout.

So now that this page is created, you can go ahead and log in and have the session created properly. You will notice this is a page from the JSecurity plug-in but using our template, as shown in Figure 7-4. This is how most of these plug-ins work.

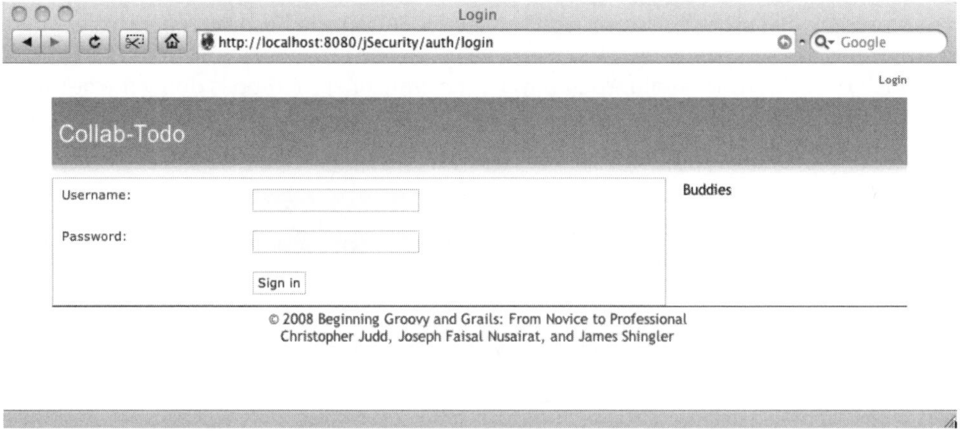

Figure 7-4. *The login page for JSecurity-authenticated application*

Locking Down the Controller

We now have the authentication mechanism set up. When you log in, it will not only authenticate via JSecurity, but it will also put the `User` object into the session; however, in reality we have not done anything yet to secure our pages.

The task at hand is to secure our controllers. We should, in theory, secure them all, but here we will focus on only the `TodoController` and look at a variety of ways to secure the page. All of these techniques have a central theme. First, you need to extend the `JSecAuthBase` class. Second, you need to overwrite the restrictions settings. In Listing 7-7, we have the base outline of what the `TodoController` will look like with these two modifications.

Listing 7-7. *TodoController Updated with the JSecurity Authentication Skeleton*

```
class TodoController extends JsecAuthBase {
    static accessControl = {
        // Insert authentication here
    }

    // . . . the rest of the methods . . .
}
```

Now we will begin the process of putting data into the accessControl block. The next examples will focus on that part of the class. As we've discussed, you can use role-based restrictions or permissions-based restrictions for access control.

The idea behind role-based restrictions is that you restrict access to the controller based on a user's membership to the role. With JSecurity, you can do this in three ways:

- Restrict access to the entire controller to the role. For example, to secure the whole class for anyone with the role General, add this line:

  ```
  role(name: 'General')
  ```

- Restrict access to one of the actions. Let's say you want to secure only the delete method, but the rest of the class can be wide open. You would add an action parameter to the role:

  ```
  role(name: 'General', action: 'delete')
  ```

- Restrict access to multiple actions. If you want to secure more than one method, you do not define multiple actions. Instead, you define an only: string. This example secures the create, update, and delete actions:

  ```
  role(name: 'General', only: [ 'create', 'update', 'delete' ])
  ```

As you can see, securing with roles is fairly simple. And you can add multiple role definitions to the accessControl block; you are not limited to defining just one role here.

The other type of security is permissions. Permissions really are about the same level of difficulty to create as roles. In fact, the permissions look much like the last two roles we created. Here is how you would create a permission on the view and just the view:

```
permission(perm: new BasicPermission('myTarget', [ 'view' ]), action: 'view')
```

And here is how you specify multiple permissions:

```
permission(perm: new BasicPermission('myTarget', [ 'modify' ]),
            only: [ 'edit', 'update' ])
```

Advanced Usage

When we wrote these examples, we assumed we were going to authenticate against an underlying database. That is one of the reasons we needed to add our own filter in the AuthController, as we did not want to tie our Todo objects to the underlying database.

As mentioned earlier in this chapter, quite often you will not want to rely on a single database for security. Sometimes, you will want to go against another system or an LDAP provider. This is where *realms* come into play. You may have noticed that when you ran the grails create-db-realm command earlier, a new directory called realms was created under grails-app. The purpose of this directory is to assist in calling out to other authentication methods.

Creating a new realm is relatively simple. First, you create a realm Groovy class. You can name it whatever you like, as long as it ends with the name Realm. We recommend naming realms after each provider you are going against; for example, if it's LDAP, call it LDAPRealm. Next, you define a few methods for it. Since we do not have interfaces for Groovy objects, it will be up to you to make sure the names are all lined up correctly with the parameters. In Listing 7-8, we have defined the skeleton structure you will need to create your realm.

Listing 7-8. *The Base Outline Structure of Our LDAP Realm*

```
class LDAPRealm {
    /**
     * This is the class of the token that will be used for our authentication.
     * If this property is not found, then realm is not used when determining
     * authentication.
     */
    static authTokenClass = org.jsecurity.authc.UsernamePasswordToken

    /**
     * If this method is present, then it will be used to authenticate against
     * the realm it takes part in. The token passed in has to be an instance
     * of authTokenClass.
     * If the authentication is successful, it will return a class that is an
     * instance of org.jsecurity.authc.AuthenticationInfo.
     * If the authentication fails, it will throw the exception
     * org.jsecurity.authc.AuthenticationException.
     */
    def authenticate(authToken)

    /**
     * Will determine if a particular user has a role or not. Returns
     * true if they do, false if they don't.
```

```
    * The first parameter passed in is a user of instance of
    * java.security.Principal.The second parameter is the name of the role.
    */
   def hasRole(principal, roleName)

/**
    * Will determine if a particular user has a permission or not. Returns
    * true if they do, false if they don't.
    * The first parameter passed in is a user of instance of
    * java.security.Principal. The second parameter is the name of the permission.
    */
   def isPermitted(principal, permission)
}
```

JSecurity is a very good basic security plug-in. It is not too heavy yet provides a wide range of functionality when it comes to roles and permissions. You might consider using JSecurity rather than the custom implementation described in the previous section if your security requirements are simple, because it can save time and you know the code has been tested.

CAS

Our third option is unique from our other choices in that it is the only one that cannot work as a stand-alone solution. The CAS Grails plug-in is a fairly simple wrapper for the Java CAS client[6] for use with a CAS server.

CAS is the Central Authentication Server developed at Yale. It is designed to allow for a single authentication system. This is useful when you have numerous organizations or systems that want to authenticate against the same system. For example, an insurance company could be selling home insurance, auto insurance, investment accounts, and term life insurance. Each of these items could be run from different business units. Each of these business units will be developing its own web site, so their users have access to their individual accounts. One of the biggest challenges of companies that have this type of setup is to avoid having the sites look like they are totally separate. They will want to allow a single sign-on. It would be annoying for your users to have to keep registering and using different usernames and passwords for the various systems.

Another issue with corporate multiple-application development is that the applications may not all be written using the same language. You could have some applications in Java, others in .NET, and maybe even a couple Rails applications. CAS is provider-agnostic

---

6. http://www.ja-sig.org/products/cas/client/javaclient/index.html

and can be consumed by a variety of languages. This means you could have a .NET application, Java application, Rails application, and so on all use the same authentication.

Since our application is not part of a multiple-application environment, the level of sophistication provided by CAS is totally unnecessary. In this section, we will go over some basic implementations and usage of the plug-in itself. While you will be able to deploy and run the sample code, it will not actually authenticate against anything (we don't have a CAS server).

■**Note** This section is provided to demonstrate the use of the plug-in, and should not be considered a CAS client/server tutorial. A basic understanding of the CAS client/server architecture may be needed in order to fully understand the plug-in. If you want to learn more, you can check out the main CAS web site.[7]

CAS Installation

The installation for the CAS plug-in is straightforward and does not create any additional artifacts in the `grails-app` directory; all that is created is in the `plugins` directory. The plug-in can either be downloaded at `http://grails.org/CAS+Client+Plugin` or installed with the following command:

```
> grails install-plugin cas-client
```

CAS Configuration

Since this application is using an outside authentication system, configuring it is rather simple. You just need to define the URLs of the CAS servers. These definitions will go in `grails-app/conf/Config.groovy`, as shown in Listing 7-9.

Listing 7-9. *The Config.groovy File with the CAS Configurations*

```
// cas client configuration, required by CasClientPlugin
cas {
    urlPattern = '/someurl/*'
//    urlPattern = ['/oneurl/*', '/another', '/anotheranother/*']
    disabled = false
}
```

---

7. http://www.ja-sig.org/products/cas/

```
// log4j configuration
log4j {
    // . . . removed for brevity . . .
}

environments {
    development {
        cas.loginUrl = 'https://localhost:8080/casSecurity/login'
        cas.validateUrl = 'https://localhost:8080/casSecurity/serviceValidate'
        cas.serverName = 'localhost:8080'
        cas.serviceUrl = 'http://dev.casclient.demo.com/access'
         log4j {
            logger {
                grails.'app.controller'="trace,stdout,logfile"
                grails.app="error,stdout"
            }
        }
    }
    // . . . production and test removed . . .
}
```

Here, we added two sections to the Config.groovy file. The first one is a required item for the CAS plug-in, which defines a URL pattern. The second is in the environments section, and it is important when you want to access the CAS server itself. It defines all the URLs to be used for filtering. These attributes once again go into web.xml, but they are added automatically during compilation of the Grails application. Table 7-7 shows the additional configuration options as well as the corresponding web.xml init-param values.

Table 7-7. *CAS URL Definition Entries*

Config.groovy Entry	Required	Web.xml Reference Value
cas.urlPattern	Yes	
cas.loginUrl	Yes	edu.yale.its.tp.cas.client.filter.loginUrl
cas.validateUrl	Yes	edu.yale.its.tp.cas.client.filter.validateUrl
cas.serverName	Yes	edu.yale.its.tp.cas.client.filter.serverName
cas.serviceUrl	Yes	edu.yale.its.tp.cas.client.filter.serviceUrl
cas.proxyCallbackUrl	No	edu.yale.its.tp.cas.client.filter.proxyCallbackUrl
cas.authorizedProxy	No	edu.yale.its.tp.cas.client.filter.authorizedProxy
cas.renew	No	edu.yale.its.tp.cas.client.filter.renew
cas.wrapRequest	No	edu.yale.its.tp.cas.client.filter.wrapRequest
cas.disabled	No	

■**Caution** `cas.serverName` and `cas.serviceUrl` are mutually exclusive. You need to fill in one or the other, but not both.

In addition, Listing 7-9 defines one other field—the `cas.disabled` flag. It works as you may have guessed. If you set it to `true`, the plug-in is disabled; if it is set to `false`, the plug-in is enabled.

CAS Usage

The usage of the CAS security is actually entirely up to you. The main goal is to pull the name of the logged-in user for the controller. You can then secure the controllers either through filters or by extending the base controller classes. Listing 7-10 illustrates how to pull the user from the session.

Listing 7-10. *Retrieving the Username from the Session*

```
def username = session?.getAttribute(CASFilter.CAS_FILTER_USER)
```

You could then use this in a base class's interceptor to perform a validation, or you could use it in a custom filter to perform the check.

The CAS security plug-in is quite easy to use and allows for simple authentication against a middle system. As we pointed out, this can be very useful in a big corporate system where you care about authentication. But what if you also want permission- and role-based access? If this is a concern, our next plug-in should be of some interest to you. The Acegi plug-in will allow you to do CAS authentication and add even more security functionality.

Spring Security (aka Acegi Security)

Last but not least, we are going to discuss how to implement security in Grails with a tried-and-true favorite from the Spring Portfolio: Spring Security, also known as Acegi Security.[8] The Spring Security framework is a subproject of the Spring Framework and was designed to give developers a single place to go for security when using Spring. Incidentally, this is also the security framework we will be using for our sample project throughout the rest of the book.

---

8. http://www.acegisecurity.org

One of the nicest things about the Spring Security framework is its flexibility. While it applies patterns to secure certain areas, it also provides a multitude of options especially for authentication. For example, out of the box, you are able to interface to the following authentication systems:

- LDAP

- CAS

- Java Authentication and Authorization Service (JAAS)

- CAPTCHA login security

The flexibility Spring Security has is one of the main reasons for its growing popularity when it comes to securing Spring applications. (Remember that Grails uses Spring as its Inversion of Control, or IoC, pattern, and, as such, Grails is in many ways a glorified Spring application.)

Acegi Installation

Installation of the Acegi plug-in is a relatively painless process. Either download the plug-in from `http://grails.org/Acegi+on+Grails` or issue the following command:

```
> grails install-plugin acegi
```

The plug-in will install without making any changes to the `grails-app` file system.

As with JSecurity, we use a few command-line options to create some Groovy classes to help set up the security apparatus. The first creates the domains:

```
> grails create-auth-domains
```

This command creates the `Person`, `Authority`, and `Requestmap` domain classes. These classes will be used for all our interactions with Grails.

You can change the domain names by appending the command with the alternative names, in the order of `Person-Authority-Requestmap`. For example, to change `Person` and `Authority` to `User` and `Role`, respectively, use the following command:

```
> grails create-auth-domains User Role.
```

Note that this is not the only way to change the objects referenced. We'll explain an alternative in the "Acegi Domain Customization" section later in this chapter.

None of the objects to manage the classes were created with the classes. For our examples, we do not need the additional controllers and views to manage them. If you want them, you can create them with this command:

```
> grails generate-manager
```

Since Spring Security is adding quite a bit of functionality, you can expect quite a few additions installed with the plug-in, including extra domain objects, controllers, and views. This can be considered a good thing or a bad thing. Some may consider it bad because you have your user and role objects predetermined for you. If you wanted to, you could work around the controllers and view pages.

The point of this plug-in is to help you automate and implement Spring Security as easily as possible. If you require customizations of the security-based objects, we suggest either writing a class to wrap the given security classes or adding Spring Security yourself. For our application, we want to use the Grails Acegi plug-in in all its glory.

As with the other plug-ins, let's start with the domain classes it adds.

Acegi Domain Classes

The domain for the Acegi plug-in adds items necessary for authentication. Three domain classes are added: `Person`, `Authority`, and `Requestmap`. These domains will be persisted to the database as their tables. In addition, the database will contain a few other tables to connect the items.

Person

The most important of the domain classes for you to deal with is the `Person` class. Table 7-8 shows the attributes of the `Person` object.

Table 7-8. *Person Attributes*

Attribute	Description
username	Login username; should be a unique name
password	Hashed password to log in with
userRealName	Real name of a user; another way to help identify the user
enabled	Flag to determine whether this user should be able to log in
email	E-mail address of the user
email_show	Flag to determine whether this user's e-mail address should be displayed
description	Description of the user; you can use this to store whatever you want
authorities	Used to store the roles/permissions that the person can access

All the `Person` attributes are not nullable, so you will need to make sure to set values for everything, except the two Boolean values: `enabled` and `email_show`. However, these two are `false` by default. This means that if you do not explicitly set `enabled` to `true`, you are going to have a user that cannot log in, which we doubt is anyone's goal.

Authority

The Authority class is in charge of creating roles that can be used for privilege creation later on. Roles are not associated on a one-to-one basis with the Person object. The Person object can have multiple roles assigned to it. This allows you a lot of flexibility. The Authority class has only two attributes, as you can see in Table 7-9.

Table 7-9. *Authority Attributes*

Attribute	Description
description	Description of the role you are creating
authority	Name for the role; should be unique (although this is not enforced from a constraint level)

By standard convention, you should label all of your authorities starting with ROLE_, although it's really up to you what you call them. While it can be confusing that an Authority class has an attribute labeled authority, you can think of it as a name attribute.

Requestmap

The Requestmap class is used to define which pages to secure and which kind of permission to secure it with. Its attributes are listed in Table 7-10.

Table 7-10. *Requestmap Attributes*

Attribute	Description
url	Relative URL of the resource to protect
configAttribute	Permission needed to access the resource

The url will be a relative URL, so you do not need to define the application context. The URL form controls how security is applied:

- To secure an entire site, use /**.

- To secure an entire controller, use */controller/***. For example, /todo/** secures any action called on the Todo controller.

- To secure a specific action on the controller, use */controller/action/***. For example, /user/list/** secures any calls made to the list action of the User controller.

As you can see, this can give you quite a bit of flexibility in defining how you want to secure your application.

The next part is where you use the roles you defined previously. `configAttribute` contains the attribute you are securing against. Now what may strike you at first is that this is a string field and not an actual `Authority` object. The reason for this is not due to an oversight of the developers, but because the roles you define are not the only items you can place in the `configAttribute`. There are predefined security attributes, which are more general-purpose items that allow the distinction between a new user, a returning user, and an anonymous user. Table 7-11 shows the predefined `Requestmap` attributes.

Table 7-11. *Preconfigured Requestmap Attributes*

Attribute	Description
IS_AUTHENTICATED_FULLY	Do not remember me and anonymous
IS_AUTHENTICATED_REMEMBERED	Remember me or is fully authenticated
IS_AUTHENTICATED_ANONYMOUSLY	Remember me, anonymous, or fully authenticated

Acegi Domain Data

Now that we have the domains defined, let's get to work. Again, we'll first create some temporary data in the `Bootstrap.groovy` file. We will add `User`, `Authority`, and `Requestmap` objects. A few of these steps will resemble our creation of data earlier with the JSecurity plug-in.

User Definition

Let's start out with the users. For this application, we will create two users: a regular user and an admin user. For the Acegi plug-in, passwords use md5Hex encryption. First, initialize a password that we will use for both:

```
def pass = DU.md5Hex("pass")
```

Now that we have an encrypted password, let's create our users.

```
def person = new Person(username: "user", userRealName: "Joseph Nusairat",
  email: "jnusairat@integrallis.com", description: "Joseph's Account",
  passwd: pass, enabled: true).save()
def admin = new Person(username: "admin", userRealName: "Administrator",
  email: "cjudd@juddsolutions.com", description: "Our admin", passwd: pass,
  enabled: true).save()
```

Notice we set the `enabled` flag to `true` so we can use these users immediately.

Authority Definition

Next, let's create a few authority classes. We create one for user and one for admin, named ROLE_USER and ROLE_ADMIN, respectively.

```
def userAuth =
  new Authority(authority:"ROLE_USER", description: "Authenticated User").save()
def su =
  new Authority(authority:"ROLE_ADMIN", description: "Administrator Role").save()
```

We now need to assign the roles to the users, since they are attached as lists. We add the ROLE_USER to our user and the ROLE_ADMIN to our admin.

```
userAuth.addToPeople(person)
su.addToPeople(admin)
```

Requestmap Definition

Our final item to create is Requestmap. Remember that these are the entries that control access to the site. We are not going to set up every permutation, but we will create a couple examples to play with.

```
new Requestmap(url:"/**",configAttribute:"IS_AUTHENTICATED_ANONYMOUSLY").save()
new Requestmap(url:"/todo/**",configAttribute:"IS_AUTHENTICATED_FULLY").save()
new Requestmap(url:"/user/list/**",configAttribute:"ROLE_ADMIN").save()
```

Acegi Domain Customization

As we mentioned earlier, you can change the names of the domain objects you are creating. This is great early on in the project, when you have not yet defined the domains. However, in our situation, we are not that lucky—we defined part of the domains back in Chapter 4. We could take the domains out, create them via the tool, and then add them back in our customizations—but that would be rather silly.

Luckily there is an easier way. When the Acegi plug-in creates the domain objects (even the custom-named ones), the way it knows which class to call and which field to call is via a mapped file. In grails-app/config, you'll find an AcegiConfig.groovy file, which handles the configurations. The default file is shown in Listing 7-11.

Listing 7-11. *The AcegiConfig.groovy Configuration File*

```groovy
acegi {
  loadAcegi=true

  algorithm="MD5"
  //use Base64 text ( true or false )
  encodeHashAsBase64=false
  errorPage="null"

  /** login user domain class name and fields */
  loginUserDomainClass="Person"
  userName="username"
  password="passwd"
  enabled="enabled"
  relationalAuthorities = "authorities"
  /* you can specify method for to retrieve the roles.
   * (you need to set relationalAuthorities=null)
   */
  //getAuthoritiesMethod=null //"getMoreAuthorities"

  /**
   * Authority domain class authority field name
   * authorityFieldInList
   */
  authorityDomainClass="Authority"
  authorityField="authority"

  /** use RequestMap from DomainClass */
  useRequestMapDomainClass = true
  /** Requestmap domain class (if useRequestMapDomainClass = true) */
  requestMapClass="Requestmap"
  requestMapPathField="url"
  requestMapConfigAttributeField="configAttribute"

  /**
   * To use email notification for user registration, set the following userMail to
   * true and config your mail settings. Note you also need to implement the script
   * grails generate-registration.
   */
  useMail = false
  mailHost = "localhost"
```

```
    mailUsername = "user@localhost"
    mailPassword = "sungod"
    mailProtocol = "smtp"
    mailFrom = "user@localhost"

    /** AJAX request header */
    ajaxHeader="X-Requested-With"

    /** default user's role for user registration */
    defaultRole="ROLE_USER"

    /** use basicProcessingFilter */
    basicProcessingFilter=false
    /** use switchUserProcessingFilter */
    switchUserProcessingFilter=false
}
```

In this file, you can define the following:

- Whether Acegi Security is enabled

- The type of encryption to use

- The names for the mapping of the authenticated classes and properties

- E-mail protocols for registration

- Whether the processing filters are activated

As you can see, this flexibility helps with integration of the software. For our example, we will not use the Person class; instead, we will add fields to our existing User class.

Acegi Security Usage

So now that we have all of our data loaded, let's start up the application server and head to the to-do page at http://localhost:8080/acegiSecurity/todo. You will see that you are redirected from the get-go, as shown in Figure 7-5. Behind the scenes, this differs greatly from how the JSecurity plug-in works. Recall that with JSecurity, we defined our access controller at the individual controller level. With the Acegi plug-in, we define it in the Requestmap, which will use a filter behind the scenes.

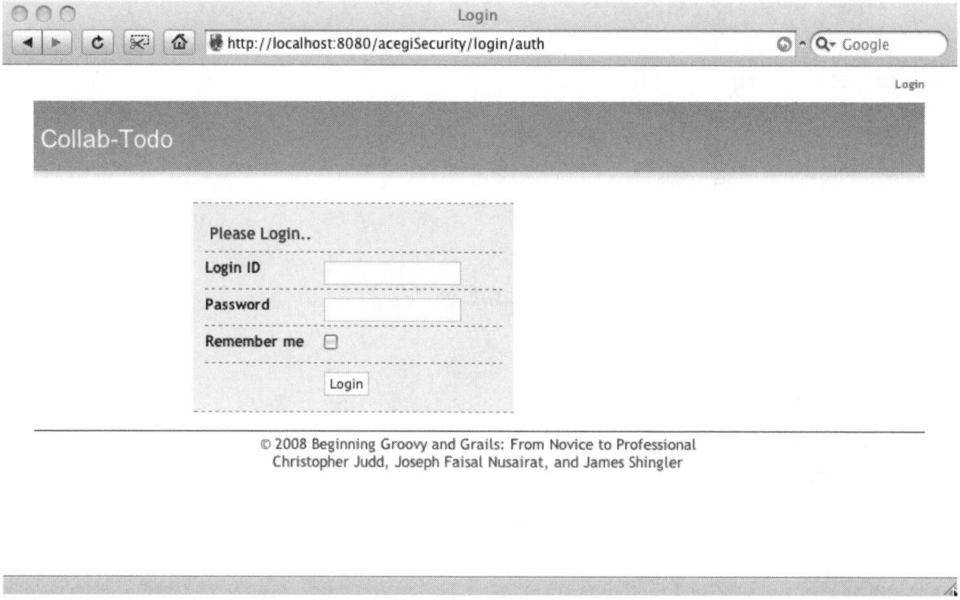

Figure 7-5. *The login page for the Acegi plug-in*

Once you log in, you will be redirected to the to-do page. So what can we do from here? The tag libraries will make things easier.

The normal Acegi security plug-in has many custom tag libraries available. The Acegi plug-in team has re-created these with Groovy syntax to be Grails plug-ins, as listed in Table 7-12.

Table 7-12. *Acegi Plug-in Tag Libraries*

Tag	Description
g:loggedInUserInfo	With the parameter field, this plug-in will display the currently logged in user.
g:isLoggedIn	Used as a body encapsulation; the body will be displayed only when the user is logged in.
g:isNotLoggedIn	Used as a body encapsulation; the body will be displayed only when the user is *not* logged in.
g:ifAllGranted	With the parameter role, the body will be displayed if all the roles have been granted.
g:ifAnyGranted	With the parameter role, the body will be displayed if any of the roles has been granted.
g:ifNotGranted	With the parameter role, the body will be displayed only if none of the roles has been granted.

We can use these tag libraries with our application as necessary. We will start by updating the _topbar.gsp page using the isLoggedIn and isNotLoggedIn tag libraries, as shown in Listing 7-12.

Listing 7-12. *The _topbar.gsp Page Updated with Acegi Tag Libraries*

```
<div id="menu">
  <nobr>
    <g:isLoggedIn>
      <b>${session.user?.firstName} ${session.user?.lastName} </b> |
      <g:link controller="user" action="logout">
        <g:message code="topbar.logout" />
      </g:link>
    </g:isLoggedIn>
    <g:isNotLoggedIn>
      <g:link controller="user" action="login">
        <g:message code="topbar.login" />
      </g:link>
    </g:isNotLoggedIn>
  </nobr>
</div>
```

Notice that we did *not* use the loggedInUserInfo tag library. The purpose of this tag is to display who is logged in; however, it displays only one field, and we want to display the last and first name. Luckily, the Acegi plug-in puts the User object into the session for us once it is authenticated, so we are able to have access to it in our GSP.

Summary

Security is important to any application. While most of the Grails security plug-ins are relatively new and some may not be completely mature, they all are based on frameworks that have been built over time. Each of these frameworks is progressing and will be adding functionality rapidly until they achieve at least 1.0 release.

Choosing a security plug-in for our application was actually difficult. We went back and forth between Acegi, JSecurity, and a custom approach. In the end, Acegi won out, mainly for two reasons:

- It has advanced functionality that makes it more fun is use.

- Its ability to use basic authentication will be necessary in order to use our RESTful web services in Chapter 9.

The coverage of other plug-ins should help you to select which plug-in is best for your own application.

Now that we have security fully in place, we will be able to embrace some more user functionality in the next chapter, which covers Ajax and other fun Web 2.0 items.

■■■

CHAPTER 8

Web 2.0—Ajax and Friends

So far in this book, we have relied on a few basic items to create our site, and, as of right now, it is fully functioning. Users have the ability to log in, create to-dos, create buddies, and so on. And while these make for a good application, good applications will not generate revenue. The Web is filled with many bad applications, quite a few good ones, and far and few between excellent ones. In this and the following two chapters, we will try to add some excellence to our web application by applying some Web 2.0 techniques.

What do we mean by *excellence*? Some developers try to cram every Ajax component and every Web 2.0 concept under the sun into their applications. Many times, this approach can fail. You end up overcomplicating the page and making it difficult to use. In this chapter's examples, we will try to toe the line between enhancing the page and making it unmanageable. Each component we will add will supply functionality that the users should be able to enjoy.

We will start it off slowly with some basic plug-ins that add some Web 2.0 functionality. From there, we will add a mail service, which we will use in this chapter and in Chapter 10, which covers reporting. After that, we will dive into some good old-fashioned Ajax and demonstrate the flexibility of Ajax in Grails. We will finish up with an RSS feed, which can be useful if you want to have your to-dos displayed on an RSS reader like iGoogle.

Advanced Presentation Components

Currently, our sample application's to-do page is pretty basic, as shown in Figure 8-1. We can improve the application by adding functionality here.

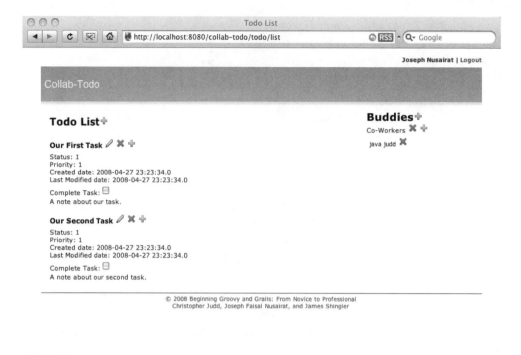

Figure 8-1. *The current to-do page in Collab-Todo*

We will focus on three areas that will make this page more useful to users:

- Allow for the use of rich text in the to-do notes.

- Make the to-dos searchable.

- Allow for uploading a file associated with a to-do.

To add these features, we will make use of an ever-growing list of plug-ins for Grails.

Adding Rich-Text Capabilities

Currently, to-do note entry is very limited. You cannot style text (such as italics or bold-face) or format it (say, into a bulleted list). We have a few ways to address this need:

HTML: Allow users to insert their own HTML code, but that would be a bad idea. Not only would it require users to know how to do this, but if they made a mistake, it could throw off the entire layout of the page by not closing the HTML tags.

Text editor: Add a rich text editor. This type of editor can provide near Microsoft Word–type functionality to a web site. Not only can you allow rich text, but you can also let the users upload images, Flash movies, and even files to your web application. The FCK editor plug-in[1] is a good example of this sort of editor. Figure 8-2 shows an example of the FCK editor embedded into an application. Although this is, as Borat would say, "very nice," it is a bit of overkill for our needs. Not only that, it might break some of the smooth lines of our page.

Figure 8-2. *The FCK editor plug-in in action*

---

1. http://grails.codehaus.org/FCK+editor+plugin

Wiki markup: Systems like Wikipedia and even regular homegrown content management systems (CMS) are turning to using a markup language for their rich content. This allows a generally more simplified system of displaying and formatting text. You can add styles like bold and italicized text, as well as formatting like bulleted and numbered lists. You can even use more advanced formatting for code display, such as a dashed border with a header. Using wiki markup is becoming a popular solution for web sites, and this is the approach we'll take with our application.

■**Note** A downside to wikis is that there is no set standard. So every wiki will implement the items differently. Some wikis can be very similar, while others will differ greatly.

While there are many wiki markup solutions, we are going to use Radeox, because Grails has a plug-in wrapper for it.[2] The Radeox plug-in uses SnipSnap as its wiki engine.

As with other Grails plug-ins, you can install the Radeox plug-in by downloading from its site at `http://www.grails.org/Radeox+plugin` or by using this command:

```
> grails install-plugin radeox
```

■**Note** At the time of this writing, the plug-in required one tweak to make it work: add a `getName()` method to the `GroovyMacro.groovy` file in the plug-in.

Let's start by adjusting our `Bootstrap.groovy` file to bold the word *task* in our notes. To do this, we surround the word we want to bold with double underscores (__), as shown in Listing 8-1.[3]

Listing 8-1. *A Note Format Adjustment in Bootstrap.groovy*

```
todo =
  new Todo(owner: user1, category: cat1, name: 'Our First Task',
          createDate: new Date(), startDate: new Date(), priority: '1',
          status: '1', dueDate: new Date() + 7, lastModifiedDate: new Date(),
          note: 'A note about our __task__.').save()
```

---

2. http://www.grails.org/Radeox+plugin
3. See http://snipsnap.org/space/snipsnap-help for SnipSnap text-formatting markup guidance.

If you now view the page, you won't see the formatting added to the sentence. In order to have Radeox format the text, you need to update the note section of the to-do page and surround it with the `<g:radeoxRender>` tag, as shown in Listing 8-2.

Listing 8-2. *The _detail.gsp Page Note Section Updated with the Radeox Tag*

```
<g:radeoxRender>${todo?.note}</g:radeoxRender>
```

Now when the page is rendered, you will see the note with **task**, as shown in Figure 8-3.

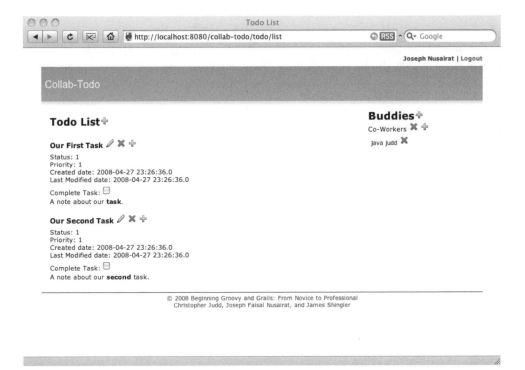

Figure 8-3. *The to-do page with the Radeox plug-in in use*

Adding Search Capabilities

Currently, the only way to search for a particular task is to literally open up every task and see what is in there. While this may work if you have a small number of tasks, it will quickly become cumbersome as the application grows—especially if the keyword you are looking for is buried in the notes.

As in previous chapters, we are not only going to make use of a plug-in, but a plug-in that is based on tried-and-true Java technologies. The Searchable plug-in is based on the

OpenSymphony Compass Search Engine framework,[4] which in turn uses Apache Lucene under the covers.

The Searchable plug-in is supplied with Grails. Install it by issuing the following command:

```
> grails install-plugin searchable
```

■**Note** At the time of this writing, the Searchable plug-in had a mapping issue. To get it to work, you *may* need to copy the directory `plugins/searchable-0.4.1/grails-app/views/searchable` to your main `grails-app/views` directory. This will allow the search views to be local.

The Searchable plug-is a snap to set up and use. The plug-in allows you to decide which domain objects should be searchable. We want to make the to-dos searchable, so we add the line `static searchable = true` to our Todo domain object, as shown in Listing 8-3.

Listing 8-3. *Marking Our Todo As Searchable in domain/Todo.groovy*

```
class Todo {

    static searchable = true
    // . . . continued . . .
}
```

And that is really all we need to do. So what does that give us?

If you go to `http://localhost:8080/collab-todo/searchable`, you will see the default searchable page. You can type in a word to search for and get the results. Figure 8-4 shows the results of searching for *task*.

---

4. http://www.opensymphony.com/compass/

Figure 8-4. *The results of searching for the word "task"*

You will notice that some of our items do not show up well. This is because these items were formatted with wiki markup to be used with our Radeox plug-in. This really is not acceptable, so let's take care of that now. To fix this, we need to modify the search view directly. We just need to change one line in `grails-app/searchable/index.gsp`—line 142, as shown Listing 8-4 (which is a partial listing of the file with the modified line bolded).

Listing 8-4. *Adding the Radeox Call to the Searchable Page (views/searchable/index.gsp)*

```
<div class="result">
    <g:set var="className" value="${ClassUtils.getShortName(result.getClass())}" />
    <g:set var="link" value=
        "${createLink(controller: className[0].toLowerCase() + className[1..-1],
        action: 'show', id: result.id)}" />
    <div class="name"><a href="${link}">${className} #${result.id}</a></div>
    <g:set var="desc" value="${result.toString()}" />
    <g:if test="${desc.size() > 120}">
        <g:set var="desc" value="${desc[0..120] + '...'}" />
    </g:if>
```

```
    <div class="desc">
        <g:radeoxRender>${desc.encodeAsHTML()}</g:radeoxRender>
    </div>
    <div class="displayLink">${link}</div>
</div>
```

All that we had to do was wrap the response with the Radeox renderer. As shown in Figure 8-5, the response will now be formatted properly.

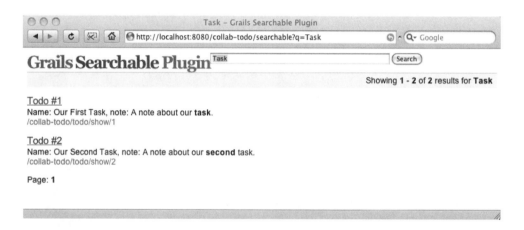

Figure 8-5. *The Grails Searchable plug-in with the Radeox formatting*

Allowing File Uploads

Some web applications allow users to upload files. For our application, we'll add the ability to upload a file for each of the to-dos, and then retrieve (download) that file later. The uploaded files can be stored either on the application server or the database itself. For our example, we are going to store the file in the database, mainly due to ease of doing so and because we're working with only one file, so space is not an issue.

Uploading the File

Grails will use Spring's file upload capability to help upload the file. Uploading a file is a fairly simple process, requiring the following steps:

- Review necessary properties on the Todo domain.

- Add a link to upload it in our list page.

- Add configurations to the Spring resources.xml file.

- Create the necessary code in our controller to store and retrieve the file.

In order to store the data, all you are required to have is a `byte[]` for data. But when you return the data, the end user probably wants to have the original name of the file. In addition, being specific about the type of data returned will help the browser know how to process the data. For example, if it's a PDF, the browser will automatically know to open it as a PDF. To handle this, in Chapter 5, we added the variable `associatedFile byte[]` and `Strings` of `fileName` and `contentType` to our `Todo` domain object, as shown in Listing 8-5.

Listing 8-5. *Updating the Todo Domain Object (in domain/Todo.groovy)*

```groovy
class Todo {

    User owner
    Category category
    String name
    String note
    Date createDate
    Date startDate
    Date dueDate
    Date completeDate
    Date lastModifiedDate
    String priority
    String status
    byte[] associatedFile
    String fileName
    String contentType


    . . .
}
```

Once you restart the server, it will automatically create the entry in the database as a BLOB, or TINYBLOB if you are using MySQL.

▓**Caution** If you are using MySQL, to allow most files to upload, you will need to change the default of TINYBLOB for the database column to LONGBLOB.

The next part is to add a section to our page to upload the file. As shown in Listing 8-6, we add a file upload tag after the due date.

Listing 8-6. *The File Upload Tag for the Todo (in views/todo/list.gsp)*

```
<tr class='prop'>
  <td valign='top' class='name'><label for='dueDate'>File:</label></td>
  <td valign='top'
      class='value ${hasErrors(bean:todo,field:'asociatedFile','errors')}'>
    <input type="file" name="asociatedFile" />
  </td>
</tr>
```

Performing file uploads also requires a change in the form tag itself. You must change the form to a multipart request. To do this, add the form tag shown in Listing 8-7.

Listing 8-7. *The Multipart Tag for the Form (in views/todo/list.gsp)*

```
enctype="multipart/form-data"
```

Figure 8-6 shows an example of the result of our additions: a to-do being created, with a file selected to upload.

As we said earlier, we are making use of Spring for our file upload capability, and you will see when we update the controller next that there are calls to Spring objects. However, in order to use the Spring objects, we need to add a bean in Spring's `resources.xml` file. This is where we define Spring resources to be used in Grails. Add the lines shown in Listing 8-8 to `conf/spring/resources.xml`.

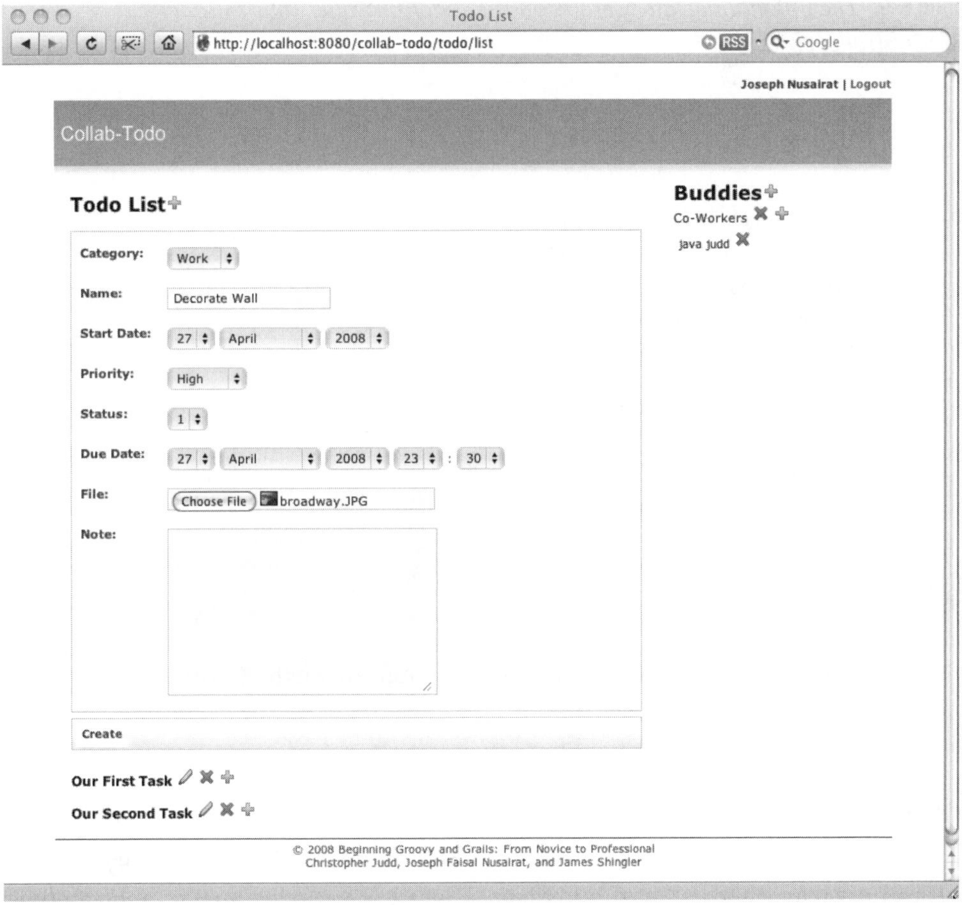

Figure 8-6. *Choosing a file to upload with a new to-do*

Listing 8-8. *Adding a Bean to conf/spring/resources.xml*

```
<bean class="org.springframework.web.multipart.commons.CommonsMultipartResolver">
    <property name="maxUploadSize"><value>1000000</value></property>
</bean>
```

This bean definition also allows you to specify an optional maximum for the file upload size, so that Spring can prevent too big of a file from being uploaded.

The final step is to actually save the file. This is not too complicated, but it does require making use of some Spring objects. We will cast the request coming in as a `MultipartHttpServletRequest` and retrieve the items off the file as necessary. Listing 8-9 shows the new method to handle the file upload.

Listing 8-9. *The uploadFileData Method on the TodoController (in controllers/TodoController.groovy)*

```groovy
import org.springframework.web.multipart.MultipartHttpServletRequest;
import org.springframework.web.multipart.commons.CommonsMultipartFile;
. . .
def uploadFileData = { todo ->
    if (request instanceof MultipartHttpServletRequest) {
        MultipartHttpServletRequest multiRequest
            = (MultipartHttpServletRequest)request;
        CommonsMultipartFile file =
            (CommonsMultipartFile)multiRequest.getFile("associatedFile");
        // Save the object items.
        todo.fileName = file.originalFilename
        todo.contentType = file.contentType
        todo.associatedFile = file.bytes
    }
}
```

Simply call this method before you persist on your save method in order to set the appropriate properties on the Todo.

Downloading the File

Now that it is stored, we are going to want to be able to retrieve the file on the fly. The file that is returned from the database is in a byte[], hence you can use any common method of response rendering to render the returned item. When you return a file, you put the byte[] into the output stream of the response, setting some header data. A basic example of a file return is shown in Listing 8-10.

Listing 8-10. *A Download File Method for TodoController (in controller/TodoController.groovy)*

```groovy
def downloadFile = {
    def todo = Todo.get( params.id )
    response.setHeader("Content-disposition",
        "attachment; filename=${todo.fileName}")
    response.contentType = todo.contentType
    response.outputStream << todo.associatedFile
}
```

This method can be called by a link on our to-do page, just by passing in the ID of the to-do. As you can see in the method, the header and contentType returns are why we needed to save those two items in the first place.

■**Caution** Later in the chapter, we will switch our to-do add page to be an Ajax form submit. When that happens, you will not be able to upload a file. This is in part due to the way Ajax sends data over to the controller. At that point in our sample application, we will need to move the file upload outside the normal form submit. You can see how that is done in this book's downloadable source code.

Adding Mail Services

Another common feature of web sites is the ability to send e-mail from them. We will add this capability to our application. For right now, we will use the mail service to send an e-mail when a user registers. In Chapter 10, we will use it again to send reports.

If you are familiar with the Spring e-mail service, you will be right at home with the Grails system, since it uses Spring Mail under the covers.

■**Note** There are proposals to make the Grail mail system more DSL-like. If you want to follow the latest developments, check out the Mail from Grails page.[5]

We will create an e-mail service, and then adjust our user registration process to call it and send an e-mail. This requires the following steps:

- Create the service to send an e-mail.

- Create the authenticator to be used for logging in to an SMTP server.

- Update the Spring resources.xml file.

Creating the E-Mail Service

Because Grails uses Spring's e-mail support, we will be using the org.springframework.mail. MailSender class to actually send the e-mail. In order to make this easier for all of us, we are going to wrap the call to the class in a service. The service will provide an easy generic set of parameters to send the e-mail. That way, the callers do not need to worry about creating MIME messages. Listing 8-11 shows the EMailAuthenticatedService.

---

5. http://grails.codehaus.org/Mail+from+Grails

Listing 8-11. *The EMailAuthenticatedService, Responsible for Sending E-Mail*

```
01. import org.apache.log4j.Logger;
02.
03. import org.springframework.core.io.InputStreamResource
04. import org.springframework.core.io.ByteArrayResource
05.
06. import org.springframework.mail.MailException
07. import org.springframework.mail.MailSender
08. import org.springframework.mail.javamail.MimeMessageHelper
09.
10. import javax.mail.internet.MimeMessage
11. import javax.mail.internet.InternetAddress;
12.


13. class EMailAuthenticatedService {
14.     boolean transactional = false
15.     MailSender mailSender
16.
17.     def sendEmail = { mail, eMailProperties, attachements ->
18.         MimeMessage mimeMessage = mailSender.createMimeMessage()
19.
20.         MimeMessageHelper helper
                    = new MimeMessageHelper(mimeMessage, true, "ISO-8859-1")
21.         helper.from = eMailProperties.from
22.         helper.to = getInternetAddresses(mail.to)
23.         helper.subject = mail.subject
24.         helper.setText(mail.text, true);
25.         if(mail.bcc) helper.bcc = getInternetAddresses(mail.bcc)
26.         if(mail.cc) helper.cc = getInternetAddresses(mail.cc)
27.
28.         attachements.each { key, value ->
29.             helper.addAttachment(key, new ByteArrayResource(value))
30.         }
31.
32.         mailSender.send(mimeMessage)
33.     }
34.
35.     private InternetAddress[] getInternetAddresses(List emails) {
36.         InternetAddress[] mailAddresses = new InternetAddress[emails.size()]
37.         emails.eachWithIndex {mail, i ->
38.             mailAddresses[i] = new InternetAddress(mail)
```

```
39.          }
40.          return mailAddresses
41.      }
42. }
```

On line 15, we have a reference to `MailSender`. Since this is not set explicitly, you can assume it will be injected by Grails. You will see later how we reference `MailSender` in Spring's `resources.xml` file.

The only public method starts on line 17. This will be the method that any clients using the service will use. The parameters passed to it are simple. We are going to send a mail object, which will be passed to the method as a `Map`.

Creating the Mail Sender

The `EMailAuthenticatedSender` has a `MailSender` as an injectable component. This is actually relatively easy to create but does require a few steps. We need to add a few entries into `resources.xml` and one new service. We are going to work this a bit in reverse—we will build up the top entries, and then go through their dependents.

We begin by defining the `mailSender` in `resources.xml`, as shown in Listing 8-12.

Listing 8-12. *mailSender Defined in resources.xml*

```xml
<bean id="mailSender" class="org.springframework.mail.javamail.JavaMailSenderImpl">
  <property name="host" value="smtp.apress.com" />
  <property name="session" ref="mailSession" />
</bean>
```

As you can see, the `mailSender` itself defines two variables: a `host` and a `session`. The `host` is a `String` bean identifying the host we are sending the e-mail through. For a production server, it could very easily be localhost or anther host on the network. In our example, we are using a fictional Apress SMTP server.

The session is a bit more complex and will require us to define another injectable object. So, we need to add another bean, `mailSession`, in our `resources.xml` file, as shown in Listing 8-13.

Listing 8-13. *mailSession Defined in resources.xml*

```xml
<bean id="mailSession" class="javax.mail.Session" factory-method="getInstance">
  <constructor-arg>
    <props>
      <prop key="mail.smtp.auth">true</prop>
      <!-- If SSL needed...
```

```
      <prop key="mail.smtp.socketFactory.port">465</prop>
      <prop key="mail.smtp.socketFactory.class">
        javax.net.ssl.SSLSocketFactory
      </prop>
      <prop key="mail.smtp.socketFactory.fallback">
        false
      </prop>
      -->
    </props>
  </constructor-arg>
  <constructor-arg ref="smtpAuthenticator" />
</bean>
```

Here, we have defined the session to work with a non-SSL source, but as you can see by the commented-out code, switching to an SSL source will be quite easy as well.

As you may have guessed, we have yet another item to inject, the smtpAuthenticator. We need to create an object and define the bean for it. First let's define the bean in resources.xml, as shown in Listing 8-14.

Listing 8-14. *smtpAuthenticator Defined in resources.xml*

```
<bean id="smtpAuthenticator" class="SmtpAuthenticator">
  <constructor-arg value="xxx@xxx.net" />
  <constructor-arg value="xxxxxx" />
</bean>
```

We have defined a constructor that takes in a username and a password (blanked out because, well, we don't need everyone checking our e-mail).

Now we need to create a bean for this as well. We are going to create this class in the services folder, and will simply extend javax.mail.Authenticator. Listing 8-15 shows our authentication bean.

Listing 8-15. *The Custom SmtpAuthenticator Bean*

```
import javax.mail.Authenticator

class SmtpAuthenticator extends Authenticator {

  private String username;
  private String password;
```

```
  public SmtpAuthenticator(String username, String password) {
    super();
    this.username = username;
    this.password = password;
  }

  public javax.mail.PasswordAuthentication getPasswordAuthentication() {
    return new javax.mail.PasswordAuthentication(username, password);
  }
}
```

Updating the Registration Page

Now that our bean and all of its subcomponents have been defined, it's time to put it to use. We will modify the registration page to send an e-mail message. Listing 8-16 shows the method that we will use.

Listing 8-16. *Registration Page to Send E-mail (in controller/UserController.groovy)*

```
private sendAcknowledgment = { user ->
    // Let's first design the email that we want to send
    def emailTpl = this.class.classloader.getResource(
        "web-app/WEB-INF/templates/regisrationEmail.gtpl")
    def binding = ["user": user]
    def engine = new SimpleTemplateEngine()
    def template = engine.createTemplate(emailTpl).make(binding)
    def body = template.toString()

    // Set up the email to send.
    def email = [
        to: [user.email],
        subject: "Your Collab-Todo Report",
        text: body
    ]

    try {
        // Check if we "need" attachments
        eMailAuthenticatedService.sendEmail(email, [])
```

```
} catch (MailException ex) {
    log.error("Failed to send emails", ex)
    return false
}
true
}
```

This e-mail call is actually relatively simple. We will pass in a map defining the To and Subject lines and text. The email message body is generated by using a Groovy template engine on the file `registrationEmail.gptl`.

Note that you can reuse this code in other places to send e-mail messages.

Tag Libraries

Tag libraries provide sets of custom actions that you perform inside pages. Generally, the actions are repetitive or would be too long to write scriptlets within the page.

You have seen many of the Grails built-in tag libraries in use in our examples so far. We have used these tags to output data, render lists, and so on, and we will continue to use them throughout the book. See the "Grails Tags" section in Chapter 5 for an overview of the Grails tags.

Here, we will cover how to create your own custom tag library. If you have created tag libraries in the past with Java frameworks, you know that it is actually quite a pain. Your tag library class must extend a base class. You then need to define the tag and its attributes in your tag library definition. Optionally, you can then reference that tag library in the `web.xml`. Finally, you reference the specific tag you are using in the page itself. Wow—that's quite a bit of work just to create something that may be only a formatter. Fortunately, creating a tag library with Grails is simpler than that.

You may have noticed that on our application's to-do page, the option to add a to-do is always shown. But users may go to that page and just want to see the list. It would be good to be able to hide the add section and open it when necessary. We can create a tag library to handle this. It will mark an area with `div` tags and allow the user to click a JavaScript link to open that section. Creating this will require two sets of code segments: one to display the JavaScript and the other to actually call that JavaScript for any `div` section. Normally, with JSP, this would require two classes and a host of XML. Thanks to Grails, we can handle this with one class and no XML.

Creating the Tag Library

Tag libraries reside in the `grails-app/taglib` folder, so that is where we will create our new tag library. Listing 8-17 shows the outline of our tag library with all the global objects we will be using.

Listing 8-17. *The ShowHideTagLib Outline*

```
class ShowHideTagLib {


}
```

As you can see, this doesn't contain much, and that's because this is all we need for
the basic outline.

We are actually creating two separate tag libraries. While this is normally done with
different classes, with Grails, we merely have separate methods. Listing 8-18 shows the
methods we are adding to ShowHideTagLib.

Listing 8-18. *The Contents of ShowHideTagLib*

```
def showHide = { attrs, body ->

    def divId = attrs['update']
    out << """<a href="javascript:showhide('$divId');">${body()}</a>"""
}

def preLoadShowHide = { attrs, body ->
    out << """<script language="javascript">
        <!--

        function showhide(layer_ref) {

            // Let's get the state.
            var state = document.getElementById(layer_ref).style.display;

            if (state == 'block') {
                state = 'none';
            } else {
                state = 'block';
            }

            if (document.all) { //IS IE 4 or 5 (or 6 beta)
                eval( "document.all." + layer_ref + ".style.display = state");
            }

            if (document.layers) { //IS NETSCAPE 4 or below
                document.layers[layer_ref].display = state;
            }
```

```
                    if (document.getElementById &&!document.all) {
                        hza = document.getElementById(layer_ref);
                        hza.style.display = state;
                    }
                }
                //-->
                </script>
            """

    }
```

Here, we have two tag library calls. Each of them shows how great it is to use Groovy when creating tag libraries.

Since creating tag libraries requires the output of the code to be HTML markups, this generally involves quite a bit of string building. Not only that, but when you have output with quotation marks, you need to escape them with \ throughout the code. Yuck! However, with Groovy, we can use triple quotes. The triple quote style allows us to not only fully embed strings with markups, but also to return characters and referenced values.

The first method, showHide, passes in two objects: attrs and body. The body is simply the section of the page between the opening and closing bracket of your tag library. The attrs is a map of attributes you want to pass into the method. With regular JSP tag libraries, you need define them individual as getters and setters on the page, and in the tag library XML. With Grails and Groovy, that is not necessary. As you can see, we have mapped a value called update, which is the div tag section we want activated.

The second method, preLoadShowHide, actually doesn't contain any dynamic code per se. We are simply outputting the JavaScript in there.

Referencing the Tag Library

Referencing the tag library is simple as well. By default, the tag library is referenced in the g namespace—the same one in which all the built-in Grails tags are referenced. Then the method name is used as the tag's reference name. Listing 8-19 shows the calls to the tags in todo/list.gsp.

Listing 8-19. *Excerpts from todo/list.gsp Showing the Calls to the Custom Tags*

```
<g:preLoadShowHide/>
<g:javascript library="scriptaculous" />
<div class="body">
<h2>Todo List<g:showHide update="addToDo">
    <img border=0 src="${createLinkTo(dir:'images',file:'add_obj.gif')}"
        alt="[ADD]"/>
</g:showHide>
```

But what if you don't want to use the g namespace? Perhaps you are bundling the application as a tag library and are worried about name conflicts, or you simply want to remember it's not part of the core Grails functionality. In order to change the namespace used, add a static namespace reference in your tag library. For example, to use the namespace todo for our code, you would add the following line to ShowHideTagLib:

```
static namespace = 'todo'
```

Ajax in Grails

We certainly could not have a Web 2.0 chapter without including a discussion of Ajax. *Ajax* stands for Asynchronous JavaScript and XML, which oddly enough, is not a 100% accurate definition. Although Ajax is usually asynchronous, usually written in JavaScript, and often deals with transmission of XML, none of these items is a *must* for it. You can send Ajax messages synchronously, you do not have to use JavaScript to send them, and your response can be an XML file but can also be a regular string.

■**Note** The term *Ajax* was originally coined by Jesse James Garrett. But the technology was first developed by Microsoft in an attempt to deal with remote scripting.

One of the biggest "secrets" about Ajax is that, for the most part, it's really not that complex, at least conceptually. There is nothing you can do with Ajax that you could not do in a normal application; however, using Ajax can help your application not only perform better, but also give a richer user experience.

The core of Ajax is just sending data to the server and parsing the data on the return without forcing the display to refresh. The complexity lies in making use of the data, and this is where you start to see frameworks emerge. The fact is that these frameworks are not 100% Ajax—if they were, they wouldn't be very big. Instead, these frameworks wrap Ajax with JavaScript UI enhancements. Some of the calls won't even involve Ajax. However, here we will refer to these frameworks as *Ajax frameworks*.

Using Ajax Frameworks in Grails

Popular Ajax frameworks include Prototype, Dojo, script.aculo.us, and Yahoo! User Interface (YUI) Library. Even Google has come onboard with its own rather complex Ajax framework, Google Web Toolkit (GWT).

Most of the popular web frameworks have implemented Ajax. The majority of these did not create their own Ajax framework, but merely wrapped code from previous Ajax frameworks. Ruby on Rails uses script.aculo.us, Tapestry's Tacos uses Dojo, and so on. So what does Grails use? The answer is all of the above.

In an effort to provide maximum flexibility, Grails currently accepts all of the frameworks out there. So what does this mean? Is this good or bad? It's a bit of both. While it allows us more flexibility in choosing a framework, in the end, we need to write more code than other frameworks usually demand, especially when it comes to the JavaScript UI portions of the Ajax items. If you are familiar with other Java or Rails Ajax uses, this will become apparent to you in the upcoming examples.

Using an Ajax framework is relatively simple. You define at the top of your page (or in the main page) which Ajax framework to use with a `<g:javascript>` tag. The following define Prototype, YUI, script.aculo.us, and Dojo, respectively:

```
<g:javascript library="prototype" />
```

```
<g:javascript library="yahoo" />
```

```
<g:javascript library="scriptaculous" />
```

```
<g:javascript library="dojo" />
```

The only slight difference is if you want to use Dojo. Since Dojo is a notoriously large framework, it has not been included by default with Grails. You will need to download and install it with the following command:

```
> grails install-dojo
```

Each of these frameworks has its own custom UI components. If you are familiar with Rails or Tapestry's Tacos, you know that they generally provide complete support for the underlying framework. In other words, there is usually a tag library wrapper for the whole framework. This makes it easy to not only support the Ajax components, but also the JavaScript components. Unfortunately, this is not the case in Grails. Grails supports just the standard Ajax components, as listed in Table 8-1. However, this does give us a good subset of components to use.

Table 8-1. *Ajax Components in Grails*

Tag	Description
remoteField	Creates a text field that sends its value to a remote link when it changes
remoteFunction	Creates a remote JavaScript function that can be assigned to a DOM event
remoteLink	Creates a link that calls a remote function
formRemote	Creates a form that executes an Ajax call on submission
javascript	Loads a JavaScript function
submitToRemote	Creates a button that submits the form as an Ajax call

For our examples, we are going to use script.aculo.us. We chose this framework because it supports the UI features we want to use. Also, since Grails is often compared to Ruby on Rails, which uses script.aculo.us, we thought that using the same Ajax framework would help provide a more direct comparison.

Now we will use Ajax to spice up our to-do page. We will go over three basic examples:

- Rendering parts of pages with form submissions

- Editing a field in place dynamically

- Showing a drop-down list of choices while typing in place (using the autocomplete feature)

Some of these will be simpler than others to implement. These examples will give you a good starting point for creating your own Ajax components.

Dynamic Rendering of Data

Our first example demonstrates using one of the most basic and popular types of Ajax components. This is where you type data into the page, submit it, remotely call the server, process the data, and re-render only a portion of the page. For our example, we are going to modify the to-do add page to do a partial page re-rendering. Now when adding a new to-do, instead of doing an entire page refresh, the page will dynamically render the to-do list section of the page.

In order to perform this, we need to take a few steps, the first of which is not necessarily Ajax-specific:

- Move the list section of the page into its own page (called a *template* or *partial page*).

- Change our current add call to do an Ajax remote call instead of submitting the whole page.

- Change the TodoController's return to render the new page we created instead of the whole page.

■Note One of the big issues you will run into when performing the dynamic rendering of data is *partial page updates*. Partial page updating refers to re-rendering a part of the page. Some frameworks, like Tapestry's Tacos, allow you to perform this in line. However, the majority of web frameworks, including Grails and Ruby on Rails, force you to call to another page. In reality, this is not a big deal. It does add to the number of GSPs you need to write, but on the plus side, it keeps the GSPs clean.

Rendering a Template

Rendering a page from another page is actually fairly simple. First, we need a page to call from, which obviously must be a GSP page. We will use the `<g:render />` tag library to define the area of the page that will be calling out to another GSP page. Grails refers to these partial pages as *templates*.

Our first step is to take our list of to-dos in `todo/list.gsp` and pull that section out to its own page. We will replace the list with what is in Listing 8-20. Also, instead of taking the entire code, we will take everything but the `for` loop. This is because we can tell the renderer to render a collection.

Listing 8-20. *A Template of todo/list.gsp with the Modified To-Do List Display*

```
<div id="todoList">
  <g:render template="detail" var="todo" collection="${todoList}" />
</div>
```

Here, we simply tell Grails to take our collection labeled `todoList` and iterate through the list, rendering the `detail` page each time for every item in the collection. The item in the collection is then referenced in the page by the variable `var`.

▓**Caution** By default, the `var` field is optional. If you did not use the field, you would be able to access the information in the template using the reserved word `it`. However, while this does work, it can present problems if your template references other templates or other tag libraries. So we suggest that you always use `var` when creating the renders.

Creating a Template

The name of the page we are creating will not actually be `detail.gsp`. Instead, Grails chooses the page to render by taking the rendered template attribute and adding underscores at the beginning to indicate the page is a template. The page must also be located in the same directory as the calling controller. Thus, for this example, we will create `_detail.gsp` in the `todo` directory, as shown in Listing 8-21.

Listing 8-21. *The _detail.gsp Page*

```
<div id="todoDetail${todo.id}" class="todo">

  <div class="todoTitle">${todo.name?.encodeAsHTML()}
    <g:link action="edit" id="${todo.id}">
```

```
            <img border=0
              src="${createLinkTo(dir:'images',file:'write_obj.gif')}" alt="[EDIT]"/>
        </g:link>
         <g:remoteLink
                 action="removeTask"
                 id="${todo.id}"
                 update="todoDetail$todo.id"
                 onComplete="highlight('todoDetail$todo.id');">
             <img border=0 src="${createLinkTo(dir:'images',file:'delete_obj.gif')}"
                 alt="[EDIT]"/>
         </g:remoteLink>

          <g:showHide update="todoDetailFull${todo.id}">
          <img border=0
                  src="${createLinkTo(dir:'images',file:'add_obj.gif')}"
                  alt="[Show All]"/></g:showHide>
    </div>

    <div id="todoDetailFull${todo.id}" class="todo" style="display:none">
      Status: ${todo.status?.encodeAsHTML()} <br />
      Priority: ${todo.priority?.encodeAsHTML()} <br />
      Created date: ${todo.createDate?.encodeAsHTML()} <br />
      Last Modified date: ${todo.lastModifiedDate?.encodeAsHTML()} <br />

      <g:if test="${todo.completeDate == null}">
          Complete Task: <input type="checkbox"
                                 onclick="${remoteFunction(
                                         action:'completeTask',
                                         id:todo.id,
                                         update:'todoDetail' + todo.id,
                                         onComplete:'highlight(\'todoDetail' +
todo.id+'\')' )};"/> <br />
      </g:if>
      <g:else>
          Completed Date: ${todo.completeDate?.encodeAsHTML()} <br />
      </g:else>
        <!-- show notes -- mark in the code that we should use a todo -->
        <g:radeoxRender>${todo?.note}</g:radeoxRender>
      <!-- update:[success:'great', failure:'ohno'], -->
        <!--
```

```
    <g:remoteLink action="showNotes" id="${todo.id}"
        update="todoDetailNote${todo.id}">
      Notes
    </g:remoteLink><br/>
    <div id="todoDetailNote${todo.id}">
    </div>
    -->
  </div>

</div>
```

Our first step is complete. In reality, there is nothing in the page that is Ajax-enabled yet. Right now, the page works exactly as it did before, and in theory, you could have used these techniques to help segregate the code.

Making the Page Dynamic

Now we will do the partial page form rendering, which is a two-step process:

- Change the form to take an Ajax form tag.

- Have the save call on the controller render the tag instead of the whole page.

For the first part, change the form encapsulation in list.gsp to the code shown in Listing 8-22.

Listing 8-22. *Adding an Ajax Form Tag (in views/todo/list.gsp)*

```
<g:formRemote name="todoForm"
             url="[controller:'todo',action:'save']"
             update="todoList"
             onComplete="showhide('addToDo')"
             enctype="multipart/form-data">
  . . .
</g:formRemote>
```

This calls the save action on our TodoController, and then on completion, hides the add section. In addition, the update attribute will tell us which <div> section we are updating. In Listing 8-21, notice that we surrounded our rendered items with the <div> tag todoList. This will be the section that the Ajax JavaScript will re-render upon return.

The changes to the save action are equally as easy. Instead of the standard return, where we redirect to the list page, we have a line to get the collection and call out to render the GSP we marked, as shown in Listing 8-23.

Listing 8-23. *Rendering Just the Tag (in views/todo/list.gsp)*

```
render(template:'detail',  var: 'todo', collection:listByOwner())
```

As you can see, besides having to move some data, this was all relatively simple as can be. And that is all that is needed. If you go back to the page now, it will do an update without needing to return the whole page.

■Note In the downloadable code, you will find that we have also changed the buddy list sections to do partial page re-rendering. So when you create a new buddy list or add a buddy to a list, those sections will be re-rendered as well.

Editing a Field in Place

The previous example involved editing an entire form; however, this is not always necessary. Sometimes all we need is to alter one field, or we want to allow users to update one field at a time.

In our application, when you add a buddy, the nickName (which is the name displayed on the screen) stored in BuddyListMember defaults to the name of the buddy. What if you wanted the nickName to be something different? It would be a bit silly to have to go all the way to an edit page just to change one field. Also, what if, in the case of buddy list members, you had many buddies in different lists that you wanted to update quickly? The easiest way would be to just click the name and be able to change the name on the fly. In this section, we'll add editing-in-place capabilities for these items.

In the previous section, we relied entirely on the Grails Ajax tag libraries. In fact, the previous code would have not changed whether we used script.aculo.us, Dojo, or another Ajax framework. However, that all changes for this and the following section, where we will be making use of calls specific to script.aculo.us.

For our example, we are going to use the buddy list name itself, although this will work with any of the dynamic fields on the page. When you click the name, the name will switch to an input box with ok and cancel buttons.

■Note As we mentioned earlier, we have also implemented the dynamic rendering for the buddy list and the buddies. This is why the GSP code is in a different place than in previous chapters.

First, let's update the code. The code in question is in common/_buddyList.gsp. So we will change it from a regular display to a custom tag library, as shown in Listing 8-24.

Listing 8-24. *The Buddy List Name Display Updated for Editing in Place (in views/common/_buddyListMember.gsp)*

```
<g:editInPlace id="buddyListName${list.id}"
            url="[controller: 'buddyList', action: 'editName', id:list.id]"
            rows="1"
            cols= "10"
            paramName="name">${list.name}</g:editInPlace>
```

Our custom tag library will be defining a few items: the ID of the area we are updating, the standard URL, and the parameter from the body of the text that will be passed through. The rows and columns are used to define the size of the input box itself.

Tip If you are developing an application where the field could potentially be very small or very large, you may want to create a method in the tag library that would dynamically size it based on the text length.

Let's move on to the tag library itself, which is shown in Listing 8-25.

Listing 8-25. *The AjaxTag Library with the editInPlace Method*

```
class AjaxTagLib {

    def editInPlace = { attrs, body ->
        def rows = attrs.rows ? attrs.rows : 0;
        def cols = attrs.cols ? attrs.cols : 0;
        def id = attrs.remove('id')
        out << "<span id='${id}'>"
        out << body()
        out << "</span>"
        out << "<script type='text/javascript'>"
        out << "new Ajax.InPlaceEditor('${id}', '"
        out << createLink(attrs)
        out << "',{"
        if(rows)
            out << "rows:${rows},"
        if(cols)
            out << "cols:${cols},"
```

```
        if(attrs.paramName) {
            out <<  """callback: function(form, value) {
                return '${attrs.paramName}=' + escape(value) }"""
        }
        out << "});"
        out << "</script>"
    }
}
```

As you may have noticed, we took the script.aculo.us call and converted it into a tag library. There's nothing too complex here, but it makes the page much more readable in the end.

The final step is the creation of the method to actually change the name. This method will be located in the BuddyListController, and will update the buddy list with a new name, save it, and re-render the section. Listing 8-26 shows this editName method.

Listing 8-26. *The editName Method in the BuddyListController (in controller/BuddyListController.groovy)*

```
def editName = {

    log.info "Update buddy list name"

    // Retrieve member
    def buddyList = BuddyList.get(params.id)
    buddyList.name = params.name

    // Render a new page.
    render params.name
}
```

Now let's take a look at this method in action. Figure 8-7 shows what happens after you click a buddy name.

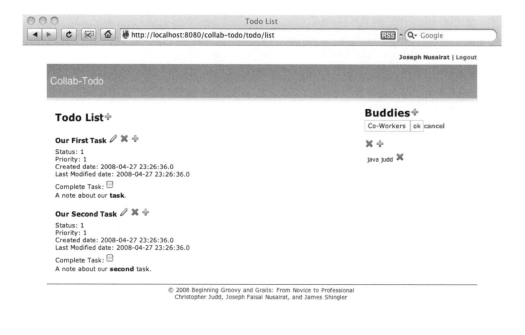

Figure 8-7. *Editing in place*

After you click ok, you will see indications that the changes are being applied (a "working" icon and then some highlighting), and then the update will be made. Figure 8-8 shows an example of changing "Co-Workers" to "Fav Workers."

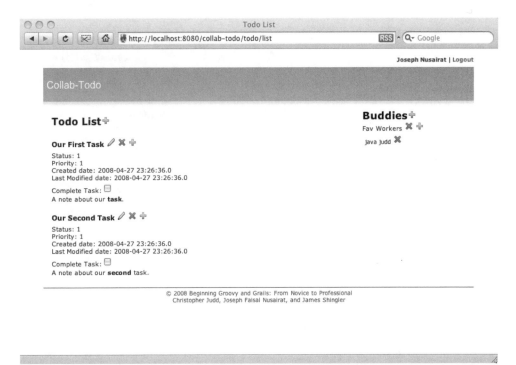

Figure 8-8. *The buddy list name is changed to Fav Workers.*

As you can see, this code is fairly simple, and with the tag library, we can easily insert this logic anywhere into our application.

Using the Autocomplete Feature

The final Ajax feature we will add is dynamic rendering of drop-downs. This is another fairly new and cool feature being employed by web sites. The autocomplete feature allows a drop-down list of matching selections to be displayed and updated as the user types. This can be good for helping users complete an entry that must be exact. Here, we will use this feature for adding buddies to an existing buddy list.

Figure 8-9 shows an example of how autocomplete will work once we have completed this example, On the page, we expanded the add section and started to type in the text field, beginning with the letter *j*. In this case, since each of the authors' names (first or last) starts with a *J*, it found all of us. From here, you can select the buddy you want to add and press Enter, and he will be added to the list.

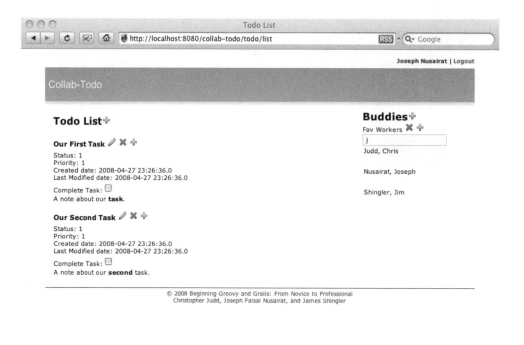

Figure 8-9. *Our drop-down box after typing in "j"*

Before the Ajax functionality, there was a simple form submit. We are going to adjust this using two techniques we have already covered: change the form to a `<g:formRemote>` tag and use an Ajax call specific to script.aculo.us. Listing 8-27 shows the added remote form tag, complete with the definition of the area we are going to update.

Listing 8-27. *The Remote Form Call for Adding a Buddy to the Buddy List (in views/common/_buddyList.gsp)*

```
<g:formRemote name="buddyListForm${list.id}"
            url="[controller:'buddyListMember',action:'add']"
            update="buddyListMembers${list.id}"
            onComplete="showhide('buddyListAdd${list.id}')">
   . . .
</g:formRemote>
```

Now we get to the script.aculo.us part. Here, the code can get a bit trickier. We are going to adjust the input text box to have an ID assigned to it. After that, we will start an Ajax call to monitor any input to it. If text is typed, it will make an Ajax call and create the drop-down list you saw in Figure 8-8. The code that performs this operation is shown in Listing 8-28.

Listing 8-28. *Ajax Code to Create the Dynamic Drop-Down (in views/common/_buddyList.gsp)*

```
<span id="indicator1" style="display: none">
  <img src="/collab-todo/images/spinner.gif" alt="Working..." />
</span>
<div id="autocomplete_choices${list.id}" class="autocomplete"></div>

<script type="text/javascript">
  new Ajax.Autocompleter("autocomplete${list.id}",
                         "autocomplete_choices${list.id}",
                         "/collab-todo/user/findUsers",
                         {afterUpdateElement : getSelectionId${list.id}});

  function getSelectionId${list.id}(text, li) {
    document.buddyListForm${list.id}.userNameId.value = li.id;
  }
</script>
```

Since our methods no longer redirect to a new page, we need to change the final render so that it renders the buddy list subpage again. This is accomplished with the line of code shown in Listing 8-29.

Listing 8-29. *Rendering the Subpage (in views/common/_buddyList.gsp)*

```
render(template:'/common/buddyListMember', var: 'buddy',
      collection:BuddyListMember.findAllByBuddyList(member.buddyList))
```

Since we are doing a dynamic lookup of names, this is not the only method we need. We will create a new method that will use the Criteria query operation, similar to the one we looked at in Chapter 6. This method will find the users based on what the user is typing and will look for the first name, last name, or username, and then return the list, as shown in Listing 8-30.

Listing 8-30. *The UserController findUsers Method (in controller/UserController.groovy)*

```
def findUsers = {
    // Let's query the database for any close matches to this
    def users = User.createCriteria().list {
        or {
            like("userName", "%${params.userId}%")
            like("firstName", "%${params.userId}%")
            like("lastName", "%${params.userId}%")
```

```
        }
        order("lastName")
        order("firstName")
    }

    // Let's build our output XML
    def writer = new StringWriter()

    // Build it
    new groovy.xml.MarkupBuilder(writer).ul {
        for (u in users) {
            li(id: u.id, "${u.lastName}, $u.firstName")
        }
    }
    render writer.toString()
}
```

The Criteria query was only half of the work. The other half is to tell the browser how to render the information we are passing back. By default, for autocomplete, script.aculo.us expects an unnumbered list to be returned to it. Once it receives that, it can properly parse the return. Luckily for us, there is a really easy way to create an unnumbered list or any XML with Groovy. We can use the MarkupBuilder to create a bulleted list of unordered elements, so that the string returned in Listing 8-30 will actually look like the following:

```
<ul>
<li>Nusairat, Joseph</li>
<li>Judd, Chris</li>
<li>Shingler, Jim</li>
</ul>
```

Now we have one final task to perform. If you have been coding along with the example, and have entered the code and tried to render it, you will get a drop-down list, but it will be difficult to read. This is because the default style is used. The solution to this is quite simple: for the autocomplete items, we will create a CSS style that will help set it apart. We will use yellow with some bold when highlighting, as shown in Listing 8-31.

Listing 8-31. *CSS Style Addition for the Dynamic Drop-Down (in main.css)*

```
div.autocomplete {
  position:absolute;
  width:250px;
  background-color:white;
  border:1px solid #888;
```

```
    margin:0px;
    padding:0px;
}
div.autocomplete ul {
    list-style-type:none;
    margin:0px;
    padding:0px;
}
div.autocomplete ul li.selected { background-color: #ffb;}
div.autocomplete ul li {
    list-style-type:none;
    display:block;
    margin:0;
    padding:2px;
    height:32px;
    cursor:pointer;
}
```

Once you have updated the `main.css` file, your code should render correctly and save correctly as well.

RSS Feeds

RSS feeds have become an increasingly popular feature to incorporate on a web site. What has contributed to RSS feed popularity is the increasing number of RSS readers out there, including the new iGoogle[6] and the RSS Web Clip in Gmail. So we are going to go over creating a basic RSS reader. This will be an extremely basic example; in a real-world application, you would want to add more items for security checking.

Creating an RSS feed basically requires creating an XML output in a fairly strict format. The reader then takes that XML and parses it for content.

We could do this by hand, but the format based on the feeds can be somewhat complex, and you would also need to write quite a bit of repetitive code. Luckily, there is as plug-in that will help us cheat a bit and create the feeds. The Feeds plug-in[7] supports creating feeds in the popular RSS and Atom formats (with multiple versions of each supported). Start by installing the plug-in:

```
> grails install-plugin feeds
```

---

6. http://www.google.com/ig
7. http://grails.codehaus.org/Feeds+Plugin

The next step is to create a controller with one method in it. This method will be rendering the XML in a way that the renderer can understand. For this example, we will use the Atom format to format the output. Listing 8-32 shows our RSSController with a feed method.

Listing 8-32. *Our RSSController with the feed Method (in controller/RssController.groovy)*

```groovy
import feedsplugin.FeedBuilder

class RssController {

    def feed = {
        render(feedType:"atom") { // optional - , feedVersion:"2.0") {
            title = "Todo List"
            link = http://localhost:8080/collab-todo/rss

            Todo.list(sort: "name", order: "asc").each {
                def todo = it
                entry(it.name) {
                    title = "${todo.name}"
                    link = "http://localhost:8080/collab-todo/todo/view/${todo.id}"
                    author = "${todo.owner.lastName}, ${todo.owner.firstName}"
                }
            }
        }
    }
}
```

Here we use a standard renderer, and in it we define a few items. We define the title and the link. Then we iterate through a list of items queried from the database sorted in ascending order. For each item, we need to define an entry. The entry has three items on it: the title for it, a URL link for it, and its contents. Table 8-2 lists a few of the common fields you would expect to have in a feed.

Table 8-2. *Some Common Fields for a Feed*

Field Name	Description
publishedDate	The date the entry of the field is published
categories	The list of categories related to the entry
author	The name of the author of the entry
link	The link to a full description of the entry
title	The title of the entry

In our example, we used `title`, `link`, and `author`. We sorted based on creation date (actually, we could have sorted based on anything). Note that if you supply `publishedDate`, then your feeder may automatically sort on that date instead. An example of the output for this example is shown in Figure 8-10.

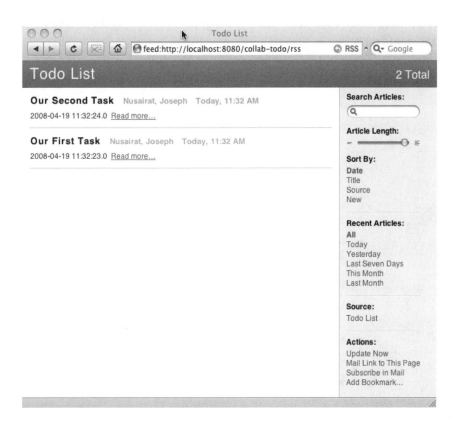

Figure 8-10. *Our RSS reader in a Safari browser*

Summary

This chapter was the start of transforming our working to-do application into a more robust application. We added features that not only make it more useful, but also make it more visually appealing as well as easier to use. These characteristics are extremely important for a web site.

Consider two web sites that both let you monitor your money: `http://www.mint.com` and `https://moneycenter.yodlee.com`. The latter, in our opinion, is far more useful and has more features. However, most people enjoy `mint.com`, simply because it is more user-friendly and eye-catching. As you develop Grails (and other) applications, keep that in mind. Sometimes what makes a site a winner is not what it has, but how easy and enjoyable it is for the users.

The purpose of this chapter was to expose you to a variety of more advanced web-styling techniques for our application. There are more Ajax techniques and plug-ins available on the Grails site. We suggest taking a peek to see if any meet your needs. And if they don't, you always have the option of creating your own plug-in and joining the Grails community that way.

In the next few chapters, we will expand the to-do application and add even more functionality, including reporting and batch jobs.

CHAPTER 9

■ ■ ■

Web Services

Up until this point, you have seen how you can use Grails to develop user-oriented web applications. This chapter focuses on how to use web services to expose your application functionality to other applications. You can also use the techniques discussed in this chapter to drive Web 2.0 Ajax-enabled web applications, like those discussed in Chapter 8.

Originally, web services grew in popularity as a means for system integration. But with the recent popularity of sites such as Google Maps[1] and Amazon.com,[2] and social networking sites like Facebook,[3] there is an expectation that public APIs should be offered so users can create new and innovative client applications. When these clients combine multiple services from multiple providers, they are referred to as *mashups*.[4] They can include command-line applications, desktop applications, web applications, or some type of widget.

In this chapter, you will learn how to expose your application functionality as a Representational State Transfer (REST) web service by extending the Collab-Todo application to provide access to domain objects. This RESTful web service will be able to return either XML or JavaScript Object Notation (JSON), depending on the needs of the client application. This web service will also be designed to take advantage of convention over configuration for exposing CRUD functionality for any Grails domain model, similar to the way Grails scaffolding uses conventions to generate web interfaces. Finally, you will discover how to write simple client applications capable of taking advantage of the web service. In Chapter 13, the web services exposed in this chapter will be utilized by a desktop application developed in Groovy.

---

1. http://www.google.com/maps
2. http://www.amazon.com
3. http://www.facebook.com/
4. http://en.wikipedia.org/wiki/Mashup_(web_application_hybrid)

RESTful Web Services

REST is not a standard or specification. Rather, it is an architectural style or set of principles for exposing stateless CRUD-type services, commonly via HTTP. The primary principles are as follows:

- Entities must be accessable via a URI with a unique identifier.

- Access is achieved via standard methods such as HTTP's GET, POST, PUT, and DELETE.

- Communication between the client and the service should be stateless.

- Associated entities should be linked together.

You can distill these principles to provide URLs with nouns. The pattern for a URL looks like this:

```
http://<server>/<context>/<entity>/<id>
```

where the entity could be the Grails domain model, and the id is the unique identifier of the domain instance. An example in the Collab-Todo application might look like this:

```
http://localhost:8080/collab-todo/todo/1
```

In this example, a representation of the Todo object with an id of 1 could get returned as XML, as shown in Listing 9-1.

Listing 9-1. *XML Representation of a Todo Object Returned from a RESTful Web Service*

```
<todo id="1">
  <completedDate>2007-12-11 11:08:00.0</completedDate>
  <createDate>2007-12-11 00:15:00.0</createDate>
  <dueDate>2007-12-11 11:08:00.0</dueDate>
  <name>Expose Web Service</name>
  <note>Expose Todo domain as a RESTful Web Service.</note>
  <owner id="1"/>
  <priority>1</priority>
  <status>1</status>
</todo>
```

Another alternative might be to return a representation as JSON, like the example shown in Listing 9-2.

Listing 9-2. *JSON Representation of a Todo Object Returned from a RESTful Web Service*

```
{
    "id": 1,
    "completedDate": new Date(1197389280000),
    "status": "1",
    "priority": "1",
    "name": "Expose Web Service",
    "owner": 1,
    "class": "Todo",
    "createDate": new Date(1197350100000),
    "dueDate": new Date(1197389280000),
    "note": "Expose Todo domain as a RESTful Web Service."
}
```

In both Listings 9-1 and 9-2, you see that the Todo representation includes all the properties of the object, including the IDs of referenced domain models like owner.

Notice the REST URLs are similar to the standard Grails convention-over-configuration URLs introduced in Chapter 4. The one difference is the lack of the action, or verb. RESTful accessed via HTTP uses the standard HTTP methods of GET, POST, PUT, or DELETE to specify the action. Table 9-1 provides a mapping of CRUD actions to SQL statements, HTTP methods, and Grails URL conventions.

Table 9-1. *Relationship Between SQL Statements, HTTP Methods, and Grails Conventions*

Action	SQL Statements	HTTP Method	Grails Convention
Create	INSERT	PUT	create
Read	SELECT	GET	show
Update	UPDATE	POST	update
Delete	DELETE	DELETE	delete
Collection	SELECT		list

The relationships described in Table 9-1 are pretty self-explanatory and follow the REST principles, except for the last action of the collection. Because REST is purely focused on CRUD, it doesn't really address things like searching or returning lists. So the collection is borrowed from the Grails concept of the list action and can easily be implemented by doing a REST read without an ID, similar to the following:

```
http://localhost/collab-todo/todo
```

The result of this URL would include a representation of all Todo objects as XML, as shown in Listing 9-3.

Listing 9-3. *XML Representation of a Collection of Todo Objects Returned from a RESTful Web Service*

```
<list>
  <todo id="1">
    <completedDate>2007-12-11 11:08:00.0</completedDate>
    <createDate>2007-12-11 00:15:00.0</createDate>
    <dueDate>2007-12-11 11:08:00.0</dueDate>
    <name>Expose Web Service</name>
    <note>Expose Todo domain as a RESTful Web Service.</note>
    <owner id="1"/>
    <priority>1</priority>
    <status>1</status>
  </todo>
  <todo id="2">
    <completedDate>2007-12-11 11:49:00.0</completedDate>
    <createDate>2007-12-11 00:15:00.0</createDate>
    <dueDate>2007-12-11 11:49:00.0</dueDate>
    <name>Expose Collection of Todo objects</name>
    <note>Add a mechanism to return more than just a single todo.</note>
    <owner id="1"/>
    <priority>1</priority>
    <status>1</status>
  </todo>
</list>
```

Notice that in Listing 9-3, two Todo objects are returned within a `<list>` element representing the collection.

RESTful in Grails

Grails provides several features that make implementing a RESTful web service in Grails easy. First, it provides the ability to map URLs. In the case of RESTful web services, you want to map URLs and HTTP methods to specific controller actions. Second, Grails provides some utility methods to encode any Grails domain object as XML or JSON.

In this section, you will discover how you can use the URL mappings, encoding, and the Grails conventions to create a `RestController`, which returns XML or JSON representations for any Grails domain class, similar to how scaffolding is able to generate any web interface.

URL Mapping

As you learned in the previous section, URLs are a major aspect of the RESTful web service architectural style. So it should come as no surprise that URL mappings are involved. But before we explain how to map RESTful web services, let's look at the default URL mappings.

Default URL Mappings

You can find the URL mappings' configuration file, `UrlMappings.groovy`, with the other configuration files in `grails-app/conf/`. It uses a simple domain-specific language to map URLs. Listing 9-4 shows the default contents of the file.

Listing 9-4. *Default UrlMappings.groovy*

```
01 class UrlMappings {
02     static mappings = {
03         "/$controller/$action?/$id?"{
04             constraints {
05                 // apply constraints here
06             }
07         }
08     }
09 }
```

In case you thought the Grails URL convention was magic, well, it isn't. Line 3 of Listing 9-4 reveals how the convention is mapped to a URL. The first path element, `$controller`, as explained in Chapters 4 and 5, identifies which controller will handle

---

5. http://grails.codehaus.org/Plugins
6. http://grails.codehaus.org/REST+plugin

the request. $action optionally (as noted by the ? operator, similar to the safe dereferencing operator in Groovy) identifies the action on the controller to perform the request. Finally, $id optionally specifies the unique identifier of a domain object associated with the controller to be acted upon. So, as a reminder, the following URL would be interpreted as invoking the show action on the TodoController class to display the Todo domain class with an index of 1:

```
http://localhost:8080/collab-todo/todo/show/1
```

Listing 9-4 shows how this configuration file maps the default URLs. It is completely customizable if you don't like the default or if you want to create some additional mappings for things such as RESTful web services. Mappings are explained in the next section.

RESTful Mappings

The basic concept behind RESTful URL mappings is simple. Just map a URL and an HTTP method to a controller and an action. However, because we want to expose our services as both XML and JSON, we will add a slight twist and include the format type that we want as the base path of our URL. This technique also simplifies making the generic RestController in the next section, because using a common base URL can always be mapped to the RestController. So the URL to invoke a RESTful web service that returns an XML representation like that found in Listing 9-1 would look like this:

```
http://localhost:8080/collab-todo/rest/todo/1
```

and the URL for returning a JSON representation like that found in Listing 9-2 would look like this:

```
http://localhost:8080/collab-todo/json/todo/1
```

You can implement this mapping by adding an additional URL mapping to UrlMappings.groovy. Listing 9-5 shows what the mapping looks like.

Listing 9-5. *RESTful URL Mapping*

```
01 "/$rest/$controller/$id?"{
02     controller = "rest"
03     action = [GET:"show", PUT:"create", POST:"update", DELETE:"delete"]
04     constraints {
05         rest(inList:["rest","json"])
06     }
07 }
```

Line 1 of Listing 9-5 shows the format of the URL. It includes a required $rest, which is the resulting format type, followed by the required $controller and an optional $id. Because $rest should only allow the two format types we are expecting, line 5 uses an inList constraint much like the constraints discussed in the GORM discussions of Chapter 6. Anything other than a rest or a json will cause an HTTP 404 (Not Found) error. Line 2 specifies that the RestController will handle any URL with this mapping. Finally, line 3 maps the HTTP methods to Grails conventional actions on the RestController.

RestController

Because Grails already has conventions around CRUD as well as dynamic typing provided by Groovy, implementing a generic RESTful controller that can return XML or JSON representations of any domain model is relatively simple. We'll begin coverage of the RestController by explaining the common implementation used by all actions. We'll then explain each action and its associated client, which calls the RESTful service.

Common Functionality

The common functionality of the RestController is implemented as an interceptor, as discussed in Chapter 5, along with two helper methods. Listing 9-6 contains a complete listing of the common functionality.

Listing 9-6. *RestController*

```
import static org.apache.commons.lang.StringUtils.*
import org.codehaus.groovy.runtime.InvokerHelper
import org.codehaus.groovy.grails.commons.GrailsDomainClass
import Error

/**
 * Scaffolding like controller for exposing RESTful web services
 * for any domain object in both XML and JSON formats.
 */
class RestController {
  private GrailsDomainClass domainClass
  private String domainClassName

  // RESTful actions excluded
```

```
def beforeInterceptor = {
  domainClassName = capitalize(params.controller)
  domainClass = grailsApplication.getArtefact("Domain", domainClassName)
}

private invoke(method, parameters) {
  InvokerHelper.invokeStaticMethod(domainClass.getClazz(), method, parameters)
}

private format(obj) {
  def restType = (params.rest == "rest")?"XML":"JSON"
  render obj."encodeAs$restType"()
}
}
```

The `beforeInterceptor` found in Listing 9-6 is invoked before any of the action meth-ods are called. It's responsible for converting the `$controller` portion of the URL into a domain class name and a reference to a `GrailsDomainClass`, which are stored into private variables of the controller. You can use the `domainClassName` later for logging and error mes-sages. The name is derived from using an interesting Groovy import technique. Since the controller in the URL is lowercased, you must uppercase it before doing the lookup. To do this, you use the static Apache Commons Lang `StringUtils` `capitalize()` method. Rather than specifying the utility class when the static method is called, an import in Groovy can also reference a class, making the syntax appear as if the static helper method is actually a local method. A reference to the actual domain class is necessary so the `RestController` can call dynamic GORM methods. Getting access to that domain class by name involves looking it up. However, because Grails domain classes are not in the standard classloader, you cannot use `Class.forName()`. Instead, controllers have an injected `grailsApplication` with a `getArtefact()` method, which you can use to look up a Grails artifact based on type. In this case, the type is domain. You can also use this technique to look up controllers, tag libraries, and so on.

■Note The `RestController` class is framework-oriented, so it uses some more internal things such as `grailsApplication.getArtefact()` and `InvokerHelper` to behave generically. If you get into writing Grails plug-ins, you will use these type of techniques more often than in normal application development.

In Listing 9-6, the helper methods are the `invoke()` method and `format()` method. The `invoke()` method uses the `InvokeHelper` helper class to simplify making calls to the static methods on the domain class. The methods on the domain class that are invoked by the `RestController` are all GORM-related. The format method uses the `$rest` portion of the URL to determine which Grails encodeAsXXX() methods it will call on the domain class. Grails includes encodeAsXML() and encodeAsJSON() methods on all domain objects.

There is one other class involved in the common functionality, and that is the Error domain class found in Listing 9-7.

Listing 9-7. *Error Domain Class*

```
class Error {

  String message

}
```

Yes, the Groovy Error class in Listing 9-7 is a domain class found in the grails-app/domain directory. Making it a domain class causes Grails to attach the encoding methods, therefore enabling XML or JSON to be returned if an error occurs during the invocation of a RESTful web service.

RESTful show

The show action has double duty. It displays both a single domain model and a collection of domain models. Listing 9-8 exhibits the show action implementation.

Listing 9-8. *show Action*

```
def show = {
  def result
  if(params.id) {
    result = invoke("get", params.id)
  } else {
    if(!params.max) params.max = 10
    result = invoke("list", params)
  }

  format(result)
}
```

In Listing 9-8, you should notice that the action uses params to determine if an ID was passed in the URL. If it was, the GORM get() method is called for that single domain model. If it wasn't, the action calls the GORM list() method to return all of the domain objects. The results will be something like those found in Listings 9-1, 9-2, and 9-3, depending on how it was invoked. Also, notice that just like scaffolding, the action only returns a maximum of

10 domain objects by default. Using URL parameters, you can override that, just like you can with scaffolding. So adding ?max=20 to the end of the URL would return at maximum 20 domain classes, but it does break the spirit of REST.

Listing 9-9 contains example code of a client application that calls the show action and returns a single domain model.

Listing 9-9. *RESTful GET Client (GetRestClient.groovy)*

```groovy
import groovy.util.XmlSlurper

def slurper = new XmlSlurper()

def url = "http://localhost:8080/collab-todo/rest/todo/1"
def conn = new URL(url).openConnection()
conn.requestMethod = "GET"
conn.doOutput = true

if (conn.responseCode == conn.HTTP_OK) {
  def response

  conn.inputStream.withStream {
    response = slurper.parse(it)
  }

  def id = response.@id
  println "$id - $response.name"
}
conn.disconnect()
```

There are a couple of things to notice in Listing 9-9. First, the example uses the standard Java URL and URLConnection classes defined in the java.net package. This will be true of all client applications through the rest of the chapter. You could also use other HTTP client frameworks, such as Apache HttpClient.[7] Second, notice the request method of GET was used. Finally, the Groovy XmlSlurper class was used to parse the returned XML. This allows you to use the XPath notation to access things such as the name element and the id attribute of the result, like the XML result shown in Listing 9-1.

---

7. http://jakarta.apache.org/httpcomponents/httpclient-3.x/

RESTful delete

Because DELETE is so similar to GET, both the action code and the client code are very similar to that shown in the previous show action section. Listing 9-10 shows the delete action implementation.

Listing 9-10. *delete Action*

```
def delete = {

  def result = invoke("get", params.id);

  if(result) {
    result.delete()
  } else {
    result = new Error(message: "${domainClassName} not found with id ${params.id}")
  }

  format(result)
}
```

In Listing 9-10, the GORM get() method is called on the domain class. If it is found, it will be deleted. If it isn't, it will return an error message. Listing 9-11 shows the client code that would call the delete RESTful web service.

Listing 9-11. *RESTful DELETE Client (DeleteRestClient.groovy)*

```
def url = "http://localhost:8080/collab-todo/rest/todo/1"
def conn = new URL(url).openConnection()
conn.requestMethod = "DELETE"
conn.doOutput = true

if (conn.responseCode == conn.HTTP_OK) {
  input = conn.inputStream
  input.eachLine {
    println it
  }
}
conn.disconnect()
```

The only difference between Listing 9-11 and Listing 9-9 is that the request method used in Listing 9-11 is DELETE, and instead of using the XmlSlurper, the contents of the result are just printed to the console, which will either be an XML or JSON result of the deleted domain object that looks like either Listing 9-1 or 9-2, respectively, or an error message.

RESTful update

A POST is used to update the existing domain models in the RESTful paradigm. Listing 9-12 shows the implementation of the method that updates the domain models.

Listing 9-12. *update Action*

```
def update = {

  def result
  def domain = invoke("get", params.id)
  if(domain) {
    domain.properties = params
    if(!domain.hasErrors() && domain.save()) {
      result = domain
    } else {
      result = new Error(message: "${domainClassName} could not be saved")
    }
  } else {
    result = new Error(message: "${domainClassName} not found with id ${params.id}")
  }

  format(result)
}
```

Like previous examples, Listing 9-12 invokes the GORM get() method to return the domain model to update. If a domain model is returned, all the parameters passed from the client are copied to the domain. Assuming there are no errors, the domain model is saved. Listing 9-13 shows a client that would call the POST.

Listing 9-13. *RESTful POST Client (PostRestClient.groovy)*

```
def url = "http://localhost:8080/collab-todo/rest/todo"
def conn = new URL(url).openConnection()
conn.requestMethod = "POST"

conn.doOutput = true
conn.doInput = true
```

```
def data = "id=1&note=" + new Date()

conn.outputStream.withWriter { out ->
  out.write(data)
  out.flush()
}

if (conn.responseCode == conn.HTTP_OK) {
  input = conn.inputStream
  input.eachLine {
    println it
  }
}
conn.disconnect()
```

Notice that Listing 9-13 uses a POST method this time. Also, pay attention to the fact the data is passed to the service as name/value pairs separated by &s. At a minimum, you must use the id parameter so the service knows what domain model to operate on. You can also append other names to reflect changes to the domain. Because this is a POST, the container automatically parses the name/value pairs and puts them into params. The results will either be an XML or a JSON representation of the updated domain object that looks like Listing 9-1 or 9-2, respectively, or an error message.

RESTful create

Finally, the most complicated of the RESTful services: the create service. Listing 9-14 shows the implementation.

Listing 9-14. *create Action*

```
def create = {
  def result
  def domain = InvokerHelper.invokeConstructorOf(domainClass.getClazz(), null)

  def input = ""
  request.inputStream.eachLine {
    input += it
  }
```

```
  // convert input to name/value pairs
  if(input  && input != '') {
    input.tokenize('&').each {
      def nvp = it.tokenize('=');
      params.put(nvp[0],nvp[1]);
    }
  }
  domain.properties = params

  if(!domain.hasErrors() && domain.save()) {
    result = domain
  } else {
    result = new Error(message: "${domainClassName} could not be created")
  }

  format(result)
}
```

Listing 9-14 begins by using InvokerHelper to call a constructor on the domain class. Unlike POST, PUT's input stream of name/value pairs is not automatically added to the params. You must do this programmatically. In this case, two tokenizers are used to parse the input stream. After that, the rest of the implementation follows the update example found in Listing 9-12. Listing 9-15 demonstrates a client application that does a PUT.

Listing 9-15. *RESTful PUT Client (PutRestClient.groovy)*

```
def url = "http://localhost:8080/collab-todo/rest/todo"
def conn = new URL(url).openConnection()
conn.requestMethod = "PUT"

conn.doOutput = true
conn.doInput = true

def data = "name=fred&note=cool&owner.id=1&priority=1&status=1&"+
 "createDate=struct&createDate_hour=00&createDate_month=12&" +
 "createDate_minute=15&createDate_year=2007&createDate_day=11"

conn.outputStream.withWriter { out ->
  out.write(data)
  out.flush()
}
```

```
if (conn.responseCode == conn.HTTP_OK) {
  input = conn.inputStream
  input.eachLine {
    println it
  }
}
conn.disconnect()
```

Listing 9-15 is nearly identical to Listing 9-13, except that the PUT request method and a more complicated set of data are passed to the service. In this example, the data includes the created date being passed. Notice that each element of the date/time must be passed as a separate parameter. In addition, the createDate parameter itself must have a value of struct. The results will either be an XML or JSON representation of the created domain object that looks like Listing 9-1 or 9-2, respectively, or an error message.

Summary

In this chapter, you learned about the architectural style of RESTful web services as well has how to expose domain models as RESTful web services. As you build your applications, look for opportunities to expose functionality to your customers in this way. You may be amazed at the innovations you never even imagined. In Chapter 13, you will see one such innovation of a Groovy desktop application that consumes the web services developed in this chapter.

CHAPTER 10

■ ■ ■

Reporting

In most projects, reporting is something that is overlooked until the last minute. Everyone is focused on getting information into the system and making the views look and feel right. Then someone starts using the application and says, "Wouldn't it be good if users could print out a copy of the information to take with them and refer to throughout their day?" "Oops, we didn't think about that." (Insert chirping crickets here.)

It makes sense that users would want to take their to-do information with them. But you're in a hurry and want to get this application rolled out quickly. What do you do?

In this chapter, you will learn how to create a reporting facility using the Collab-Todo domain and a popular open source reporting engine, JasperReports.[1] Creating a reporting facility will give you a slightly different view of Grails. You will use dynamic invocation to retrieve data for the report and pass the data to JasperReports. Along the way, you will see how easy it is to use third-party libraries in a Grails application.

The Report

The goal of this chapter is to allow users to run a report that contains their list of to-do items. Figure 10-1 shows an example of the report you will create and integrate into the Collab-Todo application.

---

1. http://www.jasperforge.org

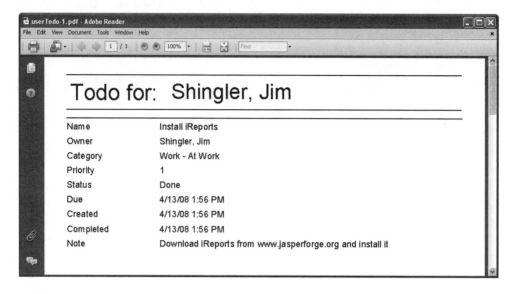

Figure 10-1. *PDF of the to-do report*

This simple PDF report displays a user's to-do items.

Overview of the Reporting Function

Now that you know what the desired result is, how do you get there? Start by adding some technical constraints to help frame the solution:

- You want to be able to create multiple reports.

- You want the report to be available in multiple formats, including PDF, HTML, TXT, RTF, XLS, CSV, and XML.

- You believe in the DRY (principle and want to maintain a separation of concerns and encapsulation.

- You want to leverage the Grails domain model and dynamic methods to retrieve the report data.

Taking these technical constraints into consideration, you can construct the solution illustrated in Figure 10-2.

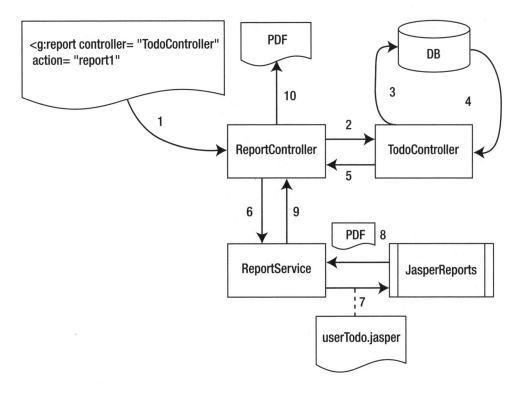

Figure 10-2. *Reporting facility overview*

The first component in the top-left part of Figure 10-2 represents an HTML page. The HTML page needs to provide a way for users to indicate that they want to generate a report. You accomplish this by creating a report tag. You could just hard-code all the logic required to invoke the next step in the process, but knowing that you will have multiple reports, that would be a lot of copying, pasting, and tweaking. It wouldn't be very user friendly to the HTML developer either. By creating a tag, you're able to encapsulate all of the invocation knowledge.

Just like most links in Grails, a tag invokes an action on a controller. If you consider the technical constraints, the controller should have very little knowledge about the actual report to be created. It should control (pun intended) the execution of the reporting process. In this case, it calls the TodoController to gather the data for the report.

The TodoController uses dynamic finder methods on the Todo class to retrieve the report data from the database and returns the result to the ReportController. Now that the ReportController has data for the report, it calls the ReportService to create the report.

The ReportService prepares the data, locates the appropriate report template, and invokes the report engine, JasperReports. The report engine merges the data and the template to create the report. It returns the report to the ReportService, which in turn returns the report to the ReportController. The ReportController then wraps the report in the appropriate headers and returns it to the browser to be displayed.

This is just an overview. Lots of questions are probably going through your head right now. The rest of the chapter will explore each step in more detail and will hopefully answer most, if not all, of your questions.

DYNAMIC FINDERS OR EMBEDDED SQL?

A question that needs to be addressed straightaway is, "Why does the `ReportController` pass the report data to the report instead of the report looking up the data using a simple SQL statement embedded in the report template?" The answer is pretty simple. That would be a perfectly legitimate approach in many situations (see the "An Alternate Approach" section at the end of the chapter), but using the dynamic finder and the domain model provides a couple of advantages.

First, when the domain model becomes more complicated, writing the SQL to navigate all of the tables and relationships is error prone and difficult. You already defined all of this information in the domain model using GORM, so why not just reuse it?

Second, your goal is to learn Grails, and using embedded SQL would cause you to miss out on using dynamic finders and dynamically calling the appropriate action on the `TodoController` to gather the data.

Now that you have an idea of how to approach creating the reporting facility, you need to add JasperReports to the application and create the report template. The next couple of sections will take you through that process. With that accomplished, you will construct the individual components and tie everything together. By the end of this chapter, you will have a pretty nice reporting facility that will allow you to easily create reports in multiple output formats.

Reporting Tools

In this section, you will receive a high-level overview of JasperReports (the runtime reporting engine) and iReports (the report designer). You will install iReports and add the appropriate JasperReports libraries to the application.

Overview

JasperReports is a popular open source Java reporting engine from JasperSoft.[2] You can use JasperReports to define robust, professional reports that include graphics and charts. You set up and define JasperReports reports using XML. The reporting engine uses the

---

2. `http://www.jaspersoft.com`

report definition and a data source to produce a report in a variety of output formats, including PDF, XML, HTML, CSV, XLS, RTF, and TXT.

JasperReports uses third-party libraries to render reports. The engine itself is not an executable application. It is intended to be embedded into a client or server-side application. The application is responsible for passing the XML report definition, data source, parameters, and configuration information to a report exporter. The exporter returns a ByteArrayOutputStream containing the report content to the application. In the case of a typical server application, the application sets the appropriate content type on an HTML response and streams the results to the browser.

■**Tip** JasperReports relies on Abstract Window Toolkit (AWT) to render the report. If you intend to run Collab-Todo in a Linux/Unix environment without graphics support, you will need to specify the headless environment by setting –Djava.awt.headless=true. You can do this by setting the JAVA_OPT environmental variable (e.g., JAVA_OPT='–Djava.awt.headless=true').

The XML report definition, known as a *report template* in Jasper terms, defines the content and layout of the report. You can define the report by hand using an XML editor, but this would be time consuming and error prone. Luckily, JasperSoft created iReports, a graphic report designer for JasperReports that defines and compiles JasperReports. It is much easier to build reports using iReports than it is to build the XML report definition by hand.

■**Note** A full exploration of JasperReports and iReports is beyond the scope of this book. In addition to the JasperSoft web site, the Apress books *The Definitive Guide to JapserReports*[3] and *The Definitive Guide to iReports*[4] are good sources of information.

Installing JasperReports and iReports

Installing JasperReports and iReports is easy. You can download iReports from the iReports home page[5] or from SourceForge.[6] Download and execute the Windows installer version.

---

3. Teodor Danciu and Lucian Chirita, *The Definitive Guide to JasperReports* (Berkeley, CA: Apress, 2007).

4. Giulio Toffoli, *The Definitive Guide to iReports* (Berkeley, CA: Apress, 2007).

5. http://jasperforge.org/sf/projects/ireport

6. http://sourceforge.net/projects/ireport

■**Note** If you're using an operating system other than Windows, you will need to download the `.zip` or `.tar` file and install it manually by unzipping or unpacking it into an appropriate location.

The Windows installer installs iReports in the directory of your choice; remember where it's installed. iReports includes JasperReports and all of the required third-party libraries. Copy the following files from the `iReports/lib` directory to the `collab-todo/lib` directory:

- `poi-x.x.x-FINAL-x.jar`

- `commons-beanutils-x.x.jar`

- `commons-collections-x.x.jar`

- `commons-dbcp-x.x.x.jar`

- `commons-digester-x.x.jar`

- `commons-logging-x.x.x.jar`

- `commons-logging-api-x.x.x.jar`

- `commons-pool-x.x.jar`

- `itext-x.x.x.jar`

- `jasperreports-x.x.x.jar`

Grails uses these JAR files to invoke JasperReports.

Creating the To-Do Report

Now that iReports is installed, you're ready to build the to-do report, as shown in Figure 10-1. You will take the following steps to create the report:

1. Define a JavaBeans data source for Collab-Todo.

2. Create the first iteration of the report using the iReport Wizard.

3. Enhance the report.

4. Compile the report.

Defining the Data Source

If you recall from the overview, the ReportController gathers the report data from another controller and ultimately passes the data to the reporting engine. This means that instead of using a JDBC database connection, the report uses a JavaBeans data source. Let's define the data source:

1. From iReports, select the Data ➤ Connections/Data Sources menu option. You will be presented with a list of currently defined and example data sources.

2. Click the New button to define a new data source. You will be presented with a "Connections properties" dialog box.

3. Select the "JavaBeans set data source" option from the list of available data sources, and click the Next button. You will be presented with the "JavaBeans set data source" options.

4. Set the name to Collab-Todo and blank out the factory class and static method fields. Figure 10-3 shows the contents of this page.

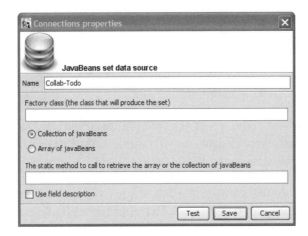

Figure 10-3. *The "JavaBeans set data source" page*

5. Click the Save button. You should see your new data source in the list of available data sources.

6. Close this window.

You're now ready to define the report using the wizard.

Using iReports

Now that you've defined a data source, you're ready to start building the report. If you're already familiar with iReports, you can skim through this section and move on to "The Report Tag" section.

MAKING IREPORTS AWARE OF THE COLLAB-TODO CLASSES

iReports uses the Collab-Todo domain class to create the report, so you need to make iReports aware of the domain classes. Ideally, you would just add the location of the Collab-Todo classes to the iReports classpath. At the time of writing, however, a bug in iReports prevents this from working as desired. You have to decide if you'd like to manually describe the JavaBean fields within iReports, or if you'd like to create a JAR file of the classes and put it in the iReports `lib` directory.

For our purposes, it's easier and less error-prone to create a JAR file of the Collab-Todo classes. By default, the Collab-Todo classes should be located in `USER_HOME/.grails/1.0.2/projects/collab-todo/classes`. You can use your favorite JAR/ZIP tool to create a JAR of the classes and place it in the iReports `lib` directory. This will make iReports aware of the Collab-Todo domain classes.

If you're familiar with iReports, you can go ahead and create the report however you see fit. However, we're assuming that you're new to iReports, so follow these steps to use the iReports Wizard.

1. Select the File ➤ Report Wizard menu option.

2. Specify the data that you want in the report. For your purposes, you want to set the Connections/Data Sources field to Collab-Todo, if it isn't already. This tells iReports that you're using a JavaBeans data source.

3. Tell iReports the domain class that contains the data. You're creating a to-do report, so the "JavaBean class" field should be set to Todo. The wizard should look something like Figure 10-4.

Figure 10-4. *Specifying the data source*

4. Assuming that you followed the instructions in the "Making iReports Aware of the Collab-Todo Classes" sidebar, when you click the Next button, you will be given the opportunity to select the fields that should be included in the report. The wizard should look something like Figure 10-5.

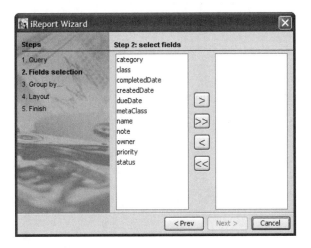

Figure 10-5. *Selecting fields*

Add all of the fields except for the class and metaClass, and click the Next button. The metaClass is internal Grails metadata and wouldn't be appropriate for a report. The next screen lists the fields and their datatypes. Click the Next button to continue.

5. You should now be on step 3, "Group by." You don't have any work to do here, so click the Next button to move to step 4, Layout.

6. The wizard lets you pick from some predefined layouts. As a starting point, check "Columnar layout" and highlight classicC.xml. Your screen should look something like Figure 10-6.

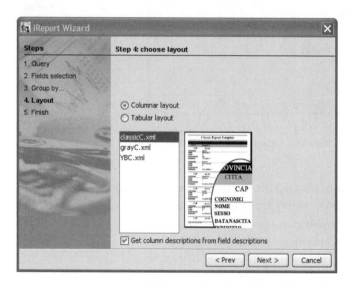

Figure 10-6. *Selecting the layout*

7. Click the Next button to move to step 5, Finish. Click the Finish button to generate the report template. You should have a report template that looks like Figure 10-7.

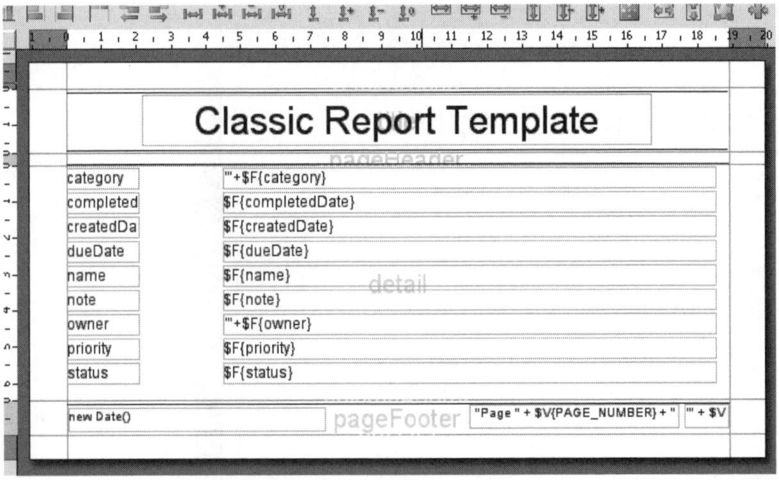

Figure 10-7. *The to-do report template*

Congratulations; you have your first report. It isn't pretty, but it is functional. At this point, you could compile the report and run it. If that's what you would like to do, skip forward to "Compiling the Report." Next, you will make the report a little more usable.

As you can see, iReports used the attribute names to create the labels. As a first step toward making the report a little more usable, type in your own text for the labels. You may have to resize the field by dragging the right side of the label.

Enhancing the Report

As you can see, iReports used the Todo property names to create the labels. You should rearrange the labels and fields to an order that makes more sense. You may want to copy the example shown in Figure 10-8.

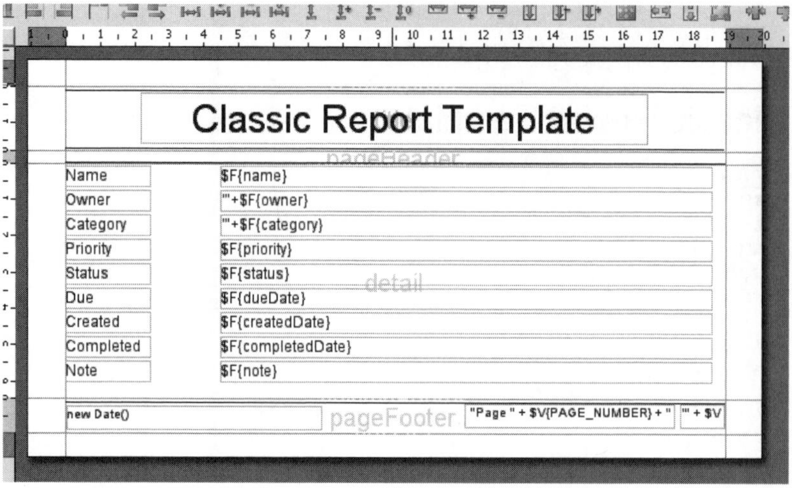

Figure 10-8. *Rearranged labels and fields*

The report is starting to look better, but you could do more. Follow these steps to enhance the report:

1. Take a good look at the Note field. It's a little small, so expand it by dragging the bottom edge of the field down.

2. The title could use a little work, so add the username, which is passed to the report as a parameter. To define the username, right-click the parameter entry in the Document Structure window and select Add ➤ Parameter. iReports displays a pop-up window that lets you input the parameter name. Set the Parameter Name field to userName, as shown in Figure 10-9.

Figure 10-9. *Setting up the parameter*

3. Now that you have defined the parameter, you can use it in the report header. Insert the userName parameter into the header by dragging it from the list of parameters in the Document Structure window to the report header. Also, change the current text to read "Todo for:." Figure 10-10 shows an example of the new header.

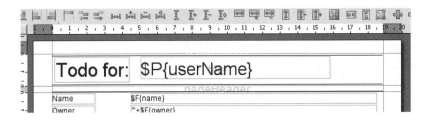

Figure 10-10. *The new header*

4. Save the report as `userTodo.jrxml` in the Collab-Todo application directory.

You're now ready to compile the report and start integrating it into the application.

Compiling the Report

Now that you've set up the report, it's time to make it available to the application. You need to compile it and copy the compiled file to the appropriate application directory.

Select Build ➤ Compile in iReports. You will see the results of the compilation at the bottom of iReports in the output console. Hopefully, the build is successful the first time, but if it isn't, work through the error messages and try again. Once you have a successful build, copy the `userTodo.jasper` file from the iReports home directory to the `collab-todo/web-app/reports` directory.

The Report Tag

You have used several tags, but now it's time to create your own. If you have developed tags before, you will be pleasantly surprised by how easy it is in Grails. You will create a report tag library to hold the report tag and then implement the tag as a closure.

Tag Library Overview

It is a best practice to group tags by topic into a tag library. In this case, all report tags are grouped together in the `grails-app/taglib/ReportTagLib.groovy`. Notice the Grails conventions again: tag libraries end with `TagLib.groovy` and are located in the `grails-app/taglib` directory. The following command illustrates creating the tag library:

```
> grails create-tag-lib Report
```

The results of the command can be seen here:

```
Welcome to Grails 1.0-2 - http://grails.org/
Licensed under Apache Standard License 2.0
Grails home is set to: C:\Apps\grails\grails-1.0-2

Base Directory: C:\workspace \collab-todo
Environment set to development
Running script C:\Apps\grails\grails-1.0-RC1\scripts\CreateTagLib.groovy
    [copy] Copying 1 file to C:\workspace\collab-todo\grails-app\taglib
Created TagLib for Report
    [copy] Copying 1 file to C:\workspace\collab-todo\test\integration
Created TagLibTests for Report
```

As you have come to expect, Grails created the tag library and an integration test. The next step is to create the tag.

Creating the Tag

As you saw in Chapter 8, a tag is a closure that has two arguments: a map of tag attributes and the body of the tag. Listing 10-1 illustrates the tag library class.

Listing 10-1. *Tag Library Class*

```
class ReportTagLib {

    def report = { attrs, body ->

    . . .

    }
}
```

Now you have to figure out what to put between the curly braces. You know you have to let the users choose in which format they want to receive the report, and you know that you have to invoke the ReportController to generate the report. With this in mind, you can start designing the tag inputs. Let's take a look at it from a usage point of view. Listing 10-2 illustrates how that tag might look inside a view.

Listing 10-2. *Report Tag*

```
<g:report id="todoReport" controller="TodoController"
          action="userTodo" report="userTodo"
          format="PDF,HTML,CSV,XLS,RTF,TXT,XML">
  <input type="hidden" name="userName" value="${todoList[0]?.owner}" />
</g:report>
```

Based upon the requirements, this should make some sense. The report tag has an id attribute to uniquely identify it. The controller and action attributes work together to specify which action to run to get the report data. The report attribute specifies which report to generate, and the format attribute supplies a list of report formats for users to select. The hidden input determines which user's information to gather. With this information, you can turn your attention back to the tag implementation. The tag body gives you a pretty good hint about the implementation. The tag generates a <form> element that invokes the ReportController's index action. The format attribute is used to display icons representing each of the report formats. Listing 10-3 contains the implementation of the report tag.

Listing 10-3. *Report Tag Implementation*

```
01  def report = { attrs, body ->
02
03    validateAttributes(attrs)
04    def appPath = grailsAttributes.getApplicationUri(request)
05
06    out << """
07        <form id=\"${attrs['id']}\" name=\"${attrs['report']}\"
08          action=\"${appPath}/report\">
09        <input type=\"hidden\" name=\"format\"/>
10        <input type=\"hidden\" name=\"file\" value=\"${attrs['report']}\"/>
11        <input type=\"hidden\" name=\"_controller\"
12          value=\"${attrs['controller']}\"/>
13        <input type=\"hidden\" name=\"_action\" value=\"${attrs['action']}\"/>
14    """
15    TreeSet formats = attrs['format'].split(",")
16    formats.each{
17      out << """
18        <a href=\"#${attrs['report']}Report\"
19                  onClick=\"document.getElementById('${attrs['id']}').
20                    format.value = '${it}';
21                    document.getElementById('${attrs['id']}').submit()\">
22        <img width=\"16px\" height=\"16px\" border=\"0\"
23                  src=\"${appPath}/images/icons/${it}.gif\" />
24        </a>
```

```
25     """
26   }
27   out << body()
28   out << "</form>"
29 }
30
31 private void validateAttributes(attrs) {
32   //Verify the 'id' attribute
33   if(attrs.id == null)
34     throw new Exception("The 'id' attribute in 'report' tag mustn't be 'null'")
35
36   //Verify the 'format' attribute
37   def availableFormats = ["CSV","HTML","RTF","XLS","PDF","TXT","XML"]
38   attrs.format.toUpperCase().split(",").each{
39     if(!availableFormats.contains(it)){
40       throw new Exception("""Value ${it} is a invalid format attribute.
41            Only ${availableFormats} are permitted""")
42     }
43   }
44 }
```

Let's take a look at the tag implementation line by line. In line 1, the tag takes two arguments: an attribute map and the body. Because you specified the report formats on the tag, the tag in line 3 has to validate that you specified supported report formats. Line 4 creates a local variable for the application path. Lines 6–14 create the form and hidden input fields to allow tag attributes to be passed to the ReportController. But wait, where was out defined? The out variable is a handle to the output stream that is injected by Grails.

Lines 15–25 iterate over the tag format attribute to create icons for each of the report formats. If you look closely, you will see that when the user selects the report format, the hidden input field format is set and the form is submitted. Line 27 outputs the tag body, and line 28 completes the form definition. Lines 31–44 are the body of the validateAttributes method called on line 3. This method iterates through the tag format attribute to validate that you specified valid report formats.

The ReportController and the ReportService

As you saw in Figure 10-1, the ReportController follows these three steps to create the report:

1. Gather data for the report by invoking a controller/action.

2. Locate a compiled report

3. Ask the ReportService to generate the report, and wrap the output with the appropriate content type.

Start by running the following code to create the ReportController:

```
> grails create-controller Report
```

Now you need to implement the three steps listed previously. Listing 10-4 illustrates gathering the report data.

Listing 10-4. *Gathering the Report Data*

```
import org.springframework.context.ApplicationContext;
import org.codehaus.groovy.grails.web.servlet.GrailsApplicationAttributes

class ReportController {
    ReportService reportService

    def index = {
        // Gather data for the report.
        // 1) Find the controller
        ApplicationContext ctx = (ApplicationContext) session.
            getServletContext().
            getAttribute(GrailsApplicationAttributes.APPLICATION_CONTEXT);
        def controller = ctx.getBean("${params._controller}");

        // 2) Invoke the action
        def inputCollection = controller."${params._action}"(params)
        params.inputCollection = inputCollection
```

The first step in gathering data for the report is to dynamically invoke the action supplied by the report tag. The tag specifies the controller and the action to be invoked to gather the data. The controller and the action to invoke are passed in the params map. The problem is that the values are just strings. You use the Spring application context to get an instance of the controller. Then you invoke the action on the controller, passing the params map to it.

Next, you need to locate the report. The compiled reports are located in the web-app/ reports directory. Listing 10-5 illustrates using the servletContext to locate and load the report.

Listing 10-5. *Locating and Loading the Report*

```
// Find the compiled report
def reportFileName = reportService.reportFileName("${params.file}")
def reportFile = servletContext.getResource(reportFileName)
```

```
if(reportFile == null){
    throw new FileNotFoundException("""\"${reportFileName}\" file must be in
        reports repository.""")
}
```

Finally, you need to generate the report and wrap the output with the proper content type. The `ReportController` calls the `ReportService` to generate the report. You could collapse the service into the controller, but the controller's purpose is to control, not do the actual work. The controller should delegate the actual work to some other component. Delegating the actual report generation to the report service maintains a separation of concerns and encapsulates knowledge of the JasperReports libraries into a single location, the `ReportService`. Listing 10-6 illustrates delegating to the `ReportService` and wrapping the output in the appropriate context type.

Listing 10-6. *Calling the ReportService*

```
// Call the ReportService to invoke the reporting engine
    switch(params.format){
        case "PDF":
            createPdfFile(reportService.generateReport(reportFile,
                reportService.PDF_FORMAT,params ).toByteArray(),params.file)
            break
        case "HTML":
            render(text:reportService.generateReport(reportFile,
                reportService.HTML_FORMAT,params),contentType:"text/html")
            break
        case "CSV":
            render(text:reportService.generateReport(reportFile,
                reportService.CSV_FORMAT,params),contentType:"text")
            break
        case "XLS":
            createXlsFile(reportService.generateReport(reportFile,
                reportService.XLS_FORMAT,params).toByteArray(),params.file)
            break
        case "RTF":
            createRtfFile(reportService.generateReport(reportFile,
                reportService.RTF_FORMAT,params).toByteArray(),params.file)
            break
        case "XML":
            render(text:reportService.generateReport(reportFile,
                reportService.XML_FORMAT,params),contentType:"text")
            break
```

```
    case "TXT":
        render(text:reportService.generateReport(reportFile,
            reportService.TEXT_FORMAT,params),contentType:"text")
        break
    default:
        throw new Exception("Invalid format")
        break
    }
}


/**
 * Output a PDF response
 */
def createPdfFile = { contentBinary, fileName ->
    response.setHeader("Content-disposition", "attachment; filename=" +
        fileName + ".pdf");
    response.contentType = "application/pdf"
    response.outputStream << contentBinary
}


/**
 * Output an Excel response
 */
def createXlsFile = { contentBinary, fileName ->
    response.setHeader("Content-disposition", "attachment; filename=" +
        fileName + ".xls");
    response.contentType = "application/vnd.ms-excel"
    response.outputStream << contentBinary
}


/**
 * Output an RTF response
 */
def createRtfFile = { contentBinary, fileName ->
    response.setHeader("Content-disposition", "attachment; filename=" +
        fileName + ".rtf");
    response.contentType = "application/rtf"
    response.outputStream << contentBinary
}
```

Now that you have the controller, you need to set up the ReportService. You can create the ReportService by running this command:

```
> grails create-service Report
```

The main functionality in the ReportService is encapsulation of the logic to generate the report using the JasperReports API. Listing 10-7 contains the ReportService.

Listing 10-7. *ReportService*

```
01  import java.io.ByteArrayOutputStream
02  import java.io.InputStream
03  import java.sql.Connection
04  import java.sql.Timestamp
05  import java.util.HashMap
06
07  import net.sf.jasperreports.engine.JRException
08  import net.sf.jasperreports.engine.JRExporter
09  import net.sf.jasperreports.engine.JasperPrint
10  import net.sf.jasperreports.engine.JasperFillManager
11  import net.sf.jasperreports.engine.JRExporterParameter
12  import net.sf.jasperreports.engine.export.JRCsvExporter
13  import net.sf.jasperreports.engine.export.JRHtmlExporter
14  import net.sf.jasperreports.engine.export.JRHtmlExporterParameter
15  import net.sf.jasperreports.engine.export.JRPdfExporter
16  import net.sf.jasperreports.engine.export.JRXlsExporter
17  import net.sf.jasperreports.engine.export.JRXmlExporter
18  import net.sf.jasperreports.engine.export.JRRtfExporter
19  import net.sf.jasperreports.engine.export.JRTextExporter
20  import net.sf.jasperreports.engine.export.JRTextExporterParameter
21  import net.sf.jasperreports.engine.data.JRBeanCollectionDataSource
22
23  class ReportService {
24
25    boolean transactional = true
26
27    int PDF_FORMAT = 1;
28    int HTML_FORMAT = 2;
29    int TEXT_FORMAT = 3;
30    int CSV_FORMAT = 4;
31    int XLS_FORMAT = 5;
32    int RTF_FORMAT = 6;
33    int XML_FORMAT = 7;
34
35
```

```
36
37   /**
38    * Generate the Report
39    */
40   def generateReport = {jasperFile, format, parameters ->
41
42     // Setup the Data Source
43     JRBeanCollectionDataSource ds = new JRBeanCollectionDataSource(
44           parameters.inputCollection);
45
46     InputStream input = jasperFile.openStream()
47     JRExporter exporter
48     ByteArrayOutputStream byteArray = new ByteArrayOutputStream()
49     JasperPrint jasperPrint = JasperFillManager.fillReport(input, parameters,ds)
50     switch (format) {
51       case PDF_FORMAT:
52         exporter = new JRPdfExporter()
53         break
54       case HTML_FORMAT:
55         exporter = new JRHtmlExporter()
56         exporter.setParameter(JRHtmlExporterParameter.
57             IS_USING_IMAGES_TO_ALIGN, false)
58         break
59       case CSV_FORMAT:
60         exporter = new JRCsvExporter()
61         break
62       case TEXT_FORMAT:
63         exporter = new JRTextExporter()
64         exporter.setParameter(JRTextExporterParameter.CHARACTER_WIDTH,
65             new Integer(10));
66         exporter.setParameter(JRTextExporterParameter.CHARACTER_HEIGHT,
67             new Integer(10));
68         break
69       case XLS_FORMAT:
70         exporter = new JRXlsExporter()
71         break
72       case RTF_FORMAT:
73         exporter = new JRRtfExporter()
74         break
75       case XML_FORMAT:
76         exporter = new JRXmlExporter()
77         break
```

```
78        default:
79          throw new Exception("Unknown report format")
80      }
81      exporter.setParameter(JRExporterParameter.OUTPUT_STREAM, byteArray)
82      exporter.setParameter(JRExporterParameter.JASPER_PRINT, jasperPrint)
83      exporter.exportReport()
84      return byteArray
85    }
86
87    def reportFileName = { reportName ->
88        return "/reports/"+reportName+".jasper"
89    }
90 }
```

Let's walk through this. Line 40 is the beginning of the generateReport closure. As you can see, generateReport takes three input parameters: the report template, the report format, and parameters. Lines 42–44 define and populate a JavaBeans collection data source. If you look closely, you will see that the data source is populated from an input collection contained with the parameters. This is the collection that the ReportController created.

Lines 46–48 do some additional setup. Line 49 passes the report template, parameters, and JavaBeans data source to the reporting engine. Lines 50–80 set up the appropriate rendering component based upon the report format type requested, while lines 81–82 set some additional parameters on the renderer. Line 83 is where the real magic happens: it causes the report to be generated. The results are returned to the caller on line 84.

In Listing 10-5, you may recall seeing something like the following:

```
reportService.reportFileName($params.file)
```

Lines 87–89 contain the implementation of this method, which, as you can tell, is pretty basic. You simply prepend the directory and append the file extension to create the report file name. You could easily have done this in the ReportController, but you really don't want the ReportController to know that you're using JasperReports. By doing it this way, you maintain a separation of concerns and encapsulation.

You're now ready to tie it all together and see the result of your work.

Tying It All Together

You're about to see the result of your work. You installed iReports and copied the appropriate libraries to the application. You created the report and the report tag library. You created the ReportService and the ReportController. The only thing left to do is to write the code that gathers the report data and hook the report tag into the application.

Gathering the Report Data

Recall from "The Report Tag" section that the tag allows you to specify the controller and the action to call to gather the report data. In this case, you'll specify the TodoController and the userTodo action, so you'll need to create a userTodo action on the TodoController. Listing 10-8 contains the content of the action.

Listing 10-8. *Gathering the Report Data*

```
def userTodo = {
     def user = User.get(session.user.id)
     return Todo.findAllByOwner(user)
}
```

The code in Listing 10-8 finds all the to-dos for the current user and returns the results. Now, you have to hook the report tag into the application.

Adding the Report Tag to the Application

The last step is to add the report tag to the Todo List view and then edit the Todo List view (grails-app/views/todo/list.gsp). At the bottom of the file, after the paginate logic, add the report tag. Follow Listing 10-9 as an example.

Listing 10-9. *Adding the Report Tag*

```
. . .
<div class="paginateButtons">
  <g:paginate total="${Todo.count()}" />
</div>
  <g:report id="todoReport" controller="TodoController"
            action="userTodo" report="userTodo"
            format="PDF,HTML,CSV,XLS,RTF,TXT,XML">
    <input type="hidden" name="userName" value="${todoList[0]?.owner}" />
  </g:report>
</div>
</body>
</html>
```

Now let's take a look at the results. Start the application, log in, and select the PDF icon. Figure 10-11 shows the report.

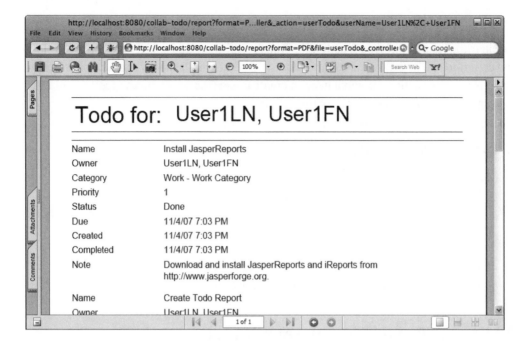

Figure 10-11. *The report*

Congratulations, you have successfully built a reporting facility. Now that you have one, it would be a shame to not reuse it.

The Report List

You have done a lot of good work; you have constructed all of the core components of a reporting facility and enhanced a view with the report tag to give users access to reports. You also saw how to use the following command to pass report parameters to the data collection action:

```
<input type="hidden" name="userName" value="${todoList[0]?.owner}" />
```

In this case, the parameter was a hidden field, but it could have just as easily been a visible input field.

It would be reasonable for users to say that they want to be able to specify a due-date range and to only show to-do items that are within the range. What would it take to fulfill such a request? Well, you would need to construct a Reports List view and hook it into the application. This view would need to list all of the available reports. If a report doesn't require any additional parameters, you could execute it directly from the Reports List view. If a report requires additional parameters, it will launch another page that allows users to specify the input parameters for the report.

The best thing is, you can reuse all of the components you just created. Pretty cool. Given the fact that this is all a rehash of everything you have learned, we are going to leave this as an exercise for you to develop on your own. However, if you get in a jam, check out the application source code for this chapter in the Source Code/Download area of the Apress web site (http://www.apress.com). We have included just such a solution in the application.

An Alternate Approach

Earlier in the chapter, we discussed using the domain model to give data to the reports or using embedded SQL. We decided to use the domain model approach for several good reasons, but the alternative is worth considering.

Marcos Fábio Pereira created a Jasper plug-in for Grails. As a matter of fact, Marcos' work provided some of the inspiration for this chapter. So here is a big shout-out to Marcos: thank you Marcos; your good work is appreciated.

The Jasper plug-in takes the embedded SQL approach. Depending upon your circumstances, this may be a good solution for you. You can take a look at the Jasper plug-in by running:

```
> grails list-plugins
```

and locating the Jasper entry. Then run:

```
> grails install-plugin Jasper 0.5
```

A look at the Jasper tag will get you started.

Summary

You accomplished a lot in this chapter. Instead of building a static solution for one report, you built a dynamic reporting facility that supports multiple reports and multiple formats, and accepts input to drive the selection of report data.

In the process of building the reporting facility, you installed and configured the JasperReports reporting engine and the iReports report designer. You used iReports to define and compile the report template.

You then moved on to creating a report tag library. You created the ReportController for the report tag to call. The ReportController took care of facilitating the data collection and invoking the ReportService to generate the report. In the ReportService, you wrapped the Todo domain objects in a JavaBeans data source, and you passed the data source, parameters, and report template to the JasperReports reporting engine for processing.

The reporting engine returned a binary version of the report, which the `ReportController` then returned to the user.

This chapter allowed you to learn some new things, and it reinforced some things you learned earlier. It showed you how to build a reporting facility that supports multiple reports and formats. The next chapter leverages the `ReportService` in a nightly batch job to generate and e-mail user to-do reports.

CHAPTER 11

■■■

Batch Processing

Grails is more than just a web framework—it is an application framework. And almost all applications contain functionality that must be executed on a periodic basis (every 15 minutes, once an hour, twice a day, daily, weekly, month, quarterly, yearly). This is known as *batch processing*.

The Grails team anticipated the need for batch processing and decided to leverage a popular open source third-party enterprise job scheduling library: Quartz,[1] from OpenSymphony. Since the Spring Framework is a core component of Grails, and the Spring Framework already includes a Quartz integration, this was a natural choice. A Quartz Grails plug-in makes it easy to use the Quartz library.

Quartz is similar to the Unix cron facility in that it provides the ability to execute a job in the future. However, Quartz is different from the Unix cron facility because it runs within the application server and has full access to all of the application components.

This chapter explores batch-processing functionality. We will start by installing the Quartz plug-in and creating a simple job. Then we will move on to creating a sample batch-reporting facility.

Installing the Quartz Plug-in

As we mentioned, Grails leverages Quartz for job-scheduling functionality. The Quartz plug-in[2] integrates Quartz into Grails and makes Quartz easy to use.

To begin, from within the project directory, execute the following command:

```
>grails install-plugin quartz
```

---

1. http://www.opensymphony.com/quartz
2. http://grails.org/Quartz+plugin

This installs the plug-in:

```
Welcome to Grails 1.0 - http://grails.org/
Licensed under Apache Standard License 2.0
Grails home is set to: C:\Apps\grails\grails-1.0

Base Directory: <<WORKSPACE>>\collab-todo

Environment set to development
Running script C:\Apps\grails\grails-1.0\scripts\InstallPlugin.groovy
    [mkdir] Created dir: <<USER_HOME>>\.grails\1.0 \plugins\quartz
      [get] Getting: http://plugins.grails.org/grails-quartz/tags/RELEASE_0_2/gr
ails-quartz-0.2.zip
      [get] To: <<USER_HOME>>\.grails\1.0 \plugins\quartz\grails-quartz-0.2.zip
...............................
     [copy] Copying 1 file to <<WORKSPACE>>\collab-todo\plugins
    [mkdir] Created dir: <<WORKSPACE>>\collab-todo\plugins\quartz-0.2
    [unzip] Expanding: <<WORKSPACE>>\collab-todo\plugins\grails-quartz-0.2.zip
into <<WORKSPACE>>\collab-todo\plugins\quartz-0.2
Executing quartz-0.2 plugin post-install script ...
    [mkdir] Created dir: <<WORKSPACE>>\collab-todo\grails-app\jobs
Compiling plugin quartz-0.2 ... ...
Compiling 9 source files to <<USER_HOME>>\.grails\1.0 \projects\collab-todo\classes
Plugin quartz-0.2 installed
Plug-in provides the following new scripts:
-----------------------------------------
grails create-job
```

As you can see, the plug-in installation created the quartz-0.2 directory under the plugins directory, created the jobs directory under grails-app, and added a create-job script to the Grails command line.

Creating a Job

A *job* is a program that contains the code you wish to run. In Grails, the job defines what to do and when to do it.

As a simple demonstration of Quartz in action, let's create a job that prints a message and the current time. The first step is to create the job, as follows:

```
> grails create-job first
```

The command generates the `FirstJob` class, in the `grails/job` directory:

```
class FirstJob {
    def timeout = 5000l      // execute job once in 5 seconds

    def execute() {
    // execute task
    }
}
```

■Note Look closely at the `timeout` value, and you'll see an `l` after the `5000`. The `l` makes the variable a `Long`. Also notice that `create-job` follows conventions just like other `create-*` commands, and appends the suffix `Job` to the end of the job name.

The `create-job` command creates a skeleton job that is preconfigured to run once, five seconds after the application server starts. So, five seconds after the server starts, the code in the `execute()` method will be executed. Add the following code to the `execute()` method:

```
println "Hello from FirstJob: "+ new Date()
```

Listing 11-1 shows the completed `FirstJob` class.

Listing 11-1. *Completed FirstJob*

```
class FirstJob {
    def timeout = 5000l      // execute job once in 5 seconds

    def execute() {
        println "Hello from FirstJob: "+ new Date()
    }
```

Start the application by issuing the following command:

```
> grails run-app
```

While the comment for the `timeout` property in Listing 11-1 could be interpreted to mean that the `FirstJob` is executed only once, you can see from the output that it is executed every five seconds:

```
Welcome to Grails 1.0 - http://grails.org/
Licensed under Apache Standard License 2.0
Grails home is set to: C:\Apps\grails\grails-1.0


. . .


Loading with installed plug-ins: ["QuartzGrailsPlugin", "WebtestGrailsPlugin"] .
. . .
Running Grails application..


. . .


Server running. Browse to http://localhost:8080/collab-todo
Hello from FirstJob: Sun Dec 16 11:23:08 EST 2007
Hello from FirstJob: Sun Dec 16 11:23:13 EST 2007
Hello from FirstJob: Sun Dec 16 11:23:18 EST 2007
```

Now that you've seen how to create a simple job, let's move on to something a bit more useful: a batch-reporting facility.

Building a Batch-Reporting Facility

As an example, we will build a batch-reporting facility that generates to-do reports and e-mails them to the user nightly. We will leverage a couple of services created in earlier chapters: EMailAuthenticatedService from Chapter 8 and ReportService from Chapter 10. Figure 11-1 shows is an overview of the nightly reporting process.

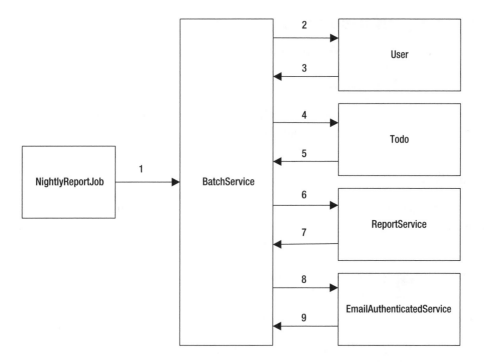

Figure 11-1. *Nightly reporting process*

The process starts with the NightlyReportJob. When the NightlyReportJob is invoked by Quartz, it immediately invokes the BatchService. The BatchService is the main control routine. It facilitates the interaction with other solution components. First, the BatchService retrieves all User objects that have an e-mail address. For each user, the BatchService retrieves the Todo objects. The BatchService then uses the ReportService to generate a PDF report. Finally, the BatchService uses the EmailAuthenticatedService to send the user an e-mail attachment of the report.

Building the batch-reporting facility requires the following steps:

- Create and configure the execution of the NightlyReportJob.

- Retrieve the user's to-dos.

- Invoke the report service (created in Chapter 10).

- Invoke the e-mail service (created in Chapter 8).

Creating a Nightly Reporting Job

Issue the following command to create the `NightlyReportJob`:

```
> grails create-job NightlyReport
```

In addition to the `timeout` property, which you saw earlier in the `FirstJob` job, several additional properties can be used to control job execution.

Setting the Name and Group

The `name` and `group` properties are used to help you identify jobs when interacting with the Quartz scheduler:

```
class NightlyReportJob {
    def name = "NightlyReport" // Job name
    def group = "CollabTodo"   // Job group
```

■**Note** Grails automatically binds the Hibernate session to the jobs. Having a bound session allows the job to retrieve data from the database. If for some (rare) reason, you don't want Grails to do this, you can tell Grails to not bind a Hibernate session by setting the `sessionRequired` property to `false`.

Controlling Execution Frequency

There are two techniques for controlling the job execution frequency:

Use the `startDelay` *and* `timeout` *properties*: These two properties allow you to control the execution frequency of the job. The `startDelay` property delays starting the job for a number of milliseconds after the application starts up. This can be useful when you need to let the system start up before the job starts. Grails defaults the `startDelay` property to 0. The `timeout` property is the number of milliseconds between executions of the job. Grails defaults the `timeout` property to 60,000 milliseconds, or 1 minute.

Use the `cronExpression` *property*: For all of the Unix geeks out there, this works just as you would expect. It is a string that describes the execution frequency using a crontab format. If you're not familiar with this approach, don't worry—we'll explain the format in more detail here.

Both techniques have their place in controlling execution frequency. Determining which technique to use depends on the job requirements. If the job can be handled by a timer, then setting the `startDelay` and `timeout` properties should be sufficient, as in this example:

```
def startDelay = 20000     // Wait 20 seconds to start the job
def timeout = 60000        // Execute job once every 60 seconds
```

If the job is very time-sensitive, then using the `cronExpression` property is probably more appropriate. But note that during development and initial testing of the job, you will probably want to use the `startDelay`/`timeout` technique, and then switch to the `cronExpression` approach later.

■**Caution** Depending on the execution frequency and duration of the job, It's possible to have multiple instances of a job executing concurrently. This could happen if a job is long running and still running when the `cronExpression` property causes it be invoked again. Having jobs running concurrently may or may not be desirable. By default, the Quartz plug-in permits the job to run concurrently. Most of the time, you probably won't want to allow a job to run concurrently. You can change this behavior by setting the `concurrent` property on the job to `false`.

A cron expression tells the job scheduler when to run the job. The `cronExpression` property value is composed of six fields, separated by whitespace, representing seconds, minutes, hours, day, month, day of week, and an optional seventh field for the year. A cron expression expresses the fields left to right:

```
Seconds Minutes Hours DayOfMonth Month DayOfWeek Year
```

For example, we define a `cronExpression` property to have the job run 1:00 a.m. every day as follows:

```
def cronExpression = "0 0 1 * * *"  // Run every day at 1:00 a.m.
```

Table 11-1 describes the cron expression fields, and Table 11-2 summarizes some of the more commonly used special characters.[3]

---

3. See the Quartz documentation for a more complete explanation of the special characters:
    `http://www.opensymphony.com/quartz/wikidocs/CronTriggers Tutorial.html`

Table 11-1. *Cron Expression Fields*

Field	Values	Special Characters
Seconds	0–59	, - * /
Minutes	0–59	, - * /
Hours	0–23	, - * /
DayOfMonth	1–31	, - * ? / L W C
Month	1–12 or JAN–DEC	, - * /
DayOfWeek	1–7 or SUN–SAT	, - * ? / L #
Year (optional)	Empty or 1970–2099	, - * /

Table 11-2. *Cron Expression Special Characters*

Character	Function	Example
*	All values—matches all allowed values within a field.	* in the Hours field matches every hour of the day, 0–23.
?	No specific value—used to specify something in one of the two fields in which it is allowed, but not the other.	To execute a job on the tenth day of the month, no matter what day of the week that is, put 10 in the DayOfMonth field and ? in the DayOfWeek field.
-	Used to specify a range of values.	2-6 in the DayOfWeek field causes the job to be invoked on Monday, Tuesday, Wednesday, Thursday, and Friday.
,	Used to create a list of values.	MON,WED,FRI in the DayOfWeek field causes the job to be invoked on Monday, Wednesday, and Friday.
/	Used to specify increments. The character before the slash indicates when to start. The character after the slash represents the increment.	0/15 in the Minutes field causes the job to be invoked on the quarter hour—0, 15, 30, and 45 minutes.

Cron expressions are very powerful. With a little imagination, you can specify a multitude of times. Table 11-3 shows some sample cron expressions.

Table 11-3. *Cron Expression Examples*

Expression	Meaning
0 0 1 * * ?	Invoke at 1:00 a.m. every day
0 15 2 ? * *	Invoke at 2:15 a.m. every day
0 15 2 * * ?	Invoke at 2:15 a.m. every day

Expression	Meaning
0 15 2 * * ? *	Invoke at 2:15 a.m. every day
0 15 2 * * ? 2008	Invoke at 2:15 a.m. every day during the year 2008
0 * 13 * * ?	Invoke every minute starting at 1 p.m. and ending at 1:59 p.m., every day
0 0/5 14 * * ?	Invoke every 5 minutes starting at 2 p.m. and ending at 2:55 p.m., every day
0 0/5 14,18 * * ?	Invoke every 5 minutes starting at 2 p.m. and ending at 2:55 p.m., and invoke every 5 minutes starting at 6 p.m. and ending at 6:55 p.m., every day
0 0-5 14 * * ?	Invoke every minute starting at 2 p.m. and ending at 2:05 p.m., every day
0 10,45 14 ? 3 WED	Invoke at 2:10 p.m. and at 2:45 p.m. every Wednesday in the month of March
0 15 2 ? * MON-FRI	Invoke at 2:15 a.m. every Monday, Tuesday, Wednesday, Thursday, and Friday
0 15 2 15 * ?	Invoke at 2:15 a.m. on the fifteenth day of every month
0 0 12 1/5 * ?	Invoke at 12 p.m. (noon) every 5 days every month, starting on the first day of the month
0 11 11 25 12 ?	Invoke every December 25 at 11:11 a.m.

Listing 11-2 shows the definition for the NightlyReportJob. Notice that it includes both techniques for controlling execution frequency, with the startDelay/timeout definitions commented out.

Listing 11-2. *NightlyReportJob Name, Group, and Execution Frequency Configuration*

```
class NightlyReportJob {
  def cronExpression = "0 0 1 * * *" // Run every day at 1:00 a.m.

  def name = "Nightly"               // Job name
  def group = "CollabTodo"           // Job group

//  def startDelay = 20000           // Wait 20 seconds to start the job
//  def timeout = 60000              // Execute job once every 60 seconds
```

You can see why the Grails team chose to integrate Quartz instead of creating something new. It is very powerful. Armed with this knowledge, you are ready to move on and implement the core logic of the nightly report job.

Retrieving the User's To-Dos

The next step is to leverage Spring's auto-wired dependency injection to inject the BatchService into the job, as follows:

```
> grails create-service Batch
```

Listing 11-3 illustrates injection and execution of the BatchService.

Listing 11-3. *NightlyReportJob with Batch Service*

```
class NightlyReportJob {
  def cronExpression = "0 0 1 * * *" // Run every day at 1:00 a.m.

  def name = "Nightly"              // Job name
  def group = "CollabTodo"          // Job group

//  def startDelay = 20000          // Wait 20 seconds to start the job
//  def timeout = 60000             // Execute job once every 60 seconds

  def batchService

  def execute() {
     log.info "Starting Nightly Job: "+new Date()
     batchService.nightlyReports.call()
     log.info "Finished Nightly Job: "+new Date()
  }
}
```

The code is straightforward. It defines when the job is to run and delegate to the BatchService.

The next step is to create the nightly closure on the batch service. It will contain the code to retrieve the user's to-dos. Listing 11-4 illustrates adding the nightly closure and retrieving the user's to-dos.

Listing 11-4. *Batch Service Nightly Closure*

```
class BatchService

   . . .
```

```
/*
 *  Runs nightly reports
 */
def nightlyReports = {
    log.info "Running Nightly Reports Batch Job: "+new Date()

    // 1. Gather user w/ email addresses.
    def users = User.withCriteria {
            isNotNull('email')
    }


    users?.each { user ->
        // 2. Invoke report service for each user.
        //     Can't reuse ReportController because it makes too
        //     many assumptions, such as access to session.class.
        //
        //     Reuse Report Service and pass appropriate params.
        // Gather the data to be reported.
        def inputCollection = Todo.findAllByOwner(user)

        // To be completed in the next section

    }

    log.info "Completed Nightly Reports Batch Job:  "+new Date()
}
```

The `BatchService.nightlyReports` gets all users with an e-mail address, and then for each user, gets their to-dos and prepares to invoke the report service.

Invoking the Report Service

In Chapter 10, you used JasperReports to build a report facility. You can reuse components of the report facility to create a to-do report PDF to attach to the e-mail.

Your first thought might be to use the `ReportController`. Well, that doesn't work. The report controller is dependent on the HTTP session and renders the PDF to the output stream. You need to go one level deeper and use the `ReportService` directly.

We have already retrieved the user's to-dos. Now all we need to do is pass the to-dos, report template, and a username parameter to the report service. The highlighted section of Listing 11-5 illustrates the required steps.

Listing 11-5. *Invoke the Report Service*

```
class BatchService {
  ReportService reportService  // Inject ReportService

  def nightlyReports = {

    . . .

    users?.each { user ->
        // 2. Invoke Report Service for each user.
        //    Reuse Report Service and pass appropriate params.
        // Gather the data to be reported.
        def inputCollection = Todo.findAllByOwner(user)
        Map params = new HashMap()
        params.inputCollection = inputCollection
        params.userName = user.firstName+" "+user.lastName

        // Load the report file.
        def reportFile = this.class.getClassLoader().getResource(
                "web-app/reports/userTodo.jasper")
        ByteArrayOutputStream byteArray = reportService.generateReport(reportFile,
                reportService.PDF_FORMAT,params )

        Map attachments = new HashMap()
        attachments.put("TodoReport.pdf", byteArray.toByteArray())

        // 3. Email results to the user.
        sendNotificationEmail(user, attachments)

    }
  }
}
```

The new code works as follows:

- Injects the ReportService into the BatchService.

- Creates a HashMap of parameters that will be passed to the ReportService. The parameters include the list of to-dos for the current user.

- Loads the JasperReports template from the classpath.

- Invokes reportService.generateReport to pass the report template, report format (PDF), and parameters.

Now that you have a PDF report, the next step is to e-mail it to the user.

Invoking the E-Mail Service

In Chapter 8, you implemented an SMTP e-mail service, called EMailAuthenticatedService. You can use your e-mail service to send the to-do report to the user. Listing 11-6 contains the code required to create and send the e-mail.

Listing 11-6. *Sending the E-mail*

```
01  class BatchService implements ApplicationContextAware {
02    boolean transactional = false
03
04    public void setApplicationContext(ApplicationContext applicationContext) {
05      this.applicationContext = applicationContext
06    }
07    def ApplicationContext applicationContext
08    def EMailAuthenticatedService EMailAuthenticatedService   // injected
09
10    ReportService reportService
11
12    def nightlyReports = {
13
14    . . .
15
16          // Load the report file
17          def reportFile = this.class.getClassLoader().getResource(
18              "web-app/reports/userTodo.jasper")
19          ByteArrayOutputStream byteArray =
20              reportService.generateReport(reportFile,
21              reportService.PDF_FORMAT,params )
22
23          Map attachments = new HashMap()
24          attachments.put("TodoReport.pdf", byteArray.toByteArray())
25
26          // 3. Email results to the user.
27          sendNotificationEmail(user, attachments)
28      }
29      log.info "Completed Nightly Batch Job:  "+new Date()
30    }
31
```

```
32   def private sendNotificationEmail = {User user, Map attachments ->
33     def emailTpl = this.class.getClassLoader().getResource(
34         "web-app/WEB-INF/nightlyReportsEmail.gtpl")
35     def binding = ["user": user]
36     def engine = new SimpleTemplateEngine()
37     def template = engine.createTemplate(emailTpl).make(binding)
38     def body = template.toString()

39     def email = [
40           to: [user.email],
41       subject: "Your Collab-Todo Report",
42       text:    body
43     ]
44     try {
45       EMailProperties eMailProperties =
46           applicationContext.getBean("eMailProperties")
47       eMailAuthenticatedService.sendEmail(email, eMailProperties, attachments)
48     } catch (MailException ex) {
49       log.error("Failed to send emails", ex)
50     }
51   }
52 }
```

The highlighted lines contain the changes made to the batch service. Lines 1 and 4–7 make the batch service (Spring) application context-aware; in other words, the Spring application context is injected into the service. You will use the application context later to look up some information. Line 8 takes advantages of Spring auto-wiring to inject the EmailAuthenticatedService. Lines 23 and 24 add the PDF report to a map of attachments for e-mail. Line 27 invokes a local sendNotificationEmail closure.

Lines 32–51 contain the code to send the to-do report e-mail to the user. Line 33 loads an e-mail template. Lines 36–38 use the Groovy SimpleTemplateEngine[4] to generate the e-mail body. Lines 39–43 define a map of e-mail parameters that will be passed to the e-mail service. Line 45 uses the Spring application context to look up e-mail properties, including the "from" address. Line 47 invokes the e-mail service, sending the e-mail map, e-mail properties, and the attachments.

---

4. http://groovy.codehaus.org/Groovy+Templates

Summary

This chapter demonstrated Grails' ability to reuse open source, third-party Java libraries. You installed the Quartz plug-in, created a simple job, and saw how to control the frequency of execution using the `timeout` property.

Next, you started to build the batch-reporting facility. You created a `NightlyReportJob` and configured it to run at 1:00 a.m. using the `cronExpression` property. You learned that cron expressions are very robust and provide fine-grained control over when the `NightlyReportJob` is invoked.

The `NightlyReportJob` delegated to a batch service that was injected using Spring autowiring injection and invoked `nightlyReports`. `nightlyReports` iterated through a list of users, gathered their to-dos, invoked the report service built in Chapter 10 to generate a PDF attachment, and e-mailed the attachment to the user using the `EmailAuthenticatedService` built in Chapter 8.

This chapter provided a brief introduction to the Quartz package. For more information, check out the Quartz web site.[5]

---

5. `http://www.opensymphony.com/quartz`

CHAPTER 12

■ ■ ■

Deploying and Upgrading

The previous chapters have been related to developing Grails applications. One of the strengths of Grails is that it comes bundled with everything you need to begin developing and testing your application. Grails embeds a web container (Jetty) and a relational database (HSQLDB). All you have to do is execute the Grails `run-app` target, and you have your entire runtime environment. However, at some point in time, you will want to expose your application to your users. The embedded runtime environment is for development and testing only, and it is not intended to scale or support the load necessary in a production environment.

This chapter focuses on deploying Grails applications to Java EE application servers and more robust database servers. It also covers some other miscellaneous, operational aspects, such as upgrading a Grails application when a new version of the Grails framework is released and automating tasks using Gant.

Deploying Grails Applications

Deploying a Grails application involves three steps. First, you need to configure the application. This typically involves environment-specific configurations. Second, you package the application. For Grails applications, this means bundling all the code and related artifacts into a WAR file. The final step is to actually deploy the application to an application server or web container.

Using Environments

Many organizations have multiple environments or gates that an application must pass through before reaching production and users. At a minimum, each application should have to pass through development, test, and production environments. The development environment is the developer's machine. In the test environment, which mimics production, somebody other than the developer completes quality assurance by validating that the application meets requirements and generally works. The production environment is where real users use the application. In each of these environments, you're likely to have environment-specific configurations and, rarer, behavioral differences. For example, in development, you may want to point to a local HSQLDB in-memory database, but in the test and production environments, you may need to point at a remote server database such as MySQL.[1]

As you might expect, Grails follows these best practices and is aware of these three environments. You can use these environments when calling the `grails` command line as the second parameter or in configuration files such as `DataSource.groovy` and `Config.groovy`, which you'll see in the next section. Table 12-1 shows the mapping per environment.

Table 12-1. *Environment Mappings*

Environment	Command Line	Configuration File Reference
Development	`dev`	`development`
Test	`test`	`test`
Production	`prod`	`production`

Depending on the size of the organization and the criticalness of the application or the system, you may have additional environments such as integration testing (IT), user acceptance testing (UAT), and performance testing (PT). You can use custom environments as well. The only requirement is that the `grails.env` system property must be passed to the `grails` command line. For example, the following would specify the performance environment:

```
> grails -Dgrails.env=PT run-app
```

Understanding Grails Configurations

Grails contains four primary configuration categories. The first is URL mapping, which we explained and demonstrated thoroughly in Chapter 9, so we won't be revisiting it here. The second is behavior when the application starts up and shuts down. The third and fourth are data source and logging configurations. You can find all these configurations in the `grails-app/config` directory.

Startup and Shutdown Behavior

Sometimes when an application starts up and/or shuts down, you need to do things such as acquire and release resources, respectively, or cache data. Grails makes this possible in the `grails-app/config/BootStrap.groovy` file, which you first saw in Chapter 7. Listing 12-1

---

1. http://www.mysql.org/

is an example of a BootStrap.groovy file. It includes comments where startup and shutdown code would go.

Listing 12-1. *Using BootStrap.groovy to Perform Startup and Shutdown Activities*

```
class BootStrap {

  def init = { servletContext ->
     // perform startup activities here
  }

  def destroy = {
    // perform shutdown activities here
  }
}
```

The init action is invoked when the application starts up or is redeployed. The javax.servlet.ServletContext[2] is passed in, providing access to the application attributes, initialization parameters configured in web.xml, the context path, and more. The destroy action is invoked when the application is shut down, but it is not guaranteed to be called. For example, it is not likely the destroy method will be called when the application server is shut down, but it is likely to be called when the application is redeployed or undeployed.

■**Note** As discussed and demonstrated in Chapter 7's "Bootstrapping" sidebar, you can use the GrailsUtil. environment() to determine which environment the application is running in and perform the appropriate bootstrapping code.

Data Source Configurations

By default, Grails is configured out of the box to use an embedded, in-memory HSQLDB database. This is not likely to be the database used in the test and production environments and possibly not even in most development environments, because as you've seen, each time the application restarts, the database gets re-created in memory and is therefore empty. It's more likely that an application will use a server database such as MySQL, Oracle,[3] DB2,[4] Microsoft SQL Server,[5] or maybe even Apache Derby.[6] It might

---

2. http://java.sun.com/products/servlet/2.5/docs/servlet-2_5-mr2/javax/servlet/ServletContext.html
3. http://www.oracle.com
4. http://www.ibm.com/db2
5. http://www.microsoft.com/sql/
6. http://db.apache.org/derby/

even use HSQLDB in a file mode. Any Hibernate-supported database[7] should be able to be used.

You can set database and Hibernate configurations in the `grails-app/config/DataSource.groovy` file. Listing 12-2 shows an example of a `DataSource.groovy` file that has been customized to include a production database configuration for a local MySQL database.

Note You can find installation and configuration instructions for MySQL at `http://www.beginninggroovyandgrails.com`.

Listing 12-2. *DataSource.groovy Containing a MySQL Production Configuration*

```
01 dataSource {
02     pooled = false
03     driverClassName = "org.hsqldb.jdbcDriver"
04     username = "sa"
05     password = ""
06 }
07 hibernate {
08     cache.use_second_level_cache=true
09     cache.use_query_cache=true
10     cache.provider_class='org.hibernate.cache.EhCacheProvider'
11 }
12 // environment specific settings
13 environments {
14     development {
15         dataSource {
16             dbCreate = "create-drop" // one of 'create', 'create-drop','update'
17             url = "jdbc:hsqldb:mem:devDB"
18         }
19     }
20     test {
21         dataSource {
22             dbCreate = "update"
23             url = "jdbc:hsqldb:mem:testDb"
24         }
25     }
```

---

7. http://www.hibernate.org/80.html

```
26     production {
27         dataSource {
28             pooled = true
29             driverClassName = "com.mysql.jdbc.Driver"
30             username = "root"
31             password = "<password>"
32             dbCreate = "update"
33             url = "jdbc:mysql://localhost:3306/collab_todo"
34         }
35     }
36 }
```

The configuration file in Listing 12-2 is separated into three main parts: dataSource (lines 1–6), hibernate (lines 7–11), and environment-specific settings (lines 12–36). The dataSource section provides default database settings that environment-specific settings may override or append to. Other than the pooled property, these default settings all relate to standard JDBC configuration information, such as the JDBC driver class name, the username, and the password for the database.

The hibernate section relates to Hibernate-specific settings. By default, it configures Hibernate caching settings. See the Hibernate documentation[8] for more configuration options.

Finally, the environment-specific settings can provide specific data source or Hibernate configurations for a particular named environment. Notice in lines 28–33 that the production dataSource is configured to use a MySQL database by setting the driverClassName and url to be MySQL-specific. It also overrides the pooled property by setting it to true, since most production environments have more concurrent needs than a developer's workstation. Finally, note that the dbCreate property is configured only for update. This means that at deployment time, Hibernate will update any of the tables it is able to, but it will leave the existing data intact. On the other hand, the default development configuration will create the table at startup and destroy the tables and data when the application is shut down.

The DataSource.groovy configuration file is not the only application configuration that you must complete to support connection to the database. You also must include the database driver JAR in the classpath of the application. The easiest way to do this is to simply copy the JAR(s) to the project lib directory. At deployment or packaging time, Grails will copy the JAR file to the WEB-INF/lib directory. For a MySQL database, you would need to copy the mysql-connector-java-X.X.X-bin.jar file to the lib directory.

---

8. http://www.hibernate.org/hib_docs/reference/en/html/session-configuration.html

Logging Configurations

Logging is an important part of gathering feedback about the state of an application. As you learned in Chapter 5, Grails provides logging support using the Apache Commons Logging component[9] and Apache log4j.[10] You can make the log4j configurations, as well as a couple other configurations, in grails-app/config/Config.groovy. Listing 12-3 shows the default version of Config.groovy.

Listing 12-3. *Config.groovy File Containing Logging Configurations*

```
01 // log4j configuration
02 log4j {
03   appender.stdout = "org.apache.log4j.ConsoleAppender"
04   appender.'stdout.layout'="org.apache.log4j.PatternLayout"
05   appender.'stdout.layout.ConversionPattern'='[%r] %c{2} %m%n'
06   rootLogger="error,stdout"
07   logger {
08     grails="info,stdout"
09     org {
10       codehaus.groovy.grails.web.servlet="off,stdout"  //  controllers
11       codehaus.groovy.grails.web.pages="off,stdout" //  GSP
12       codehaus.groovy.grails.web.sitemesh="off,stdout" //  layouts
13       codehaus.groovy.grails."web.mapping.filter"="off,stdout" // URL mapping
14       codehaus.groovy.grails."web.mapping"="off,stdout" // URL mapping
15       codehaus.groovy.grails.commons="off,stdout" // core / classloading
16       codehaus.groovy.grails.plugins="off,stdout" // plugins
17       codehaus.groovy.grails.orm.hibernate="info,stdout" // hibernate integration
18       springframework="off,stdout"
19       hibernate="off,stdout"
20     }
21   }
22   additivity.'default' = false
23   additivity {
24     grails=false
25     org {
26       codehaus.groovy.grails=false
27       springframework=false
28       hibernate=false
```

---

9. http://commons.apache.org/logging/
10. http://logging.apache.org/log4j/1.2/

```
29    }
30   }
31 }
32
33 // The following properties have been added by the Upgrade process...
34 grails.views.default.codec="none" // none, html, base64
35 grails.views.gsp.encoding="UTF-8"
```

In Listing 12-3, lines 2–31 configure log4j, while the remaining lines set some default configurations for views. When the application logs a message, something has to be done with the message. Lines 3–5 configure a `ConsoleAppender`, which takes the message and writes it to standard out with the format defined by the pattern in line 5. Line 6 instructs log4j to send only messages with severities of `error` or greater to the appender unless explicitly overwritten. Lines 7–20 show examples of overriding some logging. For example, on line 8, the `grails` logger says to include anything with a log level of `info` or above, while line 10 turns off `org.codehaus.groovy.grails.web.servlet` completely.

■**Note** There are a lot of configuration options for log4j. Check out the "Short introduction to log4j"[11] for more details.

Grails provides some special loggers for the different types of artifacts that it already understands by conventions. Table 12-2 documents the special loggers you will find helpful for seeing your log messages.

Table 12-2. *Special Grails Artifact Loggers*

Logger	Description
grails.app.controller	Configures logging for all your controllers
grails.app.domain	Configures logging for all your domains
grails.app.service	Configures logging for all your services
grails.app.tagLib	Configures logging for all your tag libraries

The most likely log configuration you will want to make is adding environment-specific logging for your artifacts; you can use the loggers described in Table 12-2. For example, in your development environment, you may want to log messages at a debug

---

11. http://logging.apache.org/log4j/1.2/manual.html

level (as shown in Listing 12-4), but in your production environment, you may want to log fewer messages for performance reasons and to ensure that the log file doesn't consume all your disk space.

Listing 12-4. *Example of Adding Logging Specific to Your Development Environment*

```
environments {
  development {
    log4j {
      logger {
        grails {
          app.controller="debug"
        }
      }
    }
  }
}
```

Listing 12-4 shows an example of logging all controllers at a debug level. You can simply add this configuration to the end of the Config.groovy file and then restart the application for the new development-specific logging configuration to take effect.

Packaging the Application for Deployment

After you complete the application functionality for an iteration or a release, you or your build master will have to package your application so it can be deployed on a machine other than your computer. At the most basic level, all you have to do is run the Grails war target to create a deployable WAR file. In reality, though, you should follow a more disciplined process to make it easier to identify the version of your application as it goes through environments. We recommended you follow this procedure for milestone releases:

1. Update the code from your version control repository to make sure it's in sync with the head/trunk.

2. Run unit and smoke tests to verify that the release is ready.

3. Increment the app.version property in application.properties either manually or by using the grails set-version target to identify a milestone release number, such as X.X.X.

4. Clean the project using the `grails clean` target to make sure there are no leftover artifacts.

5. Package the application into a WAR file using the `grails war` target and an environment designation—for example, `grails prod war`. This creates a WAR file in the root of the project with a name containing the project name and version number.

6. Increment the `app.version` property and append a `-SNAPSHOT` in `application.properties` either manually or by using the `grails set-version` target to indicate this version is a work in progress and not a milestone release.

7. Commit the `application.properties` file back into your version control repository.

Now you have a WAR file ready for deployment. We'll discuss how to deploy it in the next section.

Deploying to an Application Server

A Grails application packaged as a WAR file can be deployed to Java EE application servers such as JBoss,[12] GlassFish,[13] Apache Geronimo,[14] BEA WebLogic,[15] or IBM WebSphere,[16] or to a web container such as Apache Tomcat[17] or Jetty.[18] Deployment between containers varies greatly, so consult your application server or web container documentation for details. However, standard mechanisms include special deployment directories where the WAR can be copied, a web-based administrator console, a command-line client, and/or Apache Ant tasks. Grails does not provide anything for simplifying deployments, so the next section explains how you can write your own script to automate the process.

■**Note** The Grails FAQ[19] has specific configurations and tips for deploying Grails applications to some common application servers.

---

12. http://labs.jboss.com/jbossas/

13. https://glassfish.dev.java.net/

14. http://geronimo.apache.org/

15. http://www.bea.com

16. http://www.ibm.com/software/websphere

17. http://tomcat.apache.org/

18. http://www.mortbay.org/

19. http://www.grails.org/FAQ

HTTPS

Many applications require that the information passed from the browser to the server be encrypted to ensure the data is not intercepted along the way. This is usually done using a secure HTTP connection, otherwise known as HTTP over Secure Socket Layer (SSL), or HTTPS. Configuring HTTPS is an application server–specific configuration, so you should check your application server documentation to learn how to configure it. However, it can be critical to test your application within an HTTPS context, so Grails provides the ability to start your Grails application using HTTPS instead of HTTP. Instead of executing `grails run-app`, you use `grails-run-https`. This starts your server so it is available under port 8080 as well as port 8443 using an HTTPS protocol—for example, `https://localhost:8443/collab-todo/`. Running the server in this mode causes a temporary certificate to be generated, as shown in the following figure. You'll be prompted with an unknown certifying authority error, which makes this method unsuitable for production use but fine for testing.

Automating Tasks with Gant

Development is full of cycles and repetitive tasks, such as compiling, packaging, and deploying. Performing such tasks manually can be boring and error prone. It is considered a best practice to automate such tasks. Many books have been written to this effect, and many frameworks have been developed to solve the problem. In fact, one of the primary conventions for Grails is the `grails` command line, which is used to automate common tasks in Grails development. The Grails command line utilizes Gant,[20] a build system that uses the Groovy language to script Apache Ant[21] tasks rather than Ant's XML format. Ant, and therefore Gant, are primarily made up of name collections of tasks referred to as *targets*, which you can execute to complete a unit of work.

■**Note** Neal Ford,[22] author and frequent speaker on the "No Fluff Just Stuff" symposium series,[23] describes the importance of automation as, "Doing work like a manual laborer makes you dumber, figuring out how to automate it makes you smarter so be a craftsman not a laborer."

As you have seen throughout this book, the Grails command line provides a lot of functionality. However, it may not automate every task you perform during your development. For example, there is no task for deploying, and yet it is common to deploy your application to infrastructure that matches the application server and database you use in a production environment. So from time to time, you may want to simplify your development efforts by creating your own Gant scripts or modifying existing ones.

Grails makes it easy to incorporate your scripts into your development process. After all, every Grails command-line task is itself a Gant script already. The Grails command line uses the following directories to locate scripts for execution and incorporate them into the help system:

- USER_HOME/.grails/scripts

- PROJECT_HOME/scripts

- PROJECT_HOME/plugins/*/scripts

- GRAILS_HOME/scripts

---

20. http://gant.codehaus.org
21. http://ant.apache.org
22. http://www.nfjs-exchange.com/neal-ford
23. http://www.nofluffjuststuff.com

After writing your Gant script, you can place it in one of these directories, and it will automatically be available from the Grails command line and in the Grails help list.

Grails does not include a deployment script, because there are too many application servers and configuration options to keep up. Listing 12-5 shows an example of a simple script you can use to deploy a WAR file to an application server that supports automatic deployments via a deployment directory like JBoss has.

■Note You can find installation and configuration instructions for JBoss at `http://www.` `beginninggroovyandgrails.com.`

Listing 12-5. *Basic Deployment Script Deploy.groovy*

```
01 /**
02 * Gant script that copies a WAR file to an application
03 * server deployment directory.
04 */
05
06 Ant.property(environment:"env")
07 grailsHome = Ant.antProject.properties."env.GRAILS_HOME"
08
09 includeTargets << new File ( "${grailsHome}/scripts/War.groovy" )
10
11 target ('default':'''Copies a WAR archive to a Java EE app server's deploy
12 directory.
13
14 Example:
15 grails deploy
16 grails prod deploy
17 ''') {
18   deploy()
19 }
20
21 target (deploy: "The implementation target") {
22   depends( war )
23
24   def deployDir = Ant.antProject.properties.'deploy.dir'
25
26   Ant.copy(todir:"${deployDir}", overwrite:true) {
27     fileset(dir:"${basedir}", includes:"*.war")
```

```
28   }
29
30   event("StatusFinal", ["Done copying WAR to ${deployDir}"])
31 }
```

The `Deploy.groovy` script shown in Listing 12-5 begins by loading all system environment variables and then storing the `GRAILS_HOME` environment variable into a local variable
on lines 6 and 7. Line 9 imports another Gant script—specifically, the `War.groovy` script. The
deploy script is dependent on the `War.groovy` script to build the WAR file, so it has something to deploy.

Lines 11–19 represent the first of two targets in this script. The first target is the `default`
target, which means if no other target is specified, this will be the one executed. Since Grails
calls the `default` target, it will definitely be the one executed. Notice that the `default` name
is in single quotes; this is because the word `default` is a reserved word in Groovy. Quotes are
not normally needed for target names. Following the name is the target description, which
the Grails help system uses. The only behavior the default target has is to call the `deploy`
target.

The `deploy` target, shown on lines 21–31, does all the real work. It begins by calling
the `war` target from the `War.groovy` script. After the WAR file has been created, it looks up
the `deploy.dir` property. It then copies the WAR file to the location of this property. You
can put the destination of the WAR file in the `application.properties` file, since the Grails
command line loads it automatically. Lines 26–28 use the Ant `copy` task to copy all WAR
files to the deployment directory. Finally, a message is printed to the system out to indicate to the user that the script is complete and which directory the WAR file has been
copied to.

Running the following target performs the deployment by copying the WAR file to
your application server:

```
> grails deploy
```

■Note If you need to deploy to a remote application server, you might be able to use Apache Ant's Secure
Copy Protocol (SCP) task to copy a WAR to a remote server running Secure Shell (SSH).

Upgrading Grails Applications

Early in the development of the Grails framework, it must have become obvious that the
framework would go through many iterations and that some mechanism was needed to
ensure that applications could migrate easily to new releases of the Grails framework. As
with many of the Grails conventions, this is accomplished through a Grails target, `upgrade`.

During the startup of an application using the run-app target, Grails checks the application metadata found in the application.properties file (see Listing 12-6) located in the root of the project directory structure for the app.grails.version number.

Listing 12-6. *The application.properties File*

```
#Do not edit app.grails.* properties, they may change automatically.
#DO NOT put application configuration in here, it is not the right place!
#Fri Dec 28 22:26:01 EST 2007
app.version=0.1
app.servlet.version=2.4
app.grails.version=1.0
app.name=collab-todo
```

If the currently configured version of Grails doesn't match the application metadata's app.grails.version number, Grails will display the following message:

```
Application expects grails version [1.0], but GRAILS_HOME is version [1.0.2] –
use the correct Grails version or run 'grails upgrade' if this Grails version is
newer than the version your application expects.
```

Upgrading the application is as easy as running grails upgrade.

■**Caution** When upgrading, Grails may overwrite existing files. It's a good idea to ensure your application is in sync with your version control repository before running the upgrade target.

Summary

This chapter covered a lot of the operational aspects of developing Grails applications. Many of the topics related to things that happen after the code is written or to helping facilitate the development process. The topics included packaging and deploying the application as well as configuring environmental data sources and logging. It also covered how to automate your daily development processes and upgrade your applications to work with new versions of Grails. This chapter also ends the server-side discussion of Grails. The remaining chapter discusses aspects of writing clients that may utilize the deployed application.

CHAPTER 13

■■■

Alternative Clients

In Chapter 9, you developed a RESTful web services facility for the Collab-Todo application. You're now able to go to your browser, type in the URL, and perform basic CRUD operations against the domain objects using XML or JSON. In this chapter, you're going to see how you can use Groovy to consume the web services.

The first part of this chapter will take a look at writing Groovy scripts to consume the web services from the command line. The second part of this chapter will build upon the first part to build a rich Groovy client, using a Swing application that leverages the web services.

Overview

In Chapter 9, you developed a RESTful web service to perform CRUD operations using XML or JSON. Figure 13-1 is an overview of the components you will be developing in this chapter.

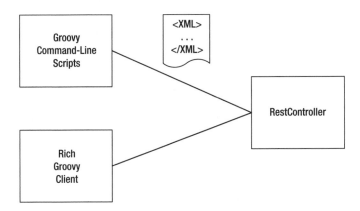

Figure 13-1. *Overview*

Setup

In this chapter, you will use Groovy to create the Groovy command-line scripts and rich Groovy client. In Chapter 1, you installed Groovy. To complete this chapter, you need to download and install some additional libraries that aren't part of the Groovy installation. The libraries you need to complete this chapter are SwingXBuilder,[1] SwingX,[2] JGoodies[3] Forms, and Glazed Lists.[4] After you download the libraries, you have three choices of where to install them:[5] on your `CLASSPATH` environment variable, in `<GROOVY_HOME>\lib`, or in `<USER_HOME>\groovy\lib`.

SwingXBuilder is a Groovy builder used to construct Swing user interfaces. SwingXBuilder uses the SwingLabs (SwingX) components. The SwingXBuilder and SwingX components make it much easier to build the Swing application than it would be to construct it by hand. JGoodies FormLayout is a popular Swing layout manager that uses a grid approach; you'll use it to position components within the Swing application. Glazed Lists is an extremely powerful Swing table component that you'll use to display to-do item summary information.

Use the information in Table 13-1 to download and install the libraries.

Table 13-1. *Additional Libraries*

Library	Download URL
SwingXBuilder	`http://docs.codehaus.org/download/attachments/80916/` `swingxbuilder-0.1.5.jar?version=1`
SwingX	`https://swingx.dev.java.net/files/documents/2981/76227/` `swingx-0.9.1.zip`[6]
JGoodies Forms	`https://glazedlists.dev.java.net/files/documents/1073/94614/` `glazedlists_java14.jar`
Glazed Lists	`http://www.jgoodies.com/download/libraries/forms/forms-1_2_0.zip`

---

1. `http://groovy.codehaus.org/SwingXBuilder`
2. `http://swinglabs.org/`
3. `http://www.jgoodies.com/`
4. `http://publicobject.com/glazedlists/`
5. `http://groovy.codehaus.org/faq.html#classpath`
6. You will need to unzip the file and copy the JAR files in the `dist` and `lib\optional` directories to the appropriate location for your particular setup.

■Note During the installation of Groovy, if you selected the Install Additional Modules options, you'll only need to download the JGoodies Forms and Glazed Lists libraries. In addition, if you selected the File Associations and PATHEXT options, you will be able to run scripts by typing the name of the script. For example, you can execute `MyScript.groovy` by typing `MyScripts` at the command line.

You now have the core components required to build the command-line scripts and the rich Groovy client.

Command-Line Scripts

All throughout the book, you have been using Groovy to build the Collab-Todo application. You have been using the Groovy language to build domain objects, controllers, and services, but that isn't the only way to use Groovy, as you saw in Chapters 1–3.

Command-Line Overview

Wouldn't it be nice if you had the ability to run CRUD operations on your to-do items from the command line? In this section, you will create the scripts to do just that. Chapter 9 introduced four client applications (`GetRestClient.groovy`, `PutRestClient.groovy`, `PostRestClient.groovy`, and `DeleteRestClient.groovy`) to demonstrate accessing the RESTful web service. You will use these as a starting point and make some enhancements.

Reading To-Do Items

Let's create a script that will invoke the RESTful web service facility created in Chapter 9 and display the results in a simple text format. The `GetRestClient.groovy` script from Chapter 9 is a good starting point. The script needs to be enhanced in the following manner: it should accept the user ID and password as arguments, it should create the appropriate authorization header, and it should format the output. The bold portions of Listing 13-1 illustrate the enhancements made to `GetRestClient.groovy` to create `GetAllTodos.groovy`, the enhanced RESTful web service client.

Listing 13-1. *GetAllTodos.groovy*

```
01 import groovy.util.XmlSlurper
02
03 if (args.size() < 2 )
04 {
```

```
05    //USAGE()
06    println """Usage: groovy GetAllTodos userid password"""
07    System.exit(1)
08 }
09
10 // Define some thing we will need.
11 def userid = args[0]
12 def password = args[1]
13 def url = "http://localhost:8080/collab-todo/rest/todo"
14 def slurper = new XmlSlurper()
15
16 println "\nGetting All Todos for ${userid}:"
17
18 def conn = new URL(url).openConnection()
19 conn.requestMethod = "GET"
20 conn.doOutput = true
21
22 if (userid && password) {
23     conn.setRequestProperty("Authorization", "Basic ${userid}:${password}")
24 }
25
26 if (conn.responseCode == conn.HTTP_OK) {
27   def response
28
29   conn.inputStream.withStream {
30     response = slurper.parse(it)
31   }
32   println "\nNo. of Todo Records: ${response.todo.size()}"
33   response.todo.each {
34     println "-----------------------------------"
35     println "Id:             ${it.@id}"
36     println "Name:           $it.name"
37     println "Note:           $it.note"
38     println "Owner:          ${it.owner.@id}"
39     println "Create Date:    $it.createDate"
40     println "Completed Date: $it.completedDate"
41     println "Due Date:       $it.dueDate"
42     println "Priority:       $it.priority"
43     println "Status:         $it.status"
44   }
45 }
46
47 conn.disconnect()
```

Lines 3–8 verify that the script is invoked with two arguments and displays a usage message if two arguments are not provided. Lines 11 and 12 assign the arguments to two local variables: `userid` and `password`. Lines 22–24 set up the connection/requests authorization header using `userid` and `password`. Line 26 accesses the web service and checks that it gave a valid response. If the response is valid, the script moves to lines 29–31, which read the XML response into a local variable using the `XmlSlurper`. Lines 32–44 iterate through each `Todo` item and display the item's content.

> **Note** You can learn more about the `XmlSlurper` at `http://groovy.codehaus.org/Reading+XML+using+Groovy%27s+XmlSlurper`, or check out the Groovy API documents in the `html` directory under `GROOVY_HOME`.

OTHER WAYS TO READ XML

As you might have guessed, you can read XML several ways using Groovy. This chapter uses Groovy's `XmlSlurper` to read XML. In addition to using any of the great Java XML libraries, you can also use Groovy's `XmlParser`[7] or `DOMCategory`.[8] You can find more information on processing XML with Groovy at `http://groovy.codehaus.org/Processing+XML`.

Run the script by typing this command from a command line:

```
> groovy GetAllTodos user1 password
```

Assuming you did everything correctly, the output should look similar to this:

```
Getting All Todos:

No. of Todo Records: 2
-------------------------------------
Id:            3
Name:          User1 Todo 1
Note:          User1 Todo 1 Note
Owner:         2
Create Date:   2008-01-13 11:06:00.0
```

7. `http://groovy.codehaus.org/Reading+XML+using+Groovy%27s+XmlParser`
8. `http://groovy.codehaus.org/Reading+XML+using+Groovy%27s+DOMCategory`

```
Completed Date: 2008-01-13 11:06:00.0
Due Date:       2008-01-13 11:06:00.0
Priority:       1
Status:         1
------------------------------------
Id:             4
Name:           User1 Todo 2
Note:           User 1 Todo 2 Note
Owner:          2
Create Date:    2008-01-13 11:06:00.0
Completed Date: 2008-01-13 11:06:00.0
Due Date:       2008-01-13 11:06:00.0
Priority:       2
Status:         1
```

This technique contains two security issues:

- *The users type in their user ID and password at the command line, so they may be exposed in a process list*: A better approach is to prompt the script for the information. The upcoming Listing 13-2 uses this approach.

- *The request is transmitted to the web service in clear text*: Any person who might be sniffing the web service port would see the authorization header that contains the user ID and password. A solution to this issue is to run the service under SSL (HTTPS). See Chapter 12 for more information on deploying and running with HTTPS.

Creating To-Do Items

Now that you know how to read to-do items, it's time to move on to creating new items. The process is the reverse of reading. You will make some enhancements to the PutRestClient.groovy script from Chapter 9, then you will prompt for the user ID, password, and to-do information. The bold portions of Listing 13-2 illustrate the enhancements made to PutRestClient.groovy to create CreateTodo.groovy, the enhanced RESTful web service client.

Listing 13-2. *CreateTodo.groovy*

```
01 import jline.ConsoleReader
02 import groovy.util.XmlSlurper
03
04 ConsoleReader cr = new jline.ConsoleReader()
```

```
05
06 // Prompt for UserID and Password
07 print "User id : "
08 def userid = cr.readLine();
09 print "Password: "
10 def password = cr.readLine(new Character('*' as char));
11
12 def url = "http://localhost:8080/collab-todo/rest/todo"
13 def userInfoUrl = "http://localhost:8080/collab-todo/userInfo?rest=rest"
14 def slurper = new XmlSlurper()
15
16 // Get the User Info
17 // It will be used later
18 def user_id
19 def user_firstName
20 def user_lastName
21 def conn = new URL(userInfoUrl).openConnection()
22 conn.requestMethod = "GET"
23 conn.doOutput = true
24
25 if (userid && password) {
26     conn.setRequestProperty("Authorization", "Basic ${userid}:${password}")
27 }
28
29 if (conn.responseCode == conn.HTTP_OK) {
30     def response
31
32     conn.inputStream.withStream {
33         response = slurper.parse(it)
34         user_id = response.@id
35         user_firstName = response.firstName
36         user_lastName = response.lastName
37     }
38 }
39
40 //  Create the to-do
41 conn = new URL(url).cpenConnection()
42 conn.requestMethod = "PUT"
43 conn.doOutput = true
44 conn.doInput = true
45
46 if (userid && password) {
```

```
47      conn.setRequestProperty("Authorization", "Basic ${userid}:${password}")
48 }
49
50 // Values for CreatedDate
51 Calendar createDate = Calendar.getInstance();
52 def cdYear = createDate.get(Calendar.YEAR)
53 def cdMonth = createDate.get(Calendar.MONTH) + 1
54 def cdDay = createDate.get(Calendar.DAY_OF_MONTH)
55 def cdHour = createDate.get(Calendar.HOUR_OF_DAY)
56 def cdMin = createDate.get(Calendar.MINUTE)
57
58 // Prompt for Todo Information
59 println ""
60 print "Name:      "
61 def name = cr.readLine();
62 print "Priority: "
63 def priority = cr.readLine();
64 print "Status:    "
65 def status = cr.readLine();
66 print "Note:      "
67 def note = cr.readLine();
68
69 def data = "name=${name}&note=${note}&owner.id=${user_id}\
70 &priority=${priority}&status=${status}&createDate=struct\
71 &createDate_hour=${cdHour}&createDate_month=${cdMonth}\
72 &createDate_minute=${cdMin}&createDate_year=${cdYear}\
73 &createDate_day=${cdDay}"
74
75 conn.outputStream.withWriter {out ->
76      out.write(data)
77      out.flush()
78 }
79
80 if (conn.responseCode == conn.HTTP_OK) {
81      input = conn.inputStream
82      input.eachLine {
83          println it
84      }
85 }
86 conn.disconnect()
```

Line 4 creates a JLine `ConsoleReader`. JLine[9] is a nice little utility that is included in the full Groovy install. You use `ConsoleReader` to read information that the user inputs. Lines 6–10 prompt for and read `userid` and `password`. Take a close look at line 10 and notice `'*'`; this is the echo character for the user input. Changing the echo character prevents the user's password from being displayed on the console.

Lines 21–38 call the user information web service to retrieve the user information that you'll use to create a new to-do item. The user information web service is a simple web service that we created to facilitate this process. For the sake of brevity, we won't go into the details of the web service; it is included in the code samples for this chapter in the Source Code/Download area of the Apress web site (`http://www.apress.com`).

Lines 50–56 create a `Calendar` object so that you can set the created date to the current date and time. Lines 58–67 prompt for the to-do information. Lines 69–73 use string interpolation to insert the values entered by the user into the query string that is sent to the web service on line 76.

Run the script by typing `groovy CreateTodo` from a command line. You will be prompted for a user ID and password. Next, fill in the to-do item name, the priority, the status, and a note. You can verify that the request to create to-dos succeeded by rerunning the `GetAllTodos` script.

Deleting To-Do Items

If you can create to-do items, then it only makes sense that you should be able to delete them as well. Once again, you will leverage the work you did in Chapter 9, with one minor enhancement. You will prompt for the user ID, password, and to-do item ID to be deleted. The bold portions of Listing 13-3 illustrate the enhancements made to `DeleteRestClient.groovy` to create `DeleteTodo.groovy`, the enhanced RESTful web service client.

Listing 13-3. *DeleteTodo.groovy*

```
01 import jline.ConsoleReader
02
03 ConsoleReader cr = new jline.ConsoleReader()
04
05 // Prompt for UserID and Password
06 def userid = cr.readLine("User id : ")
07 def password = cr.readLine("Password: ", new Character('*'as char))
08 println ""
09 def todo_id = cr.readLine("Todo Item id: ")
```

---

9. `http://jline.sourceforge.net/`

```
10
11 def url = "http://localhost:8080/collab-todo/rest/todo/${todo_id}"
12 def conn = new URL(url).openConnection()
13 conn.requestMethod = "DELETE"
14 conn.doOutput = true
15
16 if (userid && password) {
17     conn.setRequestProperty("Authorization", "Basic ${userid}:${password}")
18 }
19
20 if (conn.responseCode == conn.HTTP_OK) {
21     input = conn.inputStream
22     input.eachLine {
23       println it
24     }
25 }
26
27 conn.disconnect()
```

Lines 5–9 prompt for the user ID, password, and to-do item ID to be deleted. Line 11 adds the to-do item ID to the URL. The only other part of this script that wasn't in the Chapter 9 version is the addition of the authorization header.

Run the script by typing groovy DeleteTodo from a command line. You will be prompted for the user ID, password, and to-do item ID to be deleted. You can verify that the to-do item was deleted by rerunning the GetAllTodos script.

Updating To-Do Items

Last, but not least, let's update an existing to-do item. This script is a pretty significant update to the Chapter 9 version, PostRestClient.groovy. The enhancements include prompting for the user ID, password, and to-do item ID to be updated; retrieving the current values for the to-do item to be updated; and prompting the user for the changes. The bold portions of Listing 13-4 illustrate the enhancements made to PostRestClient.groovy to create UpdateTodo.groovy, the enhanced RESTful web service client.

Listing 13-4. *UpdateTodo.groovy*

```
01 import jline.ConsoleReader
02
03 ConsoleReader cr = new jline.ConsoleReader()
04
05 // Prompt for UserID and Password
```

```
06 def userid = cr.readLine("User id : ")
07 def password = cr.readLine("Password: ", new Character('*' as char))
08 println ""
09 def todo_id = cr.readLine("Todo Item id: ")
10
11 // Things that can be updated
12 def id
13 def name
14 def priority
15 def status
16
17 // Get the current values
18 def url = "http://localhost:8080/collab-todo/rest/todo/${todo_id}"
19 def slurper = new XmlSlurper()
20
21 def conn = new URL(url).openConnection()
22 conn.requestMethod = "GET"
23 conn.doOutput = true
24 conn.setRequestProperty("Authorization", "Basic ${userid}:${password}")
25
26 if (conn.responseCode == conn.HTTP_OK) {
27   def response
28
29   conn.inputStream.withStream {
30     response = slurper.parse(it)
31   }
32   response.each {
33       id = it.@id
34       name = it.name
35       priority = it.priority
36       status = it.status
37 }
38 }
39
40 conn.disconnect()
41
42 // Prompt for Changes with current values
43 def tname = cr.readLine("Name (${name}): ")
44 name = tname ? tname : name
45 def tstatus = cr.readLine("Status (${status}): ")
46 status = tstatus ? tstatus : status
47 def tpriority = cr.readLine("Priority (${priority}): ")
48 priority = tpriority ? tpriority : priority
```

```
49
50 // Update the Todo
51 url = "http://localhost:8080/collab-todo/rest/todo"
52 conn = new URL(url).openConnection()
53 requestMethod = "POST"
54 conn.doOutput = true
55 conn.doInput = true
56
57 def data = "id=${id}&name=${name}&status=${status}&priority=${priority}"
58
59 conn.outputStream.withWriter { out ->
60   out.write(data)
61   out.flush()
62 }
63
64 if (conn.responseCode == conn.HTTP_OK) {
65   input = conn.inputStream
66   input.eachLine {println it }
67 }
68 conn.disconnect()
```

Lines 1–40 should look very similar to GetAllTodos.groovy. Lines 32–37 process the XML that is returned. In this case, the XML is the current to-do. The XML values are saved to local variables for use by lines 42–48, which prompt the user for changes to the to-do information. The prompt contains the current value. If the user presses Enter without making a change, the script will use the current value. The last point of interest is line 57, where the values are added to the query string.

To run the script, type groovy UpdateTodo from a command line. You will be prompted for the user ID, password, and to-do item ID to be updated. Next, you will be given the opportunity update the to-do's name, status, and priority. The current value of each field is displayed in the prompt. If you would like to keep the current value, just press Enter, and the current value will be retained. You can rerun the GetAllTodos script to verify that your updated was processed.

Command-Line Script Summary

This section illustrated the usage of command-line scripts to interact with the web service created in Chapter 9. You took the sample client scripts from Chapter 9 and enhanced them to be more usable. The enhancements included prompting for the user ID and password, creating an authorization header, and formatting the output.

The result is a simple, fast, command-line script to create, read, update, and delete to-do items in the Collab-Todo application. In the next section, you will take what you learned and create a rich Groovy client using the Groovy Swing facilities.

Rich Groovy Client

Creating a rich client with Groovy and Swing is a very wide and deep topic. There is no way we can cover it in one chapter. The goal in this section is to give you a small sample of the types of things possible using Groovy, SwingXBuilder, and a couple of popular open source Java libraries (SwingX, Glazed Lists, and JGoodies Forms). You will create a simple Collab-Todo application that leverages the RESTful web services.

Overview

The application will allow usersto log in, display their to-do items, add new to-do items, update to-do items, and delete to-do items. When the application is complete, it will look like Figure 13-2.

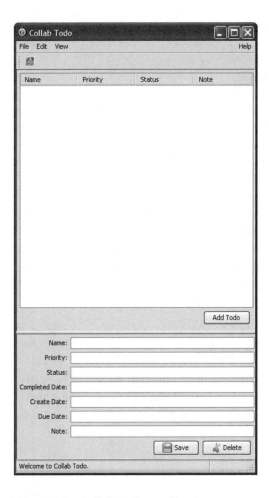

Figure 13-2. *Collab-Todo application*

■**Note** The application leverages open source libraries; we will not be going into a detailed discussion about the code and the proper usage of the libraries. You can find tutorials and documentation about the libraries on their respective web sites. The complete source for the application is included in the Source Code/Download area of the Apress web site (http://www.apress.com).

Options, Alternatives, and Considerations

You'll need to make a lot of decisions when building a client application. These are just a few of the core questions you'll need to answer:

- What presentation technology should you use?

- What presentation components and frameworks should you use?

- How should the application code be structured?

Choosing the Appropriate Presentation Technology

Groovy can do anything Java can do. If you think about the goal of developing the user interface from a Java perspective, you have two options: Swing or Standard Widget Toolkit (SWT). Either choice would work. You could just start coding Groovy and use Swing or SWT the same way you would in a normal Java program. However, if you've ever coded Swing or SWT, you probably aren't too excited right now.

Groovy uses builders[10] to make the job easier. It has both the Swing family of builders (SwingBuilder,[11] SwingXBuilder, and JideBuilder[12]) and the SWT builder (SwtBuilder[13]). Using Groovy and a builder will make the job of creating a client application much easier.

In general, Java developers are more likely to be familiar with Swing than SWT. Therefore, we'll show you how to use Swing as the presentation technology and SwingXBuilder to make it easier. SwingXBuilder extends SwingBuilder and provides access to all of the power of SwingBuilder, plus the Swing components from the folks at SwingLabs.[14]

Choosing the Presentation Components and Frameworks

Take a look at Figure 13-2. It shows a frame with a menu bar, toolbar, status bar, sortable table, labels, and text fields. When you use the system, you'll also see a login dialog and

---

10. Refer to Chapter 3 for a review of builders.

11. http://groovy.codehaus.org/Swing+Builder

12. http://groovy.codehaus.org/JideBuilder

13. http://groovy.codehaus.org/GroovySWT

14. http://www.swinglabs.org

a tips dialog. You could code all of this by hand using plain Swing, but you don't need to. Instead, you can leverage some open source components and frameworks to make your job easier.

SwingXBuilder and the SwingLabs components are a good choice for the login dialog, tips dialog, and status bar. The Glazed Lists table component can help you make a great sortable table, and JGoodies Forms helps you arrange the components on the frame.

■**Note** Check out both `JideBuilder` and JIDE Common Layer,[15] which has some really good UI components. In addition, if you're into 2-D graphics, take a look at `GraphicsBuilder`.[16] `JideBuilder` and `GraphicsBuilder` are both courtesy of Andres Almiray.[17]

Structuring the Application

There are as many opinions about the best way to structure an application as there are Java developers. Many times, the features and characteristics of a language lead to some structures working better than others. However, it's important to remember that all approaches have pros and cons. We really don't have time to investigate all of the alternatives, so let's stand on the shoulders of giants and follow in their footsteps by adopting the approach the SwingX team used to organize the SwingX version of Groovy Console.

If you investigate the SwingXBuilder code base, you will discover a SwingX implementation of the Groovy Console. It is a port/refactor of the Groovy Console from the SwingBuilder implementation to the SwingXBuilder implementation. You can find the SwingXBuilder Groovy Console source code in the `demos/console` directory of the SwingXBuilder source code. James Williams,[18] the creator of SwingXBuilder, did a nice job organizing the SwingXBuilder Groovy Console code. Well-organized code makes writing an application much easier. We will use the same code organization for the Collab-Todo application.

Figure 13-3 provides a high-level overview of the Collab-Todo application's structure.

---

15. `https://jide-oss.dev.java.net/`

16. `http://groovy.codehaus.org/GraphicsBuilder`

17. `http://www.jroller.com/aalmiray/`

18. `http://www.jameswilliams.be`

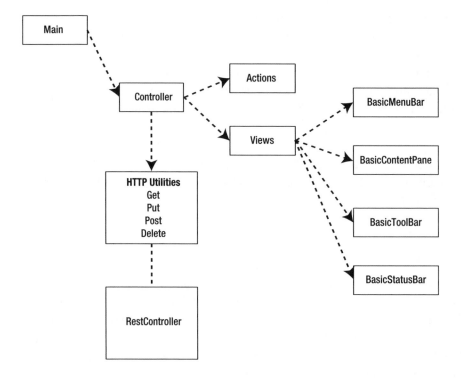

Figure 13-3. *Structure of the Collab-Todo application*

While the `Controller` and the `BasicContentPane` are the most important modules, a brief overview of all the modules is in order.

Main

The `Main` module is the entry point into the application. It creates the `Controller` and invokes the `Controller`'s run closure.

Controller

The `Controller` module is exactly what it sounds like. It is the "C" of MVC. It is responsible for initiating the construction of the view and defining the application's actions and commands. It contains the application logic.

Actions

The `Actions` module defines the actions used within the application. The actions are tied to closures located in the `Controller`.

Views

The Views module is responsible for some simple view definition information and initiating the construction of the BasicMenuBar, the BasicToolBar, the BasicContentPane, and the BasicStatusBar. It represents the "V" of MVC.

BasicMenuBar

The BasicMenuBar contains the menus and menu items, and it ties the menu items to the appropriate actions.

BasicToolBar

The BasicToolBar is a graphical representation of important or frequently used actions. In the case of the Collab-Todo application, the only entry on the toolbar is the login button.

BasicContentPane

The BasicContentPane is the major graphical component of the application. It contains the to-do summary table and the to-do details. It also contains buttons that allow the user to add, save, and delete to-dos.

BasicStatusBar

The BasicStatusBar is a message area at the bottom of the screen.

HTTP Utilities

The HTTP utilities are helper classes to assist with the web service interactions. The utilities are used to manage the model (the "M" part of MVC).

RestController

The RestController represents the web services from Chapter 9.

Builder Overview

A Swing user interface can be thought of as a composite or a tree of graphical components. If you have programmed with Swing, you're undoubtedly familiar with the never-ending pattern of adding a component to its parent. It can be a complex, verbose mess. Groovy tackles the mess using builders.

If you have spent any time with Groovy, you have probably seen or used `MarkupBuilder` to construct an HTML or XML document. Builders can be used equally as well to build a Swing UI.

The easiest way to gain appreciation for SwingXBuilder is to see an example. Listing 13-5 shows how to use SwingXBuilder to create a simple user interface.

Listing 13-5. *Creating a Simple UI Using SwingXBuilder*

```groovy
package com.apress.bgg.ui

import groovy.swing.SwingXBuilder
import static javax.swing.WindowConstants.EXIT_ON_CLOSE
import javax.swing.*

class SimpleUI {

    static void main(args) {
        def simpleUI = new SimpleUI()
        simpleUI.run()
    }

    def swing
    def count = 0

    def run = {
        swing = new SwingXBuilder()
        swing.lookAndFeel('system')

        // create the actions
        swing.action(id: 'exitAction',
          name: 'Exit',
          closure: this.&exit,
          mnemonic: 'x',
          accelerator: 'F4',
          shortDescription: 'Exit SimpleUI'
        )
        swing.action(id: 'aboutAction',
          name: 'About',
          closure: this.&showAbout,
          mnemonic: 'A',
```

```
              accelerator: 'F1',
              shortDescription: 'Find out about SimpleUI'
          )
        swing.action(id: 'clickAction',
          name: 'Click',
          closure: this.&click,
          shortDescription: 'Increment the Click Count'
          )


        // Define the Frame
        swing.frame(id:'simpleUIFrame', title: 'SimpleUI',
              location: [100,100],
              defaultCloseOperation: EXIT_ON_CLOSE
          ) {
        // Define the Menubar
        menuBar {
            menu(text: 'File', mnemonic: 'F') {
                menuItem(exitAction)
            }
            glue()
            menu(text: 'Help', mnemonic: 'H') {
                menuItem(aboutAction)
            }
        }

        // Define some stuff
        button(id:'clickButton', text:"Click Me", action: clickAction)
        // INSERT MORE STUFF HERE
          }

        swing.simpleUIFrame.pack()
        swing.simpleUIFrame.show()
}

void click(event) {
  count++
  swing.clickButton.text = "Clicked ${count} time(s)."
}
```

```
    void showAbout(event) {
       JOptionPane.showMessageDialog(swing.simpleUIFrame,
       '''This is the SimpleUI Application''')
    }

    void exit(event) {
       System.exit(0)
    }
}
```

Executing the SimpleUI application creates the user interface shown in Figure 13-4.

Figure 13-4. *The SimpleUI application*

The SimpleUI application creates a Swing user interface that features a menu bar that contains a File menu, a Help menu, and a button in the content area. The text on the button changes every time the user clicks it. When the program starts, it invokes the run closure to build the UI. The run closure sets up the builder, then uses the builder to create three actions that will be used within the UI. Then the closure uses the builder to create the frame. The frame contains a menu bar, which contains the File and Help menus. Each of the menus contains menu items that reference the previously created actions. The frame also contains a button labeled Click Me, and a reference to the clickAction action.

If you take a closer look at the actions, you will notice that a parameter named closure was passed to the builder when creating the actions. In the case of clickAction, the closure to be executed is click. The click closure increments a counter and sets the button's text.

Now that you have a basic feel for using SwingXBuilder to create a user interface, we will return to the Collab-Todo application. We will focus on the Controller module, creating the view, and the HTTP utilities.

Creating the Main Module

All applications have a starting point, and Groovy Swing applications are no exception. Listing 13-6 illustrates the Collab-Todo application's startup.

Listing 13-6. *The Main Routine*

```
package com.apress.bgg.ui

import org.codehaus.groovy.runtime.StackTraceUtils
import com.apress.bgg.ui.Controller

class Main {
    static void main(args) {

        . . .

        def controller = new Controller()
        controller.run()
    }
}
```

As you can see, Controller performs the real startup and initialization. Main instantiates the Controller and invokes the run closure.

Creating the Controller Module

Just as in a web application, the Controller is the heart and mind of the application and creates the actions and views. It contains closures that are invoked by the actions. Listing 13-7 is a high-level view of the Controller.

Listing 13-7. *High-Level View of the Controller*

```
package com.apress.bgg.ui

import groovy.swing.SwingXBuilder
import groovy.util.slurpersupport.GPathResult

import java.awt.Component
import java.awt.Cursor
import javax.swing.*
import java.util.prefs.Preferences

import org.jdesktop.swingx.JXLoginPane
import org.jdesktop.swingx.JXTipOfTheDay
import org.jdesktop.swingx.tips.TipOfTheDayModel
import org.jdesktop.swingx.tips.TipLoader
```

```
import ca.odell.glazedlists.*
import ca.odell.glazedlists.gui.*
import ca.odell.glazedlists.swing.*

import com.apress.bgg.services.CTLoginService

import com.apress.bgg.http.utils.Get
import com.apress.bgg.http.utils.Delete
import com.apress.bgg.http.utils.Post
import com.apress.bgg.http.utils.Put

class Controller {
  . . .
  def run = {
      todoEventList = new BasicEventList()

      swing = new SwingXBuilder()

      // adjust the look and feel aspects.
      swing.lookAndFeel('system')

      // add controller to the SwingBuilder bindings
      swing.controller = controller

      // create the actions
      swing.build(Actions)

      // create the view
      swing.build(Views)

      swing.consoleFrame.pack()
      swing.consoleFrame.show()
  }

  void exit(event) { System.exit(0) }

  void doTips() { . . . }
  void showTips(event) { . . . }
  void showAbout(event) { . . . }
  void showLogin(event) { . . .
  void fullStackTraces(EventObject evt) { . . .}
  void showToolbar(EventObject evt) { . . . }
```

```
def status = { message -> swing.status.text = "$message" }

void loadData(){ . . . }
void deleteTodo(event) { . . .}
void saveTodo(event) { . . . }
void addTodo(event) { . . . }
}
```

When the application starts, the Main module instantiates the Controller and invokes the Controller's run closure. The run closure uses SwingXBuilder to construct the UI and then puts it on the screen. Everything else in the Controller is application logic that is tied to actions.

The nonbold closures are standard code that you would expect to see for handling the login dialog, displaying tips, displaying the About dialog, and handling other miscellaneous actions. The loadData, deleteTodo, and saveTodo closures interact with the web service using the HTTP utilities, which we'll cover shortly.

When the user logs in, the application invokes loadData to retrieve the user's to-do items. Listing 13-8 illustrates using the HTTP utility Get to retrieve the user's information.

Listing 13-8. *Loading Data from the RESTful Web Service*

```
void loadData(){
  status "Loading Data"

  def get = new Get(url: APP_URL,
      userName: loginService.name,
      password: new String(loginService.password))

   def todos = new XmlSlurper().parseText( get.text )

  todoEventList.clear()
  todoEventList.addAll( todos.todo.list() )

  status "Finished Loading Data"
}
```

The closure puts a message on the status bar, creates the Get HTTP utility to interact with the web services, and parses the resulting XML with XMLSlurper. The results are then added to the todo collection, which notifies the application of new data using change events so that the screen can be updated. Finally, the status message is updated.

The user can delete to-do items by selecting the to-do from the summary table and then selecting the Delete button. The Delete button invokes deleteAction, which runs deleteTodo. Listing 13-9 illustrates the implementation of the delete logic.

Listing 13-9. *Deleting a To-Do*

```
void deleteTodo(event) {
    def delete = new Delete(url: APP_URL+"/${selectedTodo().@id}",
        userName: loginService.name,
        password: new String(loginService.password))
    delete.text
    loadData()
}
```

The deleteTodo closure creates a Delete HTTP utility to interact with the web services. It then invokes the web services and repopulates the user's information. If you recall, when using web services to delete information, the ID of the item to be deleted is appended to the URL, and the request method is set to DELETE. The bold code shown in Listing 13-9 retrieves the ID of the currently selected to-do using a helper method.

The user can add a new to-do item by clicking the Add button. This adds a blank to-do to the summary table. The user selects the blank to-do from the summary table and then enters the to-do details. Next, the user clicks the Save button to save the new to-do. The Save button invokes saveAction, which runs saveTodo. Listing 13-10 illustrates the implementation of the save logic.

Listing 13-10. *Saving a To-Do*

```
void saveTodo(event) {
    selectedTodo().name = swing.nameTextField?.text
    selectedTodo().priority = swing.priorityTextField?.text
    selectedTodo().status = swing.statusTextField?.text
    selectedTodo().completedDate = swing.completedTextField?.text
    selectedTodo().createDate = swing.createTextField?.text
    selectedTodo().dueDate = swing.dueTextField?.text
    selectedTodo().note = swing.noteTextField?.text

    // Save or Update?
    // if don't have an ID, then save else update
    if (selectedTodo().@id) {
        def put = new Put(url: APP_URL,
            userName: loginService.name,
            password: new String(loginService.password))
```

```
            put.queryString.add("name", selectedTodo().name)
            put.queryString.add("priority", selectedTodo().priority)
            put.queryString.add("status", selectedTodo().status)
            put.queryString.add("note", selectedTodo().note)

            // Construct a create date
            // Values for createDate
            Calendar createDate = Calendar.getInstance();
            def cdYear = createDate.get(Calendar.YEAR)
            def cdMonth = createDate.get(Calendar.MONTH)+1
            def cdDay = createDate.get(Calendar.DAY_OF_MONTH)
            def cdHour = createDate.get(Calendar.HOUR_OF_DAY)
            def cdMin = createDate.get(Calendar.MINUTE)

            put.queryString.add("createDate",
                    "struct&createDate_hour=${cdHour}&createDate_month=${cdMonth}&
                     createDate_minute=${cdMin}&createDate_year=${cdYear}&
                     createDate_day=${cdDay}")
            put.content = content
            put.text
        } else {
            // Update
            . . . .
        }
        loadData()
}
```

The saveTodo closure saves the screen values of the to-do details to local variables, and
it populates an XML string using the values. Then, the closure determines if the intent is to
save a new to-do or update an existing one. If the currently selected to-do doesn't have an
ID, then the closure saves it.

Next, you create a Put HTTP utility to interact with web service, populate the request
with the XML string and a create date, and invoke the service. Finally, you use the loadData
closure to repopulate the user's information.

In this section, you've learned about the more important portions of the Controller.
You have seen how to use SwingXBuilder to construct the view components and how the
Controller interacts with the web services. The next step is to look deeper into the view
creation.

Creating the View

Most IT people like to think that UI programming is easy. The truth of the matter is that it isn't as easy as everyone thinks it is. Creating a good, well-organized UI can be tough work and require lots of code. However, the Swing and SwingX builders and some open source Swing component libraries make the job much easier.

The `Controller` creates SwingXBuilder, and it also creates actions and views by passing `Actions` and `Views` scripts to the builder. You accomplish this by using the builder's `build` closure. The `build` closure allows you to pass a script as a closure, and it allows the code to be divided into separate modules, resulting in a code base that is easier to manage. If you take a look at `Actions.groovy` and `Views.groovy`, located in the `com\apress\bgg\ui` directory, you will see that they are scripts. You saw how to create actions in the SimpleUI application, so now let's focus on creating the views. Listing 13-11 is a partial listing of Views script.

Listing 13-11. *The Views Script*

```
package com.apress.bgg.ui
. . .
frame(
    title: 'Collab Todo',
    location: [100,100],
    iconImage: imageIcon(Controller.ICON_PATH).image,
    defaultCloseOperation: DO_NOTHING_ON_CLOSE,
    id:'consoleFrame'
) {
    build(menuBarClass)
    build(toolBarClass)
    build(contentPaneClass)
    build(statusBarClass)
```

The script creates and configures a frame and then uses the builder's `build` closure to construct the menu bar, toolbar, content pane, and status bar. Now let's take a look at the content pane. The content pane is responsible for constructing the main portion of the user interface. The content pane is composed of two parts: a summary table and the details. Listing 13-12 is a partial listing of the script used to construct the content pane.

Listing 13-12. *Constructing the Content Pane*

```
01 package com.apress.bgg.ui.view
02 . . .
03 swing = controller.swing
```

```
04
05 def selectedIndex = 0
06
07 // Create Sorted List for use by the table
08 EventList todoEventList = controller.todoEventList
09 SortedList sortedTodos = new SortedList(todoEventList,
10        { a, b -> b.name.text() <=> a.name.text() } as Comparator)
11
12 /*
13 * Helper method to get the current model/row
14 */
15 def selectedTodo = {
16   selectedIndex = swing.table.selectedRow
17     if( selectedIndex != -1 ){
18         selectedIndex = sortedTodos?.getSourceIndex(selectedIndex)
19         return todoEventList[selectedIndex]
20     }
21 }
22 controller.selectedTodo = selectedTodo
23
24 /*
25 * Define a Summary Table
26 */
27 def columnNames = ["Name","Priority","Status","Note"]
28 def summaryTable = scrollPane(){
29     table( id: 'table', model:
30        new EventTableModel( sortedTodos, [
31           getColumnCount: { return columnNames.size() },
32           getColumnName: { index ->
33              columnNames[index]
34           },
35           getColumnValue: { object, index ->
36                object."${columnNames[index].toLowerCase()}".text()
37           }] as TableFormat))
38     def tableSorter = new TableComparatorChooser(swing.table,
39        sortedTodos, AbstractTableComparatorChooser.SINGLE_COLUMN )
40 }
41
42 splitPane(id: 'splitPane', resizeWeight: 0.50F,
43     orientation: VERTICAL_SPLIT)
44 {
45
```

```
46        // Set up the Summary Table form using JGoodies Forms
47        FormLayout layout = new FormLayout(
48                "3dlu, 200dlu, 3dlu, pref, 3dlu, pref,3dlu", // columns
49                "3dlu, p, 3dlu, p, 3dlu, p, 3dlu");      // rows
50        CellConstraints cc2 = new CellConstraints()
51
52        panel(layout: layout){
53            widget( constraints: cc2.xyw(2,2,6), id: "summaryTable" , summaryTable)
54            widget( constraints: cc2.xy(6,4), id: "addButton",
55                    new JButton(addAction))
56        }
57
58        // Set up the to-do details form using JGoodies Forms
59        FormLayout layout2 = new FormLayout(
60            "3dlu,right:pref, 3dlu, 90dlu, 3dlu, pref, 3dlu, pref, 3dlu", // columns
61            "3dlu, p, 3dlu, p, 3dlu, p, 3dlu, p, 3dlu, p, 3dlu, p, 3dlu, p, 3dlu,
62            p, 3dlu"); // rows
63        CellConstraints cc = new CellConstraints()
64
65        // Define the detail panel
66        // container( new FormDebugPanel(layout: layout2) ){
67        panel( layout: layout2 ){
68            label( constraints: cc.xy(2,2), text: "Name:" )
69            widget( constraints: cc.xyw(4,2,6),
70              new JTextField(columns:20), id: "nameTextField" )
71            label( constraints: cc.xy(2,4), text: "Priority:" )
72            widget( constraints: cc.xyw(4,4,6),
73              new JTextField(columns:20), id: "priorityTextField" )
74            label( constraints: cc.xy(2,6), text: "Status:" )
75            widget( constraints: cc.xyw(4,6,6),
76              new JTextField(columns:20), id: "statusTextField" )
77            label( constraints: cc.xy(2,8), text: "Completed Date:" )
78            widget( constraints: cc.xyw(4,8,6),
79              new JTextField(columns:20), id: "completedTextField" )
80            label( constraints: cc.xy(2,10), text: "Create Date:" )
81            widget( constraints: cc.xyw(4,10,6),
82              new JTextField(columns:20), id: "createTextField" )
83            label( constraints: cc.xy(2,12), text: "Due Date:" )
84            widget( constraints: cc.xyw(4,12,6),
85              new JTextField(columns:20), id: "dueTextField" )
86            label( constraints: cc.xy(2,14), text: "Note:" )
87            widget( constraints: cc.xyw(4,14,6),
```

```
88              new JTextField(columns:40), id: "noteTextField" )
89          widget( constraints: cc2.xy(6,16), id: "saveButton",
90            new JButton(saveAction))
91          widget( constraints: cc2.xy(8,16), id: "deleteButton",
92            new JButton(deleteAction))
93      }
94
95      // Data Bind the fields (view) to the model.
96      // sourceValue = model
97      // target      = view
98      bind(source:swing.table.selectionModel, sourceEvent:'valueChanged',
99          sourceValue: { selectedTodo()?.name },
100         target: swing.nameTextField, targetProperty: 'text')
101     bind(source:swing.table.selectionModel, sourceEvent:'valueChanged',
102         sourceValue: { selectedTodo()?.priority },
103         target: swing.priorityTextField, targetProperty: 'text')
104    bind(source:swing.table.selectionModel, sourceEvent:'valueChanged',
105         sourceValue: { selectedTodo()?.status },
106         target: swing.statusTextField, targetProperty: 'text')
107     bind(source:swing.table.selectionModel, sourceEvent:'valueChanged',
108         sourceValue: { selectedTodo()?.completedDate },
109         target: swing.completedTextField, targetProperty: 'text')
110     bind(source:swing.table.selectionModel, sourceEvent:'valueChanged',
111         sourceValue: { selectedTodo()?.createDate },
112         target: swing.createTextField, targetProperty: 'text')
113     bind(source:swing.table.selectionModel, sourceEvent:'valueChanged',
114         sourceValue: { selectedTodo()?.dueDate },
115         target: swing.dueTextField, targetProperty: 'text')
116     bind(source:swing.table.selectionModel, sourceEvent:'valueChanged',
117         sourceValue: { selectedTodo()?.note },
118         target: swing.noteTextField, targetProperty: 'text')
119 }
```

The summary table is a sortable table that supports property change events. Creating this functionality from scratch would be error prone and require a lot of work. Instead, you can use the Glazed Lists table component to do the heavy lifting. Lines 7–10 get the list of to-dos from the Controller and wrap them with a sortable list. Lines 27–39 create the table inside of a scroll pane.

The next step is to lay out the top portion of the content pane and add the table and the Add button. There are many different ways to lay out the form. For this example, we're using the JGoodies FormLayout component, which uses a grid approach to position the components. Lines 47–50 define the grid. Line 52 creates a panel using the JGoodies

FormLayout manager. Lines 53 and 54 add the table and the Add button. Using the JGoodies FormLayout manager requires using the builder's `widget` closure to add the table and the Add button at specified locations in the grid.

The to-do detail section of the content pane is a simple list of to-do details and the Save and Delete buttons. Lines 58–62 define the layout grid for the detail area. Line 67 creates a panel using the detail layout manager. Lines 68–92 add the to-do details to the panel as a label and a text field. As explained previously, using the JGoodies FormLayout manager requires using the builder's `widget` closure.

When the user selects a row from the summary table, the to-do item's details should be displayed in the details section. You could do this with an event listener, but a better, more contemporary, approach is to use the builder's data-binding abilities. Lines 98–118 define the data binding between the list of to-dos supporting the table and the to-do detail fields. Whenever the user selects a row in the table, the table's selection model changes and fires off a `valueChanged` event. Whenever there is a `valueChanged` event on the table's selection model, the data binding populates the to-do detail fields with the to-do's value and displays the results.

We have barely scratched the surface of what is possible using Groovy, builders, and open source component libraries. The important thing to remember is that "Groovy is Java," and that allows you to use any of the Java components and libraries you want to build an application. The next section will explore the HTTP utilities that are used to interact with the web service.

HTTP Utilities (Get, Put, Post, and Delete)

In the "Command-Line Scripts" section of this chapter, you learned how to create four to-do scripts that correspond to the four HTTP request methods. These scripts worked well, but they were specific to the task at hand—that is, interacting with the Collab-Todo web service to maintain to-do items.

The Collab-Todo rich client also needs to interact with the web service. You can use the same technique to create a couple of utility objects to perform the web service interactions. Listing 13-13 illustrates the results of refactoring the `GetAllTodos` script into a `Get` utility class.

Listing 13-13. *HTTP Get Utility*

```
package com.apress.bgg.http.utils

class Get{
  String url
  QueryString queryString = new QueryString()
  String text
```

```
def userName
def password

String getText(){
  def response
  def conn = new URL(toString()).openConnection()
  conn.requestMethod = "GET"
  conn.doOutput = true

  if (userName && password) {
      conn.setRequestProperty("Authorization", "Basic ${userName}:${password}")
  }

  if (conn.responseCode == conn.HTTP_OK) {
      response = conn.content.text
  } else {
      response =  "URL: " + this.toString() + "\n" +
        "RESPONSE CODE: " + responseCode
  }
  conn.disconnect()
  return response
}

  String toString(){
  return url + "?" + queryString.toString()
  }
}
```

There isn't anything special about the implementation, which is very similar to the GetAllTodos script. It takes a URL, a username, a password, and, optionally, some query parameters. Listing 13-14 illustrates its usage.

Listing 13-14. *Usage of the Get Utility*

```
def get = new Get(url: "http://localhost:8080/collab-todo/rest/todo",
    userName: loginService.name,
    password: new String(loginService.password))
def todos = new XmlSlurper().parseText(get.getText())
```

We won't cover the details of the Put, Post, and Delete classes, but they follow the same approach and are included in the Source Code/Download area of the Apress web site (http://www.apress.com).

Summary

In this chapter, you created command-line scripts and a rich client written in Groovy to interact with the Collab-Todo web services. This required you to download and install the full Groovy installation, which provides access to additional Groovy modules and open source libraries.

The command-line scripts leveraged Chapter 9's web service client scripts, which you extended to give the user the ability to log in to the web services and view all of the to-dos, create a to-do, update a to-do, and delete a to-do.

Next, you turned your attention to creating a rich client application using SwingXBuilder, JGoodies FormLayout manager, and the Glazed Lists table component. You started by writing a simple application that counted button clicks. This simple application gave you a basic understanding of SwingXBuilder and the process of creating the actions, menus, and buttons. With this information, you were able to start constructing the user interface portion of the application.

You started building the application by creating a `Controller` that was responsible for building the view, executing the application logic, and interacting with the web services. The `Controller` delegated the construction of the view to the `Views` script, which used SwingXBuilder to build the menus, toolbar, content pane, and status bar. The content pane was the main focus. The content pane script created the summary table, the detail fields, and the Add, Delete, and Save buttons. You used the JGoodies FormLayout manager to position these items on the screen.

Finally, you interacted with the Collab-Todo web service. You took what you learned from creating the command-line scripts to create a couple of HTTP utility classes to perform the web service calls. You now have a rich client application to maintain your to-dos.

The purpose of this chapter was to help you see that Groovy and Grails aren't just web application frameworks. Our goal was to give you a sample of what is possible. You are only limited by your imagination.

Index

You Need the Companion eBook

We believe this Apress title will prove so indispensable that you'll want to carry it with you everywhere, which is why we are offering the companion eBook (in PDF format) for $10 to customers who purchase this book now. Convenient and fully searchable, the PDF version of any content-rich, page-heavy Apress book makes a valuable addition to your programming library. You can easily find and copy code—or perform examples by quickly toggling between instructions and the application. Even simultaneously tackling a donut, diet soda, and complex code becomes simplified with hands-free eBooks!

Once you purchase your book, getting the $10 companion eBook is simple:

❶ Visit **www.apress.com/promo/tendollars/**.

❷ Complete a basic registration form to receive a randomly generated question about this title.

❸ Answer the question correctly in 60 seconds, and you will receive a promotional code to redeem for the $10.00 eBook.

THE EXPERT'S VOICE™

2855 TELEGRAPH AVENUE | SUITE 600 | BERKELEY, CA 94705

Offer valid through 12/08.